SUBVERTING COLONIAL AUTHORITY

Challenges

to

Spanish

Rule

in

Eighteenth-

Century

Southern

Andes

SUBVERTING COLONIAL AUTHORITY

SERGIO SERULNIKOV

Duke University Press   Durham and London 2003

© 2003 Duke

University Press

All rights reserved

Printed in the

United States

of America on

acid-free paper ∞

Typeset in Galliard

by Keystone

Typesetting, Inc.

Library of Congress

Cataloging-in-

Publication Data

appear on the last

printed page of

this book.

2nd printing, 2005

Contents

Acknowledgments

WHILE WORKING ON THIS BOOK, I benefited from the help of many institutions and individuals. The Social Science Research Council (SSRC), the Consejo de Investigaciones Científicas y Técnicas de la Argentina (CONICET), the John Carter Brown Library, the Fundación Antorchas, Boston College, and the National Endowment for the Humanities offered financial support for the research and writing. I want to thank the staffs of the Archivo Nacional de Bolivia in Sucre, especially its former Director Lic. Rene Arce Aguirre, and the Archivo General de la Nación de Buenos Aires for their cooperation.

I would like to express my appreciation to the History Department at the State University of New York at Stony Brook, where I wrote the dissertation on which this book is based. I am particularly indebted to Paul Gootenberg, Ian Roxborough, and Barbara Weinstein for their advice and support. A special note of gratitude is due to Brooke Larson, who contributed in various ways to design this research and improve its final product. In Buenos Aires, colleagues and friends at the Programa de Historia de America Latina (PROHAL) belonging to the Instituto de Historia Argentina y Americana "Dr. Emilio Ravignani," Universidad de Buenos Aires, provided a stimulating intellectual environment. I am grateful to its director, Enrique Tandeter, who was involved in this project from its very beginnings. The confidence of my colleagues at Boston College greatly helped me to bring this work to completion.

Many colleagues and friends offered fruitful comments and criticism on different sections of this study over the years. Among those, I want to mention

Fernando Boro, John Coatsworth, Francie Chasen-López, Roberto Fernández, Ariel de la Fuente, Pepe Gordillo, Leonardo Hernández, Christine Hunefeldt, Juan Carlos Korol, Jorge Hidalgo Lehuede, Nils Jacobsen, Kevin Kenny, Deborah Levenson-Estrada, Gene Lebovics, Nacho Lewkovitz, Jane Mangan, Cecilia Méndez, Scarlett O'Phelan Godoy, Juan Manuel Palacios, Prasannan Parthasarathi, Gustavo Paz, Tristan Platt, Mariano Plotkin, Ana Maria Presta, Andrés Regiani, Juan Jose Santos, Roberto Schmit, Karen Spalding, Sinclair Thomson, John Tutino, Charles Walker, and Kathleen Wilson. The three anonymous readers for Duke University Press provided much valuable insights and suggestions on the manuscript. I owe my deepest gratitude, intellectual and otherwise, to my wife Silvana Palermo.

THIS BOOK EXPLORES THE CHANGING forms of colonial domination and peasant politics in the province of Chayanta, an important Aymara cultural zone in an area of present-day Bolivia known as northern Potosí. The study begins in the 1740s with the opening of a new cycle of demographic, agrarian, and commercial growth, and it concludes in the early 1780s when a mass Indian uprising shook the foundation of Spanish rule in the Andes. The socioeconomic and political characteristics of this region make it a particularly rich case study for the analysis of subaltern politics and culture. An overwhelmingly indigenous area, the social fabric of the Andean community exhibited in northern Potosí an unmatched resilience to colonial and postcolonial regimes. As such, these rural groups have become the focus of a wealth of anthropological and ethnohistorical studies.[1] Politically, the region was one of the main scenarios of rebel activity during the pan-Andean insurrection of the early 1780s. As the most massive and radical indigenous uprising since the beginning of colonial times, this insurgency swept an extensive area stretching from south Ecuador to the north of Chile and Argentina. Native peoples organized large armies and laid siege to some of the most populated cities in the region. The ideology of the movement is no less striking: 250 years after the Spanish conquest,

Map 1. Peru and Bolivia (selected cities and towns).

the Andes witnessed the outbreak of a mass insurrection aimed at reestablishing pre-Hispanic polities, particularly the Inca empire.

Although Túpac Amaru became the most recognizable symbol of insurgency across the Andes, the rebellion was not a single homogeneous movement. It was formed by the conjunction of three main regional upheavals, each with a history and dynamic of its own: the rebellion led by Túpac Amaru of Quechua peoples from Cuzco, the old center of the Inca empire; the insurrection of Aymara highland communities from La Paz, a growing commercial region in eighteenth-century southern Andes; and the Indian uprising of northern Potosí. By examining the movement led by Tomás Katari between 1777 and 1781 in Chayanta, the least-known of the three upheavals, we can see the exceptional cycle of political unrest and cultural revivalism from a different perspective than those studies focused on the other two areas of rebellion. Unlike the overt insurrectionary conspiracies of Túpac Amaru and Túpac Katari, occurrences in Chayanta represented a gradual process of social unrest. They escalated from a routine and successful legal claim against illegitimate native authorities presented by the rural communities of Macha before the *audiencia* (high court) of Charcas in 1777, to the siege of the same city three years later by thousands of Andean peasants from several provinces of the southern Andes. And in contrast to its counterparts in Cuzco and La Paz, where most rebels sought a complete rupture with colonial institutions and society, the Chayanta movement never rejected altogether the existing system of justice and government until the last stages of the conflict. Local riots and ethnic insurrection, legal strategies and mass violence, form in the context of the Chayanta movement a continuum of social defiance.[2]

By tracing the advent of this kind of anticolonial politics, in this study I address three questions that speak to larger debates in eighteenth-century colonial history and the cultural anthropology of the Andean world. First, I analyze long-term patterns of social conflict rooted in local political cultures and regionally based power relations.[3] In so doing, I attempt to shift the focus from insurgency itself—usually conceived as exceptional moments of rupture—to the changing forms, social meanings, and political contexts of collective violence. This approach seems especially relevant for the Andean colonial world where there were definite continuities between village disturbances and large-scale insurrections. Although often compared to the peasant riots in the Mexican countryside analyzed by William Taylor (1979: 113–51), I contend that Andean village revolts were not isolated episodes of social unrest conveying a "localocentric" worldview. Parochialism, in other words, was not a necessary feature of Andean routines of contention. The centralized system of government and surplus appropriation, peasant social autonomy and physical mobility, and homogenizing juridical notions of Indianness often endowed community mobilization with radical ideological undertones. Local disputes could ignite a process of peasant politicization because the most common sources of discontent (forced distribution of goods, scarcity of lands, taxes, church fees, and abusive provincial Spanish governors) tended to be perceived as expressions of general trends.[4] Virtually all social conflict in eighteenth-century Andes pushed indigenous peoples to deal with different instances of the colonial administration, to experience the gap between norms and power, and to test the balances of force between peasants and rural elites. The dynamic of these processes is important in understanding the roots of Indian insurgency not only in negative terms (the climate for large-scale upheavals created by the failure of village revolts) but also in positive terms: the forms whereby routine dissension at the local level shaped the nature of mass rebellion. To understand why (and how) Indians moved from community uprisings to millennial expectations of social and cosmological change, those discrete political histories must be reconstructed.

In this study I show that insurgency in northern Potosí was preceded by two fairly long conjunctures in the 1740s and 1770s of widespread, public, albeit not necessarily violent, confrontation with rural overlords over taxes, ecclesiastical fees, assignment of labor obligations, land distribution, and ethnic political autonomy, among other issues. These struggles bear remarkably little resemblance to the "spasmodic, localized, often extremely violent, and short-lived" nature of contemporary village riots in Mexico (Van Young 1989: 91). Instead, as peasant notions of political legitimacy were matched with the realities of colonial rule, a collective experience of contention was evolving whereby the indigenous communities expanded their ideological horizons beyond the community level and their repertoires of struggle beyond passive resistance or spasmodic violence. Not only was the Chayanta rebellion of 1780–1781 encouraged by the success of some of those previous protest movements, but some of its distinctive political tenets (the full enforcement of Indian communities' corporative rights, among them), as well as modes of collective action (the overlapping of mass mobilization with judicial litigation), directly derived from the dynamic of those local conflicts.

A second general theme is the workings of Spanish colonial rule at its most concrete and socially significant level: that of the administration of justice in the Indian towns. I try to reconstruct how colonial law, courts, and judicial procedures functioned in practice, to borrow Edward Thompson's words, as "institutional expressions of social relations" (in Taylor 1985: 147). In analyzing the relationship between empire, colonial government, and village society, my approach is akin to recent investigations dealing with the linkage between state-building processes and peasant movements and consciousness in nineteenth- and early-twentieth-century Latin America.[5] As has been noted, state hegemony needs to be examined from two interrelated perspectives: as processes rather than as stable structures of domination, and as inherently ambivalent endeavors rather than as cohesive ideological models. Elite hegemonic projects, in other words, are less a set of institutions than a series of contested practical interpretations. In this study I delve into the ideological and political factors that conditioned the process of the intervention of Spanish high courts in rural affairs, the shifting systems of alliances and factionalism within the rural elites, and the development of repertoires of contention and judicial politics among the indigenous communities. It is my general thesis that during the late Bourbon era of political transformation, the intensification of intraelite strife between imperial, regional, and local government agencies, as well as the crown and the Catholic Church, and the growth of peasant protests reshaped the perceived role of the Spanish institutions. From its traditional place as an arena of conflict between competing interest groups, the state administration gradually became the focus of struggles over the foundations of colonial legitimacy.

Finally, in this book I offer a historical argument for the emergence of ethnic consciousness and solidarity in the context of a growing crisis of cultural hegemony, rather than in an "Andean utopia" associated with the propagation of millenarian notions of change and messianic expectations.[6] The embracing of nativist projects of epochal transformation linked to the Inca king's "second coming" and to the revitalization of Tawantinsuyu imperial memories was the outcome rather than the starting point of the demise of the structure of colonial authority. Northern Potosí peasants were able to overcome entrenched tendencies toward ethnic fragmentation, and they constituted themselves as political actors in the very process of using both law and force successfully to assess the Indians' rights to make colonial authorities accountable and to enforce Andean communities' corporative prerogatives. Along the way, these peasants not only widened collective identities but also redefined and disputed colonial elites' representations of indigenous societies as pliant objects of European rule or, conversely, autonomous cultural isolates. I intend to show that beyond certain forms of political oppression and economic exploitation, what eventually came to be at stake was the very historical experience of ethnic submission, those "appropriate objects of a colonialist chain of command, authorized versions of otherness" (Bhabha 1984: 129) by which colonized peoples are represented in Western discourse.

NORTHERN POTOSÍ INDIGENOUS COMMUNITIES

Northern Potosí was located near two important Spanish settlements in the southern Andes—the mining center of Potosí, one of the largest silver producers in the world from the sixteenth through the eighteenth centuries, and the administrative city of La Plata, the seat of the audiencia of Charcas, the highest colonial court in the area. A province predominantly populated by indigenous communities, this region constituted a major source of state revenues as well as a source of labor for the mining industry through the tribute and the *mita* (rotation draft labor) systems. Several ethnic groups with roots in the pre-Hispanic kingdoms grouped in the Charka-Karakara confederation

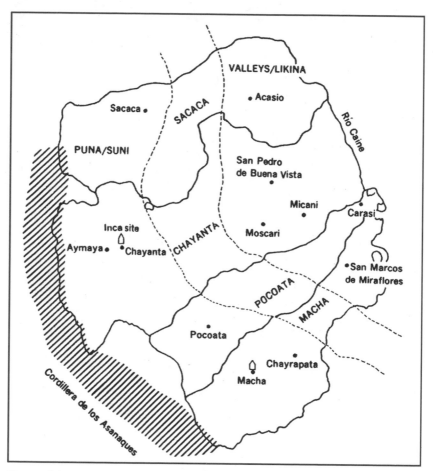

Map 2. Schematic map of the ethnic strips of northern Potosí. Source: Olivia Harris, "Ecological Duality and the Role of the Center: Northern Potosí," in *Andean Ecology and Civilization: An Interdisciplinary Perspective on Andean Ecological Complementarity*, ed. Shozo Masuda, Izumi Shimada, and Craig Morris (Tokyo: University of Tokyo Press, 1995), 316. • Sixteenth-century rural village (*pueblo de reducción*), - - - - *taypirana/chauupirana* (middle region).

inhabited the colonial province of Chayanta. The province roughly covered the territory of four precolonial Aymara nations: Sacaca, Macha, Pocoata, and Chayanta (map 2). The ethnic groups had a segmentary organization whose lower organizational level was composed of the landholding groups known as *ayllus*. Each of these ayllus belonged to one of the two moieties (Anansaya, "upper half," and Urinsaya, "lower half") that made up the larger ethnic groups. This segmentary organization was cemented by webs of reciprocity, communal labor, and ritual. In addition, northern Potosí peasants practiced, as did most Andean peoples, a land tenure model that anthropologist John Murra (1975) has defined as a "vertical archipelago system." According to this economic system, each ayllu had direct access to fields in different altitudes of the Andean landscape. Ecological complementarity allowed Andean groups a large measure of self-sufficiency.

By the late sixteenth century, after the sweeping reforms implemented by Viceroy Francisco de Toledo put an end to the early encomienda system, the institutional organization of the Chayanta province began to take its final shape under Spanish rule. The native communities were organized in *repartimientos* (Indian districts), most of which encompassed communities scattered across distant puna and valley lands. (For the spatial distribution and an index of the repartimientos in the eighteenth century, see map 3 and table 1.) A Spanish-like rural village, *pueblo de reducción*, usually located within the highland territories of the respective communities, served as the capital of each repartimiento. The ethnic composition of the repartimientos presents a vast array of situations regarding their degree of continuity vis-à-vis the precolonial times.[7] Thus, the repartimientos of Sacaca, Pocoata, and Macha approximately encompassed the old pre-Hispanic nations. By contrast, the repartimiento of Chayanta grouped six ethnic groups (Laymi, Chullpa, Puraca, Chayantaca, Sicoya, and Caracha) that, while once members of the homonymous Aymara kingdom, became politically independent from one another. This means that while during the colonial period the terms "Sacaca," "Pocoata," or "Macha" designated repartimientos (and the puna villages that served as their capitals) as well as actual native polities (i.e., dispersed, multiecological communities comprised of about ten minor ayllus grouped into two moieties), Chayanta designated an administrative entity alone.[8] Aymaya, Jukumani, and Panacachi, three other groups of the precolonial kingdom of Chayanta, became two separate repartimientos.[9] Finally, the native groups comprising the repartimientos of Moscari and San Pedro de Buena Vista present still a disparate feature because they emerged during the colonial era as a result of the grouping of households that belonged to some of the pre-Hispanic units. Unlike the rest of the repartimientos, moreover, the Auquimarca and Cayana communities (San Pedro repartimiento) were purely lowland groups, and the Moscari community possessed contiguous puna and valley lands. Table 1 provides a simplified but useful summary of this arrangement.[10]

It is important to observe that this administrative scheme combined Andean and European political notions. As mentioned, the very structure of the repartimiento somehow reproduced indigenous patterns of settlement by recognizing

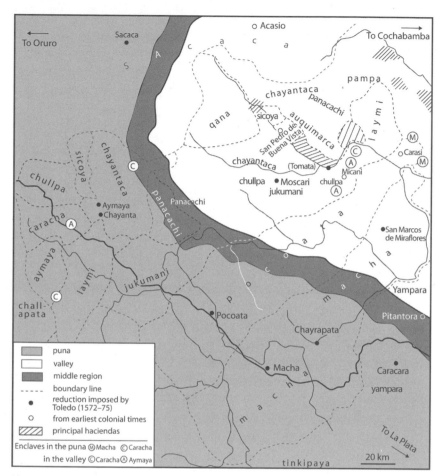

Map 3. The ayllus of northern Potosí. Source: Olivia Harris and Tristan Platt, "Mirrors and Maize: The Concept of Yanatin among the Macha of Bolivia," in *Anthropological History of Andean Politics*, ed. John Murra, Nathan Wachtel, and Jacques Revel (Cambridge: Cambridge University Press, 1986), 234.

Andean vertical organization. Colonial censuses incorporated the households of the valley districts into their respective highland ethnic groups. In cases of repartimientos encompassing more than one ethnic group (Chayanta or Aymaya, for example) the peasant families (whether they resided in their puna seats or in the multiethnic valleys of Micani, Carasi, or San Pedro de Buena Vista) were listed within their respective ethnic groups. Thus, although the repartimientos were originally conceived as fiscal units, for those multiethnic repartimientos the colonial state recognized, in practice, the political and fiscal autonomy of their respective communities. In the case of Macha, Sacaca, and

Table 1. Major Repartimientos of Chayanta

Repartimiento Name	Ethnic Group	Valley Districts (Parishes)						Tributaries (1772)*
		San Pedro de Buena Vista	Carasi	Micani	San Marcos de Mira-flores	Acasio	Parica	
Pocoata	Pocoata		X	X				577
Macha	Macha		X		X			587
Sacaca	Sacaca					X		707
Chayanta	Laymi		X	X				
	Puraca		X					
	Chullpa			X				
	Chayantaca	X						
	Caracha			X				
	Sicoya	X						1823
Aymaya	Aymaya			X				
	Jukumani			X				445
Panacachi	Panacachi						X	235
San Pedro de Buena Vista**	Auquimarca	X						
	Cayana	X						229
Moscari***	Moscari	X						451
Total								5054

* AGN, XIII, 23–3–1, Primer Cuaderno.
** Includes only valley lands.
*** Includes contiguous puna and valley lands.

Pocoata the Indians were grouped into moieties (Anansaya/Urinsaya) and their constituent minor ayllus. Because Andean chiefs at various community organizational levels (ayllus, moieties, and/or ethnic groups) were responsible for collecting tribute and selecting the mita team from puna and valley households alike, their role in the allocation of lands, administration of common resources, performance of ritual, and maintenance of forms of ecological complementarity was reinforced.[11] It is apparent that the correspondence between colonial administrative units and real social polities greatly contributed to the long-term historical endurance of the northern Potosí groups.[12] Furthermore, the rural villages founded in the late sixteenth century (pueblos de reducción) as seat of the repartimientos never accomplished their original goal of serving as places of indigenous residence to facilitate the political, economic, and religious control of the native population. One of the most spectacular failures of the Toledean reforms was precisely the resettlement of the Andean population in Spanish-like towns. Peasant families by all accounts continued to live in their traditional rural hamlets alongside their agricultural lands.[13] Rural villages were mostly inhabited by civil officials, parish priests, and mestizo and Spanish residents working in agriculture, commerce, tax collection, and so forth.

Spanish criteria of territoriality, on the other hand, were reflected in the creation of a system of town-council officials (*cabildo indígena*) modeled on Castilian municipal government, and ritual sponsors and church assistants (*doctrina de indios*) in each of the puna and valley villages. Ecclesiastical districts, unlike administrative jurisdictions like repartimientos, seldom conformed to Andean social patterns because they were essentially based on contiguous residence. The discrepancies between Andean and European modes of spatial organization were manifested in two forms. First, valley parishes (e.g., the territory around the village of Micani) would generally encompass disparate groups, while puna parishes (e.g., the territory around the village of San Pedro de Macha) had only segments of a single group. Second, given the extended Andean practice of "double domicile," puna families served as ritual sponsors in the valley parishes and vice versa following seasonal migrations.[14] In other words, ethnic affiliation, not contiguous residence, continued to determine social identities and access to land (the Indians living in the valley of Carasi, for example, did not derive their landholding rights from their belonging to the town but rather to their belonging to their home communities of Pocoata, Macha, Laymi, and Puraca). It needs to be noted, however, that this network of village officeholders added a novel and influential element to traditional political arrangements. In contrast to the hereditary ethnic lords, *alcaldes* (mayors), *alguaciles* (constables), *alfereces* (standard-bearers), and *mayordomos* (stewards) were rotating and elective posts. Parish priests and nonindigenous elite town-dwellers might have a direct influence over these municipal indigenous authorities. Rural villages, moreover, became important places for ritual (Catholic festivals) and collective gatherings linked to the delivery of tribute and mita obligations. The religious and fiscal calendar, plus the existence of a residentially based authority system, bestowed rural towns (particularly multiethnic ones) with a larger social significance than administrative centers. In terms of political mobilization, the pueblos de reducción could have facilitated the expansion of protest movements because disparate communities shared common Spanish civil and ecclesiastical local authorities. They did it, too, by providing sites of social interaction: in northern Potosí, as elsewhere in the Andean and Mexican countryside, religious festivals and other community meetings served as prime opportunities for social unrest. Disturbances, in brief, could not only spread spatially across the highland and valley territories of the rebellious communities, but also socially from one group to another sharing the same parish.

The preservation of traditional principles of social organization was not incompatible with participation in the colonial markets. The Andean ideals of reciprocity and self-sufficiency could develop within the context of a growing mercantile economy. An index of this phenomenon is that by the end of eighteenth century, Chayanta, along with Cochabamba, became the main supplier of grain to the city of Potosí, the larger market in the southern Andes. Unlike the Cochabamba valleys dominated by large landed estates, however, agricultural production in Chayanta heavily rested on the Indian communities (Larson 1997; Platt 1982b). Historical records — as will be shown for the cases of Moscari, Pocoata, Macha, and others — reveal that one of the crucial mechanisms of agricultural commercialization in this area was the sale of grains produced in valley and highland fields cultivated collectively by the members of the ayllus. The income from these common lands (*comunes*) was destined to cover collective needs (from tribute and litigation costs to coca leaves). It has been demonstrated, for instance, that in the 1790s the Auquimarcas sold in the colonial markets 58 percent of the maize and wheat produced in their comunes.[15] What can be seen here, therefore, is a pattern of economic development that sharply differs from what structuralist approaches would predict. According to these interpretations, the expansion of the European mercantile economy would end up either dissolving the ethnic economies and commodifying their labor force, or pushing native communities into an isolated economic sector resting on a "natural," self-contained economy, linked to the markets only by the force of state coercion. But, as numerous investigations of Indian participation in colonial markets have widely demonstrated, there was not that kind of dual economy during the eighteenth century.[16] What was found in northern Potosí is native society that did undergo a deep process of fragmentation since the Spanish conquest but that also was able to preserve the fundamental bases of their social organization by successfully participating in labor and commodity markets, renting communal lands and mills, and engaging in other strategies of economic and social reproduction.

THE ANDES IN THE EIGHTEENTH CENTURY

Toward the mid-1740s, northern Potosí seemed to be entering an era of intense rural agitation. If the logic of archives reflects in any degree the density of historical processes then the increase in the number and nature of litigation records unquestionably indicates the intensification of social tensions. No doubt the province of Chayanta was not an exceptional case but followed regional-wide trends. A brief overview of the socioeconomic changes taking place during this period will help to frame this historical process.

Historians have characterized the 1740s as the starting point of a wave of rural disturbances that eventually would culminate with the great Túpac Amaru rebellions of the early 1780s. "The age of Andean insurrection" is the term historian Steve Stern (1987b) has used to define the 1742 to 1782 years.[17] Several factors account for this phenomenon. The most apparent reason was the expansion of the forced distribution of commodities (*reparto de mercancías*), a commercial monopoly exerted by the provincial Spanish governors (*corregidores*) over the native peoples under their jurisdiction.[18] Historical literature has shown that since the seventeenth century this system turned into one of the most effective means of economic exploitation of the indigenous communities. As the highest administrative and judicial authorities in the rural villages, the corregidores were in an excellent position to set the amounts and prices of the goods forcefully sold to the Indians, as well as putting state power behind the collection of debts. The cash demand imposed on the rural communities compelled their participation in colonial markets as sellers of agricultural products and as a labor force. Furthermore, the reparto had significant indirect effects on local power structures and, consequently, social stability. The system gave rise to an increasing intervention of corregidores in the appointment of friendly caciques willing and able to insure its smooth operation; imposed extraordinary strains in the relationship between ethnic authorities and Andean communities concerning the allotment and payment of the distributed goods; and bred strife among different segments of the rural elites, especially corregidores and parish priests, for the appropriation of peasant labor and agricultural surpluses. The reparto was also the main incentive behind the crown's sale of corregimientos, and it was the origin of financial and commercial alliances between Lima merchants (who provided capital and imported commodities) and Spanish provincial authorities throughout the countryside.[19] In the 1750s, the crown finally legalized this commercial monopoly in an effort to set limits to the amounts and prices of the effects. But the legalization of the reparto did nothing but provide a final boost to the system, which in turn unleashed intense rural agitation.

The second third of the eighteenth century marked a turning point in the social and economic history of the region in other important respects as well. A series of indicators suggest the onset of a period of demographic, agricultural, and mining growth. To begin with, these years witnessed a strong increase in the Andean population following the severe demographic crisis provoked by the great epidemics of 1719–1721. According to Noble David Cook's estimates, the population of Peru grew by an annual average rate of 1.32 percent between 1754 and 1782 (cited in Tandeter 1995: 8–13). This trend is clearly visible in the

Table 2. Originario and Forastero Populations, Province of Chayanta

Census Year	Originarios	Forasteros	Tributaries	Total Population
1573	—	—	5,759	30,605
1683	4,440	3,557	7,997	26,467
Ca. 1738	2,298	1,753	4,051	—
Ca. 1746	2,360	1,802	4,162	—
1751	2,570	1,996	4,566	20,547
1772–77	2,481	3,637	6,118	27,531
1786	1,801	6,618	8,419	37,885
1792–94	—	—	—	43,934
1796–99	—	—	—	47,241
1804–7	—	—	—	35,584

Sources: Figures for the censuses of 1573 and 1683 are in Sánchez-Albornoz 1978: 29. The figures for 1738, 1746, and 1751 are in AGN, XIII, 18–9–2; the list for 1780, which includes the counts made between 1772 and 1777, are in AGN, XIII, 18–10–1, Leg. 84, Libro 1. The census of 1786 is in AGN, XIII, 18–10–3. The figures for the final three censuses are in Santamaría 1977: 254. Note: The number of tributaries in 1738 and 1746 is approximate because only the total tribute is available, from which I have estimated the number of originarios and forasteros by projecting the same ratios of the 1751 visita. The total population of 1751, 1772–77, and 1786 is also estimated, and is a result of multiplying the number of tributaries by 4.5.

Chayanta province. Table 2 summarizes the number of tributaries starting with the *visitas generales* (general population inspections) carried out under Viceroys Francisco de Toledo in 1573 and Duque de la Palata in 1683 and ending with the censuses undertaken in the early nineteenth century.

Table 2 shows that between 1751 and the 1770s, assessed from comparable census-taking processes, the number of tributaries increased by an average rate of about 2.4 percent per annum. By this period, the Chayanta tribute population had started to recover its seventeenth-century levels.[20] Several studies based on sources more reliable than fiscal records confirm these general trends. The analysis of parish registers of baptisms and deaths in the northern Potosí villages of Sacaca and Acasio reveals a sustained and continuous pattern of growth of the Andean population from the beginning of the 1750s until the last decade of the century, even though by the end of this period it only recovered the levels that had existed before the plague of 1719–1721 (Tandeter 1995: 8–13).

This demographic growth inexorably engendered agrarian tensions across the region. Deprived of the significant amount of land that had been transferred to Spanish entrepreneurs (and sometimes to the native nobility) during the nadir of the Indian population in the mid-seventeenth century, the Andean communities now faced a scarcity of resources. This led to increasing disputes over land property rights. Several regional studies coincided in pointing out the increase in tensions between communities and haciendas that surfaced in those years.[21] Agrarian strains manifested also in the substantial increases in the category of landless *forasteros* (literally, immigrant Indians no longer living with their original ethnic groups) across the Andes (Tandeter 1995: 20). The Chayanta population mirrored this trend: from the second third of the century on, and particularly from 1751, there was a remarkable rise in the number of forasteros (table 2), which contrasts with the relative stability and even decline in the number of *originarios* (literally, Indians living with their original ethnic groups). This evolution points to a crucial agrarian development, because in eighteenth-century northern Potosí the distinction between originarios and forasteros (or *agregados*, an exchangeable term in this region) was not mainly based on genealogical considerations (the place of origin of the Indians or their ancestors) but on the type of plots the tributaries occupied. Forasteros, in other words, were not necessarily past or recent migrants but rather Indians who received fewer or less-fertile land parcels.[22] This fiscal category mostly signaled an agrarian not a migratory status. Sharp increases in the number and percentage of forasteros meant, for the most part, that more peasant households were left without enough plots to continue to be categorized as originarios. It is possible, then, that demographic pressures caused the same economic trend that Tristan Platt (1982b: 53–56) has documented for northern Potosí a century later: population growth was followed by a subdivision of the plots of originarios into several agregado *tasas* (the set of puna and/or valley fields assigned to the families).[23] Therefore, the rise in the forastero population is not so much a ratio of migratory movements as a sign of the intensifying subdivision of land with its inexorable impact on decreasing rural productivity.

This trend of agrarian compression is behind the land disputes that engulfed many villages in northern Potosí during this period. As examined in this volume, confrontations between indigenous peoples and Spanish hacienda owners sprang up at this time. More often yet, echoing the predominance of the Andean ayllu in this area, agrarian tensions manifested in intense feuds within and between peasant communities and in protests against caciques. I have shown elsewhere (2000), for instance, that families and ayllus of the group Pocoata engaged in fierce disputes over community boundaries and household land allocations from the 1730s onward. This alarming state of affairs prompted a provincial corregidor in 1754 to urge the viceroy of Peru to adopt concrete measures to curb the growth of landless Indian families.[24] In 1766, another corregidor went as far as to propose to the viceroy the restitution to the Indian communities of fields that had been transferred to private haciendas, "to place on these lands all the Indians that now have few plots, or are landless, and who are considered agregados. In this way, they would pass to the category of originarios."[25] Ten years later, still another provincial magistrate warned that, as a result of population growth, the originario Indians lacked enough plots to meet the tribute dues assigned to this fiscal category. In order to decrease the tax burden of these indigenous families, he suggested that those originario families should be legally recategorized as forasteros.[26]

During this time agricultural and mining production experienced a period of expansion that matched the population growth. By the second half of the eighteenth century, the main silver deposits of the Andes, Potosí and Cerro de Pasco, had expanded their output. Likewise, analyses of the tithe series in various Andean regions also indicate increases in the production of maize, wheat, wine, and brandy in the Spanish haciendas.[27] Agricultural production in lands controlled by indigenous communities expanded as well. A study of the series of *veintenas* (the payment of one-twentieth of European grains harvested in indigenous lands) of several Chayanta Indian communities demonstrates that around the mid-1750s peasant production started to increase at even higher rates than did hacienda production (Tandeter 1995: 15). By the end of the century, as mentioned above, Chayanta had become one of the main suppliers of wheat to the Potosí market.

And yet, once more, mining and agrarian growth did not necessarily translate into an increase in living standards for the rural population. During this period the southern Andes experienced the beginning of a deflationary price cycle that hurt the peasant economy insofar as indigenous communities, both in the Andes and in Mexico, tended to participate in urban markets as sellers of agricultural produce rather than as consumers of goods. The declining prices, consequently, must have lowered the net returns of the peasant economy, even within the context of agrarian growth (Tandeter and Wachtel 1989). This ominous trend probably deepened as the successful efforts of the Bourbon administration to raise tribute revenues and, especially, the expansion of the forced distribution of goods increased the cash obligations of the native peoples.[28] Furthermore, rises in the rate of the *alcabala* (sales tax) and the setting up of customhouses (*aduanas*) to insure its collection—a policy that bred widespread urban revolts in some of the major Andean cities—sharply undermined the indigenous participation in regional markets.[29] The revamping of the Potosí mining industry, in turn, unlike the boom of its counterpart in Mexico that was stimulated by tax reductions and state subsidies, relied in large part on the imposition of new and harsher modes of exploitation on the mita workers.[30]

This complex array of market, fiscal, and agrarian trends seems to account for the paradoxical situation experienced by Andean society during the second half of the eighteenth century: the fact that a process of population and production growth, plus a cycle of price stagnation and decline (a reverse of the situation causing massive social unrest in Europe) went hand in hand with what Enrique Tandeter (1995: 22) has defined as "a crisis in the living standards of the Andean indigenous communities." It is this crisis that provides the context for the escalation of rural protests and turmoil.

This study combines narrative and analytical modes of historical writing. As a political history, the exposition roughly follows a chronological order. Each chapter, however, is centered on a particular cluster of political, socioeconomic, and ethnohistorical issues. Underlying the work is the idea that a civilization can be examined not only through large institutional, economic, and social categories but also through an in-depth analysis of particular groups. Hence, the study of social relations and interaction among concrete historical actors is favored in this volume. Socioeconomic trends (fiscal pressures, commercial monopolies, demographic growth, migration, etc.) and mental structures (neo-Inca ideologies, millennial prophesies, ideal visions of community/state relationship) provide the context of social agency, not agency itself. In understanding the process whereby Andean peoples constituted themselves as political actors, I propose to follow, over a long period of time, the way northern Potosí communities engaged state institutions, related their specific hardships to the rules that were supposed to govern social relations, expressed their own visions of justice, and tried to promote community mobilization and solidarity over internal divisions.

In chapter 1 I look at the first crisis of domination in northern Potosí in the late 1740s, which was brought about by widespread, mostly successful, struggles over control of ethnic chieftainships. I show the emergence of contentious peasant notions of the legitimacy of caciques as well as the effects on power relations in the countryside of the ideological dissension within the colonial administration. In the following chapter I reconstruct the activities of a cacique named Florencio Lupa of the group Moscari, the first and most prominent target of collective violence during the rebellion of 1780. I trace his career from his advent as native chief of Moscari in the early 1750s to the early 1770s, when, through his appointment as cacique of two other ethnic groups, Panacachi and Pocoata, he became the beneficiary of the most ambitious experiment in social control ever attempted in the region: the formation of a multiethnic chieftainship. In chapter 3 I explore the impact of the implementation of the Bourbon reforms, the most profound reformulation of the colonial pact since the Toledean reforms, on existing social arrangements in the northern Potosí villages during the 1770s. Whereas the relation between Bourbon absolutism and social protest usually has been analyzed in terms of mounting economic grievances, my study is concerned with the ways new state mechanisms of domination contributed to mold new forms of peasant contention. I contend that Bourbon rationalizing programs increased peasant burdens and set up new mechanisms of social discipline, but also empowered native peoples to contest the institutions of local government by heightening antagonisms between royal official and provincial ruling groups, as well as between secular and ecclesiastical magistrates. As discussed in the chapter, the fierce (and successful) resistance of the Pocoata communities to the encroachment on their right to self-rule provoked by the appointment of Florencio Lupa, and the ensuing uprising led by Tomás Katari of their Macha neighbors against their own ethnic chiefs are striking illustrations of the unwitting consequences of this process of political empowerment.

The indigenous rebellion of 1778–1781 is analyzed in the last three chapters. My central aim is to trace the transition from everyday forms of colonial politics to the politics of anticolonialism. Through a detailed narrative of the events, I will show how peasant mobilization began as an expansion of customary struggles over the command of community government and, in the course of three years, turn it into a large-scale upheaval unique in the region in terms of geographical reach and political radicalization. This thorough collapse of the legitimacy of Spanish rule in the area goes a long way in explaining the rapid embrace of neo-Inca nativist projects following the eruption of the Túpac Amaru insurrection in late 1780. And yet, the fusion of a discrete local political history with pan-Andean expectations of epochal changes made for an extremely complex process. The encounter of these two insurgent outlooks gave rise to ideological ambiguities that in the end would greatly contribute to sealing the fate of the indigenous movement. A comparison between the different regional sites of rebel activity, which I develop in the conclusion to this study help to locate this specific ideological trajectory in the larger scenario of Andean insurgency.

1

Political

Legitimacy

in Mid-

Eighteenth-

Century

Andean

Villages

IN MID-1747, A GROUP OF INDIANS OF CHULLPA, one of
the six ethnic groups that comprised the Chayanta repartimiento, traveled to
the city of La Plata to ask the audiencia of Charcas for the dismissal of their
cacique, Dionisio Choque. While it was not the first overt confrontation between communities and native chiefs at the time, this conflict would have particular repercussions. As a member of a well-established family of Chullpa
ethnic lords, Dionisio Choque had in the 1720s succeeded his father, Pedro
Choque, who had been cacique since the late seventeenth century.[1] In confront-
ing Dionisio Choque, the Chullpas resorted to a judicial strategy that would
thereafter become a cornerstone of peasant contention in northern Potosí, even
in the midst of the great insurrection of 1780: they exhibited before the Charcas
court a document with the names, place of residence, and minor ayllu membership of fifty-five tributaries that paid their taxes to the cacique but were not
registered in official tax rolls.[2] These "concealed" Indians would have increased
the state revenues by 452 pesos per year. Equally important, this litigation by
the Chullpas brought to the forefront the sharp disagreements within the colonial administration in the Andes. Despite the opposition of the provincial corregidor, Agustín Pérez de Vargas, the audiencia ministers, the highest authority

in the region, backed indigenous claims by ordering not only Dionisio Choque's removal from office but also his detention in the court jail in La Plata.

The success of this protest set in motion widespread defiance of rural ruling groups. Following the example of the Chullpas, Indians of the Caracha community managed to have their cacique, Pedro Yavira, discharged in 1747 through a denunciation over fiscal fraud. Yavira identified himself as *cacique propietario*, which meant that his position had been recognized by the audiencia or the viceroy because of his noble lineage. One year later, after numerous collective petitions in Chayanta and La Plata, their neighbors in Puraca succeeded in replacing Marcos Tococari (who had held the post for eighteen years) with one of the protest leaders, an Indian named Sebastián Auca. By this time, fifteen native chiefs and *hilacatas* (tribute collectors) of the six ethnic groups that composed that the Chayanta repartimiento — Puraca, Chullpa, Laymi, Chayantaca, Caracha, and Sicoya — threatened to resign if Indian dissent were not suppressed. Protests were likewise made by four caciques of Macha and one of Pocoata. In March 1750, the Jukumanis (Aymaya repartimiento) blatantly overlooked their native chief by delivering the tribute payments to an Indian whom they themselves had elected. Discontent among the Chullpas and Puracas, on the other hand, continued after the removal of their respective caciques because corregidor Pérez de Vargas had put a mestizo named Gregorio Jorge de Medina in the place of Dionisio Choque and demanded that the Puracas formally disavow their previous charges of tribute embezzlement in exchange for the appointment of Sebastián Auca. In mid-1750, after a new wave of protests, Pérez de Vargas's successor, Pablo de Aoíz, was eventually forced to remove Gregorio Jorge de Medina and to carry out a population recount that demonstrated the concealment of taxpayers in both Chullpa and Puraca. Then, in 1751 and 1752, the native lord of Chayantaca, Pedro Espíritu Portugal, and of Pocoata, Blas Cori, were driven out of office. The latter, who had faced litigation since at least 1744, was, like Dionisio Choque of Chullpa in 1747, placed under arrest in La Plata's court jail.[3] Summarizing the current state of affairs, one of the caciques who had managed to keep his post, chief of Sicoya Francisco Callisaya, urged the grandson of a former cacique "to take his place as governor, for his people were behaving in a very arrogant and quarrelsome manner with him."[4]

In short, northern Potosí experienced during these years extended challenges to the community system of rule. Equally significant, as the beleaguered Andean chiefs enjoyed the firm support of the corregidores, parish priests, and most Spanish town-dwellers — and as the high court of Charcas became actively involved in these occurrences — rural disturbances exceeded the level of intra-ethnic disputes or mere local affairs and turned into conflicts over the institutions of village government. In fact, the breakdown of political subordination bred by community/cacique strife expanded to other important economic spheres. Between 1751 and 1753, some Indians denounced the forced distribution of goods carried out by the corregidor, as well as the abuses perpetrated in the collection of veintenas—the tax levied on wheat and livestock raised on Indian lands. In July 1748, a hacendado in the valley of Carasi, along with several Indian tenants, violently assaulted a *diezmero* (tithe collector) and some of the indigenous and Spanish officials escorting him. As indicated by a corregidor's lieutenant, this attack rapidly spread to other areas of Carasi (a district populated by Laymis, Puracas, Pocoatas, and Machas) where "more than fifty Indians rose against the diezmero . . . [in view of the fact] that no exemplary measure was taken for the continence and subjection, calmness and peace, of the Province and the people who inhabit it."[5] In a society where state power relied on scarce means of coercion, those in charge of conducting the daily business of government in the Andean countryside—a few Spaniards in an overwhelmingly indigenous world—knew all too well the potential impact of open political defiance.

"Popular views of authority and the law were forged in the crucible of conflict," John Brewer and John Styles (1983: 15) observe in their study on the interaction between society and government in eighteenth-century England. In this chapter I argue that the events of the late 1740s, the first crisis of domination in northern Potosí during the eighteenth century, prefigure in many regards the attitudes toward authority and the law dramatically played out during the mass Indian uprising three decades later. Although little violence occurred, these years witnessed collective demonstrations of force, overt and subtle expressions of insubordination, and tenacious indigenous judicial politics. In response to the perceived violation of community rights, the Andean peasants thus developed certain routines of contention, i.e., certain established modes of collective action in the public realm of colonial institutions and in the rural world emerged.[6] More generally, the crisis of ethnic chieftainships is linked to the emergence of a principle of political legitimacy that underwrote, implicitly or explicitly, Indian rights to select the caciques according to their purported capacity to preserve the social and economic fabric of the Andean ayllu. This contractual principle of authority stood in open contradiction to the two dominant mechanisms of access to the post: hereditary rights and discretional appointment by provincial corregidores. Indian dissension, on the other hand, rendered visible the profound ideological discrepancies over the nature of colonial rule within the Spanish administration and the practical effects of those discrepancies. State officials were faced with the underlying dilemmas of colonialism in the Andes: the consequences of ruling by force given the limited coercive resources, as well as the consequences of tolerating institutionalized expressions of dissidence given the propensity of social unrest to spread out due to the free interaction between indigenous communities and their high levels of everyday autonomy and physical mobility. The way the Spanish government would tackle this dilemma was in large part to determine the evolution of social relationships in northern Potosí until the eruption of mass insurgency in 1780.

ETHNIC GROUPS OF THE CHAYANTA REPARTIMIENTO

Because rural agitation during the 1740s was mostly focused on some of the six ethnic groups that made up the Chayanta repartimiento, a brief ethnohistorical overview is in order here. By the eighteenth century, Chayanta was the largest repartimiento of the province. In 1750, 25 percent of the indigenous population of the province were located there, and in the early 1770s its communities contributed 9,880 pesos per annum to the royal treasury, roughly 27 percent of the total tribute collection of the province (see table 3). It is crucial to note, however, that unlike Macha, Pocoata, and Sacaca, which retained their political identity throughout colonial times, the pre-Hispanic Chayanta kingdoms broke up into its eight constituting ethnic groups: Chullpa, Laymi-Puraca, Caracha, Chayantaca, and Sicoya (Chayanta repartimiento), Aymaya and Jukumani (Aymaya repartimiento), and Panacachi.[7] By the eighteenth century, the Laymi and Puraca were two separate groups with their own caciques, although, as noted below, starting from the 1760s a Laymi cacique governed over the two communities. Certainly this process of fragmentation did not affect the mainte-

Table 3. Originario and Forastero Populations,
Repartimiento of Chayanta

Tributaries	Ca. 1740	1746	1751	1772	1786
Originarios	772	808	856	871	636
Forasteros	198	207	219	952	864
Total	970	1,015	1,075	1,823	1,500

Source: The information for the years 1740, 1746, and 1751 is from AGN, XIII, 18–9–2; the census of 1772 is in AGN, XIII, 23–3–1, Cuaderno Primero; the census of 1786 is in AGN, XIII, 18–10–4. Note: The number of tributaries in 1740 and 1746 is approximate because data are only available for the total amount of tribute, from which I have calculated the number of tributaries. The jump in Chayanta's tributaries between 1751 and 1772 (as well as the decrease registered in 1786) can largely be attributed to the fact that the 1772 population recount was done by an outside official.

Table 4. Originario and Forastero Populations Residing in Puna and Valleys, Repartimiento of Chayanta, 1786

Ethnic Group	Minor Ayllus	Puna		Carasi		San Pedro de Buena Vista		Micani		Total
		Orig.	Forast.	Orig.	Forast.	Orig.	Forast.	Orig.	Forast.	
Lami	Collana	52	34	—	—	—	—	5	10	—
	Laymi	62	57	34	36	—	—	—	—	—
	Sulcata	25	15	—	—	—	—	—	—	—
Subtotal		139	106	34	36	—	—	5	10	330
Puraca		109	48	89	57	—	—	—	—	303
Chullpa	Collana	8	42	—	—	—	—	4	9	—
	Sulcata	8	25	—	—	—	—	—	—	—
Subtotal		16	67	—	—	—	—	4	9	96
Chayantaca		50	218	—	—	18	42	—	—	328
Caracha		90	61	—	—	—	—	39	37	227
Sicoya		37	156	—	—	6	17	—	—	216
Total		441	656	123	93	24	59	48	56	1,500

Source: AGN, XIII, 18–10–4.

nance of the traditional Andean pattern of ecological complementarity. The communities owned continuous puna lands where they cultivated several varieties of tubers, beans, wheat, and barley and grazed their livestock, as well as discontinuous territories in the valleys of Carasi, Micani, and San Pedro de Buena Vista (table 4). In these multiethnic lowland territories, Indians cultivated maize, wheat, fruits, and horticultural products.[8]

The highland town of Chayanta, the provincial capital, was divided in two parishes, Laymi and Chayantaca. The Laymi parish was comprised of the groups Laymi, Puraca, and Chullpa, and the Chayantaca parish of the groups Chayantaca, Sicoya, and Caracha. As described in an eighteenth-century account, the population of the village of Espíritu Santo of Chayanta "is divided into two parishes housed in a single church of which the right side or the side of the gospel belongs to the Laymis and the left side or side of the epistle belongs to the Chayantacas, each parish has its own altars, wrought silver and ornaments, with the exception of the high altar which is commonly shared by both parishes."[9] Although the original aim of the foundation of this village, a product of the general resettlement of the Indian population carried out under Viceroy Toledo, was never accomplished, it did become an important ritual center.[10] The Indians from Chayanta dealt with the same Spanish civil authorities, *curas doctrineros* (parish priests), Spanish and mestizo *vecinos* (residents), and town-council officeholders. They also shared some of the most important collective celebrations related to Catholic festivals and the fiscal calendar (especially community gatherings for the payment of tributes). Traces of these ties exist still today: the present-day town of Chayanta holds ritual battles, or *tinkus*, where members of the different ethnic groups confront each other, and where the three ethnic groups of Laymi and Chayantaca get together to confront the other moiety (Harris 1996: 265).

LEGITIMACY CRISIS OF LOCAL AUTHORITY

By the mid-eighteenth century, as discussed in the introduction, the viceroyalty of Peru witnessed the beginning of a long cycle of social turmoil promoted, among other factors, by the expansion of the forced sale of goods, a growing fiscal burden (tribute and alcabala), declining prices, and land shortages associated with the general growth of the indigenous population. While northern Potosí participates in this historical trend, rural discontent surfaced, for the most part, through numerous confrontations between communities and caciques. The intensity and recurrence of these conflicts speaks to the crucial social features of this rural universe.

First and foremost is the pivotal role of the ethnic chiefs in the social reproduction of the Andean community. In northern Potosí, native lords continued to wield a large influence on the articulation of the ayllus with the outside world — the colonial state, local power groups, regional markets, and neighboring Indian communities — through a series of practices: the collection of tribute in tune with Andean cultural norms linking the amount of the tasa (head tax) to land allocations, marital status, and performance of labor and religious services; the election of mita workers, ritual sponsors, and church servants according to an integrated system of turns; the commercialization of peasant surpluses, prominently those produced in common lands (comunes); the lease of community fields and grain mills; the intervention in the corregidores' forced sale of goods; and the defense of ethnic territories in boundary conflicts. Native chiefs, moreover, allocated agrarian resources following manifold land tenure rights: highland plots distributed annually to the domestic units to produce specific crops (*mantas*), fields cultivated by the community for collective needs (comunes), and parcels assigned to peasant households according to a combination of demographic (size of the families), social (participation in festival sponsorships), and agrarian (land availability) factors.[11] Symbolic action was also a fundamental attribute of authority. Historical records reveal that the caciques played a major role in rituals, Catholic festivals, and communal gatherings through institutionalized generosity. As a result of these entrenched arrangements, agrarian, fiscal, and market pressures on the ethnic economies tended to have a direct repercussion on community/cacique relationships. It should be noted here that this was not the case throughout the Andes. In the Quito region, for instance, the decay of native chieftainships starting in the late seventeenth century caused the government of the Andean community to be characterized, according to Karen Powers (1995: 151), by "its extreme departure from all Andean expectations of good leadership and its disavowal of the communities' interests." In Andagua, a province of Arequipa, the leaders of social networks coalesced around ancestor-mummy cults, and regional trade overtook most of the functions traditionally accomplished by the caciques, who then began to function, and to be perceived, as local colonial officials (Salomon 1987).

It is possible that a second system of authority within the Andean communities, the members of the indigenous *cabildo* (town council) and the church servants and ritual sponsors, set limits to the power of the northern Potosí caciques. Certainly, services in cabildo posts and confraternities carried great social prestige and became, along with other community obligations like tribute and mita, a means to secure access to community lands. Yet whatever the tensions between these two authority systems, there is little evidence that the alcaldes and other town-council officeholders assumed in northern Potosí the kind of political and economic roles they took, for instance, in southern Peru in the aftermath of the suppression of the Túpac Amaru rebellion. There, the caciques' loss of jurisdiction over tribute collection, peasant resistance, and new state policies gave rise to the gradual replacement of traditional Andean lords by *alcaldes varayoks* (Indian mayors).[12] Whereas civil-religious town hierarchies, along with offices such as mita captain and tribute collector, served to legitimize claims to chieftainships, there is little evidence that northern Potosí Indians demanded or envisioned the elimination of caciques and their replacement for a system of residence-based rotating officeholders.[13] In this area, the native lords at different levels of the community (ayllus, moieties, and/or ethnic groups) were essential for organizing the distribution of economic levies and resources among peasant households scattered through distant highland and valley town/parish districts. As I discuss in chapter 3, it appears, moreover, that the caciques and hilacatas appointed the members of the cabildo and confraternities.

The continuing centrality of the caciques in the economic, political, and ritual life of the Andean communities was matched by a second fundamental factor: the demise of hereditary chieftainships. In eighteenth-century northern Potosí, most of the native lords did not belong to a noble lineage. As in the rest of the Andes, the corregidores' aggressive policy of appointing "interim caciques" in order to facilitate their forced distribution of goods drastically diminished the number of proprietary caciques. Actually, although several of the caciques deposed between 1747 and 1753 had been in office for many years, only the Caracha chief appears to have possessed the title *en propiedad*. But, more important still, those native chiefs who did belong to traditional families of Andean lords, far from embodying the ethnic autonomy and historical memory of the group, were the most assimilated to the structures of colonial power. Centuries of kin relations, commercial partnerships, and social interaction with Spanish rural dwellers and government officials turned most indigenous elite groups into private hacendados and culturally hispanicized mestizos. Not surprisingly, in the course of this period, hereditary lords like the Ayaviri Cuisara of Sacaca, Ayra Chinchi of Pocoata, or Florencio Lupa of Moscari would be among the main targets of peasant violence.[14]

A crucial phenomenon emerged out of this process. The political discrediting of the native aristocracy expanded to the very principle on which its authority rested: the Indians no longer considered hereditary rights as a sufficient (or necessary) basis of community rule.[15] In contrast to the "fever of titles and genealogies" experienced by the indigenous elite in other Andean regions in response to the multiplication of "interim caciques" (O'Phelan Godoy 1998: 19), protest leaders in northern Potosí did not cast the conflict in terms of their superior *derechos de sangre* (hereditary rights). By contrast, while in the short run the arbitrary appointment of caciques served the corregidores' commercial ventures, it could have contributed to removing from the institution the aristocratic undertones that the *señores naturales* (Andean lords) had preserved after the Spanish conquest.[16] It was not the nobility claims but notions of representation that infused the challenges to native chiefs, both those designated by the corregidores and those with blood rights. To the criteria of social control underwriting the discretionary interference in community affairs by colonial magistrates, some resistance groups, with varied degrees of collective support, opposed their presumed consensus among their peers (the protesters were "acclaimed" by the community and the current caciques were "despotic") and their services to the crown (disclosure of tribute embezzlement). Native chieftainships, in short, continued to play a central role in the functioning of Andean society—all the more crucial as agrarian and fiscal pressures mounted—at the same time that chieftain ideological legitimacy was no longer subjected to somewhat rigid aristocratic principles. The control of ethnic government thus became a fundamental locus of conflict, the object of struggles between state disciplining policies and peasant representative criteria.

The disturbances of the mid-eighteenth century clearly reflected this dynamic. Sebastián Auca, head of the movement against Puraca cacique Marcos Tococari, never exhibited his hereditary rights; when explaining his rise to the chief-tainship he simply stated that "it was at the request of the community."[17] In justifying the removal of their cacique from tribute collection in March 1750, the Jukumani Indians alluded to the collective will of the community.[18] Interest-ingly, Bernabé Choque, the only Indian of Chullpa involved in the disputes who is said to be associated with a traditional noble lineage, renounced exercising "the unquestionable right that I have to the post as the first-born son of the last cacique with blood rights" in favor of other leaders of the protest (he argued that he would not be able to occupy the government of Chullpa due to the "hatred and bad will" of the rest of the caciques toward him).[19] Like lineage, personal wealth also did not figure as a defining premise of political legitimacy. Pledges of more efficiency in the collection of tribute were based less on the personal resources of the candidates — as was the case, for example, in Cochachamba where a lengthy litigation over chieftanships was taking place at the time — than on the exhibition of detailed lists of taxpayers that proved the inaccuracy of the official censuses.[20] As the fifteen caciques and hilacatas of the six ethnic groups of the Chayanta repartimiento lamented in 1748, the final purpose of the uprising was that "nobody should rule them and correct their excesses, conducting by themselves the collection of tributes and refusing to pay them [to us] voluntarily unless they are rigorously pressured to do so."[21]

To be sure, the appeal to consensual principles does not mean the actual existence of such consensus. The implicit principle that renders social action intelligible is that Indian commons had no obligation to obey ethnic authorities who did not represent them (regardless of their supposed noble lineage) but claims to community representation were not to be taken at face value. Even though rural disturbances, as shown below, emerged in a context of intensifying community/cacique tensions, and judicial litigation could not possibly be sus-tained without a measure of indigenous support, the demise of the old Andean lords did not necessarily translate into political legitimacy for their successors. From 1757 to 1762, considerably large groups of Indians requested the removal of Martín Ninavia (Chullpa), Sebastián Auca (Puraca), Melchor Fernández de Espinoza (Chayantaca), and Antonio Vilca (Caracha) — all caciques who had been appointed in the midst of the crisis of the late 1740s. Collective mobi-lization, moreover, was rather limited and moved in the tenuous border of social protest and factionalism. The protests could serve as mechanisms of social climbing, too. For instance, one of the Chullpa leaders, a family named Poli-cario, were in fact natives of Sorasora (a province of Oruro) who had settled in Chayanta in the 1720s.[22] In August 1750, after the dismissal of Gregorio Jorge de Medina, Isidro Policario, a member of the family's first generation born in

Chayanta, was appointed cacique lieutenant of Chullpa. Political strife had thus allowed the family to make the transition from forasteros to hilacatas in less than twenty years.

And yet by putting into question both hereditary rights and the corregidores' discretionary appointments the protests of the Puracas, Chullpas, Pocoatas, Jukumanis, and Carachas opened a space of contention over the concrete meaning of the Andean ayllus' corporate privilege to self-rule. They canalized, too, the increasing strains in several realms of peasant everyday life. In this sense, Indian grievances during the years 1747–1752, along with the complaints that members of the same ethnic groups continued to voice in the following years, underscore the intertwinement of the emerging principles of political legitimacy with the moral economy of the Andean ayllu.[23] As one might expect, issues of land, mita, and tribute were at the center of indigenous complaints.

Echoing the increasingly crucial role of the caciques in times of agrarian pressures and demographic growth, the management and defense of communal landholdings appeared as one of the overriding causes of Indian discontent. Thus, in the late 1740s, the Chullpa caciques Dionisio Choque and Gregorio Jorge de Medina were accused of misappropriating 150 pesos yielded by the lease of communal lands in a place called Bombo (on the border with Oruro), which were supposed to be used for collective needs.[24] Ten years later, reflecting the shortage of lands, the Indians started to complain that the communal fields were being rented to about thirty indigenous families from the province of Paria, when the Chullpas, as some Indians put it, "contribute their tributes and other obligations to which they are subjected without having a piece of land of their own."[25] In the 1760s, the Auquimarcas, a lowland group of San Pedro de Buena Vista, also accused their cacique of renting out community lands when they had become tenants in outside ayllus and haciendas because of the lack of fields.[26]

Agrarian pressures also translated in charges against the caciques for their purported inability to secure the ethnic territories in the endemic boundary conflicts with neighboring communities. The Auquimarcas themselves were embroiled in land conflicts with the Sicoyas and Chayantacas, two puna communities with valley territories in San Pedro de Buena Vista.[27] In 1757, Caracha Indians pronounced their cacique, Antonio Vilca, incompetent because, among other reasons, "he does not read or write, which is necessary to take care of us and defend us and for this reason our neighbors strip us of our lands."[28] The Puracas claimed that they lacked "lands to sow because what happens is that since [Sebastián] Auca does not know how to speak and is a complete drunk and idle, he lets any Indian who comes from outside provinces strip him of our lands."[29] The testimony alludes to families of the Condocondo community (in the province of Paria) who, led by their powerful cacique, Gregorio Llanquipacha, gradually introduced themselves in lands where the Puracas "planted their little crops" under the false excuse "that they had titles." Despite having presented approximately forty witnesses to the Chayanta corregidor, the Puracas failed to preserve their rights because of the "natural drunkenness, stupidity, and laziness" of their cacique.[30] In 1772, several Chullpa Indians, too, contended that Manuel Ninavia (Martín Ninavia's son) failed to "defend the lands in disputes over boundaries that arise . . . allowing Indians [from the Caracha, Sicoya, and Chayantaca groups] to occupy our fields in the puna."[31]

The election and treatment of the mita workers awakened various grievances. First, the Indians protested the appointment of *colquerunas* ("money-man," in Quechua), members of the community who commuted their turn in the Potosí mita for cash payments. As only the wealthiest Indians could afford to buy their exemption, this practice meant an extra burden for the poorest families who occupied their places.[32] Seven mitayos of Puraca, for instance, explained that Sebastián Auca sent "the poorest Indians . . . to the mita, since those more well off stay home thanks to this payment and fraud." To prove the charge, the Puracas exhibited a detailed list of fifteen colquerunas residing in both puna and valleys who had paid between 60 and 65 pesos in 1757.[33] The same year, the Carachas also complained that due to the appointment of colquerunas, Indians were dispatched to Potosí "before the two-year rest."[34] The Chullpas also presented a list of colquerunas named by their caciques in 1771 and 1772.[35]

Second, we know that the mita was an obligation undertaken by the community as a whole, because the worker and his family survived during their year in Potosí on the cattle, foodstuffs, and clothing that they brought from their villages (Assadourian 1979: 223–92). Many Andean communities met part of this burden through the collective cultivation of communal lands.[36] As the Puracas described it, for the mining workers to receive provisions of maize, wheat, *chuño* (dried potatoes), and other supplies, "the Indians who stay in the village plant, and whatever they harvest, it should be assigned for this purpose, without the caciques taking any part of it, other than the charitable help for these miserable Indians who have to go through such a toilsome trip."[37] Their cacique, however, was accused of using the land "as if he were its absolute owner," so that the mitayos lacked food in their trip to Potosí, a "long road that they usually have to walk, driving their cattle, with their poor children and hapless wives."[38] Likewise, the cacique of Chullpa was accused of expropriating money from the Caja de Censos, a reserve fund of the communities meant to meet their duties toward state and the church. One of the mitayos of Chullpa explained to Potosí officials that despite that "it has been always the custom that the caciques give this money to the mita captains and workers for the journey to Potosí," cacique Martín Ninavia had allowed them to leave for the mining town without the needed supplies.[39]

Perhaps the most aggravating aspect of the management of the mita system within the Indian communities was the payment of tribute after the year of service in Potosí, one of the longstanding sources of conflict between Spanish legislation and indigenous practices across the southern Andes region. As a Potosí intendant put it, in the 1780s, "one of the main reasons why the Indians loath their service in the mita is because they find it difficult to pay their tributes when they return from it" (quoted in Tandeter 1992: 76). Thus, in 1759 and 1761, twelve captains of the mita from the province of Pacajes and six from the province of Sicasica denounced their corregidor for having auctioned off the cattle belonging to the mitayos who did not pay their taxes after their return from Potosí. Both complaints reached the highest levels of government of the viceroyalty of Peru.[40] By this time, the Chullpas and Puracas gained the cooperation of numerous mitayos of Chayanta to testify against the caciques before the Potosí authorities, by promising them to obtain the recognition of their tributary exemption. It was said that Isidro Policario, Bernabé Choque, and other Chullpas had drawn the support from tens of mitayos, "arguing that they could not have two levies at the same time."[41] I will show in chapter 5 that even at the height of the rebellion of 1780, one of the main objectives of the northern Potosí communities was precisely to compel provincial authorities to implement a royal decree of 1692 freeing mita workers from tribute payments.

As mentioned earlier, most of the caciques were charged with misappropriating tribute money from unregistered Indians. In the course of the conflicts, the Chullpas, Puracas, and Pocoatas exhibited to the audiencia several lists containing the real number of taxpayers, and the Jukumanis delivered tribute money to the corregidor without the intervention of the cacique. That many other Indians followed this example in the years to come will be noted, including the example of insurgent leader Tomás Katari. No doubt this accusation had a pragmatic purpose insofar as colonial legislation allowed for the immediate removal of ethnic authorities engaged in fiscal fraud.[42] Yet the persistence of this charge, even when as in the case of Puraca the resisted cacique had already been removed, suggests that it represented more than a mere tactical resource. Tribute and mita indeed constituted the main economic and symbolic link between the Andean communities and the king. As Tristan Platt (1982b: 28–29) has shown for the nineteenth century, the northern Potosí ayllus perceived the payment of taxes to the state as a means to guarantee their collective landholding. The relationship between communities and the state could be understood as a projection, at the macro social level, of the relationship between the peasant families and their caciques, for the payment of tribute was a basic mechanism of ethnic affiliation and access to ayllu lands.[43] Consequently, apart from their legal connotations, the disclosure of new tributaries could have represented the reaffirmation of the "pact of reciprocity" linking Andean peoples and the crown, a means of reestablishing a morally disrupted social order. As a Chullpa mita worker summarized, his cacique used the peasant taxes "for his fitting sustenance, for him and not for the King our Lord, because this is what the governors usually do, and under this pretext he does not hand over the Royal tributes of these Indians, keeping them for himself as if the money belonged to him."[44]

Certainly, one should be careful when assessing the socioeconomic motives of peasant unrest. Litigation pursued a tactical goal: to convince colonial officials of the necessity of removing the caciques. The language of legal rights that the Indians needed to adopt in their judicial battles entailed the denunciation of certain practices that in other social spheres, or applied to other native authorities, might have appeared as perfectly acceptable. Tribute demands to mita workers or involvement in the repartimiento system could have been perceived as inherently unjust levies. But the leasing of community lands, the appointment of colquerunas, and the concealment of tributaries were time-honored practices that had emerged as strategies of resistance to colonial exactions. It is well known that from the outset of the colonial order in the Andes, the cash obligations of the communities forced the caciques to integrate ethnic economies based on ideals of reciprocity and self-sufficiency into the colonial markets. The historical literature has rebuffed essentialist interpretations based on the premise that the level of consensus of ethnic authorities was directly related to the degree of attachment to pre-Hispanic models of behavior.[45] Accordingly, most of the native lords did not seek to deny the existence of many of the "abuses" the Indians attributed to them; instead they tried to show that the money thus collected was destined to meet their obligations toward both the state and the community. In 1757, for example, the Puraca cacique exhibited the following list of annual expenditures necessary as part of the relations of reciprocity within the community (offerings during collective gatherings and assistance to mita workers) and colonial economic dues to the Church and the provincial corregidores.[46]

| 135 pesos | For the "cantors of the Chayanta, Carasi, and Micani parishes" |
| 25 pesos | For lodging during the priest's three annual visits to the vice-parish of Calacala, and a week during Lent" |

25 pesos	"For the lodging of the corregidores' visit"
50 pesos	For the maintenance of the captain of the mita "and double payment when it is the turn to send Captains and Hilancos from this part [Puraca]"
15 pesos	For "the transportation of the loads of the mita workers"
40 pesos	"For the feast of the tax collection, because if they are not given chicha, wine, cocoa, and brandy, they do not pay their tribute"
100 pesos	For chicha, coca, "and other treats" offered in the meeting for the enlisting and dispatch of the mitayos

Likewise, when accounting for the money produced by the lease of communal lands of Bombo and by the Caja de Censos, the Chullpa cacique said he had to spend money in three types of activities: trips, litigation, and institutionalized generosity. In 1761, Martín Ninavia explained that "the expenditures that the job of Tax collector carries are large, since I have to invest in the mules that I have to keep for my trips, in the salary of the scribe who is always with me, and in coca, brandy, and chicha which, according to custom since time immemorial, I should provide to please and honor Indians every year during the collection of the Royal tributes."[47]

In the case of the Chullpa, the Indians had the opportunity to voice their opinion about the economic nature of their native lords' expenses. They did not dispute that the cacique was obliged to distribute important amounts of coca, chicha, and brandy during collective celebrations, particularly during Easter and the gathering for the dispatch of the mita team; rather, what the Chullpas denied was that the "offerings" were indeed paid by the caciques. They argued that the community as a whole, through its labor and agricultural resources, covered the expenses. Summarizing their perspective on economic relations between the community and the cacique, the Chullpas told a judge,

> nothing comes out of [the cacique's] pocket [during festivities], because instead of supplying the mitayos he tells them to make chicha, and he buys coca selling the harvest of the plots that, under the name of commons, all the Indians sow using their own oxen and ploughs. So it comes from the same Indians' pockets because they work on it, but since the harvest is kept by the Governor, he claims that it is his expenditure. Even if there were an accurate accounting of such matters, he would have a surplus because the expenses in such celebrations are no more than twenty jugs of chicha, and two coca baskets are worth 4 reales and maybe one or two arrobas [one arroba equals about twenty-five pounds] of brandy, [*aguardiente*], which

is mainly drunk by the Governors and their principals. And he does not spend anything in mules because the Indians plant barley and take it to his home, and they do the same with maize, potatoes, and wheat which they grow in the best areas of the communal lands, so that the Governor, after living off such harvests, and paying for the said celebrations, still has some leftover to sell, even though it has not cost him a cent, other than rigorously giving orders to do so, and taking care that he keeps seed for the following year.[48]

In this remarkable description of the political economy of the Andean ayllu, the cacique emerges as a mere administrator of the income produced by the peasant economy, including that from cattle, lands, and the labor force. His access to resources appears as a delegation of responsibilities by the Indians. Generosity and redistribution, consequently, were not a favor but a duty. The cacique neither owned nor created wealth; the community produced it. This statement makes plain that what was at stake was the social meaning involved in these material and symbolic exchanges between caciques and communities. As for the commercialization of agricultural surpluses in the colonial markets, tribute embezzlement, or colqueruna appointments, those redistribution activities could not be understood outside the implicit "cultural logic" governing them, whether the use of common assets served for the defense of the indigenous community or for mere personal wealth accumulation.[49]

It could be argued, then, as has been maintained for eighteenth-century French peasantry, that it was not so much changes in the weight or nature of the economic exactions that led to social outrage but rather their perceived or actual loss of utility. In the case of France, seigneurial levies began to be "experienced as unjust and detested" as the absolutist state gradually seized some of the traditional services provided by the lords to protect the rural communities (Markoff 1996: 18–19). Likewise, as growing economic pressures (agrarian, fiscal, demographic, and so forth) and the protracted process of internal differentiation made Andean lords relinquish their perceived role as safeguards of the community welfare, their specific sources of revenues and material demands appeared as wrongful. Paraphrasing the explanation for the intensifying rural agitation prior to the French Revolution, the issue was not so much burden as such, but justice (18). In many regards, it was the illegitimacy of the caciques that rendered their practices illegitimate, not the other way around.

It is at this point that the connection between shifting peasant notions of the ideological foundations of ethnic authority and the social function of Andean lords becomes most apparent. The protest movements of the 1740s should be understood as the first wave of projects aimed at bridging the gap between the economic and political rationality of native government. As the use of common economic resources (money, workforce, agrarian surpluses) was subjected to institutionalized forms of redistribution, and as the access to the post became increasingly disengaged from the aristocratic principles that had justified the perpetuation of traditional lineages of Andean lords, the legitimacy of the caciques came to depend, by and large, on their performance. The economic reciprocity informing ayllu-cacique relations began to be translated into a contractual notion of political legitimacy whereby some indigenous groups claimed the right to demand the removal of their native authorities, and the appointment of others in their place, according to their assumed ability or inability to fulfill their duties toward the community and the state. If attacks on hereditary caciques served provincial corregidores as a means of social and economic control over the Andean peasant society, it served the Indians as a weapon to assess the contractual, reversible, representative nature of native government.

THE RISE OF A CONTENTIOUS POLITICS

Dissenting indigenous groups reshaped notions of political legitimacy by acting on them. Thus, the analysis now turns to the concrete forms of collective action through which this emerging concept of rule was played out. Indigenous dissension in northern Potosí was not channeled through localized, short-lived, spontaneous eruptions of collective violence, the usual description of the rural protests that mushroomed in the Andes during the eighteenth century, but rather through prolonged and complex judicial processes. Andean peasants would typically fight abuses of power by accusing rural overlords before high colonial courts, the audiencia of La Plata and, in the late 1750s, Potosí's officials as well. The form social conflicts assumed should not be taken, however, as an index of their low intensity. The meaning of litigation in the Spanish colonial world is best captured by an observation made by Woodrow Borah (1983) in the preface to his study on the General Indian Court in Mexico. Borah comments that while doing research during the years 1938–1939, "I saw almost daily the delegations of Mexican village peasants waiting in the presidential patio for an audience with President Lázaro Cárdenas, and realized that I was witnessing the Juzgado General de Indios still functioning in the form it had under the first Spanish viceroy" (246). For the native peoples, in effect, judicial politics was not about crime and law but about justice and rights. The issues on which Indians looked for redress encompassed such fundamental social institutions as community government, land tenure, colonial economic levies, and religious practices. Accordingly, Spanish courts acted, as Borah noted for the General Indian Court, "not so much as a court of law as a court of compromise and accommodation. It may in this respect have dealt more in justice than do courts of law" (246).

If legal battles usually revolved around large matters of political and economic rights, the process of law enforcement was much less about state coercion than about local balances of forces. In the Spanish colonial rural world, the intervention of the courts did not entail the renunciation of the use of force. On the one hand, all involved parties perceived the Indian appeals to regional courts as a forthright act of defiance to the power of rural authorities, that is, as an unmistakable sign of insubordination. As judicial procedures, on the other hand, did not contemplate the deployment of any independent law enforcement officers (the very Indian claimants had to hand court orders to commissioned judges who usually were residents of the province), court battles to obtain legal redress of grievances were often followed by battles in the Andean villages to achieve their enforcement.[50] Appealing to the Spanish justice, in short, was neither motivated by, nor resulted in, peaceful settlements of social conflicts. In many ways, such acts amounted to a public declaration of "war," the setting in motion of an overt process of confrontation, or at least its continuation through other means. As Colin MacLachlan (1988: 124) has remarked: "Investigative hearings and the courts provided a controlled arena within which to test the strength of contending parties. Although appeals to the laws and abstract notions constituted a form of pressure, without actual power a legal victory could not be sustained. When seemingly powerless Indians forced the Audiencia to recognize their communal land-holdings, they not only relied upon philosophical notions but also implied their ultimate willingness to resort to violence or some form of social disruption in defense of their expectation of justice."

The function of the Spanish justice as an institutional framework for the exercise of violence (or for threats to resort to it) becomes apparent when we consider the reaction of the local power groups in northern Potosí to indigenous legal appeals. Provincial authorities deployed all the coercive and legal resources at their disposal to resist the intrusion of higher courts in local affairs. Thus, for instance, in 1748 and 1749 the audiencia of Charcas had issued several orders to force corregidor Agustín Pérez de Vargas to remove the Chullpa cacique Gregorio Jorge de Medina, "which could not be achieved," as an audiencia's official related, "even though we finded the corregidor for his disobedience, but he tenaciously wanted to keep this person in government even at the cost of paying the fine, as he did."[51] In the case of Puraca, the corregidores, cacique Marcos Tococari, the Chayanta parish priests, and the elite town-dwellers managed to have three commissioned judges who had been appointed by the audiencia between 1747 and 1750 force the Indians to recant their former charges of fiscal fraud.[52] In April 1748, several Indians requested that testimonies be taken in the city of La Plata because, "since the governor is powerful we justly are afraid that, as he can easily bribe Spaniards, in that area there is nobody who can behave with faithfulness."[53] Although the audiencia accepted the request, they would not be able to take witnesses to the city because Indian mayors were placed in the rural hamlets to prevent people from leaving their homes, and Marcos Tococari and his compadre Manuel Chico (a mayor of Chayanta town and Laymi cacique) "had a proclamation announced in the public plaza of our town [of Chayanta] saying that any Indian that left or moved from their hamlets and fields without permission would be sentenced to lashes, jail, and expropriation of their possessions."[54] During this period, Indians from Puraca, Chullpa, and Jukumani involved in the protests would be arrested, confiscated, and in at least one case publicly whipped in the central plaza of Chayanta village.

The resilience of Indian judicial politics in this environment speaks to the intensity of social discontent and the erosion of mechanisms of political subjection. Processes of legal appeal on the scale of those developed during this period could hardly be mounted without a backstage network of cooperation. Only by relying on some webs of solidarity within the peasant society could protest groups confront reprisals and open resistance to the implementation of the regional tribunal's rulings. It is clear, for instance, that in mobilizing people for the lawsuits traditional forms of reciprocity were deployed. It was reported that the Policarios drew the collaboration of their peers through "libations as [they] are accustomed to do, asking for a service [*mingando*] and buying witnesses for their endeavors."[55] Likewise, in his condition of hilacata of Chullpa, Isidro Policario asked in 1752 two indigenous officeholders to bring Indians to testify against the cacique, offering some personal rewards and the redressing of collective demands such as the use of the communal fields of Bombo and the appointment of colquerunas.[56] Although it is impossible to quantify popular participation, two incidents that took place in the village of Chayanta in March and August 1748 — a testimony of the Pocoata cacique on the state of his relations with the community, and the rising against the Jukumani cacique — afford us a glimpse into the political tensions underlying this cycle of conflicts.

The first incident occurred during the Pascua de la Resurrección of 1748, in the midst of the Chullpas's and Puracas's protests against their caciques. The Easter celebration was an important event of the festivity calendar. During this time of the year, the communities resided in their puna hamlets until they migrated to the valleys in May to harvest wheat and maize. We know that, as with other feasts, the Easter meeting was a significant occasion of community life combining Catholic elements with Andean rituals. According to a Chayanta mestizo neighbor, during the evening of Easter a multitude of Indians gathered to sing and dance, "which results in many sins." Among other heresies usually performed in these celebrations, the Indians dared "to profane the cemetery," meaning perhaps engaging in ancestor rituals.[57] Furthermore, during these gatherings, ethnic authorities were expected to accomplish their symbolic and material obligations toward their communities through institutionalized generosity. In fact, some Chullpa Indians mentioned in passing some years later that Easter constituted, along with the meeting for the dispatch of the mita team to Potosí in August, the main annual *convites* (offerings) of chicha, brandy, and coca leaves on the part of the caciques.[58] Given the cultural significance of Easter, the incidents of 1748 offer some insight into the tensions within this Andean society. A witness of the events related that the non-Indian neighbors of Chayanta, wary of the protests against the ethnic authorities, and

> fearing that among the Indians there should be some quarrels, the night before Easter of this year, due to the number of people who gathered in the plaza of this town to sing and dance, the Alcalde Mayor don Manuel Chico with some people went out to this plaza to prevent the Indians from the abuse of dancing and singing, which have been introduced a long time ago and originated many offenses against God our Lord during that night. [Chico] ordered everybody to leave the plaza and return to their homes, and since the Indians were already aroused due to the mentioned lawsuits, they resisted the Alcalde Mayor, so that he was forced to arrest one or two of them in the public jail of that town. With this example the Indians left the plaza and the great clamor that they had created during the night was calmed down.[59]

It is evident that it was not the "offenses against God" or "the abuse of dancing and singing" but the ongoing conflicts between communities and caciques that caused the confrontation with the authorities in such a critical moment of the communal cycle of festivities. As the same account indicates, the songs, dances, and rituals were time-honored customs and, as such, the priests and the other residents in Andean villages tolerated them. Certainly, the usual role of the ethnic chiefs in the Easter celebration went far beyond indulgence. What moved Manuel Chico to cancel the celebration was not the rituals but the fear of the meaning these rituals might take as a result of the struggles against the caciques—the fact that "the Indians were already aroused due to the mentioned lawsuits." We are told by another witness that Chico "cleared the plaza using some whippings and arrests because before doing that, he was resisted, and only with these displays did the shrieks and noise cease."[60] The connection between the general climate of unrest and the Easter incident is captured in a testimony of a Chayanta neighbor, an Aymara-speaking teacher of Christian doctrine. By the time of the Easter celebration, one of the troublemakers "from the Sullcata ayllu, who did not know Christian doctrine, because this witness told him that he must learn it with a Palmeta de Tabla, he got so outraged that he threatened to go to Chuquisaca to sue both the priests and this witness, and the said Indian left without confession, because he ran away."[61]

The reference to the reluctance to attend church services is not incidental. The disputes against caciques translated into confrontations with the clergymen. The priest of the Chayantaca parish, Nicolás Virto, claimed that only a very small number of Chayantacas, Sicoyas, and Carachas had attended mass and confessions during the past Lent. The same occurred, according to the priest of the Laymi parish, with the Chullpas and Puracas, for in the course of the two months that he had spent in the indigenous hamlets, "it has cost me a great amount of work to bring them [the Indians to be indoctrinated] here either with pleas or praise since their governors and principals do not dare to bring them by force, out of fear of a disgrace, although only through force have we been able to ensure that they attend punctually."[62] He estimated that more than thirty persons would be left in 1748 without confessing or receiving communion. But according to a list that the same priest presented later, more than one hundred Laymis, Puracas, and Chullpas, both men and women, did not confess or receive communion that year.[63]

The second incident also took place in the highland Chayanta village on August 16, 1748, a few months after the Easter celebration, in the course of another important moment of the festive calendar, the cabildo for the payment of the San Juan tribute quota and the election of the mita team. Coinciding with San Roque's day, this celebration attracted a multitude of Indians from several ethnic groups because Laymis, Chullpas, Puracas, and Chayantacas had convened in the town for the delivery of tributes and mita.[64] By this time, as already mentioned, corregidor Pérez de Vargas had accepted the appointment of Sebastián Auca as Puraca cacique in the place of Marcos Tococari in exchange for dropping the litigation.[65] The disturbances occurred when Francisco de Arsiniega, a commissioned judge who owned a hacienda in the valley of San Pedro de Buena Vista, tried, with the assistance of an audiencia's clerk, to validate this maneuver.[66] Arsiniega, who thirty years later would play a prominent role in the failed efforts to suppress the mass uprising in the area, expected the Puracas to deny the existence of tribute embezzlement and to admit that the protests had been stirred by a few "ringleaders" alien to the group (the Chullpa Indians Bernabé Choque and the Policario family, as well as the Moscari cacique, Miguel Lupa).[67]

Although one of the protest leaders had already been appointed cacique, the Indians refused to cooperate with the authorities. The underlying fact of legal politics, the "willingness to resort to violence or some form of social disruption in defense of their expectation of justice," as MacLachlan put it, was thus put to test. Arsiniega himself, despite his manifest intention of downplaying the level of peasant discontent, reflected the climate of confrontation by admitting that he had not dared to take testimonies from the Indians during the San Juan cabildo: "On the sixteenth day of [August] which was when the list [of mitayos] was made and the Indians gathered in the town, we did not summon the Indians because they were all drunk since dusk to dawn *making several displays in the plaza and streets of this town [of Chayanta] as well as in the pampa and the place where the said list is carried out, many of them carrying sticks and clubs.*"[68] These threats were followed by other demonstrations of force. A large group of Puracas met four days afterward in the residence of the judge to give their testimonies. The sole fact that they insisted that their own version of the conflict should be heard reveals their conviction about the legitimacy of their claims. On August 20, Arsiniega "summoned six Indians who were among the many who had gathered in the patio of the house where the judge was lodging." While the judge attempted to divert the interrogation toward the most personal aspects of the initial denunciation against Tococari (the cacique had been accused of raping one of the Indian's daughters), the Puracas wanted to talk about the central points of contention: the tribute misappropriation and the designation of colquerunas. They ratified that,

> when the governor don Marcos Tococari goes to hand over the tribute to the corregidor of this province, of the money that he takes, he usually has about 500 pesos left over after paying them, which they assume is left over from the tributes that he charges. . . .
>
> When the Indians who go to the Potosí mita are appointed, every year the governor Marcos Tococari made up the list with forty-one Indians and sometimes thirty-five, of all these only about twenty-one actually go to Potosí, the rest he charged 80 pesos as an exemption fee from the mita.[69]

The following day a crowd convened again in Arsiniega's home in an attempt to offer testimony, but to no avail. It seems that tempers flared even more, for the Puracas, as the audiencia clerk put it, "uttered so much nonsense [*disparates*] that neither I, the interpreters, nor the judge [Arsiniega] of those proceedings could understand anything of what they were saying, only that they assured that they did not know Miguel Lupa or Juan Policario or Bernabé Choque."[70] No doubt, this "nonsense" would provide much insight into the Indians' outlook on the conflict. Yet the judges were unwilling, or unable, to register it and put an end to the inquiry.

These public expressions of dissension, on the other hand, might have represented the tip of more subtle modes of struggle. Resistance to the ethnic chiefs surfaced not only in the realm of the Spanish justice or in public ceremony, but also in a social domain that James Scott (1990: 185–201) has defined as "the hidden transcripts of power relations." In 1748, the ethnic chief of Pocoata, Blas Cori, disclosed the rupture of customary forms of obedience and cooperation to the caciques. Cori, who would later be removed and arrested by the audiencia, explained that

> to the Indians going to the Mita, I have to provide everything, so that they have the necessary support to maintain themselves. I am always subsidizing them and giving them whatever they lack and I go through lots of trouble to ensure that they go to the Mita, as if it were not just their obligation. I also marry them at my expense just to make them happy. [However] they do not want to cultivate for us plots in the common lands whether in the valley or the puna; only my relatives and compadres help me in cultivating my scarce plots, and the rest, instead, try to take away from me the pieces of land that my ancestors used to sow. If all the Indians were to cultivate my plots, I would have to pay them, and I cannot have any services from them, since they only do it for pay, and if we tell them to take care of some of our mules, they break their feet and ruin them.[71]

This statement sheds light on a range of veiled modes of deception and insubordination that normally go unsaid in the historical record but were of utmost importance for the maintenance of the caciques' authority. The words allude to the reluctant supply of "free" labor services, the reduction of the plots set aside for the use of ethnic authorities, and forms of economic sabotage. The legitimacy crisis thus translated into a breakdown of the everyday norms of reciprocity ruling the relation between caciques and Andean communities.

A final example of the undermining of political acquiescence in the rural world during these years is the revolt against the Jukumani cacique, Juan de Dios Umacaya. As noted above, in March 1750 the Jukumanis had de facto deposed their native chief by handing the tribute quota to an Indian named

Francisco Choque. Choque, as corregidor Pablo de Aoíz pointed out, "came to hand [the money] to me along with many Indians, without possessing the title of collector of the said taxes, and without me or the said governor [Umacaya] having asked him to do so."[72] The election of the new cacique discloses the pressures from Indian commoners in this process. One of the cacique's assistants recounted that, with the purpose of appeasing the Indians, Umacaya intended to appoint Francisco Choque as tax collector, but he "answered that he would first see if the people of his ayllu wanted him as their Principal Tax Collector, and that with these results he would come to see the said governor."[73] Umacaya himself conceded that "in the presence of their priest, [Umacaya] told the Indian Francisco Choque that he should go to his house and he would appoint him his Principal Tax Collector, but he never appreciated this offer nor did he ever go to the house of the deponent to reject being his Principal Tax Collector."[74] Clearly, what Francisco Choque "rejected" was not the post of tax collector but being appointed by Umacaya. In order to collect the tribute, he sought and achieved the support of the members of his community. Then, he asked the corregidor for the dismissal of the cacique. In a note from prison addressed to the parish priest, the Jukumani leader claimed that he had been arrested "for having been acclaimed in writing by the people of [Jukumani], asking the General of this province [corregidor Aoíz] to be their cacique."[75] Despite labeling him a "rebellious Indian," Aoíz acknowledged that he had received five petitions from several Jukumanis demanding the confirmation of Francisco Choque as their cacique.

The strife during the Easter celebration in the Chayanta village, the Puracas's categorical refusal to let government officials impose their version of the conflict, the Pocoatas's sabotage of the traditional economic services to the caciques, and the Jukumanis's collective mobilization all suggest that the crisis of the mid-eighteenth century was more than factional disputes aired in Spanish courts. As analyzed in the following, the undermining of political subjection in the countryside was matched by sharp ideological dissension among colonial state agencies.

THE DISCOURSE OF LAW AND THE DISCOURSE OF AUTHORITY

One of the paramount effects of the disturbances of the late 1740s was to bring to the fore the conflicts between the two major loci of colonial power in this Andean region, the audiencia of Charcas and the provincial ruling groups. This strife reflected enduring tensions in the colonial administration. The Spanish empire was governed by two contradictory principles that, however, coexisted in the everyday workings of colonialism. The first principle was consolidated in Peru by the Toledean reforms in the late sixteenth century. This conception of colonial society rested on the existence of a complex bureaucratic and administrative apparatus that could preclude the formation of a local feudal class with seigniorial economic rights and private jurisdictions. The crown took over the government and administration of justice of the rural population through a vast set of institutions and salaried civil servants. The state organized the assignment of forced labor to Spanish entrepreneurs and the collection of taxes. In ruling an empire of unprecedented territorial vastness, the crown set in motion mechanisms of bureaucratic control — modes of "legal domination" that, according to John Leddy Phelan (1967: 321), would not appear in Western Europe until the eighteenth and nineteenth centuries.

The imperial reason, the "juridico-discursive representation of power" (Gruzinski 1989: 18), met little explicit, outright opposition due to the fact that the first generation of Spanish conquerors and their offspring vanished as a political force after their defeat during the civil wars of the sixteenth century. In the Andean world, the erosion of imperial control was part of a process in which the local elites gradually gained control of state institutions through the purchase of posts and patrimonialism. The juridical conception of government and social relations thus coexisted with an equally deeply rooted conception of the state as source of private economic benefits. From this perspective, political power could not be bound by legal and institutional limitations. It should be noted, for example, that the reparto system and Indian contributions for religious celebrations, the two main sources of income of the king's and the church's representatives in the rural world, were developed beyond and against colonial legislation.

Now, in a context where the ideal of obedience to the king was unquestionable, and where the legitimacy of the bureaucracy before both the crown and the native peoples rested on its representation of the sovereignty and interests of the king in America, the concept of a public position as a commercial investment could not be articulated but through other discourse. The central motif of this discourse was that the government of native people could only be attained through mechanisms of discipline and social control to the detriment of judicial mechanisms of social mediation. In other words, colonial rule was only feasible by reasserting the power of local authorities over the juridical logic of the higher courts. The contradictions between imperial reason and private powers unfolded within imperial administration, and the actors of this conflict had, whether out of conviction or interests, two types of discourses with which to legitimize their claims: the discourse of authority and the discourse of law.

These ideological antagonisms within the Spanish colonial administration provide the broader backdrop for the confrontations between the audiencia ministers and the local groups of power in northern Potosí during the late 1740s. As already mentioned, the corregidores and caciques defended their jurisdiction on local affairs by deploying the usual repertoire of coercion in the Andean world: arrests of the leaders, threats against the Indians that cooperated with them, confiscation of goods, accusations of tribute indebtedness, and so forth. Yet, their strategies to curb social contention went beyond the simple use of violence. Provincial magistrates, ethnic authorities, parish priests, and non-Indian neighbors articulated a discourse that construed the protest movements as the outcome of an alleged general uprising to achieve the reduction of the communities' duties toward the church and the state. This rebellion would be directed by a small group of *cabecillas* (ringleaders) who had misled the other Indians with false promises. More important still, the audiencia of Charcas itself harbored this potential uprising with its positive reception to peasant grievances. The regional courts' intervention in the Andean rural world had thus endangered the basic mechanisms of colonial domination: tribute payment, observance of religious duties, and subjection to authorities.

Corregidor Pérez de Vargas, for instance, informed the audiencia that the province was in turmoil because the Indians refused to continue to obey their caciques and to pay more than 20 reales per year of tribute, a predicament that would result in a big drop in provincial tax revenues.[76] He then poignantly asked the ministers of the audiencia for instructions on how to suppress the social unrest that the court itself was supposedly stirring. In 1748, the priests of the Laymi and Chayantaca parishes, the brothers José Ignacio Virto and Nicolás Virto, wrote a letter to corregidor Vargas complaining about "how possessed by the devil and rebellious are the Indians [as result of] the turmoil nurtured by the change of their governors and the aspirants to substitute them, who in order to achieve their goals have offered to lower their tribute quota and supposed easing of other duties that they have with the parish." Widespread rural agitation stemmed, according to José Ignacio Virto, from the audiencia's favorable response to all kinds of denunciations without finding out first the real causes behind the complaints. Indian ringleaders "embroiled the others by offering not only freedom in their way of life but also spreading the word that they will get a reduction of tribute, so that they are so restless that in a short time they will destroy all the parishes and the whole province." His brother recalled that just as in Laymi parish (including Laymi, Puraca, and Chullpa) the destitution of Dionisio Choque offered an example to follow, so in the Chayantaca parish (including Chayantaca, Caracha, and Sicoya) would be the removal of the

Caracha cacique Pedro Yavira, "a noble Indian of much discernment."[77] Until the audiencia was persuaded to punish the rioters instead of the caciques, ending the unrest would be impossible, both priests concluded. The mestizos and Spaniards residing in the village of Chayanta (tax collectors, merchants, clerks, small hacendados, and assistants of the priests and corregidores, often related by kin to the caciques) endorsed this view of the ongoing conflicts before successive judges and corregidores Pérez de Vargas and Aoíz.[78]

The ethnic chiefs and hilacatas of the six ethnic groups of the Chayanta repartimiento also attributed the growing Indian unrest to audiencia policies. A few weeks after the incidents of Easter 1748, during the collection of the tribute quota in the village of Chayanta in April, they said that Dionisio Choque's imprisonment in La Plata had caused the other Indians to become "extremely arrogant, haughty, and shameless," and whenever they attempted any minor "correction" the Indians traveled to La Plata to sue them. The final purpose of the uprising was that "nobody should rule them and correct their excesses, conducting by themselves the collection of tributes and refusing to pay them [to us] voluntarily unless they are rigorously pressured to do so."[79] The cacique of Pocoata, Blas Cori, and the four caciques of the Macha ethnic group added that it had become impossible to subject the Indians because as soon as their bad habits were corrected they traveled to La Plata "to present frivolous grievances without any real value so that they could keep their extreme idleness and evil vices." The situation had no solution, Blas Cori said, due to "the extreme facility with which these [Indians] promptly present their grievances before His Highness [the president of the audiencia], calling each other to serve as witnesses of any legal proceedings that they want to thunder against." The peasant communities thus refused to meet their dues and "the province is now about to rise up."[80] Blas Cori had good reasons to despise this state of affairs: four years later he would be removed and arrested in the audiencia.

In the words of Philip Corrigan and Derek Sayer (1985: 7–8), "the idea of the state, as Weber stressed, is a *claim* to legitimacy, a means by which politically organized subjection is simultaneously accomplished and concealed, and it is constituted in large part by the activities of institutions of government themselves." They continue by stating that claims to legitimacy, as any claim, are by definition contestable, particularly by those who are the objects of regulation. Spanish colonialism in the Andes also shows us that the idea of the state — that is, the moral conceptions informing the series of administrative, economic, and political practices that government agencies perform and command others to perform — could be highly heterogeneous and mutually contradictory. Subaltern groups were not alone in disputing the ways politically organized subjection was being accomplished in the Andean villages. If the "mundane routines" and the "magnificent rituals" of rule inexorably produce "messages of domination," if the state always "talks" to its subjects, in the Spanish overseas possessions it did so in sharply disparate tongues.

The stance toward the conflict of two influential functionaries of the audiencia, the general Protector of Indians and the crown attorney, as well as the concrete measures adopted by the court during these years, indeed disclose an entirely different conception of the ways in which the government the Andean peoples should be conducted from that offered by the northern Potosí authorities. When brought to the surface, these opposing ideological outlooks, these contradictory claims to legitimacy, greatly contributed to undermine peasant acquiescence to local rulers. The Protector of Indians, Joseph López Lisperguer, had assumed the post in 1747. Reflecting his standing within the colonial administration, he became *oidor* (judge or magistrate) of the audiencia in 1751, and one year later the viceroy of Perú designated him as arbitrator in a high-profile conflict among prominent elite groups of Oruro (Burkholder and Chandler 1982: 184–85; Cornblit 1995: 88–91). In May 1748, López Lisperguer argued that he could not offer guidelines to defuse the alleged peasant rebellion because he simply did not find any evidence of the existence of "an uprising or conspiracy." From his perspective, the writings of the priests and caciques only proved "the fear that they have of being sued by the Indians, and they blame the turmoil on the frequency that the Indians appeal before the Royal Audiencia."[81] Not only did the audiencia official find no indication of an uprising, what local authorities defined as an "uprising" would be defined by him as the legitimate resort to acknowledged legal rights.

In more general terms, the Protector of Indians remarked that the indigenous right to appeal to the highest courts could not be called into question for this would grant corregidores and caciques a monopoly of power over the Andean peoples. The investigation and punishment of abuses in local government "cannot be imagined in opposition to the good government of the province since the harmony of all well-governed republics is based on rewarding the good and punishing the wrongdoing; and appealing to Higher Courts should never be deemed to be malicious and even less subversive and seditious, because sedition means mainly disobedience and it cannot promote the violence of the interiors to use legal means such as the recourse to Highest Courts."[82] In preventing the removal of ethnic authorities it was unjustifiable that "the doors would be closed to the unhappy Indians that have no other recourse than presenting their grievances to the justified pity of His Highness." Instead of giving corregidor Vargas council on how to put down the unrest, López Lisperguer contended that "the court could not resolve anything other than warning the Corregidor to watch and supervise the behavior of the Governors so that the source of the grievances would be uprooted."[83]

Audiencia attorney Joseph Casimiro Gómez García, who in 1751 would be promoted to oidor of the audiencia of Lima, one of the most prestigious positions in the Peruvian bureaucracy, also did not believe in the existence of a conspiracy. By contrast, the sole aim of the provincial authorities was to "hide and obscure" their complicity in the concealment of taxpayers and mitayos. Corregidor Pérez de Vargas, in particular, was trying to divert attention from "the forced distribution of goods [repartos] that he realized despite the legal prohibition against it."[84] One year later, Gómez García lamented that the voluminous body of legal documents gave witness to "the utmost difficulties [of the Indians] in justifying the truth of their claims, because those who should have searched for the truth have, instead, confused it further."[85] In other words, it was not the Indians that were striving to lessen their obligations toward the state, as rural ruling groups argued, rather it was the ruling groups that were conspiring against the royal treasury. As López Lisperguer pointed out, if the demonstration of tribute embezzlement proved to be impossible, it was because "most of the respectable people of the province are very interested in not allowing its disclosure."[86] So few individuals, Gómez García complained, "loved the Royal Justice" that prosecutions were always stranded "unless they are directed toward a poor soul whose bad luck has left him naked, without any protection."[87]

The failure of the colonial state to deliver the right "messages of domination," to make a morally justified exercise of authority, was compounded, according to Gómez García, by very practical obstacles in the administration of justice. Drawing on his twenty-five years of experience as audiencia attorney, he explained that the high colonial magistrates could not exert effective control over rural ruling groups because the audiencia could not, because of financial costs, appoint some "distinguished outsider" but the designation of provincial dwellers inevitably distorted the process because of their collusion with the local authorities. He concluded that "it is such a sad situation that your fiscal head admits that his efforts only lead to the increase in the amount of documents, and by no means to solving the conflicts, and although he knows what the source of illness is, he could not find out the remedy because the illness is lethal."[88]

The concrete political effects of the coexistence within the Spanish government of such disparate worldviews became particularly visible in March 1750, during the annual meeting for the payment of the Navidad tribute quota in the town of Chayanta. Two events converged on this meeting. One was the arrival of a high official of the royal treasury of Oruro, Tomás Landaeta, whom the audiencia had entrusted with carrying out, in collaboration with the ethnic authorities of Puraca, the list of "concealed" Indians that the latter had been denouncing for the last three years and arresting former cacique Marcos Tococari. As a member of a prominent family, a son and brother of corregidores of Oruro, and a functionary of the *real hacienda*, Landaeta represented, as the audiencia fiscal head would put it, the "distinguished outsider" who could finally end the futile accumulation of papers by breaking the power arrangements that precluded the exercise of authority through the law.[89] Landaeta's performance, however, would demonstrate on the contrary the engrained collusion between public service and private interests in the Andean colonial administration. When he arrived in Chayanta, the Oruro official confiscated just a few possessions from former cacique Tococari and allowed him to take refuge in the church. By contrast, Landaeta demanded 100 pesos from the ethnic authorities, 2 reales (besides their tribute) from each of the Indians who had gathered in the town for the census, and 6 reales from those passing to the *reservado* (tax-exempt) status. Naturally enough, the Puracas who had shown up "recognizing this violence disappeared and advised the others who had not shown up not to come."[90] Resentful of the resistance to his demands, Landaeta urged Sebastián Auca to display the tribute increase "right away," which was impossible because the cacique needed time to travel through the valleys and collect the tribute from the Puracas who resided in Micani and Carasi.[91] Finally, alleging the failure to deliver the promised tribute increase, Landaeta arrested Sebastián Auca and seven other Puracas under custody of Manuel Chico, the compadre of the former cacique Marcos Tococari, who had dispersed the crowd during the Easter celebration two years earlier.[92] While in jail, the Indians had to submit still additional payments to avoid confiscation of their possessions.[93]

Venality was not the only reason behind these measures. The second significant feature of this meeting was that it represented the first tribute collection under the new corregidor, Pablo de Aoíz. No doubt Aoíz had motives of his own to promote this policy. Constant journeys to the city of La Plata and the forced removal of caciques pointed to a crisis in the mechanisms of subjection. Allegations of tribute embezzlement brought to the fore, as the Charcas ministers made exceedingly clear, the contradictions between the mercantile interests of the provincial magistrates and the fiscal interests of the crown. In order to rule the province and ensure the collection of his own repartos, Aoíz needed to assert his full command over local affairs. And this was what he set out to do during the first collective meeting of the Indian communities of his tenure. Thus, although the Jukumanis, as noted above, had traveled to the Chayanta village to deliver tributes and request the appointment of their leader Francisco Choque through formal petitions, the new corregidor pronounced that "as a good example for others [Francisco Choque] should be punished publicly in the plaza with fifty lashes and a year of banishment in Potosí, to be employed in the service of the Casa de la Moneda's offices."[94] We know that Francisco Choque received his lashes in the central square of Chayanta, presumably in front of the numerous Indians gathered there for the delivering of the tribute.[95] At the same time, Aoíz forced the leaders of Puraca to recant their denunciations of fiscal fraud after Landaeta had thrown them in jail. Then, once the collection of the Navidad quota was finished, Aoíz personally transported the Puraca authorities to the town of Ocurí, from where he dispatched them to La Plata. In a letter to the audiencia ministers, he justified the public punishment of Francisco Choque on the grounds that Jukumanis's actions proved the extent to which "the province is exposed to a general commotion." He added that the seven Puraca prisoners, as well as several Chullpas who had avoided punishment because they were in La Plata asking once again for the destitution of Gregorio Jorge de Medina, should be given an exemplary punishment because the province "is in revolt by the tributary Indians, since they are almost convinced that Your Highness has reduced their tributes by half and the tribute collection of all the governors has been very difficult since Sebastián [Auca] has persuaded the Indians about this." On April 4, 1750, Sebastián Auca and six other Indians were taken under the custody of nine soldiers from the gates of the Ocurí jail to the doors of the audiencia of Charcas. "At my expense," the new corregidor stressed, "I paid for a pair of handcuffs for each one of them *so that your highness may punish the accused sternly for the good example of this province.*"[96]

But this advice the court was not ready to follow. The sharp dissension within the colonial state and the steadfastness of the Indians would not permit Pablo de Aoíz to impose his will. Rather than punishing those in custody, the audiencia would liberate them, send them back to Chayanta, and, for the good example of the province, command Pablo de Aoíz to redress their grievances. As soon as they landed in the court jail, the Puracas denied the retractions that they had been forced to swear before Landaeta and Aoíz. Sebastián Auca declared that he had only recanted from his previous statements "out of fear of the said judge."[97] A hilacata, Salvador Coio, explained that if he had not spoken about the hidden taxpayers before the corregidor or the commissioned judge, it "was because neither one nor the other had requested it from the deponent in the way that now he is being asked; rather, they had violently put him along with the others in jail without leaving them freedom to do anything."[98] The audiencia ministers believed the Puracas's version. Protector of Indians Joseph López Lisperguer argued that the behavior of Aoíz and Landaeta was nothing but "unmistakable evidence of the obstacles that have been invented so that the fraud that has been carried out against His Majesty's treasury should not be discovered." The audiencia ministers strongly condemned that the Puraca Indians had been sent to La Plata "full of handcuffs as if they were dangerous delinquents." If these maneuvers were to be accepted, no Indians would in the future wish to denounce increases in taxes since "instead of the reward that they should expect for their revelation, the first step is their harsh and tough imprisonment."[99]

In the course of July and August 1750, corregidor Aoíz would be forced to conduct new population censuses of both Puraca and Chullpa, which in part proved the veracity of the allegations of tribute misappropriation presented three years earlier. Interestingly, the new tax roll of the Puracas was carried out on August 16, during the San Juan meeting, the same day that two years earlier the Indians had made "demonstrations with sticks and clubs" due to the refusal to acknowledge the legitimacy of their claims. Following the audiencia's orders, Sebastián Auca was confirmed as Puraca cacique and three protest leaders of Chullpa (Martín Ninavia, Isidro Policario, and Miguel Caracara) were appointed cacique and hilacatas in the place of Gregorio Jorge de Medina.[100] The court commanded the corregidor to banish the latter from the town of Chayanta because of his condition as mestizo.[101] "With the mentioned Census and Reinspection," López Lisperguer concluded, "the repeated complaints of these miserable [Indians] are over. They have increased your Royal income at the expense of their own suffering and the costs of their many trips and legal proceedings that have been carried out at their expense. So they should be reimbursed as well rewarded for their fidelity."[102]

These conflicting messages of domination would have still further repercussions. While the resolution of the disputes among the Chullpas and Puracas contributed to appease the province, the challenges to local relations of power would not vanish. As mentioned previously, in 1752 and 1753 the caciques of the groups Chayantaca and Pocoata were removed. By this time, Indians of the Chullpa group protested against two collectors of veintenas (the tax on European grains and livestock produced in indigenous lands) in the communal fields of Bombo and in the highland hamlets of Chayanta. The collectors were accused of demanding payment on grains and livestock that were exempted from this levy and of collecting the tax using violence.[103] The elimination of this levy, as discussed in chapter 6, would represent one of the central aims of the rebels during 1781. Furthermore, in 1753 corregidor Aoíz would face a fairly detailed inquiry into his forced distribution of goods and other commercial ventures. It was shown that Aoíz had allotted mules, European textiles, iron tools, and other commodities through several assistants, or mayordomos, and had financed mining ventures in the province with tribute money.[104] When the Indians failed to cancel the debts, they were imprisoned and their possessions auctioned. Although the corregidor managed to avoid an indictment — the full consideration of the legal proceedings were left for the *residencia*, the customary judicial review at the end of his term — the investigation could have borne some practical effects: it was reported at the time that Aoíz was "very busy gathering the goods that we [the Indians] have disclosed he distributed in the province."[105] Not surprisingly, the investigation was promoted by the Policarios, the family of Chullpa cited as one of the main instigators of the political turmoil. Despite repeated pleas to the audiencia requesting their punishment, the court had instead commanded Aoíz to appoint Isidro Policario as hilacata of Chullpa in 1750.

As did his successors during the years leading to the general insurrection of 1780, Aoíz learned that the monopoly of the legitimate force could eventually be the outcome but never the starting point of the exercise of rule in the Andean rural world.

LESSONS LEARNED

Looking ahead historically from the late 1740s, it can be seen that the general crisis of authority represented a discrete but momentous event in the sense that encompassed several ethnic groups, touched on manifold aspects of the daily life of the Andean communities, and involved different state authorities and groups of power. It was not the magnitude of violence but rather the range of issues at stake and the level of coordination among northern Potosí groups that confers on this episode its historical significance.

The breakdown of political submission to local ruling groups bolstered two trends of paramount importance in the evolution of colonial relations of power in the region for the next thirty years. The first is the emergence, or consolidation, of notions of political legitimacy based on contractual, representative concepts of authority that paved the way for broader challenges to the social order. At the same time of the struggle over agrarian and labor surpluses, the dispute for control of ethnic chieftainships called into question the right of provincial officials to intervene in community affairs, as well as the validity of the hereditary principles underwriting the power of the indigenous aristocracy. Paradoxically, in the short term the ethnic chiefs of Puraca, Chullpa, or Caracha who emerged out of the protests could have been victims of their own success: the very process of factionalism and political unrest that served their rise to power served also to challenge them in the late 1750s and early 1760s. These caciques might also have been victims of the structural vulnerability of the office. While caciques could do little to halt large demographic, fiscal, and market trends undermining the peasant economy across the Andes, these very trends made their performance in managing community resources all the more relevant for the Indians both materially and symbolically.

In the long run, the language of rights and the repertoires of collective action that emerged during these years laid the foundation for more far-reaching disturbances. Twenty years later, the same type of political strife would give rise to mass mobilizations that ended up eroding the entire building of colonial subjection. Between 1775 and 1777, the Pocoata communities undertook an unprecedented massive mobilization against a cacique appointed by colonial officials in the place of the descendant of a traditional noble lineage of the group. Yet, once the ousting of the intruder was secured, the Indians would firmly reject the restitution of the old ethnic lords, forcing instead the designation of the leaders of the collective protest as their new caciques. The initial goal of the general indigenous insurrection of 1780 was the appointment as cacique of the Macha group of Tomás Katari, an Indian commoner whose aspiration to the post was never based on his hereditary rights. Then, in the course of the mass uprising, virtually all the northern Potosí communities relentlessly assaulted their respective caciques. Significantly, one of the few native chiefs spared of collective violence was Miguel Caracara, the Chullpa Indian who had participated in the protests of the late 1740s. Caracara had assumed the post in 1772, after strong indigenous pressure forced the corregidor to conduct one of the few public contests for the assignment of the title of cacique propietario in the province.[106] In 1781, among the papers confiscated from a Chullpa Indian who served as link with the Oruro rebels and Túpac Amaru, was found a letter addressed to Caracara by an insurgent captain.[107]

A second aspect of the political crisis of mid-century that would have important reverberations in the years to come is the overlapping of Indian dissension with antagonisms within the Spanish colonial administration. As with the modes of Indian contention, short-term and long-term repercussions must be distinguished. It is apparent that during the 1750s and early 1760s provincial authorities were determined to prevent audiencia ministers from continuing to breed social defiance. Thus, when several communities returned to La Plata between 1757 and 1762 to ask for the dismissal of their caciques, corregidor Gabriel de Larreategui (Pablo de Aoíz's successor) would forcefully refuse even to consider the charges, adducing that judicial battles only contributed to raise unrest, and stating that "a proof of this is how frequently lawsuits against the governor are repeated for the slightest reprimand."[108] Moreover, the ministers of the audiencia, wary perhaps of the effect of their previous policies, were now reluctant to intervene in these local affairs. Despite several indigenous appeals, they deferred the handling of the case to the corregidor. Undeterred by this new political atmosphere, the Puracas and Chullpas sought, and found, support in the other important regional agent of colonial government, governor of Potosí Ventura de Santelices, who on taking testimonies of protest leaders and several mitayos sent to the province a Potosí resident as judge and commanded that the Puraca cacique be brought in chains to Potosí.[109] Yet, Larreategui's determination to uproot any trace of open dissent by resorting to all the punitive weapons at his disposal (arrests, public whippings, confiscation of goods, co-optation of judges, charges of conspiracy) would this time frustrate Indian judicial politics.[110] In addition to punishing the Chullpas and Puracas, the corregidor repeatedly handcuffed and confiscated a Chayantaca Indian who had managed to replace his cacique, Fernández de Espinoza, through a denunciation of fiscal fraud before the audiencia in 1758. The Indian was soon forced to resign and Espinoza was then restored to the post.[111] Further, a still more significant form of social control emerged during these years: a cacique of the group Laymi named Marcos Soto was at the time appointed as cacique of the riotous Puracas. While both groups had strong links (in a 1683 census, Puraca still appears as the Laymi's ayllu), it seems clear that matters of social order were behind this measure.[112] Not coincidentally, Marcos Soto would be a prime target of violence during the 1780 upheaval; Puraca appears again as an independent community afterward.[113]

The corregidor, in addition, explicitly challenged the decisions of the appeals courts. In September 1757, for instance, he wrote to Governor Santelices that he was not going to permit the arrest of the Puraca cacique for he was innocent and, above all, because "any imprisonment should be carried out by me, rather than by a commissioned judge." He caustically recommended to Santelices that if he wished to defend the interests of the royal treasury, he should inflict "an exemplary punishment" on the "denouncers," not on those who were denounced, "because in encouraging restlessness and the [Indians] to shake off the yoke of obedience by tying the hands of the governors, the denouncers charge them with homicides, or tribute embezzlement, or cruel treatment of their people, spreading from one moiety to another the kind of issues that they should denounce and encouraging [the Indians] through the vicious persuasion (as I have heard) of a possible lowering of the tribute."[114]

Larreategui would eventually succeed in preventing outside institutions from interfering in the relationship between peasants and rural authorities. Their successors would not have the same fortune. During the 1770s, the propensity of the northern Potosí communities "to shake off the yoke of obedience" would be greatly enhanced by the proliferation of intra-elite conflicts fostered by the implementation of the Bourbon reforms: disputes between the state and the church over ecclesiastical fees; between treasury officials and corregidores over the increase of tribute revenues; and between the ministers of the audiencia of Charcas and the newly created viceregal court of Buenos Aires over jurisdiction on Andean affairs. As these ideological, economic, and jurisdictional battles mounted, so did the peasants' chances to challenge the fundamental mechanisms of exploitation in the Andean world through the coordination of legal politics ("spreading from one moiety to another the kind of issues that they should denounce," as corregidor Larreategui put it). In the course of his brief tenure from 1778 to 1780, corregidor Joaquín Alós would repeatedly warn, like Pérez de Vargas, Pablo de Aoíz, and Gabriel de Larreategui before him, that the intervention of appeal courts in village conflicts inexorably undermined social discipline. He, too, accused the Indians of seeking to lessen their obligations toward the state despite the fact that they, like protesters thirty years earlier, charged caciques and corregidores with tribute embezzlement. By contrast, the viceroy and ministers of the new court of Buenos Aires, like the audiencia of Charcas in the late 1740s, blamed the corregidores for the growing indigenous unrest on the grounds that they put their personal economic benefit over the crown interests and their personal political power over the authority of the appeals courts. The arguments were similar, the political environment was not: Joaquín Alós, unlike his predecessors, would be assaulted by a multitude of Indians, taken hostage, and expelled from the province for good.

In sum, the rise of a contentious politics in northern Potosí prefigured critical aspects of the dynamics of the political culture in the region. No doubt, by the mid-eighteenth century strife between communities, caciques, and government officials did not endanger still basic power balances. Yet, when some years later the colonial administration in the southern Andes confronted overt clashes between the discourse of authority and the discourse of law bred by Bourbon absolutism, along with massive social protests bred by the increasing erosion of the material and symbolic fabric of the Andean community, the outcome would be a political crisis of unprecedented magnitude—one that generated the second major institutional transformation since the reforms of Viceroy Toledo from above, and, from below, the most formidable indigenous rebellion since the times of the conquerors.

2

From a

Multiethnic

Community to

a Multiethnic

Chieftainship:

Florencio

Lupa,

Cacique of

Moscari

ON SEPTEMBER 5, 1780, barely a week after a mass uprising erupted in the village of Pocoata, panic overtook the city of La Plata. For a few hours, the city's residents—from municipal council officials to audiencia ministers to priests of the archbishopric to common people—thought that their lives were in peril. A town resident reported that during the morning "he noticed that the people's sense of alarm and restlessness grew by the second, so that they opened and closed their doors at the same time, closing them to take refuge and opening them to defend themselves, taking sticks, knives, stones, or whatever happened to be at hand as weapons."[1] According to another witness, "this city was shaken in such a way that its inhabitants believed that this was going to be the last day of their lives."[2] Rumors alleging that a group of Indians were about to attack the city were responsible for this state of general agitation. The news was that "outside the walls of the city, in the area commonly called Quirpinchaca, a considerable number of Indians [are] gathering, raising flags and playing cornets with the obvious purpose of falling into this neighborhood and invading it. People [believe] that these Indians [are] coming from the rebellious province of Chayanta."[3]

As is frequently the case with rumors that spread during times of social unrest, the fears of the residents of La Plata were greatly exaggerated. No crowd had gathered outside the gates of the city, nor did the Indians at that time have any plan to invade it. The panic was not entirely unwarranted, however. As the neighbors of the city would learn in the course of the morning, what had triggered the wave of panic was that the head of an Indian had during the night been placed on a cross in the locality of Quirpinchaca. More important still, the head was that of the native lord of Moscari, Florencio Lupa, one of the few members of the indigenous communities in the region whom the Spanish society of Charcas could identify by name, and someone whom many of its residents knew personally. For many of the functionaries and common people of La Plata, the execution and public display of the cacique's head amounted to a declaration of war.

Later in the day, Lupa's head was carried from the outskirts of the city to one of the chambers of the cabildo building (seat of the municipal council). A crowd gathered there. According to one witness, the officers "along with the town clerk went down to the cell of the jail where the head was shown wrapped in a blanket, and we recognized that it was Lupa's head and we ordered that it should be safeguarded in one of the dungeons of the jail until further notice; when we came out from that place we found that the patio was so full of people that we could not leave it."[4] One alguacil (constable) was ordered to disperse the crowd from the building out of the fear that people would break the bars of the jail in "their curiosity to see the head." According to one of the captains of the city's militia, "various people who had known the cacique while he was alive" inspected the head. Another neighbor declared that the fact that the head belonged to Lupa had been verified "through the inspection that most neighbors of this city did of the severed part of the corpse."[5]

Who was Florencio Lupa? What were the factors that turned him into a symbol of the crisis of colonial domination in the southern Andes? The career of this Moscari ethnic lord is so intertwined with the general history of northern Potosí during the thirty years leading up to the Indian insurrection that answering these questions is to delve into some of the major issues of the Andean colonial world. In this chapter I focus on the mechanisms through which, in the course of two decades, Lupa accumulated political influence and material wealth. I explore how the cacique established ties with several corregidores and other local elite groups, attempted to recover community lands from nearby Spanish haciendas, commercialized Indian agrarian and labor assets, effectively repressed internal dissension, fought other native chiefs over the government of Indian migrants, and fought parish priests over power and peasant economic resources. My analysis starts with Lupa's rise as cacique of Moscari in the early 1750s, and ends with his appointment, twenty years later, as the cacique of two other ethnic groups, the Panacachi and the Pocoata. By this time, Florencio Lupa had achieved an unparalleled political status among the northern Potosí caciques. And this concentration of power would unleash intense processes of confrontation that eventually came to a dramatic close with the exhibition of his head in the outskirts of La Plata on September 5, 1780: processes that I will examine in the next chapter because, strictly speaking, they do not belong to the history of Moscari and its cacique but rather to the history of the general Indian insurrection.

In many respects, Lupa's career is that of a paradigmatic Andean lord during the expansion of the repartimiento de mercancías system. Throughout the Andes, the rapid growth of the forced distribution of commodities required native chiefs either to collaborate with the colonial authorities or to face eviction. Certainly, Lupa displayed a high degree of accommodation to European economic and cultural models and was an efficient collector of tribute and repartos for the colonial state and provincial magistrates. The consolidation of his authority, moreover, occurred in the context of northern Potosí officials vigorously repressing the kind of collective protests that had mushroomed in the late 1740s. Nevertheless, his role went beyond that of a simple means of political and economic subjection. This study shows that far from being a passive instrument of colonial domination, Lupa was able to muster the economic resources and political influence, both within Indian society and Spanish administration, that turned his relationship with colonial provincial authorities into an alliance rather than mere subordination. In addition, although Lupa established strong ties with members of the local elite, some of his endeavors to protect (and even expand) community resources caused the animosity of priests, landowners, and other groups. His style of government and his private wealth accumulation bred deep discontent among peasants, but it is also clear that as cacique he observed traditional Andean norms of reciprocity and redistribution.

Thus, Lupa's trajectory is not that of a subordinate agent of Spanish rule in the Andes, but rather that of a powerful intermediary between colonial authorities and native peoples. His ascent rested on his successful integration in both worlds and it is my contention here that this integration explains his demise as well. Ultimately the rise of Lupa prefigured the crisis of colonial hegemony. For the colonial elites, he came to embody the Spanish government's dependence on autonomous, unreliable (and increasingly illegitimate) intermediaries. For the native peoples, he came to symbolize the increasing violation of the political and economic rights on which their acquiescence to European domination was founded.

MOSCARI

The Moscari group sprung up from a general reorganization of the Indian population implemented by Viceroy Toledo at the end of the sixteenth century. The group emerged as a multiethnic community. This means that unlike other communities in the province, the Moscari originated during the colonial regime as an amalgamation of Indian families from different ethnic groups, particularly those belonging to the pre-Hispanic nation of Chayanta that encompassed Moscari territory (see map 2).[6] According to eighteenth-century population records, Moscari was divided into four ayllus (Collana, Sulacata, Chiquito, and Chulpata) asymmetrically grouped into the moieties of Anansaya and Urinsaya (table 5). It seems, however, that this dual organization did not result in the creation of two competitive and complementary communities.[7] Each ayllu had a hilacata or *principal* (tax collector), and a single authority (*gobernador y cacique principal*) ruled the entire town assisted by a *segunda persona* (cacique's lieutenant).

Whereas most ethnic groups owned discontinuous lands in distant valleys and punas, Moscari Indians did not possess a divided territory. The Moscari region was located east of the Cordillera de Azanaques, which crosses the province from north to south; its altitude ranges from 3,000 to 3,500 meters. This intermediate ecological region (*taypirana*) between the highlands and the temperate western valleys is suitable for the cultivation of potatoes, broad beans,

Table 5. Total Population of Moscari, 1766

Ayllus	Originarios	Forasteros	Exempted	Men under 18	Women	Total
Anansaya						
Collana	13	54	21	85	171	344
Sulcata	25	70	22	132	235	484
Chiquito	58	105	53	266	530	1,012
Urinsaya						
Chulpata	32	101	43	203	347	726
Total	128	330	139	686	1,283	2,566

Source: AGN, XIII, 18–9–5.

Table 6. Originario and Forastero Population of Moscari

Tributaries	1725	1738	1746	1754	1766	1786
Originarios	136	79	91	120	128	136
Forasteros	39	135	155	224	330	573
Total	175	214	246	344	458	709

Source: The 1725 census is in AGN, XIII, 18–8–4. Figures from 1740, 1746, and 1754 are in AGN, XIII, 18–9–2; the 1766 census is in AGN, XIII, 18–9–5; the 1786 census is in AGN, XIII, 18–10–3.

and certain varieties of highland maize and wheat (Rivera Cusicanqui 1992: 83–84; Harris 2000: 99–111). Anthropologist Olivia Harris (2000: 100) has noted that the ayllus located in this zone are known today as "pure center," as compared to the ecological duality characteristic of most northern Potosí communities. As the intendant of Potosí, Juan del Pino Manrique, described it, "Moscari has punas and valleys within the jurisdiction of the parish, which permits the easy harvest of grains, since it can be done without [the residents] leaving their lands."[8] During colonial times, this location carried a further economic advantage: unlike most of their neighbors, Moscari Indians had to sustain one parish alone.

By the 1760s, the Moscari comprised 458 taxpayers, with a total population of 2,600 (table 5). It was smaller than the Sacaca, Macha, or Pocoata groups but more populous than any of the six ethnic groups of the Chayanta repartimiento. Moreover, eighteenth-century counts register sharp population increases. By the 1780s, the official number of tributaries grew three times that of the 1720s (table 6). The agrarian consequences of this demographic movement are perhaps reflected in the extraordinary rise of forasteros, which multiplied by four during this time period. As I discuss in the introduction, this trend might signal a process of land subdivision.

The Moscari district housed several Spanish haciendas. Whereas Pocoatas, Aymayas, and others coexisted with haciendas in their valley lands, the ayllus of Moscari (along with their neighbors of San Pedro de Buena Vista) interacted with Spanish estates in their nuclear territories. According to a census of 1766, Moscari encompassed eight haciendas (one of them, Pisaca, included several dispersed hamlets), which hosted 119 indigenous tenants, with a total population of 526 (table 7). As I show later, this labor force was made up of Indians from neighboring ethnic groups who continued paying their tribute to the caciques of their home communities and, to a lesser extent, of Moscari itself. Little is known about the size and productivity of these estates. Measured by their resident population—which, as historian Herbert Klein (1993: 13–19)

Table 7. Total Population of the Moscari Haciendas, 1766

Haciendas	Tenants	Exempted	Men under 18	Women	Total
Asiruri	9	3	11	21	44
Chirocari	12	7	6	23	48
Lipichicayme	4	—	1	5	10
Pisaca	21	—	7	39	67
Pisaca hamlets:					
Tutupaya	21	—	13	35	69
Guayllas	3	—	—	7	10
Arospata	2	—	—	3	5
Achocchi	12	—	10	25	47
Acoio	3	—	5	6	14
Others		26	18	41	85
Subtotal	62	26	53	156	297
Sacasaca	7	—	5	12	24
Vilacirca	21	7	18	44	90
Yareta	2	—	2	1	5
Yarquivirque	2	—	2	4	8
Total	119	43	98	266	526

Source: AGN, XIII, 18–9–5.

has noted, provides a reasonable index of the value of the Andean haciendas — their wealth and size were relatively low. In the areas comprised by the intendant of La Paz in the late eighteenth century, the bulk of the Spanish estates had a labor force of between twenty and ninety-nine Indian households.[9] With the exception of Pisaca and Vilacirca, the Moscari haciendas hosted a smaller number of tenants. Demesne agriculture, in addition, must have been limited to small parcels. It is very likely that the hacendados leased most of the estates to resident tenants, who owed them rent in cash or kind and labor services. Still, despite the limited scale of private commercial agriculture, the peasant families living in Spanish landed estates represented nearly 20 percent of the overall indigenous population of the district.

This agricultural structure endowed the Moscari community with peculiar characteristics. First, the community was comprised of traditional Indian landholders and tenants in Spanish estates. An official list from the early 1750s counted fourteen Moscari indigenous households living in private haciendas, but given the levels of underregistration they must have been in reality more numerous.[10] Although the Moscari cacique ruled over both groups, future political conflicts would prove that Spanish landlords wielded some influence over their tenants as well. Furthermore, unlike other northern Potosí peasant communities, Moscari Indians owned, aside from the lands for communal use, two haciendas in the hamlets of Hipira and Consata whose fields and grain mills were rented out. Florencio Lupa, in turn, had a private hacienda of his own located in the hamlet of Coropoya.[11] As the three haciendas were under his sole purview, the distinction between them was a matter of sharp contention. Centuries of coexistence of private and communal property, individual wealth accumulation, and intermarriage between the indigenous elite and Spanish or mestizo town-dwellers, contributed to blur the distinction between the rights that caciques enjoyed as private landlords and those they did as officeholders. After all, as several Indians were keen to remind, the hacienda and milling stations of Coropoya that Florencio Lupa held as private property also had been built in lands of the Moscari community, just as were the two communal haciendas of Hipira and Consata.[12]

The administration of these haciendas had definite political repercussions. For example, Lupa rented fields for wheat cultivation to his father-in-law, a mestizo named Santos Hinojosa, and one of the grain mills of Hipira to his segunda persona, Pedro Velazco.[13] The hacienda of Consata was rented for many years to a mestizo named Juan Chrisóstomo Ramírez, who gained the bid for the collection of the diezmos and veintenas of Moscari, Pocoata, and Panacachi — the three communities ruled by Lupa during the 1770s.[14] The personal loyalty of these individuals to the cacique would be fully displayed in the years to come.[15] As in the case of another prosperous south Andean lord, Fernández Guarachi of Machaca (province of Pacajes), it is clear that the management of communal assets allowed Lupa to cast some social relations in the village "in the European model of patron/client relations."[16] Not surprisingly, after his murder in 1780, Moscari rebels proceeded to seize the haciendas of Hipira, Consata, and Coropaya that Lupa had been exploiting for the last thirty years.[17] Juan Chrisóstomo Ramírez was among those whose grains, livestock, and other possessions were confiscated.[18] Once the upheaval was suppressed, Florencio's son, Marcelino Lupa, claimed before the audiencia to have inherited these three haciendas. Yet the current Moscari cacique — an Indian who had been involved in the uprising — along with the eight hilacatas of the community, thought otherwise: they tried to evict Marcelino from lands whose usufruct belonged to the holder of the post rather than to the former cacique's relatives.[19]

In short, three traits of Moscari should be stressed: the multiethnic origins of the town, the coexistence of haciendas and ayllus, and the institutionalized penetration of Spanish forms of property and private accumulation in village affairs. These three factors had a direct influence on the dynamics of the social conflicts in this area and on the role that its cacique would play in the process leading to the mass uprising of native peoples of northern Potosí.

FLORENCIO LUPA

From 1753 Florencio Lupa ruled the town of Moscari. A member of the Collana ayllu, he was about twenty-three years old when he took office. During the next three decades, Lupa became the most influential Andean lord in the region. Tristan Platt (1982b: 29–30) gives Florencio Lupa as the most prominent example of the general process of alienation between communities and caciques that took place in the Andes in the eighteenth century. In evaluating the causes of peasant insurgency, a Spanish resident explained that the communities were disgusted by "seeing that the collection of the Royal tribute was not in the hands of pure Indians as they are, since they are spiritless and fainthearted and do not accept others to command them, and perhaps this is the explanation of the murders that took place in Macha and Moscari of their governors Blas Bernal and Florencio Lupa who were Hispanicized mestizos with whom they always were upset."[20]

It needs to be stressed that the description of Lupa as a Hispanicized mestizo is not a mark of his lack of hereditary rights but of the loss of legitimacy of this type of Andean authority. Indeed, Florencio Lupa was one of the few caciques in northern Potosí who did belong to a traditional lineage of ethnic lords. A man named Juan Lupa appears as cacique in documents of 1614 and 1645.[21] In 1697, the audiencia granted the title of proprietary cacique to a Martín Ignacio Lupa "for being the legitimate son and grandson of the rulers of [Moscari], a direct descendent of its first caciques, according to the information contained in the documents he presented."[22] In 1753, Florencio succeeded his grandfather, Martín Lupa, as cacique propietario, which indicated that the title was recognized by superior courts.[23] Although in fact he was mestizo like most of the old indigenous noble families by this time (he himself married a mestizo woman named Apolonia Hinojosa),[24] his hereditary rights seemed to be even more outstanding when compared to other caciques. Thus, in 1779 a Spanish neighbor mentioned that "all the governors and tax collectors of the province *with the exception of the ones in Moscari* [Lupa], Sacaca and Acacio [Ayaviri Cuisara] do not have any blood rights and enjoy none of the privileges of Indians since some of them are Spanish and others are mestizos."[25]

The violent animosity against Florencio Lupa that surfaced during the 1780 rebellion did not stem, therefore, from his ethnic background or even less from his condition as a cacique arbitrarily imposed by the corregidores, but from his performance as native lord. The process of economic differentiation between the cacique and the members of the community unquestionably represented a major motive of discontent. Some of the multiple modes whereby the cacique took advantage of his post for private wealth accumulation were revealed in an in-depth inquiry into his activities of November 1769. Thus, according to the Indians, Lupa appropriated the collective cultivation of comunes — parcels that the four Moscari ayllus set aside every year for collective cultivation — for his own benefit, rather than subsidizing the mita workers, "which was meant to be its main purpose." The Chulpata ayllu, for example, had six comunes. In three of them, Indians cultivated about twenty cargas [approximately one hundred and twenty bushels] of potatoes per field employing their oxen and ploughs, and transported the crops to Lupa's house with their own draught animals. In the three remaining comunes, the Chulpata Indians planted six fanegas [one fanega approximately equals 1.6 bushels] of wheat and one carga of maize. Since the Collana ayllu only had one común, Lupa took its members to work in some of the Chulpata's.[26] Then, the cacique sold the grains and *chuño* (freeze-dried potatoes) in the markets. Besides this exaction, the cacique demanded the handing over, during the feast of San Juan and the Navidad meetings, of one chicken — rooster or hen — by every Moscari man and woman, whether married, single, or widowed.[27]

Lupa not only commercialized community agrarian surpluses in colonial markets but also traded outside goods in the Moscari hamlets. Under the excuse of carrying out the corregidores' forced sale of goods, the cacique distributed effects at his expense and for his own benefit. Those included coca, cloth, colored wool, and the storage sacks that Lupa brought in from the mining city of Oruro. One Indian assured that he, along with another peasant from the Collana ayllu, had been sent to Oruro to bring those goods for Lupa's reparto. He also had been sent to Moquegua to get brandy.[28] Interestingly enough, there was no mention of mules or iron, the two main commodities distributed by provincial magistrates, which may indicate that the cacique avoided direct competition with the corregidores' reparto.

The management of the forced-labor system represented a private source of revenues as well. As did other northern Potosí caciques, Florencio Lupa, during the enlistment of mita workers in his hacienda of Coropaya, "exempted every year twelve or sixteen Indians to whom he charges and demands 70 pesos under the title of Colqueruma."[29] More important still, the coercive commodification of the community labor force also included the dispatch of Indians to the mines and refineries of the mining center of Aullagas, the main silver-producing area in the province. This system was akin to the state-organized mita of Potosí. Little is known of the arrangement between the cacique and the Aullagas miners for this labor draft, but a Moscari Indian related that Lupa "had sent six Indians to work in the Rosario refinery [one of the largest mines in Aullagas], under the claim that the King was ordering it. For this effect he placed a stock [rollo] in the Moscari plaza and another in the house of the mayor Miguel Sola, to intimidate the Indians and force them to do that work. Lupa in fact lashed in the public plaza the Indian Pascual Churi and he also lashed Santos Guanacota and had the mayor put him in stocks, after which he forced him to go [to Aullagas]."[30] A mining worker was publicly lashed in the Moscari plaza for having fled from the silver refinery of Rosario.[31] Another Indian who had been forced to work in the Rosario refinery explained that this "mita" lasted for five months and that he received a daily wage of 4 reales, but as this work was done during the harvest time, the salary did not compensate for the abandonment of his fields.[32]

Lupa reportedly separated some young boys and girls from their parents (orphans from their relatives, according to other versions) to send them to the major urban centers in the region to work as domestic servants (called unillos and yocallas). An Indian said that his six-year-old brother had been given as a present in La Plata, and heard that Lupa had sent one unillo and one yocalla to Cochabamba.[33] Another Indian reported that he had seen how Lupa had violently separated several boys and girls from their parents in order to send them to Oruro and La Plata. To support his account, he even listed the names of eight men and women who had their children taken from them. Of one of these parents, it was said that "the cacique took a yocalla and his father is still crying for her because she was sent to [La Plata]."[34]

Finally, as mentioned earlier, the cacique drew revenues from his hacienda in Coropaya and the two communal haciendas and grain mills of Hipira and Consata. By the time of his murder, Lupa administered a total of ten milling stations, which alone must have represented a significant source of profit.[35] The mills in the two communal estates were rented for 650 pesos a year. It was said that the milling stations of Hipira, three mills for grinding maize and one for wheat, yielded between 70 and 80 pesos weekly during the harvest season from June through August, "because of the large number of millers that show up at this time."[36] It should be noted here that the Indians not only milled grain into flour for domestic consumption but also to sell in regional markets.[37] The deployment of relations of reciprocity helped, moreover, to maximize profits. Not only was the construction of the houses, fences, and alfalfa silos done by the community, but the Indians were also responsible for the maintenance of mills, houses, storage rooms, and other facilities of the three haciendas. Like mining mita and church services, the repair of the mills, damaged regularly by floods, was realized by the ayllus on a rotating basis.[38] The cleaning of the ditches and the transportation of lumber alone took two days of work. As usual in labor exchanges within the Andean communities, workers did not seem to receive monetary wages but rather provisions of coca, chicha, and food.[39] Those who failed to show up for work in the mills were issued a fine, called *costilla*, that amounted to between 1 to 4 reales according to their status as forasteros or originarios. Labor discipline was tight: an Indian stated that "when he was laying a stick over one of the rooms that they were thatching, the cacique [Lupa] asked him why he was doing it if it belonged to the other room, and made the mayors hold him and he received twelve lashes."[40]

What is at work here is one of the most significant economic trends of European colonialism in the Andes: the articulation of traditional forms of economic organization based on communal labor and reciprocity with commercial enterprises.[41] To be sure, not all the proceeds of these economic activities were for personal usufruct. In accounting for the use of the revenues of the Hipira and Consata haciendas, Lupa himself made a detailed list of the expenditures he had in order to meet state levies and institutionalized generosity. He mentioned, for instance, a sum of 114 pesos spent in brandy, coca, and chicha in the three collective meetings for the election mita workers in order "to force them to go [to Potosí], as my ancestors used to do."[42] At stake, then, was not a clear-cut opposition between mercantile and nonmercantile modes of economic behavior but a delicate balance between the use of collective resources for private wealth accumulation and for community social reproduction. Where the line was, and where it should be, was in large part a matter of perception. It is unquestionable, though, that the cacique greatly benefited from his institutional position as broker of peasant labor and agrarian assets.

An inventory of Lupa's possessions conducted in 1776 affords a last look at both his personal wealth and his adoption of Spanish lifestyle models. For example, the furnishings of the house that he had built in the hacienda of Hipira included "a small table with a drawer and a dais painted in vermilion and gold, another large table of the approximate length of two varas [one vara equals approximately thirty-three inches] with a drawer and twelve chairs with golden and well-worked backs." The document describes the house as newly constructed with a thatch roof and a small oratory where "a large golden frame with its crown having a painting of the image of the Crucifixion of Our Lord . . . a Bretania tablecloth with Cochabamba-style embroidery, a stand of painted wood . . . a cross, also of painted wood, an altar, a Chalice of golden silver . . . a silver dish with its cruets and silver bells . . . a chasuble [vestment worn by priests] of red damask with a golden snail, stole, mantle, Chalice cloth, and a used missal." In the residence of his private hacienda of Coropaya he possessed, among other objects, four pictures of the Doctors of the church, one of the Holy Trinity, one of a crucified Christ, as well as "six maps of the world and globes with golden frames." The hacienda had two grain mills with their tools and implements, a house with a hall chamber and four bedrooms, a kitchen with an oven, a chicken coop, and a large garden with fruit trees and an alfalfa storehouse under an enclosure.[43] As in the other haciendas, everything was neatly maintained. Lupa also owned a house in the town of Santiago de Moscari, the one from which he was dragged by a multitude of Indians on the night of September 3, 1780, two days before he was beheaded.

Compounding his economic practices, Lupa developed firm links with regional ruling groups and, particularly, with several Chayanta provincial magistrates. An anonymous document that circulated in La Plata in 1781, after Lupa's execution, summarizes the general perceptions about the power that the cacique had managed to muster: "In this city used to live an Indian governor named Lupa, he was so well known for his actions that he had province-wide influence. In such a way that the Corregidor who was in harmony with him, left the province in very good shape, and those who were not, he attacked them until they fell. Since he was so sovereign in his actions, all tributaries used to give him half a real per annum, which he saved to defend provincial causes. He used the money to bribe the system of justice for his just or unjust causes" (Lewin 1957: 825–26).

Although this testimony may have overestimated Lupa's political ascendancy, it is clear that his influence expanded beyond the boundaries of native society. Already in the late 1750s, the Moscari cacique managed to rebuff accusations of tribute embezzlement promoted by one of his cousins, Pedro Lupa, because of succession disputes.[44] Whereas a few years earlier this charge had caused the removal of several caciques of Chullpa, Puraca, Caracha, and Pocoata, this time both the Chayanta corregidor and the Charcas court formally pronounced Florencio Lupa innocent from any alleged wrongdoing.[45] Significantly, as the result of this litigation, charges of fiscal fraud against caciques were thereafter moved to the viceregal government of Lima, a much more inaccessible appeal court for the Indians. But not for Lupa. In the 1760s, the cacique overtook the long journey to Lima in order to address in person his judicial affairs (Penry 1996: 196).

Connivance with state officials would only deepen in the years to come. By the time of his trip to Lima, Lupa was one of the caciques appointed by the president of the Charcas audiencia to recruit troops for an expedition against the Chiriguano Indians, a lowland group who inhabited the eastern frontier of the Spanish domains (Penry 1996: 194). Then, in 1770, one Moscari Indian observed that Lupa was "compadre and dinner guest" of the corregidor; six years later, one audiencia attorney of the audiencia depicted the relationship between the Moscari cacique and the higher provincial authority as one of "collusion and alliance."[46] In 1778, for example, the Chayanta corregidor turned to him to enforce a sentence in a commercial dispute that did not involve Indians but two Spanish landowners from Moscari and Micani. Both hacendados traveled to communal hacienda of Hipira where the cacique imparted justice.[47] In a letter sent to the king in October 1780, rebel leader Tomás Katari justified Lupa's murder by arguing that "your Majesty ought to know that Lupa was the favorite of your ministers due to the gifts and bribes he used to give them, [and] that Lupa had amassed a huge fortune out of the blood he stole from the miserable Indians."[48]

I turn now to some major aspects of this process of concentration of political power and the antagonisms it bred.

RESHAPING THE ANDEAN SOCIAL LANDSCAPE:
MIGRANTS AND HACIENDAS IN MOSCARI

By the mid-1760s Florencio Lupa pursued two ambitious endeavors. The first was to incorporate into Moscari, under his government, all the tenants from other ethnic groups residing on the haciendas of the district. The second project was to recover some of the lands that the Indian community had been surrendering to private Spanish landlords since the seventeenth century. The first undertaking defied the authority of the caciques of the Indian tenants, the second defied the legal foundations of one of the few hacienda systems in northern Potosí. The number of colonial authorities who became involved in these lawsuits — two Chayanta corregidores, the audiencia of Charcas, the royal treasury officials, and the highest authority in the land, the viceroy of Peru — echoed the economic and political significance of Lupa's endeavors. The attack against ethnic chiefs and hacienda owners, albeit eventually unsuccessful, questioned two basic attributes of the social structure in this rural world: an entrenched pattern of spatial occupation of the Andean ayllu and the relationship between private and communal property.

Ethnogenesis in the Making:
The Government of Indian Migrants
Between 1764 and 1766, Lupa initiated a series of demands to change the ethnic classification of the Indian tenants of the haciendas of Moscari. It was an ex-

tremely ambitious initiative that involved the fate of more than one hundred Indian families from different ethnic groups of Chayanta and of the neighboring province of Paria. The expansionist ambitions of the cacique reflect both the range of his influence and the social dynamics of his community. It is no wonder that an initiative of this type should take place in a community characterized by its multiethnic origins — that is, a community created as the result of the grouping of Indians who had belonged to different preconquest units. In this sense, the proposed absorption of hacienda resident workers can be seen as an exceptional step in a continuing process of ethnogenesis, a process of creating a collective ethnic identity out of disparate ethnic backgrounds. Yet, the achievement of this project required the imposition of European criteria of territoriality over the Andean principles of discontinuous occupation of space. As in most regions of the Andes, ethnicity in northern Potosí did not imply contiguous residence, and coresidence did not determine common ethnic identity. As I discuss in the introduction, valley dwellers did not "belong" to the villages where they lived but rather to ethnic groups whose members were scattered through other lowland and highland areas. In this sense, Lupa's initiative endangered the very principle of verticality, the exploitation of resources located at different altitudes of the Andean landscape by the members of a single group. It also defied one of the key strategies by which Indians accommodated colonial demands: internal migration.

Indian migration within the Andes was a constitutive feature of colonial society. Since the Toledean reforms in the late sixteenth century the colonial state designed a social order based on the classification of each Indian into fixed fiscal and social categories. The migratory movements of the Andean population became one of the most important factors in the disruption of this order. The causes underlying these migrations are well known. The Spanish government placed the greatest burden of colonial exploitation on the population of Indian villages through tribute, mita labor, forced distribution of goods, parish dues, and labor services to local secular and ecclesiastical authorities. In trying to elude these levies, a growing mass of peasants migrated toward cities, haciendas, and other Indian communities from the seventeenth century onward.[49] The abandonment of Indian towns was initially interpreted as a result of personal decisions, as a symptom of the gradual destructuring of the symbolic and material links cementing the indigenous rural community. Migration, in other words, expressed the adoption of cultural models based on the individual initiatives in tune with the growing commodification of peasant economies.[50] Subsequent research has proven that, beyond the personal motivations, some migration movements must be regarded as community strategies of social reproduction. It has become increasingly apparent that many Indians classified as forasteros continued to keep their ties with their original ethnic groups by recognizing their native lords and helping their home communities meet their economic responsibilities toward the colonial state, with tribute in particular.[51] Insofar as migration did not forsake ethnic ascription, colonial migrants fulfilled in a different environment the function of the pre-Hispanic *mitimaes* (colonizers), namely, a mechanism whereby the ayllus scattered through various ecological tiers in order to meet their subsistence needs. In the colonial society, migrants provided access to the scarcest commodity, money, and, as demographic pressures mounted, land as well.

In determining the cultural logic of population displacements, testimonies about the existence of concrete links between migrants and their home ethnic authorities are crucial. But, given the fact that the purpose of migration was evasion of official registration, those bonds have left few traces. The disputes concerning the government of the Indian tenants of the Spanish haciendas located in Moscari afford a rare glimpse into this phenomenon. As a result of litigation initiated by Florencio Lupa during the years 1764–1766, three demographic surveys were undertaken of the entire Indian population living in haciendas. One of them, the count elaborated by corregidor Juan Francisco Navarro in 1766, in the drafting of which all the tenants and their families were summoned to the village of Moscari, disclosed the social identity and residence patterns of tenants, as well as the enduring ties between migrants and their home communities. It must be noted that the haciendas were located near but not within the territories of the ethnic groups to which the tenants belonged.

All the resident peasants, 119 taxpayers total, recognized their ethnic membership, which indicates that they paid tributes to the caciques of their home communities. Table 8 shows that the tenants' ethnic ascription is highly consistent with the map of the spatial distribution of northern Potosí ethnic groups, which was elaborated by Olivia Harris and Tristan Platt (1986) using ethnographic and historical data. The concentration of Aymayas, Chayantacas, Chullpas, and Panacachis seems to reflect the fact that these groups owned valley lands in areas close to Moscari. On the other hand, Challapata Indians, a group from the neighboring province of Paria, controlled puna territories that bordered on lands of the Laymis and Aymayas. It is also noteworthy that 50 families, approximately 220 persons total, belonged to the six ethnic groups of the Chayanta repartimiento. Accordingly, a census of 1683 reported that two Moscari ayllus did not send mita workers to Potosí because Laymi and Chullpa Indians, in exchange for "lands that they have been given in these [Moscari] ayllus to cultivate," supplied their quota.[52] Finally, if we add the tenants from

Table 8. Indian Tenants of the Moscari Haciendas
by Ethnic Group, 1766

Ethnic Group	Number of Tenants	Percentage of Total
Aymaya	26	21.84
Chayantaca	25	21.00
Chullpa	16	13.44
Pocoata	12	10.08
Panacachi	10	8.00
Challapata (Paria)	10	8.40
Moscari	7	5.88
Laymi	5	4.20
Sacaca	3	2.52
Caracha	2	1.68
Puraca	1	0.84
Guari	1	0.84
Sicoya	1	0.84
Total	119	99.96

Source: AGN, XIII, 18–9–5.

Note: Moscari's tenants were exempted because they were single. They paid their taxes to Florencio Lupa after the 1766 count. The analysis of the data here has been inspired by Zulawski's 1987 analysis of the 1683 census of Oruro.

the communities belonging to the Chayanta repartimiento (Laymi, Chullpa, Sicoya, and Chayantaca) to those from Aymaya and Panacachi, the Indians descending from the pre-Hispanic kingdom of Chayanta represented more than 72 percent of the total hacienda population.

The birthplaces of the tenants show that the population of the haciendas was, in most cases, quite stable (see table 9). Fifty-three Indians were born in Moscari, which means that their parents or grandparents had already established themselves in hacienda lands. In turn, 33 percent of the tenants had been born in their original ethnic groups' villages. Only seventeen Indians declared that they had not been born either in Moscari or in their original towns. These families, therefore, might have migrated several times, the first time to the tenant's place of birth and the second one to the Moscari hacienda.

Finally, it is worth noting that the residence patterns of the Indians measured according to their ethnic ascription indicate a clear trend toward common residence among members of the same groups. This tendency reinforces the notion of the ongoing bonds of identity of tenants with their home communities. Thus twenty-one out of the twenty-five families from Chayantaca lived in the Pisaca

Table 9. Indian Tenants of the Moscari Haciendas
by Ethnic Group and Place of Birth, 1766

Originaries	Born in Place of Origin	Born in Moscari	Born Elsewhere
Aymaya	2	16	8
Chayantaca	8	14	3
Chullpa	5	9	2
Pocoata	8	4	—
Panacachi	6	3	1
Challapata (Paria)	2	7	1
Moscari	6	6	1
Laymi	3	2	—
Sacaca	3	—	—
Caracha	1	—	1
Puraca	—	1	—
Guari	1	—	—
Sicoya	—	1	—
Total	39 (33%)	63 (53%)	17 (14%)

Source: AGN, XIII, 18–9–5.

Note: The Indians usually considered as their birthplace their main place of residence rather than the actual location of their birth.

hacienda, most of them in the Achocchi hamlet, where eight or nine out of its twelve residents belonged to this group. The Chullpas tended to concentrate in the Vilacirca and Chirocari haciendas, where they accounted for thirteen of their sixteen households. The Pocoatas had the highest concentration rate, because its twelve tributaries rented lands in Pisaca, ten of them in the same hamlet of Tutupaya. In the case of the Aymayas, we can also detect a certain tendency toward coresidence, although the degree of dispersion is greater. Out of twenty-six families, thirteen lived in Pisaca, nine of them in the same area. The remaining thirteen households were distributed among three haciendas. In two of these three haciendas the degree of ethnic homogeneity is also noteworthy: the four tenant families living in Lipichicayme were from Aymaya, and from the seven families that resided in the Sacasaca hacienda, three belonged to Aymaya and the other four to Challapata.

The Indian tenants of the Moscari haciendas would eventually become the focal point of an extraordinary dispute. By the mid-1760s, Florencio Lupa initiated a legal claim to ensure that all the peasants ceased to be registered in their original towns and were incorporated into the population rolls of the Moscari community. The Indians were to stop paying tribute to their caciques, thereby losing their traditional rights in their home communities. Had Lupa managed to achieve this goal, the number of Indians under his command would have increased to about one-quarter of the existing registered population of Moscari.

The dispute did not just challenge Andean migratory strategies but Andean fiscal practices as well. The cacique based his claim on the fact that the native chiefs collected 4 to 5 pesos per year from the tenants, while their names were hidden from the state population records. The amount that caciques usually drew from landless peasants or those with small land assignations was 5 pesos, as opposed to the 7 pesos that was the official tribute for forasteros (or agregados).[53] If the tenants were to be incorporated into the state tax roll, they might have to start paying 7 pesos, as the hacienda tenants belonging to the Moscari community in fact did. This discrepancy would indeed have important political repercussions in the years to come. In August 1780, as over forty indigenous men and women from various haciendas assaulted Lupa's segunda persona Pedro Velazco and other Moscari authorities, one of their main grievances was precisely that Lupa demanded 7 pesos when their due tasa was 5 pesos — that is, the amount that the other hacienda tenants submitted to their respective ethnic chiefs.[54] The concealment of these tributaries from the census lists, moreover, represented a crucial strategy of fiscal deception. Lupa himself collected taxes from unregistered Indians living outside Moscari. As some Indians observed, for many peasants appearing in the Moscari census as runaways, "even if they indeed are runaways, [Lupa] collects their tributes because he knows very well where they can be found."[55] Not surprisingly, both the Indian tenants and their caciques resisted the attempts to break their links. One of the provincial magistrates involved in the dispute said that he had received requests from the caciques of the Chayanta repartimiento, Aymaya, and the other communities to be allowed to continue to collect tribute from the tenants. Many tenants, in turn, "lamented that they would always want to recognize their origin."[56]

In pursuing this project, Florencio Lupa displayed a remarkable capacity for political maneuvering. Initially, he brought his demand to the audiencia of Charcas. The tribunal referred the case to the viceroy of Peru, Manuel de Amat, who ordered Chayanta corregidor Francisco Rodríguez Dávila to elaborate a census list of the hacienda peasants. As the corregidor was unwilling to cooperate (he delayed the remittance of the document to the viceroy in order to obstruct the proceedings), Lupa traveled to the Potosí royal treasury in July 1764 to ask for the discharge of Rodríguez Dávila from this case, and his replacement by the general lieutenant (*justicia mayor*) of Chayanta, Francisco

Antonio de Urtizberea.[57] Not accidentally, Urtizberea and Rodríguez Dávila were engaged in a confrontation over the appointment of the former by Viceroy Amat to carry out population censuses in Chayanta. The displacement of Rodríguez Dávila from a task to which corregidores were traditionally entitled had been promoted by a Spanish resident of Chayanta, Gabriel de Solís y Valdez, who served as Defender of the Royal Treasury for the revisita of the Chayanta province. Solís y Valdez, too, was involved in Lupa's initiative.

Whereas the treasury officials of Potosí, in response to Lupa's petition, ordered Urtizberea to check if the hacienda tenants figured in the records of their respective ethnic groups, the justicia mayor undertook a much more drastic measure: he decided by himself that the hacienda tenants, regardless of their ethnic affiliation, should immediately begin to pay tribute to the Moscari cacique.[58] We know in fact that the hacienda residents submitted the 1765 San Juan quota to Lupa. Equally significant, they did it at a tasa of 7 pesos per annum, the official tax for agregados, instead of 5 pesos, the amount that they had been submitting to their caciques. On receiving this money, the Moscari cacique delivered it to Urtizberea, who then proceeded to remit it to the royal treasury of Potosí. Lupa's ability to manipulate intraelite feuds for his own ends seemed to pay off.

The situation would soon take a new turn, however. In 1765, a new corregidor replacing Rodríguez Dávila sought to assert his authority by attacking Urtizberea and Solís y Valdez and undermining the aspirations of the powerful cacique. In May 1765 the new corregidor, Juan Francisco Navarro, explained to Viceroy Amat that the collusion between Urtizberea and Lupa had resulted in a large subregistration of Moscari Indians. Despite that fiscal fraud had been the excuse for both the initial appointment of Urtizberea as *juez visitador* (judge in charge of the population court) and the shift in the ethnic affiliation of the tenants, the justicia mayor had received large cash payments in exchange for granting tribute exemptions of different types.[59] Hence, in January 1766, at Viceroy Amat's command, Navarro carried out the third census of the Indians belonging to the Moscari ayllus and hacienda tenants, and dismissed Valdez as Defender of the Royal Treasury. His attitude toward Lupa was no less hostile. Because this third list included 12 additional tenant households (119 instead of 107), Navarro asked Lupa to explain why he had consented to register tributary Indians as reservados (tax exempt).[60] In an answer that reveals the resistance of the indigenous tenants to his policy, the cacique responded that "the said Fco. Antonio [Urtizberea] agreed with the humble petition of [Lupa] that he should leave a few of the hundred and some Indian tenants of the haciendas out of the census since if he did not do it, more would be lost. For it was normal that some fled from the haciendas, as it has already happened, for not paying the 7 pesos of tribute that they should now pay, since they used to pay only 5 pesos to their caciques."[61]

Lupa did not receive any punishment for his behavior, but the incorporation of hacienda residents into the Moscari rolls was revoked. In April 1766, Navarro wrote to Viceroy Amat that although it was true that tenants had hitherto not been inscribed in the tax rolls, they should not be included with the Moscari but rather placed in the population records of their respective communities. In rebuffing Urtizberea's claims that the caciques exercised no control over the hacienda tenants, Navarro observed that

> all or most of the chieftainships of this province, and even of other provinces, have most of their people spread out very far distances, such as the very far valleys where they own lands, and despite this, all those [valley] people who live very removed from their native towns, which are in the highlands, are still subject to the church. The reason for this is that when the caciques leave the valleys to go to the puna they always leave their segundas [lieutenants] in command to take care of everything that the caciques should do. The same thing happens when caciques go from the puna to the valleys. In this way, the government of the people is always well established. And if it were detected that in some towns the caciques fail to leave their segundas in command, it would be solved by forcing them to follow the example of the other caciques.[62]

In addition to these institutionalized mechanisms of control over households residing in distant areas, the affiliation of migrants to their home communities needed to be preserved because otherwise the authority of the Andean lords would be severely weakened. Were the loss of ethnic membership to be validated in this case, the corregidor argued, the caciques would be left "insecure and suspicious that the Indians would move to other towns." Even if the Indians had been born in the haciendas, their original ethnic ascription had to be recognized "because they always have reasons to leave temporarily, either to rent lands because they do not own any or have very few plots, or for other situations that cause their children to be born outside their original towns."[63] In short, making the place of birth or residence the basis for determining social and political identities would undermine one of the organizing features of the Andean societies.

Viceroy Amat eventually accepted the suggestion that the claims of the tenants and their caciques be supported. In fact, under the recommendation of several Lima officials, the viceroy decided that the tribute money already submitted to Florencio Lupa had to be returned to the Indian tenants so that they could deliver it to their respective ethnic lords. In February 1767, when the royal accountant in Lima determined, according to Navarro's census, the total tribute assessment of the Moscari community, he explicitly excluded from the count the tenants of the haciendas.[64]

Indian Communities and Haciendas:
The Disputes over Property Rights
Florencio Lupa's second endeavor was no less ambitious than the battles over governing Indian tenants: he aimed to recover some of the lands of the Moscari ayllus that had been transferred to private landowners. In the Andes, the hacienda system consolidated around the mid-seventeenth century when a general demographic decline and the growing abandonment of rural hamlets by the indigenous population increased the vacant lands.[65] In the case of Moscari, as in most of the province, a key moment in this process occurred in 1645 during an official inspection of the lands conducted by judge-revisitador Joseph de la Vega Alvarado. A list that cacique Juan Lupa submitted to Alvarado at the time shows that Moscari had 98 tribute payers, that is, less than a quarter of that a century later.[66] Due to the small number of Indians, 396 in total, Alvarado sold lands hitherto owned by the community to Spanish landowners. This privatization represented the starting point of the expansion of the hacienda system in Moscari.

In the early 1760s, Lupa campaigned to recover some of the lands that the community had surrendered. Initially, the cacique brought charges to the audiencia of Charcas against the hacendado Juan Joseph Veramendi, whose ancestors had purchased the fields of the Yarquivirque hacienda from Alvarado one century earlier at a price of 400 pesos. On behalf of the community, Lupa offered to return this amount to Veramendi in exchange for the restitution of the plots. It should be noted that by the 1750s the Moscari community rented their two haciendas for 325 pesos per annum each, so it is little wonder that corregidor Navarro considered the original sale prices as "ridiculously low."[67]

Taking advantage of his alliance with justicia mayor Francisco Antonio de Urtizberea, Lupa asked him, while he was completing the census of Moscari, to undertake a new survey and inspection of the lands occupied by the community. He argued that, as the seventeenth-century population records showed, there were "many more registered Indians now than when the original surveying and partition of the lands of the community had taken place." In January 1765, a Spanish resident commissioned by Urtizberea conducted a "measure and visual inspection" of the lands, which underscored the toll on agrarian productivity of the growing demographic pressures. It was reported that the lands belonging to the Moscari ayllus were "consistent with the old boundaries, which can be recognized with the instruments that I carried with me, but they were very impoverished and definitely profitless due to their continuous use by Indians." The peasant families could not survive with their current allotments, about fifty varas (one vara is equivalent to thirty-three inches) of land, because as the fields could not be allowed to lay fallow as often as necessary, the lands were left "fatigued and fruitless."[68] It should be noted that even the lower lands of the puna require long periods of fallow, from six to seven years, which creates the need for a much greater number of plots than the ones the Andean peasants were cultivating at any given time. Shortening the highland fallow time, anthropologist Ricardo Godoy (1990: 41) observes, "weakens and eventually destroys productivity, forcing peasants into a predicament of declining output despite intensification."[69]

Backed by the report, the cacique made the case that the Moscari ayllus required more lands because the current ones were both scarce and unproductive. Urtizberea reported to Viceroy Amat in February 1765 that this request, especially regarding the purchase of the hacienda of Yarquivirque, "was very reasonable to insure the permanence and stability of the Indians."[70] Then, corregidor Navarro, in vivid contrast to his firm opposition to the transfer of hacienda tenants to the Moscari community but in tune with his defense of Andean patterns of social organization, keenly endorsed the complaint about the scarcity of communal lands. In April 1766, as an extension of Lupa's initial petition, the corregidor prepared a report promoting a series of measures that, if followed, would have reversed a century and a half of agrarian evolution. Navarro urged Viceroy Amat to order a thorough redistribution of land on the grounds that the original sale of community plots to private landowners had been done "with the condition that if the Indians ever required the lands, these should be returned to them at the same price that the purchasers had paid." This time had come: the original possessions of the Indian communities had to be returned to them, "to place on these lands all the Indians that now have few plots, or are landless, and who are considered agregados. In this way, they would pass to the category of originarios." This change in the existing landholding and fiscal structure would accomplish an increase of the tribute of 2 pesos 6 reales per taxpayer—the difference between the tasa of agregados and that of originarios. Moreover, if a new general distribution of lands was to be announced then all the runaway Indians would voluntarily return to their home communities. "Most of the six hundred Indians who are now in hiding would become agregados," corregidor Navarro noted, "and at a tax of 7 pesos each, the total to be collected would mount to 4,200 pesos."[71] This dramatic increase in the size of the indigenous communities would in turn revamp the Potosí mining mita. Some of these resources could be used to purchase the lands from the hacendados.

The Spanish landowners voiced their opposition to the corregidor's sweeping proposal, claiming that the current value of the property was four or five times higher than the price paid by their ancestors because they had built mills on the land and extended their cultivation acreage. Navarro, however, contended that this loss should be regarded as the just price that would compensate for the damage inflicted on the peasant economy. In this sense, he proposed that landowners keep the grain mills, "which provide most of their revenues, but that which they have gained through burning brush and extending cultivation is compensated by how exhausted the lands have become, and that we should first consider the well being of the Natives both because these lands are theirs and because their well being is always recommended by His Majesty, whose own benefit we should also secure. The natives are very numerous and they do not have, as other persons, the free will to work elsewhere."[72]

In the end, no significant transfer of private estates to the Moscari ayllus seemed to have occurred. Such a sweeping plan of agrarian reform, as expected, found no support among Lima officials. Florencio Lupa's attempts at recovering hacienda lands as well as placing under his rule more than a hundred Indians from other ethnic groups still shows a sphere of action and an ability to summon solidarity within the colonial administration that largely surpassed the possibilities of the other northern Potosí caciques. The sheer financial costs of this judicial litigation must have been considerable. Naturally enough, the various sectors of local society alienated by those initiatives did not remain passive. Indeed, in 1768, shortly after these conflicts, the cacique faced the greatest challenge to his authority ever to emerge within his community until the dramatic events of 1780.

INDIANS, LANDOWNERS, AND PRIESTS: THE BACKLASH

In the late 1760s, Florencio Lupa's government was questioned by a considerable number of peasants from the four ayllus of Moscari, the parish priest, and some landowners. Assaults on Lupa were twofold. First, the cacique of Moscari was once again accused of tribute misappropriation. This time the charge was directly presented to the highest authority in the land, the viceroy of Peru, who held exclusive jurisdiction over these matters ever since the denunciation pursued by his cousin Pedro Lupa ten years before. In 1768, several Moscari Indians led by Tomás Chipata, a member of the Chulpata ayllu, asked Viceroy Amat for the removal of Florencio Lupa on the grounds of tribute embezzlement. Second, a fifty-year-old Indian called Matheo Jorge headed a protest before the audiencia of Charcas. Claiming that the cacique committed several abuses of power and misappropriated community resources for his own benefit, Jorge and his followers demanded Lupa's removal.[73] The social standing of some of the protesters also signals the scale of village factionalism. Matheo Jorge, Lázaro Chipata, and Basilio Catusiri (an Indian who testified against Lupa) had been hilacatas of the ayllus Collana and Chiquito during the past two decades. Jorge, in addition, had served several times as captain of the mita.[74]

It is clear that some prominent members of local society backed these initiatives. The priest of Moscari, Josef de Osa Palacios, was one of them. According to Lupa, one of the main accusers, Manuel Baleriano, was "a compadre of the priest" and Matheo Jorge and Tomás Chipata were under the influence of Osa Palacios and his main assistant.[75] Even before appealing to the audiencia and the viceroy, the leaders of the protest, under Osa Palacios's encouragement, had gathered testimonies in the province to force the dismissal of the cacique. This feud with Osa Palacios was certainly not circumstantial. Compounding his challenge to Spanish landlords and hacienda tenants, Florencio Lupa consistently disputed the Moscari clergymen's claims to the spiritual guidance and economic resources of the Indian community. Numerous Moscari peasants stressed that the cacique took an active role in making sure that the fees for sacraments (baptisms, marriages, and funerals) and ritual sponsorships were in accordance with official tariff lists. In fact, not only did Lupa press many legal charges against Osa Palacios for the excessive number of servants and material resources demanded by the church, but he also lowered in practice the labor services to the priest and the number of ritual sponsors for some Catholic festivals (Penry 1996: 204–5). Equally significant, Lupa kept at his expense a priest other than the official one, to ensure, he said, the proper religious instruction of the Indians.[76] In May 1769, for instance, the Indians reacted violently when Lupa separated thirty boys so that his priest would be the one to teach them Christian doctrine.[77] While Lupa's practice of allocating young children as domestic servants might account for this reaction, the cacique also argued that Osa Palacios had encouraged it because of his opposition to the priest paid by the cacique. It seems sure, in any event, that in response to this extraordinary encroachment on his jurisdiction and sources of revenues, Osa Palacios compelled Lupa to decrease his own forced distribution of goods and challenged his control of the haciendas owned by the community.[78]

Although the effect of this personal strife between the two dominant authority figures on the everyday life of the Andean peasants should not be generalized (as discussed in chapter 1, for example, the priests of the Chayanta parish were firm defenders of the caciques), Lupa's policy partook of a larger pattern of conflict: the priests of the Chayanta village had repeatedly accused his father, Miguel Lupa, of inciting the Indians against their chiefs.[79] In the early 1770s, in the context of widespread struggles over ecclesiastical levies, it was reported that Florencio Lupa sought an alliance with the Chullpa and Caracha lords Manuel Ninavia and Alejandro Yavira, "to go against all the priests of this province, as well as other people who oppose them and prevent them from exercising the lordship that, as caciques, they should have; the agreement was that they should help each other and as a result of it they initiated some legal proceedings under Lupa's direction."[80] Some years later, during the confrontation between the hacienda tenants and Moscari tribute collectors in August 1780, some Indians lamented that their cacique "was only good to publish the official list of ecclesiastical fees."[81] Not long afterward, Tomás Katari remarked that "Lupa had always been an assailant of the ministers of Jesus Christ."[82]

Not surprisingly, the hacendados also were active in their participation in the indigenous protest against Florencio Lupa. When Francisco Ruiz, the commissioned judge appointed by the audiencia to investigate the cacique's abuses, granted the Indians the opportunity to choose their own Protector of Indians, the owner of the Moscari hacienda of Sacasaca, Joseph de Sandoval, a man fluent in Quechua and Aymara, was chosen. The interpreters were hacendados as well. One of them was Juan Joseph Veramendi, the owner of the Yarquivirque hacienda whom Lupa had sued two years before.[83] Uncharacteristically for these kinds of inquiries against caciques, the judge consistently leaned in favor of the protesters. Ruiz's inquiry indeed turned into one of the most comprehensive investigations on the activities of an ethnic lord in the province. During the last week of November 1769, based on a detailed questionnaire written by Joseph de Sandoval, testimonies from seventeen Indians from the four ayllus of Moscari were recorded. They detailed, among other abuses, how Florencio Lupa carried out his own forced distribution of goods, forcefully dispatched Indian workers to the mining center of Aullagas, appropriated the yield of collective work on common lands, and embezzled part of the tribute monies because of the underregistration of taxpayers.

And yet despite the abundance of evidence no action in the end would be taken against the cacique. The conflict was played out in three scenarios: the Chayanta province, the audiencia of Charcas, and the viceregal court of Lima. The cacique found solidarity in all three milieus.

In the case of Chayanta, although Lupa was unable to avoid the active involvement of more than twenty Indians in the protest, the cacique did deploy several means of intimidation. Despite the judge's warnings, Lupa remained in town during the proceedings in order to prevent more peasants from testifying. Assisted by his segunda persona, a mulatto or mestizo named Tomás Estévez, the cacique placed several Indians in the stocks, gallows, racks, and dungeon that he had built in his own house.[84] Moreover, he mobilized the support of the ten current tribute collectors of all the Moscari ayllus, Indian mayors, and some Indian commoners who presented several writings in both Moscari and La Plata threatening an uprising if their cacique were to be removed.[85] Lupa also counted on the firm support of the acting corregidor, justicia mayor Nicolás Ursainqui, who fully backed the cacique, unlike his predecessor Martín Navarro. Despite his contempt for some elite town-dwellers, Lupa managed to have a group of Moscari Spanish residents declare before Ursainqui that the landowners had dictated Indians' depositions, and that priest Osa Palacios had traveled through the rural hamlets promising that Matheo Jorge would be their new cacique.[86] Ursainqui appointed as commissioned judge Gabriel Solís y Valdez, the same person who had promoted, along with Urtizberea, Lupa's previous initiatives. In 1769, a Collana Indian recalled that Florencio Lupa had tied his hands because "the cacique thought that I had gone [to La Plata] to act against him and in favor of Matheo Jorge, and [he] forced me to take an oath with a Judge who was there, don Gabriel Valdez, who wrote in a paper things I did not know anything about and then let me go."[87] This combination of coercion and legal appearances is also visible in the repression of Matheo Jorge, whose lands Lupa reallocated to two other Indians "to place them under the category of originarios."[88] In August 1769, Ursainqui endowed the redistribution with a legal sanction by appointing two inspectors who verified that the size of the parcels justified their subdivision.[89]

The complicity of the cacique with some audiencia ministers is also notable. A day before the first presentation of the Indians before the tribunal in June 1769, Lupa sent a letter to the audiencia's Protector of Indians, Manuel Martínez de Escobar, discrediting the Indians' grievances. Not only did Martínez de Escobar back Lupa's position, he also tried to block the appointment of a commissioned judge to investigate the charges. When the Moscari protesters returned in October 1769 for the second time to the city, they went as far as requesting that the court should appoint somebody else as their defendant instead of the "lawyers who had been appointed for Indian legal causes" because all of them were in favor of Lupa.[90] As mentioned at the beginning of this chapter, contemporary testimonies observed that Lupa "used the money to bribe the system of justice for his just or unjust causes." This collusion became exceedingly apparent when Matheo Jorge appealed to the audiencia for the last time in March 1770. Jorge announced that the inquiry of the past November had only resulted in an escalation of violence against the Indians, including Lupa's "increasingly expensive repartos." Jorge himself had been arrested and then put in the stocks for his appeals to the audiencia. In response, Protector of Indians Martínez de Escobar commanded him to present his claim before the Chayanta corregidor himself.[91]

In this petition, Jorge remarked that he had heard that Lupa was trying "very keenly [to ensure] that all the pending writs that are now in this audiencia should be transferred to Lima, because in this distant court we will not have the resources to pursue them."[92] Effectively, Lupa's explicit strategy was to transfer the entire case, along with the issue of tribute misappropriation, from the audiencia to the viceregal court of Lima. As mentioned above, Lupa himself had traveled to Lima in the 1760s. A distant tribunal, almost inaccessible to the Indians and less sensitive to social pressures, would be even more reliable than a regional court. He eventually succeeded in his efforts to gain a transfer, and in December 1769, in response to a request by Florencio Lupa before the Protector of Indians of Lima, Viceroy Manuel Amat asked the Charcas court to send the complete dossier to Lima. The audiencia initially refused to give up its jurisdiction over the matters, but as pressures from the viceroy and from Lupa himself mounted it finally conceded. In January 1771, Amat received the original dossier and ordered the audiencia to communicate to both parties that they "must come to this Superior Government to exercise their rights." This invitation, as Matheo Jorge had anticipated, is the last document on the matter.[93]

A MULTIETHNIC CHIEFTAINSHIP

In the battles over the governing of tenants and the control of hacienda lands, the leverage of the Moscari native lord can be assessed through the scale of his initiatives; in the subsequent conflict through the forces he had to reckon with—principal Indians, landowners, and priests—in order to keep his post. By the early 1770s, Florencio Lupa had effectively suppressed internal opposition and established concrete links of political cooperation with rulings groups in northern Potosí, with audiencia ministers, and with at least some contacts with members of the viceregal court of Lima. The development of this network, along with his efforts to incorporate into the tax rolls numerous unregistered Indians, eventually paved the way for an expansion of his authority with no precedents within northern Potosí. Florencio Lupa, in effect, would become the focal point of the most ambitious attempt at reformulating state/community relations during the years prior to the great Andean upheaval. A few months after the confrontation with the Moscari Indians, colonial authorities sought to use Lupa's ascendancy as a far-reaching means of social and fiscal control over the rural population. Lupa was raised to the position of cacique of two other ethnic groups, thereby becoming a sort of general intermediary between the Indians and the Spanish administration. Whereas corregidores during this period often imposed their own candidates as native chiefs, this was the first time in northern Potosí that a complete outsider was appointed as cacique of a community, and the first time for a cacique to hold the chieftainship of several communities simultaneously. Laymi cacique Marcos Soto's overtaking of the Puraca chieftainship might be considered an antecedent, but the very ethnic identity of these two groups was rather ambiguous (as discussed in chapter 1). In the case of Lupa, the formation of a multiethnic chieftainship unquestionably represented an extraordinary attempt at legally transforming the nature of the Andean lords from representatives of the community (however contested the criteria of representation and political legitimacy of these representatives might have been) to state-imposed government agents.

In 1771, Chayanta corregidor Carlos de Hereña appointed Lupa as an interim cacique of the Panacachi, a group that by the 1760s had 235 tributaries.[94] Unlike the case of the Laymi-Puraca, it is clear that the sweeping abrogation of the Panacachi's political autonomy had nothing to do with the material or symbolic bonds that might have existed between the Panacachis and the Moscaris as a result of their territorial proximity (the Panacachi's territory bordered that of the Moscari's) or their common past (both groups had distant roots in the pre-Hispanic Charka confederation). The ascent of Florencio Lupa instead rested on a more comprehensive model of the reorganization of the government of native peoples of northern Potosí. In fact, his appointment as governor of Panacachi was immediately followed by his appointment as cacique of Pocoata, with whom Moscari had even slighter links.[95] In any event, for the first time in eighteenth-century northern Potosí, two Andean communities were overly deprived from a basic political prerogative under Spanish colonialism: the right to self-rule.

The case of the Pocoata was of particular significance. Unlike the Panacachi, the Pocoata ethnic group was a large one. According to a reinspection of 1754, the Pocoata group had 941 tributaries, 633 originarios and 308 agregados. Adding the Indians registered around the village of Pocoata (the puna seat of the repartimiento), and the households residing in the Chayala, Micani, Carasi, and Surumi Valleys the census reported an overall population of 4,169.[96] This ranked the Pocoata as the second most populous ethnic group in the province after the Sacaca. In addition, Pocoata was the seat of one of the most ancient and prominent lineages of native lords in the southern Andes: the Ayra Chichi Ariuto. Certainly, the displacement of the Pocoata caciques did not emerge in a vacuum. Indeed, complex agrarian and power struggles within the Pocoata group preceded the appointment of Florencio Lupa. As I have analyzed elsewhere, an unusually large number of land conflicts among Pocoata families took place starting from the 1730s. These conflicts involved issues of community boundaries in puna and valley territories alike, family claims against ethnic chiefs' allocation of plots, collective confrontations among ayllus and moieties, and clashes over hereditary land tenure rights.[97] Although demographic growth and its direct effect, land subdivision, appears as an explicit source of tension, the sheer volume of judicial litigation signals the weakness of the ethnic structures of government, the prime means in Andean society for solving strife over agricultural resources. Intraethnic land struggles were indeed matched by indigenous protests against the Pocoata caciques, including the descendants of the Ayra Chìnchi Ariuto whose members possessed considerable amounts of fields and, in some cases, turned into private landlords.[98]

This process of intraethnic agrarian strife and social differentiation notwithstanding, the removal of all the native chiefs of Pocoata constituted an extraordinary violation of the political autonomy of the community. No political, historical, or legal reasons, other than the policy of establishing Florencio Lupa as a general intermediary between colonial authorities and indigenous peoples, could possibly legitimize this unprecedented decision. In fact, in July 1772 when taking advantage of an internal dispute in Pocoata corregidor Carlos Hereña appointed Lupa, he did so on the sole grounds that the Moscari cacique was "a person who has been acknowledged (as it is public and well known) for his zeal in the worship of God, the Royal interests, and the good government that he has given and gives to the people of his community [of Moscari]."[99] No attempts were made at elucidating the rights that entitled Lupa to hold the chieftainship of a neighboring Andean group. Accordingly, the audiencia ministers praised the decision as a means of social control, overlooking its obvious arbitrariness. In tune with his position in previous protests against Lupa, Protector of Indians Martínez de Escobar immediately pronounced the ruling an act of "utmost wisdom" because the Moscari chief would be able to teach the Pocoatas the rules of good government, "which for them is hard to understand because their extreme rusticity naturally pushes them toward a further relaxation of their costumes and less Christian and religious subjection, which should be repressed."[100] The audiencia attorney also gave his approval, and shortly thereafter the Charcas court formally validated the appointment.[101]

Perfunctory as it might have seemed at the time, the decision to bestow the Moscari cacique with such sweeping authority would have enormous consequences in the months and years to come. In September 1772, right after the annual meetings for delivery of tribute and the dispatch of the Potosí mita, a large group of Pocoatas — large enough to be described by a Spanish witness as a "multitude of Indians" — traveled to La Plata to protest the encroachment on their ethnic autonomy. But despite the massiveness of the mobilization the audiencia ministers refused to hear them. It was reported that neither the Protector of Indians nor the audiencia attorney could be entrusted with the defense of the Pocoatas because of their open partiality.[102] In fact, Martínez de Escobar tried to misrepresent the mass mobilization as aimed against the previous Pocoata caciques, particularly Diego and Dionisio Ayra. He also asked for the eviction of the Pocoatas from La Plata on the grounds that only a few Indians were legally allowed to present grievances on behalf of their communities.[103] Uncharacteristically, the Indians were even unable to voice their complaints. A very brief petition, written by Martínez de Escobar in their name, is the sole trace of this collective protest. Even this succinct document underscored that the motivation behind the trip was not, as the same official had previously claimed, to protest against their former chiefs (although the Pocoatas, as shown later, would not want their reinstatement either) but rather to repudiate the appointment of Florencio Lupa. The Pocoatas, the petition reads, rejected the Moscari cacique because he lived "at too great a distance to be able to carry out in their town [Pocoata] the duties that he has been assigned."[104] As I describe in the next chapter, when three years later the Pocoatas compelled, through mass protests and demonstrations of force, colonial authorities both in northern Potosí and La Plata to hear their views on the matter, they would have much more to say about the abolition of their right to self-rule.

In mid-1772, at any rate, Florencio Lupa became a multiethnic cacique. In 1766 his first effort to incorporate Indians from neighboring ethnic groups to Moscari had failed. Six years later, he wielded a power unparalleled by any other northern Potosí native chief since the reorganization of the native peoples implemented by Viceroy Toledo at the end of the sixteenth century. Lupa was the lord of three different ethnic groups that occupied a vast territory stretching from the highlands of Pocoatas to the punas west of the village of Chayanta and the valleys of Micani, Carasi, Moscari, and Parica. Under Lupa's command, according to official figures for 1772, were 1,263 tributaries, and he was responsible for about a quarter of the total taxes and mita workers of the province.[105]

The extraordinary prominence achieved by the Moscari lord is a remarkable example of the ability of some members of the Andean aristocracy to take full advantage of their role as brokers between the Andean peoples and the political and mercantile structures of colonialism. Lupa's position, as the series of confrontations analyzed above makes clear, was not free from serious challenges from both ends of the colonial social hierarchy. Nevertheless, in the context of a rural world increasingly prone to political unrest, Florencio Lupa came to epitomize ideals of social and economic normalization. This is what accounts for his unique political standing. In the final analysis, Lupa's appointment as cacique of Panacachi and Pocoata must be regarded as an initial step toward the imposition of these criteria of social control over the traditional corporate rights of the northern Potosí communities. The paradox, then, is that this new disciplining policy gave rise to collective mobilizations that would shake the existing social order as would no other event during the eighteenth century. The kind of moral outrage bred by this policy was underlined in May 1781 by a mestizo resident of Pocoata who had witnessed the social conflicts in the area for the past thirty years, had been wounded in one of the battles with rebel forces, and had just been appointed Protector of Indians of the province. Looking back to the causes of the general insurrection that was finally coming to a close, he did not hesitate to point to the day, nine years earlier, when Florencio Lupa had been put in charge of the collection of tributes of Pocoata.[106]

The career of Florencio Lupa tells us, however, just one side of this story. The rise of this type of indigenous authority was indeed intertwined with a political context of overarching changes in ideas and power relations at all levels of the Spanish empire. This change encompassed the organization of the old viceroyalty of Peru and the relationship between state and church and extended to the exercise of authority in the northern Potosí rural villages. This general conjuncture of political transformation that laid the foundations for the emergence of a multiethnic chieftainship and the indigenous reactions to it are the focus of the following chapter.

3

Customs

and Rules:

Bourbon

Rationalizing

Projects and

Social Conflicts

in the

1770s

IN HIS BOOK *THE LETTERED CITY*, Angel Rama (1996: 1) offers the following account of the conceptions of social order underpinning the ideals of the city of the first European settlers in the New World:

> Over the course of the sixteenth century, the Spanish conquerors became aware of having left behind the distribution of space and the way of life characteristic of the medieval Iberian cities — "organic," rather than "ordered" — where they had been born and raised. Gradually and with difficulty, they adapted themselves to a frankly rationalizing vision of the urban future, one that ordained a planned and repetitive urban landscape and also required that its inhabitants be organized to meet increasingly stringent requirements of colonization, administration, commerce, defense, and religion.

When applied to the rule and the organization of the native peoples that inhabited the territory of the old Inca empire, this rationalizing utopia took on various forms. In sharp contrast to the early colonial society, by the late sixteenth century the crown built centralized modes of economic exploitation, ordered a massive resettlement of the rural population in Spanish-like towns, and set up a myriad of civil and ecclesiastical authorities in charge of policing the native groups and administering Spanish justice.[1] Although those institutions would continue to be the hallmark of colonialism in the Andes until the end, over the course of the next 150 years the region experienced a gradual but systematic erosion of this hierarchical and rationalizing model of government and society. Andean traditional economic systems and customary social arrangements long survived attempts to reorganize the spatial distribution of the population and the structure of ethnic rule; pervasive bureaucratic institutions and a centralized fiscal system stumbled as a result of the massive sale of appointments and local officials' private entrepreneurial activities; and native rituals and religious beliefs blossomed beneath the tolerant gaze of the rural priesthood and the idiosyncrasies of Andean Catholic festivities.[2] An age of political consent, custom-oriented social relations, and baroque piety would make its quiet but inexorable way into the Andean world.

It was the absolutist monarchies that would undertake the task of refining and enforcing Renaissance models of social normalization and centralized power. As is well known, late Bourbon colonial administrators devised an ambitious program of imperial reforms to undo the historical developments that had taken place during the Hapsburg era. Bourbon enlightened absolutism sought to regain command over the colonial empire by undermining the power of local ruling groups, disciplining social practices, and imposing criteria of economic efficiency and normative conceptions of law predicated on the universal application of legal norms.[3] My central aim in this chapter is to examine the effects of this program when translated into concrete practices — specifically how power relations in the rural world were affected by the rationalizing project.

Recent studies focused on the relation between state-building processes and peasant movement and consciousness in Latin America have suggested the need to examine state hegemony (and there are few doubts that Bourbon absolutism represented a new hegemonic project, a profound reformulation of the colonial pact) as processes rather than as stable structures of domination, and as inherently ambivalent endeavors as opposed to cohesive ideological models.[4] By exploring the relationship between empire, local government, and peasant society, in this chapter I address questions that in many respects speak to those general issues of state domination. How did the ambitious Bourbon scheme of social and political transformation shape everyday colonial power relations in a particular Andean rural society? How did various ruling groups offer opposing "readings" of the changes taking place? What was the relation between the new normative trends — the increasingly aggressive rationalizing impulse — and customary social arrangements? While the relation between Bourbon absolutism and social protest has been analyzed usually in terms of the mounting economic grievances that followed increases in taxes and commercial monopolies,[5] this study is concerned with the ways whereby new state mechanisms of domination contributed to mold new peasant forms of contention. In other words, I deal here with two basic problems: how the emerging project of colonial hegemony was performed and negotiated at its most concrete level, and how subaltern groups engaged and challenged state power.

I am concerned in this chapter with four aspects of the dynamic of Bourbon reforms in the southern Andes. The first is the attempt by provincial and regional colonial authorities to set up institutionalized mechanisms of surveillance over peasant life. To address this issue I analyze a series of measures to control ethnic lords' use of the labor force, distribution of the tax burden, election of mita teams, and administration of common lands and mills. These new policies stemmed from a conflict over native chieftainships in the Chullpa group (examined in chapter 1) since the group's inception in the late 1740s. The second topic involves the local repercussions of the state regulation of ecclesiastical fees in the early 1770s. The Bourbon administration sought to curtail parish priests' command over peasant resources by issuing a standard schedule of fees and prohibiting unwilling contributions during the extensive cycle of religious celebrations. Civil officials, the clergy, and the Indians engaged in intense disputes over the meaning of those new norms. The series of tensions unleashed by the Bourbon initiatives provide the proper historical context for the third theme which involves most acute conflict between northern Potosí peasants and rural power groups prior to the rebellion of 1780: the struggle of the Pocoata Indians against the foreign cacique Florencio Lupa. This process sheds light on the way the Andean communities took full advantage of manifest dissension within the group of colonial elites over tax matters in order to advance their own agenda: the recovery of their ethnic political autonomy. The fourth topic is the opening stages of what would become a full-fledged mass insurgency, the protest movement of Macha Indians led by Tomás Katari. I examine how Machas's initiatives were shaped by their Pocoata neighbors' mobilization and, more generally, by the overall atmosphere of horizontal and vertical political contention among colonizers and colonized.

My overarching aim in this chapter is, then, to show that by looking at certain aspects of Bourbon reformism that have not been sufficiently connected to the phenomenon of peasant protest we can obtain a more thorough understanding of the process leading up to the great Andean insurrection of the 1780s. I hope to discern the role of enlightened rationalizing programs in the transition from quotidian, incremental forms of indigenous politics to the emergence of a mass anticolonial movement. I contend that some Bourbon policies or, to put it more accurately, various state initiatives that emerged in the context of the climate of ideas nurtured by enlightened rule, came to represent a major instrument of Andean resistance against entrenched structures of exploitation and political oppression in the rural villages. Certainly, as I will show, colonial rulers also used the new rationalizing project for quite different objectives. The key point, nonetheless, is that the most radical indigenous upheaval during the colonial period in this region was the outcome of the *intertwinement*, not the *clash*, between processes of social mobilization from below and political transformation from above. Seen from this particular regional context, the crisis of colonial legitimacy may have resulted less from the enforcement of a new colonial pact than from the unintended ways in which this new hegemonic project helped to collapse the old one without consolidating in the process a viable alternative. Bourbon policies increased the economic burden of Andean communities at the same time that they empowered them to contest local authority. During the 1770s provincial magistrates, rural clergymen, and Andean native chiefs repeatedly warned of the potentially catastrophic consequences of this combination, and eventually they proved to be right.

NORMALIZING ANDEAN SOCIAL RELATIONS

Beginning in the late 1760s northern Potosí society underwent a series of transformations connected to the Spanish administration's attempts to redefine social relations within the rural world and within the colonial administration. Bourbon policies followed a common "ordering urge," to use Angel Rama's expression, in an effort to impose a set of norms upon a society that during the late Hapsburg era had been increasingly subjected to a set of local customary practices and compromises formed beyond colonial law and the crown's control. What was at issue was the imposition of a new system of domination rooted in enlightened notions of rationalization and centralized power, which meant the adaptation of existing social reality to normative schemes and the subordination of the lower levels to the upper levels of the state bureaucracy.[6] Although the reorganization of fiscal, commercial, and administrative colonial structures was the most conspicuous and by and large the best-known target of Bourbon policies, in northern Potosí the reform effort concentrated on a rather less visible domain of power relationships, namely, the use of Indian agrarian assets and the distribution of the economic burden within the Andean community. During the early 1770s, peasants and authorities generated a series of debates about the jurisdiction of Spanish magistrates to oversee the management of communal resources by ethnic lords. The surveillance of caciques' activities ranged from the use of the labor force and the election of the mita team to the administration of common lands and mills and the allotment of the tribute quota to households.

A major step toward state intervention in traditional Andean economic arrangements occurred in 1772 in the context of a protracted conflict over government in the Chullpa group. As I show in chapter 1, from the late 1740s onward this community had experienced intense struggles over the administration of agrarian assets and the distribution of colonial levies among its members. In the early 1770s, a new cycle of peasant unrest, which included numerous collective appeals to Chayanta and Charcas officials, forced the replacement of the cacique Manuel Ninavia by Miguel Caracara, one of the old protest leaders, through the realization of one of the few public contests for the appointment of cacique propietarios conducted in the province. In suppressing the engrained state of rural agitation epitomized by this longstanding strife, corregidor Carlos de Hereña set out to fix strict mechanisms of control over the activities of the Andean lords. He issued a decree that penalized the appointment of colquerunas (wealthy Indians who commuted mita services through money), prohibited any transgression of the mita obligation, and regulated the use of common lands or comunes (plots worked collectively for community needs). Corregidor Hereña argued that "since time immemorial the harmful practice of naming colquerunas annually has been introduced in all the towns of this province, with the result being the total annihilation of the miserable Indians."[7] Although the caciques sustained that the 50 pesos paid by the colquerunas were spent in the cabildos (communal meetings) celebrated to select mita workers and to collect tribute, for the corregidor those gatherings only amounted to collective drinking sprees. On the other hand, the exempting of wealthy Indians from mita services altered turn rotation because the caciques put all the burden of the labor draft on the shoulders of the poorest members of the community. Furthermore, the corregidor argued that the native chiefs usually misappropriated the produce cultivated in common lands, whereas royal ordinances stipulated that these fields should be used to outfit mita workers and subsidize widows, the elderly, and the sick.

On these bases Hereña established, firstly, that the appointment of colque runas would henceforth be forbidden "and the penalty for those [caciques] who do it will be their immediate removal from the collection of the Royal tribute and dispatch of the mita, replacing them with whichever Indian had revealed [the appointments], even if he happens to be of the lower ranks."[8] Second, the ethnic authorities would also be evicted if they altered the mita rotation by replacing wealthy Indians with poor Indians. Finally, in order to insure that the harvests in common lands would be set aside for the benefit of the communities, Hereña decided that the caciques had thereafter to keep formal written records of the output and allocation of the production of common lands and mills. By doing so the native lords would become accountable for the management of communal resources any time that the corregidor deemed necessary. Issued in May 1772, this ruling was publicly read "with drum rolls and bugles" in all the northern Potosí towns and a transcript of it was sent to the caciques of each ethnic group.

Although the colquerunas and the misappropriation of agrarian revenues had stirred numerous disputes among Chullpas, Puracas, Chayantacas, Carachas, Moscaris, and Pocoatas, this decision constituted an unprecedented undertaking to legislate over realms of social life that had traditionally fallen outside the gaze of colonial administrative power. To be sure, the corregidor must have pursued his own entrepreneurial ventures with this measure, especially in order to pave the way for the manipulation of native chieftainships, a crucial issue during the expansion of the forced sale of goods. Yet the extent to which state surveillance of peasant affairs was in tune with predominant rationalizing social ideals (and not just with personal economic interests) is shown by the fact that this local initiative would immediately be embraced in the high ranks of the colonial government in the area. Soon after the publication of the decree, the audiencia of Charcas extended its applicability to all the territories under its jurisdiction, from the altiplano provinces in the La Paz region to the northern territories of present-day Chile and Argentina. Indeed, the impulse to extend the arm of state control into the rural world moved the court to set up even closer mechanisms of surveillance than those established in the initial measure. The tribunal commanded provincial magistrates to demand annually from every cacique a written, sworn account of the communities' assets, the yearly revenues, and the way surpluses had been distributed. Each year, the Andean lords were to submit the affidavits to the corregidores, and the corregidors, in turn, to the audiencia. In October 1773, the Charcas court mailed the order to all the Upper Peruvian corregidores, commanding them to publish it in every rural village and to give a copy to all the native chiefs. Its content, the audiencia emphasized, should be applied with the greatest strictness "without any tolerance or indulgence."[9]

The same kind of intrusiveness in customary peasant practices appears in disputes over the working of the tribute system within the Andean community. This trend did not spring from conflicts within the indigenous communities but from another crucial historical development: the successful strivings of the

Bourbon administration to raise fiscal revenues (Cahill 1990: 265–67; Klein 1992: 72–74). By the early 1770s, this royal policy prompted Spanish and Andean authorities to denounce the wide gap between official taxation rules and the set of cultural norms governing the tribute system within Andean society. In particular, nine native chiefs from Aymaya, Jukumani, Panacachi, and the six ethnic groups of the Chayanta repartimiento (Caracha, Chayantaca, Sicoya, Chullpa, Puraca, and Laymi) publicly blamed the peculiar set of checks and balances of the Andean fiscal regime for their inability to deliver a new tribute quota established by a recent population count.[10] This count was since 1731 the first general demographic census of the province assigned by the vice-roy of Peru to an outside official. When the revisitador, a resident of La Plata named Pedro Pereira de Castro, elaborated the first lists — those corresponding to the nine ethnic groups — the results were striking: a 68 percent rise in relation to existing rolls and an overall addition of 1,019 new taxpayers.[11] In jail for failing to fulfill their new tribute dues, the nine caciques condemned what they defined as "invincible and harmful customs that are deeply rooted among the Indians of our communities." These entrenched practices consisted, basically, of four sets of tributary norms. The first one defined fiscal liability according to ancient Andean norms that made family status and land tenure, as opposed to age, the criteria for taxation. Young men started to pay their taxes only one or two years after their marriage rather than after reaching the age of eighteen, as established by fiscal ordinances. By the same token, when the newly married couple occupied their parents' lands, their parents passed into the reservado (tax exempt) category, even if they had not reached the official retirement age of fifty. The next two rules established community norms of temporary tax exemp-tion: mita workers were free from tribute payments during their service in Potosí, as well as were Indians serving as civil or ritual authorities in any of the several highland and valley villages inhabited by these ethnic groups. Finally, the actual amount of tribute money delivered by the peasant households did not match official rates.[12] As long as these time-honored tributary customs were allowed to be in place, the nine caciques contended, the efforts to raise state revenues would not be achieved.

The existence of these practices, of course, was not a secret. Andean peoples had for centuries conducted the tribute operation within their communities in accordance with their own cultural criteria. For one thing, state population records, as historians have amply demonstrated, routinely concealed large num-bers of Indians insofar as colonial censuses were in practice the outcome of negotiations between native chiefs and the revisitador, usually the provincial corregidores.[13] Equally, the divergence between Spanish and Andean fiscal rules described by the nine caciques rendered tax rolls useless in the tribute collection process. For instance, in 1760, a hilacata of Moscari explained that he had no use for official records because "the Indians resist making full payments when they lack enough lands to pay the tax that they are supposed to pay."[14] The tasa could be as low as 2 pesos 2 reales, another hilacata added, "because they are poor and they have just started to pay the tribute, and he tolerates it because he fears that if not these Indians will run away."[15] An approximate quantitative measure of this divergence was provided by two ayllus of Macha in 1778, when they exhibited the tribute lists employed by the caciques and hilacatas: out of 237 taxpayers, 69 Indians (29 percent) paid taxes that did not match the official ones.[16] Regarding the discrepancies in tax-exemption criteria, the Puracas reported in 1750 that 64 households (out of an overall number of 162) were released from tribute in any given year because of their services as mita workers as well as town councilmen, ritual sponsors, and church servants in the puna and valley villages of Chayanta, Micani, and Carasi. Current official records at the time only registered 15 exempted Puracas.[17] Two successive reinspections of Pocoata carried out by corregidor Pablo de Aoíz in 1751 and 1754 raised the number of tribute payers from 577 to 943. In accounting for this striking difference, the corregidor explained that the new record included the names of the *mayordomos* (stewards), *priostes* (chief stewards, both male and female), *alfereces* (main ritual sponsors and standard-bearers), sacristans, altar boys, bell ringers, mita workers, "and many others of many particular posts that the people have, who according to the Royal Ordinances should pay their taxes but due to the customs that they have enjoyed, all these people, who add up to many in the three towns of the repartimiento [Pocoata and the valleys of Carasi and Micani], are exempted from them."[18]

The colonial tax system, in brief, rested on a document, the Padrón de Indios, that conceived as both a thorough registry of the Indian population and a fiscal categorization of each Indian family was a fiction. No doubt, however, it was a useful one, because it provided the crown with a measure of the agrarian surpluses to be drawn from the natives and at the same time allowed the Andean communities to preserve their own cultural norms. The point here is that this regime of indirect government entered into crisis in the 1770s, as the mounting fiscal pressure made traditional modes of accommodation between Andean and European taxation conceptions increasingly unattainable. Bourbon initiatives, in other words, turned the gap between state norms and indigenous social practices into a matter of public policy. Just as the caciques were pushed to denounce time-honored economic arrangements, the corregidores found a rationale for the dismissal of ethnic chiefs who were supposedly unable to enforce official criteria of taxation. One case that achieved some notoriety in 1771 was the expeditious removal of the cacique of the Caracha group, Alejandro Yavira y Ayaviri, one of the few caciques propietarios in the area, "for his supposed lack of suitability in collecting tribute and . . . also in dispatching Indians to the Royal Mita of Potosí."[19] A few months later, as I describe in chapter 2, the Pocoata lords, the descendant of the Ayra Chinchi lineage, were also discharged on the basis of their failure to implement current tribute norms or, as corregidor Hereña put it, "of the complete disorder in the collection of the royal tributes."[20] Little wonder that on assuming Pocoata's chieftainship the cacique of Moscari, Florencio Lupa, condemned the survival of native tributary practices and pledged to eradicate what he defined as "these vicious and chaotic customs."[21] According to one report, during the first year of his tenure Lupa announced that the communities should henceforth comply with official tax rates; the following year he set rollos (scrolls) in the main Pocoata villages to make sure of their enforcement.[22] This disciplining discourse had, after all, justified the sweeping abrogation of Pocoata's political autonomy in the first place.

What was the response of northern Potosí ayllus to colonial initiatives to discipline community practices? Andean communities responded to the imposition of new normative frameworks (and the enforcement of old ones) in a selective, discriminating way. Peasant strategies combined outright defiance of some intended reforms with the manipulation of others for their own ends.[23] State intrusion in communal tributary customs clearly counted among the policies vigorously challenged. Shortly before deciding the removal of the Pocoata lords, corregidor Nicolas Ursainqui summoned the Indians to inquire about their opposition to their chief, Diego Ayra, and in doing so he was told that their discontent "was based on the fact that their rulers, observing what had been published, demanded the rightful tribute dues." Ursainqui published a list with the current rates, but the Pocoatas rejected his intervention openly: the corregidor related that one Indian "in an out-of-control way lost his respect [for Ursainqui] with a loud and inappropriate voice, saying that the document . . . published was not right or proper."[24] Then, Florencio Lupa's efforts to reorganize the assignation of tribute dues according to Spanish concepts met fierce resistance as well. The Pocoatas bemoaned that the cacique charged church servants, mita laborers, and single males, "being apparent that this [new] custom has been very harmful and imposed by the said governor, because all these persons did not bear this burden before."[25] Condensing his cultural understanding of the economic disruption caused by the violation of the Andean conceptions of marriage, rather than age, as a fiscal rite of passage (Lupa demanded tribute from adult males still living with their relatives), an Indian contended that Lupa "has imposed the contribution of two members of a household, Father and son."[26] The Macha Indians, too, lamented that Blas Bernal, a mestizo cacique appointed in 1775, did not abide by their customary unofficial tasas "with the specious pretext that there was a new royal order establishing it."[27] In 1777, one of the initial Macha leaders complained that Bernal had demanded of him the tribute "despite that I begged him to make a reduction since I had paid 100 pesos for the sponsorship of a feast [*alferazgo*]."[28] In 1780, as peasant unrest ran rampant, numerous northern Potosí communities would forcefully demand the official acknowledgment of the tax exemption for mita workers and ritual sponsors.

Whereas, as these examples make clear, northern Potosí peasants challenged disciplining policies and asserted their right to keep traditional social arrangements regardless of how much their moral economy might contradict the colonial legislation, they were also willing to manipulate the new normative schemes to their own advantage. Thus, in 1778, when members of the ethnic group of Macha asked, before the Charcas court, for the removal of their cacique one of the charges they wanted to emphasize was the misappropriation of the revenues generated by Indian collective work in communal lands. In accordance with the decrees issued in the early 1770s, the Machas made the point that those fields were set aside from the lands assigned to the households in order to provide for mita workers during their service in Potosí.[29]

While the Pocoatas forcefully protested the assaults on their customary tribute rules, they did not hesitate to fight a traditional practice by appealing to the new legislation that established the immediate removal of those ethnic lords who continued to designate colqperunas. In 1775 numerous Pocoatas claimed before the audiencia that Lupa had designated one colqueruna from each ayllu. Although it was argued that "this grievous tax remained unheard of before," colqperunas had been being designated in Pocoata since at least from the late seventeenth century (Sanchez-Albornoz 1978: 135). Yet the Pocoatas were fully aware of the potential consequences of the 1772 decree: the leaders of the protest submitted to the audiencia a complete official transcript of that ruling, which they had requested to corregidor Hereña in September of that year.[30] Linguistic and cultural barriers did not prevent the Andean peasants from mastering the rules of political struggle within the colonial administration. Not without reason, in 1772, as soon as the decree was issued, Lupa urged the audiencia of Charcas to withdraw it immediately from the province and to send instead a previous royal decree stipulating that the "corregidores have neither faculties nor jurisdiction over the persons of the caciques."[31] Lupa knew all too well that setting fixed standards by which the cacique's management of community resources could be judged would render their authority vulnerable. And, as he had feared, the same ideological predicament that had legitimized his assent, the suppression of those "vicious and chaotic customs," was now deployed for petitioning his dismissal.

"IMPLICIT PACTS": CONSENT AND VIOLENCE IN INDIAN SERVICES TO THE CHURCH

By the beginning of the 1770s northern Potosí underwent a series of struggles over the contributions of indigenous communities to their *curas doctrineros* (parish priests). The conflict achieved a particular significance because it came to embrace several ethnic groups and became intertwined with an open confrontation between the highest civil and ecclesiastical authorities in the region: the audiencia and the archbishopric of Charcas. Viewed from the perspective of social relations in the Andean world, this process called into question the magnitude of Indian services to the clergy and, above all, the nature of those contributions, whether they were mandatory or voluntary. From the standpoint of colonial government, the conflicts expressed a wider jurisdictional battle testing the balance of force between the state and the church. As is well known, the Bourbons pursued an aggressive campaign to affirm royal jurisdiction over the church. The most spectacular outcome of this policy was, of course, the expulsion of the Jesuits in 1767, but Bourbon regalism was also intended to place Indian parishes under closer supervision.[32]

The institution of the rural parishes (*doctrina de indios*) was a fundamental locus of colonial exploitation and rule. Together with corregidores, the priests (*curas*) represented the most immediate Spanish authority figures in the rural villages. Yet, unlike the civil magistrates, the priests and their assistants (*tenientes de cura*) did reside among the Indians, often spoke native languages, had some kind of presence in the everyday life of the Andean families, and, above all, presided over crucial moments of the annual ritual cycle of the community.[33] Furthermore, the labor force and agricultural surpluses demanded by the Andean clergy constituted altogether an extraordinary economic burden. The basic income of the curas doctrineros came from the royal synod, a fixed salary deducted from Indian tributes, and, from the parish, fees for masses, births, weddings, and funerals.[34] However, the greatest source of revenues of rural parishes in northern Potosí (and probably in most of the Andes) was the complex system of rotating religious posts and personal services linked to the annual cycle of Catholic feasts.

During the colonial period, the church promoted an extensive calendar of feast-day celebrations (fiestas) in the rural villages. A report from the late eighteenth century suggests that 351 feasts per year were celebrated in northern Potosí, and 899 tributaries were involved as church servants and ritual sponsors.[35] An elaborate communal system of rotating sacred posts emerged around the celebration of religious festivities. This fiesta-cargo system, as mentioned earlier, was composed of alfereces, mayordomos, priostes, and other minor offices. The parish priests received a fixed amount of money and agricultural goods for each fiesta. The communities also assigned a rotating number of Indians for the personal service of the priest and the upkeep of the church. In major feasts each alférez should pay as much as 117 pesos and a generous basket of farm produce known as *ricuchicu*.[36] The responsibility, however, did not weigh on the individual alone: in order to meet this heavy burden the ritual sponsors received a special allocation of lands and labor from their respective ayllus.[37] By the same token, festival sponsorships seemingly counted as a turn in the mining mita and, as we have just seen, carried by custom a relief from tribute.[38] Given the linkage of religious feasts with issues of land, mita, and tribute, it is little wonder that the caciques (puna authorities, in the case of valley parishes) intervened in the election of church posts.[39] The observance of these exactions, in sum, was subjected to many of the same forms of indirect rule as done for other colonial levies. Religious festivities, moreover, followed a strict sequence of events that reveals that mass fees, mandatory payments for priests, and "alms" offered by alfereces and mayordomos were carefully distinguished. Thus, it was reported that "these alms are larger than the parish dues, and [the Indians] know that it is not for the priest, that it is for the church, and they stress that by the fact that before the feast they only bring to the priest's house the twelve pesos that belong to him, and the next day, before entering the fiesta, they request a bowl . . . and they take the alms to the church and they offer it there during the mass's offertory."[40] It was this economic complex that constituted in the case of northern Potosí the core of the conflict between peasants, priests, and civil magistrates.

Disputes over Indian contributions to the church revolved around the publication of a new ecclesiastical schedule of fees, or *arancel*. Toward the end of 1770, the audiencia announced that the elaboration of a new arancel, intended to regulate and standardize the costs of church services in the archbishopric of Charcas, had been concluded. The tariff list set the exact cost of each parish service, established a fixed rate of 12 pesos for all religious feasts, and forbade ricuchicus as a customary tradition, allowing only proven spontaneous and voluntary donations. As done elsewhere in Spanish America, the publication of the arancel has been considered by researchers to be one of the pillars of the Bourbon policy of strengthening state control over the activities of the priesthood.[41] The new legislation was designed to limit the church's monetary and labor exaction from the ethnic economies and, indirectly, to enhance state fiscal demands. On the other hand, this measure expressed a broader cultural change of sensitivity toward the way Catholic rituals were being performed. Influenced by the ideas of the Enlightenment, state officials manifested a growing distrust of popular religion, especially of expressions of "baroque piety" such as the feasts, dances, processions, and dramatic plays that the church had traditionally tolerated and indeed promoted both in urban and rural settings (Gruzinski 1993: 268–69; Estenssoro 1995: 43, 45).

As in New Spain, royal functionaries in the Andes also expected the ecclesiastical fee schedule to "eliminate the confusion of customs" by imposing "fixed rules (*reglas fijas*) and obedience to the law without interpretation" (Taylor 1996: 13). The tariff list would put an end, as audiencia ministers claimed, "to the abuses that have occurred in some parishes."[42] Yet, as in the case of Mexico, the outcome was entirely different. Very soon, royal authorities and northern Potosí peasants alike would find out that the rural priests stubbornly repudiated the new normative framework and punished those ritual sponsors who refused to deliver the customary cash payments. The conflicts that emerged in the parish of Carasi, a multiethnic valley inhabited by Laymis, Puracas, Pocoatas, and Machas, are a case in point. During the months previous to the issuance of the arancel, the Indians had repeatedly complained about the large contributions in cash, kind, and labor required by their priest, Dionisio Larrazabal, and had exhibited before the audiencia of Charcas a detailed list of the annual calendar of religious celebrations. In February 1771, on the occasion of the first feast day after the publication of the arancel (the feast of Our Lady's Purification), when Carasi parish's ritual sponsors refused to pay the customary fees Larrazabal's assistant, after threatening to confiscate their fields, forced them to submit the usual 117 pesos. When the Indians exhibited a copy of the new official tariff list, the priest ordered the cacique to punish them "without listening to any of the reasons [the Indians] gave on the bases of the mentioned arancel." In fact, the priest became increasingly annoyed, and irritated the parish he claimed that [the Indians] would always be indebted to him if [they] did not pay the mentioned 117 pesos."[43]

While the refusal to abide by the fee schedule clearly reflects the economic dimension of the struggles, an additional reprisal by the priests underscores another key element in the confrontation. According to both the priests and the peasants, because the ritual sponsors maintained their refusal to submit more than 12 pesos for the feast, Larrazabal's assistant had decided to call off the celebration. Had this conflict been solely about economic levies, that measure should have been perceived as a relief. But the curas and communities both knew that the denial to conduct the feast as usual amounted to a severe punishment. After all, the Indians traveled to La Plata not only to complain that they had been asked to pay the usual amounts but also that the celebration had been canceled because of their refusal to pay. The reason appears to lie in the nature of these gatherings. We know that although these collective celebrations followed the Catholic liturgical calendar and the priests played a central role in them, the feasts were also occasions for Andean cults of ancestors, and to worship local deities and spirits of protective hills.[44] What is more, the cancellation of the feast conveyed a strong element of symbolic violence because it deprived ritual sponsors from providing a vital service to the community. Carasi parish's alfereces remarked that, as revenge for their alleged disobedience, the priest "proceeded to celebrate the feast by himself without allowing any of us as alfereces to take out the standard." As in Andean religious feasts today, bearing the standard during the procession seems to have been a fundamental element in the ritual celebrations.[45] Thus, also in this case, Andean peasants reacted to state intervention in local affairs in a rather selective way, for they rejected the economic costs involved in the fiestas but by no means the fiestas themselves, which on the contrary they considered their own right to perform and the duty of the parish priests to observe. Hence, the opposition to lessen customary abusive fees contained as much violence as the refusal to follow the custom of celebrating the feasts altogether.[46]

The new normative framework may have sought to impose "fixed rules," but the ecclesiastical functionaries read the legislation in their own particular way. By mid-1771, the Chayanta corregidor reported that after the publication of the fee schedule, all the priests of the province "understood that the order to observe the customs regarding the offerings and donations that parishes give during feasts means to compel the parishes to give them. So they forced them to do so."[47] An attorney of the archbishopric claimed that the Andean communities' contributions during the religious celebrations were "voluntary" as long as the Indians did not refuse to give them; that is, the contributions were voluntary but, in the clergy's own words, "not too voluntary." Because this source of income was indispensable, it could not be admitted that "this contribution be *so voluntary* that the amount of the donations be left to the parishioners' own free will, who do not require too much to refuse to pay them at all, in prejudice of their spiritual well being."[48]

Could a contribution be conceived simultaneously as voluntary and compulsory? For the clergymen, feast-day fees were customary duties or "good habits," so that even if the Indians might not at that moment comply with the church dues out of their free will, they were bound to observe the burdens because at some point in the past they had voluntarily accepted them. It was the supposed free will of the dead, not the actual one of the living, that counted. Insofar as giving presents during feast days was a time-honored custom, "in no way can it be considered voluntary, or [construed] as harmful, corrupting, or abusive." The new arancel, in short, did not *permit* the observance of "customs"; it *commanded* it.[49] The historical origins of the custom endowed ricuchicus and contributions with the force of a contract rather than with the volatility of a voluntary contribution.

Hence, in May 1771 Archbishop Pedro Miguel de Argadoña established that the custom of donations and contributions for feasts "has the force of the law and parishioners are obliged to [engage in these customs] even if they are Indians." On the other hand, Argadoña argued that because according to his informants the region was "in revolt due to well-known influences," a harsh measure that would serve as a warning for everybody and "soothe the restlessness of the Indians" was in order. So he decreed that the Indians from Carasi "should give the traditional donations directly to us, which in obeying and following the custom that we are ordering them to comply with, are due for the Feast of Our Lady's Purification in the Carasi parish." In addition, the archbishop decided that "each one of them will receive twelve lashes in front of the door of the notary's offices so that their influence and the unrest they have provoked to date are completely rooted out."[50]

Opposing visions on the nature of church fees were matched by broader ideological discrepancies over the nature of colonial government. The Catholic Church magistrates not only rejected advances over their jurisdiction, but also condemned the intervention of higher judicial institutions in local social conflicts. In the same way that corregidores and caciques faced Indian collective litigation, the clergy conceived this model of rule as undermining the power of rural authorities. In this sense, the archbishop's decision to punish the agitators was more than a reaction against Bourbon regalism: it expressed opposition to a general model of colonial rule. If protesters were not severely punished, the Carasi priest contended before the audiencia, "the Indians will harass their parish priests, promote turmoil in the tribunals, and acquire the concept that priests are easily challenged and that they [the Indians] are in a favorable position of power. Then, the priests' authority will falter."[51]

Conflicting interpretations of the new schedule of fees and services gave rise during the following months to sharp disputes between secular and ecclesiastical colonial officials. In April 1771, commenting on the Carasi cura's behavior during Our Lady's Purification feast, the audiencia sent a letter to the archbishopric condemning the blatant rejection of the new legislation. It was stressed that the fees for masses had been clearly defined and that ricuchicus had been forbidden, so that "the spirit of custom" could not be used to make them compulsory. The key point was that the new legislation *permitted* but did not *require* the feast sponsors to give the customary donations and services. These alms and charities should thereafter be entirely voluntary, "and in no way can be kept the ones that [the Indians] were obliged to give under this name, since to compel the Indians to fulfill the said donations and charities is an utmost form of abuse and corruption." Consequently, the archbishop was commanded to issue an edict to be published along with the new arancel stressing that donations were voluntary and that to demand them in any form was strictly forbidden.[52]

In response to the punishment the archbishop had inflicted on the Carasi parishioners, the audiencia attorney contended that it represented "a notorious irregularity, violence, transgression, and lack of respect for the regular procedure and steps that the law establishes." More important still, Argadoña's decree contradicted the very core of the new legislation, for if the Indians were to be forced to continue their contributions in cash and kind under the excuse that they were customary, "this would be as if the said legislation had not actually reformed anything." Moreover, the daily expenditures of the churches did not justify the exorbitant contributions required for feasts. Churches, the official poignantly reminded, should be ornamented in accordance with the economic possibilities of their parishioners "without spending for fantastic splendors that God does not wish nor receive, and which are harmful to third parties."[53] Finally, in November 1771, the court decided formally to declare that the archbishop's sentence on the Carasi Indians had been illegal because it surpassed his jurisdiction by neglecting to consult with the audiencia before imposing a physical punishment.[54] Thus, the ideal of removing interpretation from the performance of colonial government translated into public, high-profile struggles over the meaning of the norms. In the political context nurtured by Bourbon reformism, what had been meant to be an exemplary punishment for the Indians became an exemplary censure of the highest ecclesiastical authority in the land.

Whether or not the civil court was right in its interpretation of jurisdictional rights, the priests knew better how an open dissension within the ranks of the colonial administration could affect authority in the Andean world. By mid-1771, it was not only the ethnic groups of the Carasi parish who protested against their priests: Aymayas and Jukumanis (Aymaya parish), Chayantacas, and Machas from the puna parish also traveled to La Plata to report the priesthood's systematic refusal to follow the arancel.

Thus, for instance, Jukumani peasants, who in early 1771 had secured from the audiencia a copy of the new tariff list, returned to La Plata to complain that when they showed the document to their priest, Dionisio Cortés, he had imprisoned and whipped the leaders of the protest, established additional levies, and "asked the individuals in charge of the collection of tithes, veintenas, and alcabalas to impose as much harm as they can on us."[55] In response, a group of twenty Jukumanis and Aymayas traveled again to La Plata in June 1771 to request the enforcement of the new fees and to warn that they would not return to their village until Cortés was deposed. Although Cortés, a particularly powerful priest in the province, would not be dismissed, much more about his economic and sacerdotal activities would be heard in the months and years to come, as I soon will show.

Indians from Chayantaca, who had asked in the archbishopric for a copy of the new list of fees, found on returning to their villages that their priest, Francisco Paredes, refused to publish the document. He limited its exposure to reading part of it during one Sunday only, continuing with "the same excesses over feasts and other dues, under the excuse of it being an ancient custom." So, as in the case of the Aymaya and Jukumani, within a few weeks several Indians returned to La Plata to denounce their priest's behavior, this time before the audiencia. With the purpose of avoiding further delays, the audiencia attorney sent a letter to Francisco Paredes warning him to observe the arancel. Yet, during the celebration of the feast of Santa Rosa in late August 1771, as an alférez asked the Chayanta priest to moderate his demands according to the new legislation, Paredes refused to lower the fees but "not before giving the alférez some strong blows screaming that the said list was useless."[56] The Indians came back once again to the city to report the story.

Although northern Potosí peasants did not speak Spanish, centuries of colonial rule had taught them ways to distinguish accurate from misleading readings of legal documents. Andean communities refused to acknowledge what the priests wanted them to acknowledge: that the new legislation had not introduced any changes in what was customary, and that customs "had the force of law," as the archbishop put it. For example, a priest of Chayanta village attested that "everything comes to disobedience, the Indians pretend that they do not understand the edicts, and they say that we read out loud, and have them believe, things that are not written in the documents."[57] Yet, there seems to have been no misunderstanding. Soon after this incident, eight Indians from the Chayanta priest's own parish showed the audiencia a complete list of the dues for feasts demanded by the priest. They insisted that the archbishop should take all necessary measures to ensure that the new fee schedule be published in Chayanta village's central square and "in the most public places" in order to guarantee its compliance and "remove the corruption during feasts, which causes us so much harm."[58]

In March 1772, two principal Indians from the Majapicha ayllu of Macha (the ayllu to which future rebel leader Tomás Katari belonged) stated the following:

> We were hoping to have some relief from the said publication of the arancel, [but] the current assistant, Don Lorenzo Morales, has been even more rigorous with us not only in the abuse of forcing us to pay fees but also in the way that he mistreats us, punishing [us] for the slightest offense through lashes and beatings . . . In this way, nowadays we are even more grieved by the said assistant than we were before, *because he has posted at the doors of the church an Arancel that is very different from the true one that was recently approved*, since no poor person can be buried free, and there is not any feast that costs less than one hundred pesos . . . and even for just tasting the salt of the food that the alfereces are required to donate to the priests, we have to pay 4 pesos to the cook, even though she has no other job than the said one.[59]

In view of the growing Indian unrest, the parish priests of northern Potosí collectively requested that the archbishop abolish the arancel. In response, Argadoña decided to suspend the issuance of copies of the tariff list despite the fact that it had already been published throughout the province. Thus, when at the beginning of October 1771 several Indians from the puna parish of Macha requested a copy of the document on behalf of their community, their petition was denied.[60] By January 1772, a group of Machas was still camped out in La Plata waiting for the arancel. The intransigence of the ecclesiastical authorities reflected their growing wariness about the political repercussions of divulging the new schedule. Why should the publication of a regulation, already sanctioned by both the audiencia and the archbishop, be suspended? The Macha priest argued that the circulation of the new schedule would cause "irreparable damage" because the notion that the contributions toward the church were unjust would take root and, consequently, would awake the Indians' collective resistance. "For everybody knows," he recalled, "their tendency to disturb the peace and to get rid of any obligation or contribution no matter how just may it be. *That is even more so when they have learned that it is indeed unjust, as we know very well from experience.*"[61]

The reason why the diffusion of the new legislation fostered widespread perceptions of the injustice of church dues was that it made explicit what had previously remained implicit: it forced the church to expose (and publicly discuss) the coercive basis underlying the colonial pact of government. Debates about contributions in cash, kind, and labor to the priesthood are a clear example of what sociologist Pierre Bourdieu (1977) has defined as "euphemization" of social relations, a process through which the compulsory transference of resources between social groups appears as a voluntary and acquiescent act of generosity. In societies in which neither sheer violence nor market relations mediate the transference of surpluses, a "normative filter" transforms modes of economic exploitation into willing assistance.[62] In the case of Andean services to the church, the social chemistry performed by this ideological process is condensed in the meaning of such concepts as "charity," "donations," or "contributions." As Andean communities expressed their opposition to continue delivering the customary set of goods and services (and sustained their opposition with concrete acts of resistance), donations and charities began to appear as mere forms of coercion. By transmuting the public representation of social relations from "voluntary" into "not too voluntary" (in the Carasi priest's words), what was before recognized as just and acceptable now became (in the Macha priest's words) "learned" as "unjust" and unacceptable.

The abolition of the new arancel was essential for the rural priests because the legislation, one of the curas contended, "went against an acquired right of the priests and against the *implicit pact* celebrated between the priests and the parishioners by which the former have the obligation to administer the Holy Sacraments and spiritual guidance to the latter, and the latter have the obligation to provide for the necessary material sustenance of the former."[63] At the hands of the Indian communities, the new legislation turned into a political weapon to reconsider that "implicit pact."

Crown officials, under the influence of current rationalizing ideas, greatly contributed to that outcome. In January 1772, facing pressure from both audiencia ministers and Andean peasants, Archbishop Argadoña was eventually forced to reassume the issuance of copies of the new schedule of fees to the Indians. Certainly, he did so under protest: in the same decree ordering the observance of the new arancel, the archbishop stressed that all the rural priests had requested its annulment and that the synod of Charcas had determined that the custom of contributions for feasts should be maintained.[64] Yet, the mere fact that church magistrates were forced to recant indicates the ongoing strengthening of Bourbon regalism. The Protector of Indians and the audiencia attorney requested that all the parish priests be informed that if they had any complaint against the arancel they should appeal to the audiencia, *"which is the only competent judge in this matter."* Furthermore, all the corregidores of Upper Peru were instructed to monitor the priests' behavior.[65]

If the aftermath of the conflict mirrored larger imperial trends toward restricting ecclesiastical immunity and enhancing state control over social affairs in general, it reflected also the ability of the northern Potosí Indian communities to mount an open challenge to local authorities. As rural priests had feared, Andean peasants knew how to take advantage of internal dissension within the colonial government and to legitimize their own aims by appealing to legal norms. In other words, they were able to use new regulations to fight abusive aspects of customary colonial levies without endangering in the process the valuable, consensual aspects of the customs. Although we do not know the degree of their success in curbing ecclesiastical levies, there may be few doubts about their success in defying the place in social life of one of the major rural power groups.

The fate of Dionisio Cortés, priest of the Aymaya parish, is perhaps the most prominent example of this process. Cortés seemed to enjoy a unique standing in village society judging by the range of his economic activities and command over his Indian parishioners. In June 1771, as noted earlier, a large group of Aymayas and Jukumanis had complained that their priest had confiscated their copy of the tariff list, publicly punished them, and pitted tithe and veintena collectors against them. Yet, reflecting his influence, Cortés managed to draw, unlike most of his colleagues, a formal exoneration from the archbishopric after two summary inquiries into these charges. In April 1772, a priest preached to the Indians in the village of Aymaya "that next time they said these false slanders, removed from any traces of truth, they would receive the rightful punishment."[66] The Indians, however, were not easily deterred. Led by Bartolomé and Francisco Bello, several Jukumanis traveled for at least a third time to La Plata to protest that Cortés continued to refuse to abide by the tariff list.[67] There, after a face-to-face meeting between the Indians and the priest in the house of the archbishopric's vicar general, Cortés returned to them their copy of the arancel. The Jukumanis, however, were warned that "they ought to abandon the reckless demands and calumnies that, due to fears, inducements, and other circumstances that they had expressed, they had been thus far promoting."[68] A perhaps unspoken aspect of the agreement between the priest and the Indians emerged when these trial records are matched with the caciques' tribute receipts of 1773: they register, along with Pedro Gallego as Aymaya cacique, Domingo Bello as Jukumani chief.[69]

Whatever the weight of intimidation, judicial manipulation, and compromise in these arrangements, they eventually fell apart once more. Between 1776 and 1778, Cortés became the target of a still broader protest that brought into focus not only his disregard for the arancel but also his economic, pastoral, and punitive activities. Cortés, the peasants repeatedly lamented, forcefully married the Indians and publicly punished those who refused to do it.[70] While this policy might have been motivated by material gain (the collection of marriage fees), it could have also aimed at curbing the extended Andean kin practice of *sirvinacuy* (trial marriage).[71] Thus, the Indians attested that forced marriages resulted in a situation where "women have a bad life, and their husbands run away from them."[72] The close surveillance of native customs such as trial marriages, adultery, or perhaps polygamy, was confirmed by an Indian mayor, Blas Colque, who reported that Cortés had had him arrested for two months with *grillos* (scrolls that Colque later handed over to the audiencia) because he was supposedly cohabiting and procreating with a woman other than his wife, whom the priest dubbed a "consenting, submissive accomplice" due to her refusal to condemn her husband.[73] A Spanish resident also observed that Cortés "administers paternal and moderate whippings to those who refused to quit their illicit friendships."[74] Cortés, on the other hand, ran a store in the Aymaya village where the Indians were obliged to purchase goods; lent money to the Indians; kept about forty mules to conduct commerce; and made extensive use of peasant labor without retribution. Several Jukumanis related that he kept two separate private jails (one for men and one for women) located inside the parish house. Those who failed to cancel debts or who dared to protest against the cacique could be arrested, beaten up, publicly humiliated, confiscated, or banished from town. Equally telling of his grasp on village affairs, the priest decided to institute two new fiestas, Dolores and Animas, with a cost of 70 pesos each, even after the conflicts over the new tariff list. The peasants argued, plausibly, that he could carry out all these illegal activities because of his longstanding association with corregidor Nicolás Ursainqui.[75]

During these years, Aymayas and Jukumanis (among them Domingo Bello, who by then identified himself as a "former cacique") came back to the audiencia several times, once at least in a group of more than fifteen Indian commoners.[76] Some of the mechanisms of mobilization for this protest were described by Joseph Roque, the Jukumani cacique who had replaced Domingo Bello. He recalled that "in the boundary marker [*mojón*] of Orcapata, at a time when a lot of people were gathered near an ancestral tomb [*chullpa*], Domingo Bello told me that we should tell everybody to go to the city of La Plata against the Sr. Cura [Domingo Cortés] so that the services and feasts of two Saints added [by the cura] and other [abuses] that the said Domingo Bello mentioned were suppressed."[77] Then the leaders traveled over the indigenous hamlets recruiting people for the initiative. Later, there was another meeting of this kind in the mojones called Quinsa Cruz.[78] We know that mojones and chullpas were places of great symbolic meaning for the Andean ayllus, places where notions of identity, memory, and ethnic authority were reaffirmed and negotiated.[79]

The protest would not immediately bear fruit. The priest counted the firm support of corregidor Nicolás Ursainqui and the Spanish residents of Aymaya. In March 1778, Domingo Bello, his father Francisco Xavier Bello, and other Indians were formally sentenced to twenty days in prison for calumnies. Cortés also was able to carve into village factionalism by mobilizing the Aymaya and Jukumani caciques Joseph Roque and Pedro Gallego, Indian mayors, and some Indians commoners. It was reported, for instance, that after complaining before the audiencia that the priest had married his daughter by force "as he is accustom to do," an Indian "was dragged along the streets in the most shameful manner, making him shout at every street corner and square the following words: *'I, Matheo Choque, a dumb and litigious Indian who went to complain about the priest, give myself these lashes in order to serve as an example for those who would go against the priest and the corregidor. They will suffer the same fate.'*"[80]

Although intimidation may have served Cortés well in these instances, when the political context changed, so did his fate. In 1781, the Aymaya priest would be among the most prominent victims of collective violence. In the context of generalized attacks on rural elites, including parish priests, during the celebration of the first Sunday of Lent a large number of Aymayas and Jukumanis, among them several members of the Bello family, would storm into the house of Cortés in the village of Aymaya and beat him to death. "Cura ladrón, que por tu causa estamos desnudos" ("Thief priest, we are naked because of you"), some Indians were said to have shouted. We are also told that following Dámaso Katari's instructions one of the Bellos had contended that "killing priests was not a sin."[81] True or not, the long experience of the struggles of the Aymayas and Jukumanis with their priest must have provided them with motives of their own to believe it.

UNPUNISHED CRIMES: BATTLES FOR SELF-RULE
AND THE LOGIC OF THE TRIBUTARY STATE

Social dissension during the years leading up to the general insurrection of northern Potosí was clearly centered in Pocoata. Some of the most ominous aspects of Bourbon enlightened policies, the assault on traditional Andean social arrangements, hit the Pocoatas in a particularly harsh way. With the appointment of a foreign cacique, the Moscari lord Florencio Lupa, the Pocoatas were suddenly faced with a formidable challenge to their ethnic autonomy. At stake was the command over a critical institution in the distribution of economic levies and productive resources among peasant households, as well as a basic political right of colonial domination: as members of the República de Indios and as loyal subjects of the Spanish monarchy, Andean communities were entitled by law to a measure of self-determination. And yet, if current disciplining policies undermined a central piece of the indigenous social fabric, another aspect of Bourbon absolutism, the Spanish crown's hunger for colonial revenues, would have the opposite effect. As in the case of ecclesiastical levies, northern Potosí peasants would mount a vigorous defense of their social values by exploiting the apparent tensions between imperial policies and local colonial government.

From the beginning of 1775, the Pocoata ayllus set in motion a long process of mobilization to remove the foreign cacique from power. Between August 1775 and February 1776, numerous members of the Pocoata communities undertook several collective journeys to La Plata, flooding the Charcas court with dozens of written petitions asking for the cacique's removal. Grievances against Florencio Lupa covered a wide range of issues. First and foremost, the Indians targeted the very foundations of the political project behind his ascent: the Pocoatas made exceedingly clear that the fact that Lupa did not belong to the ethnic group deprived him of any legitimate claim to rule. In addition to his ethnic origin, Lupa's policies also raised discontent. Thus, the Indians protested the appointment of mestizo authorities at all levels of the native system of rule, the favoring of friendly ayllus in the internal disputes over land boundaries, the violation of customary ethnic norms in the distribution and collection of the tribute burden, and the imposition of new labor services like the collective work in fields that Lupa had set aside for his own benefit. Peasant legal politics were so tenacious that even in the city Lupa sought to intimidate the protesters. Some Pocoatas reported that as they met the cacique in a street of La Plata, "he very arrogantly told us that also in this city there were rollos, prisons, and other means of punishment and that he would dispatch us to our town chained to a mule."[82]

The first direct confrontation of the Pocoatas with corregidor Nicolás Ursainqui occurred at the end of August 1775, during the annual meeting in the town of Pocoata for the celebration of the feast of San Bartolomé and the departure of the Chayanta mita team to Potosí. In the course of this important event, they handed Ursainqui a decree they had won in La Plata commanding the dismissal of the mestizo alcaldes and hilacatas appointed by Florencio Lupa. As the

Pocoatas addressed the corregidor, "the community had great expectations and was committed to obtain its enforcement, in whose pursuit the Indians had gathered to expose their grievances." These expectations were not fulfilled, however. Ursainqui, according to the Pocoatas, "proceeded to conceal and disobey the mentioned superior decree due to his well-known collusion with the cacique."[83] In retaliation for the judicial appeal, some of the Indians who led the initiative were publicly whipped and put in the rollo.

The public punishment of the protesters, far from dissuading them, triggered a new wave of collective journeys to the audiencia. Numerous Indians from both moieties, Urinsaya and Anansaya, converged in La Plata to demand the removal of Lupa, whom they portrayed as "an arrogant man who disturbs the public peace and who through maneuvers has made ineffectual the many decrees issued against him as a result of continuous complaints given rise by his disorderly and merciless conduct."[84] The Pocoatas expressed the possible political consequences of the imposition of mestizo alcaldes and hilacatas in no uncertain terms. It was said, for instance, "these mestizo and mulatto men are of a bastard nature opposed to the poor Indians. They continually [abuse] the community with their ignominious and startling insults, such that our patience is exhausted, and [our outrage] grows bigger as the Indians recognize that all these mistreatments are encouraged by Lupa."[85] The Indians offered accounts of the punishment received by the mitayos who refused to submit their tribute, the Indians who rejected their appointment as colquerunas, and those who explicitly contested Lupa's policies or had aspirations to the chieftainships. As evidence of these policies, the Pocoatas even submitted to the audiencia one of the grillos used by the cacique to punish the Indians.[86] (Just six months later it was the Aymaya mayor Blas Colque who brought to the court the grillos used by his priest, Dionisio Cortés, to discipline his parishioners.)

In discouraging popular resistance, Lupa orchestrated other, subtler means of repression. Several Pocoatas narrated that in reprisal for their protests, he had pressed the cacique of the Laymi and Puraca groups, Marcos Soto, to invade some lands that the Pocoatas had near those communities. A Laymi Indian who had recently been appointed as cacique of Puraca, Soto had then brought his cows, donkeys, mules, and other cattle to the Pocoatas's fields. These animals, besides ruining twenty loads of potatoes and two pots of maize, knocked down a stone and wood fence built by the Pocoatas. Before Lupa's impassivity, Soto brutally whipped one Pocoata Indian for trying to protect his harvest. Naturally enough, the episode appeared as particularly significant because it represented the ultimate violation of the expected behavior of an ethnic lord: the collusion with a foreign cacique to invade the lands of his own people.[87] Furthermore, although in Moscari Lupa had a longstanding feud with the clergy, his relationship with the Pocoata priests was very different. Here, for instance, the cacique agreed to mobilize communal labor to repair the church. In preventing their collective work from being capitalized in this way, the Pocoatas needed to ask the audiencia to disregard that agreement, "for in case the repair of the Holy Church is required and necessary, we the Indians are ready to do it with our work and short means."[88] An Indian from the Chanca ayllu observed that "it is the truth that the governor compels us to go to mass, to confess, and to attend doctrine. But it is also true that there are other Indians who can be Governors without demanding these new taxes and allowing Indians to keep their old customs to which they are so attached . . . It is apparent, too, that all the Indians are dissatisfied with this governor's behavior because they no longer have any break during the services to the Church since he charges them the tribute."[89] "The countless complains that against [Lupa] have been made," one of the petitions at the time summed up, "must have made [the tribunal] realize the pernicious behavior with which he manages; for it is apparent that since his assumption we do not have peace and quiet anymore, nor do we believe we will until his expulsion be secured."[90]

In April 1776, when a judge appointed by the Charcas court established himself in northern Potosí to investigate the charges against Lupa, the setting of political battles moved from La Plata to the Andean villages. Beginning in the village of Pocoata on May 4, one day after the massive gathering of the indigenous communities for the celebration of the feast of La Cruz, the most important meeting before the peasants were to migrate to the valleys for the grain harvest, Indians from different ayllus denounced Lupa's practices and demanded his removal.[91] By this time few doubts could remain about the massiveness of the protest and, consequently, the failure of the rationale behind Lupa's appointment: his ability to discipline social relations. Florencio Lupa's lawyer himself would finally concede that the cacique had suffered since his assumption of "the stubborn opposition of his inhabitants" and had had to tolerate that the Indians "had ignominiously denied him due obedience . . . to return to their old licentiousness." He continued by stating that Indian unrest "gets worse by the day as the influence of the main dissidents increasingly stirs up the already poorly predisposed spirits of the people," and, instigated by their leaders, the Indians had already made in the Andean villages a particularly ominous display of "notorious disobedience": "they removed the Rollo from the Pocoata town square."[92] The prolonged presence in the province of a source of authority independent from the corregidor and the cacique would garner even further mass support for the protest movement. As the audiencia's envoy traveled through northern Potosí puna and valley villages, he received an extraordinary number of collective and individual complaints. The content of the claims voiced before the judge give witness to the process of political radicalization underway. But what goes largely unsaid in the historical record (and yet makes it intelligible) is the social context, the face-to-face relations, the collective journeys following the judge's displacements through northern Potosí villages, the tacit shift in the balance of forces that enabled such displays of contention. Lupa himself alerted the judge to the dangers involved in not conducting his inquiry expeditiously, "[provoking] with this omission a more widespread state of unrest among the protesters, because this gave them time to go out through all the hamlets announcing with great excitement to the Indians that Your Majesty [Escudero] came to establish a reduction of tributes and other false claims."[93]

The "reduction of tributes" alluded to in the testimony actually refers to the Pocoatas's resistance to the normalization of ethnic fiscal practices (expressed in numerous complaints against the demand of tribute to mitayos, ritual sponsors, and adult males belonging to same household), and ultimately to the Pocoatas's refusal to continue delivering their taxes to the foreign cacique. The decision to no longer deliver the next tribute quota to Lupa and his collectors was formally announced first to the judge and then to the justicia mayor Nicolás Ursainqui in Carasi, a valley where the Pocoatas also possessed agricultural lands. On June 26 — two days after the celebration of the feast of San Juan — several Indians from the ayllus Hilata, Sulcavi, and Capac of Urinsaya moiety, and from Collana, Pisaca, Chacaya, and Carigua of Anansaya moiety, argued that they had brought to the audiencia numerous charges against Lupa for "his countless wrongdoings and serious crimes." As the Indians unanimously considered him a "tormentor and a harmful person," the appointment of any Indian from Pocoata in his place was absolutely pressing. Ursainqui was bluntly warned about "not allowing us to get lost by disregarding the Laws of Justice . . . We do not want by any means to deliver or to cancel those Royal Tributes to the said Lupa."[94]

Yet despite the open state of political unrest (during the judge's formal inquiry in early July alone, forty-six Pocoatas offered their testimony, which likely was the largest investigation done in the province to date), no concrete steps to remove the cacique were being taken. The success of challenges to local ruling groups depended not only on the intensity of moral outrage and the scope of collective mobilization but also on the peasants' ability to draw active support within the ranks of the Spanish administration. Eventually, Pocoatas would discover that strife among colonial rulers over peasant surpluses provided precisely the kind of issue that enabled them to find such common ground.

Thus, in late August 1776, the time of year when the Andean communities delivered the tribute quota to the corregidor, the Pocoata Indians resorted to an unprecedented strategy: they traveled to Potosí to prove the misappropriation of tribute carried out by the cacique and the corregidor by submitting the money directly to the royal treasury officers. The series of events leading to this decision have left few traces in the historical record, but they doubtlessly constituted a turning point in the way colonial domination in northern Potosí was to be exercised and perceived in the years to come. We know from later references that the Pocoatas had traveled to the audiencia by mid-August to achieve the formal appointment of the leaders of the movement (Pedro Caypa from the Urinsaya moiety and Francisco Ancona from the Anansaya moiety) as tribute collectors. Both leaders then took into their hands the tax collection and the election of the mita contingent. They also threatened Lupa in case he ventured into Pocoata territories to collect money. In fact, the cacique of Moscari not only avoided traveling to the Pocoatas's hamlets but failed to attend the traditional annual meeting celebrated in the towns of Pocoata and Macha in late August and early September, in which northern Potosí indigenous communities dispatched the mita team and submitted the tribute. Lupa later related that "the insolent spirit of these people grew so big that they seriously arranged to kill me in case I tried to make this collection, and also to kill don Nicolás Ursainqui if he took repressive measures."[95]

Whether or not the Indians really intended to murder Lupa and Ursainqui, the corregidor did prepare himself for an armed confrontation. He gathered a group of soldiers to escort him during the feast of San Bartolomé when the mita team was being dispatched in the town of Pocoata. On the same date the previous year, some Indians had been publicly punished for protesting against the foreign cacique. This time, however, was different. It was reported that if Ursainqui had not come to the place "with armed people, and had not displayed an extraordinary prudence in tolerating vituperations, insults, and provocations with which he was addressed, the Indians without a doubt would have executed what had been prepared."[96] Although Ursainqui and subsequent authorities would repeatedly depict these occurrences as a rebellion or uprising, no actual acts of violence seem to have taken place. However, the outcome of the confrontation was no less unsettling for local colonial authority. In describing what had happened, Lupa offered the following story: "When [the corregidor] attempted to appease this riot through sagacious ways, he failed because the conflict escalated to such a degree that, disregarding the royal jurisdiction with great insolence and scandal, the leaders of the riot walked to the Villa of Potosí joined by more than five hundred Indians. They took with them the tributes that they had collected without any authority to do so. Then, they delivered only part of the money in the Royal Treasury with a [population] census devised at their will."[97]

In effect, about five hundred Pocoatas (along with Panacachi Indians, who had also been under Lupa's authority since 1771) traveled to the mining town to deliver their tributes. While various northern Potosí communities had in the past exhibited population records before high courts, they had never dared to override provincial magistrates' jurisdiction by delivering the money directly to the royal treasury. And the results were remarkable. As mentioned earlier, over the previous months Lupa had claimed that the Pocoatas's leaders had gained support from the Indians by "going out through all the hamlets announcing with great excitement to the Indians that [the audiencia's commissioner] came to establish a reduction of tributes."[98] However, the census lists and the corresponding money surrendered by the Pocoatas largely surpassed their current fiscal dues. On reviewing the documents submitted by the Indians in early September 1776, Potosí treasury officials established that the tribute quota for the whole ethnic group amounted to 9,910 pesos per year. The last official demographic count of Pocoata, which had been carried out by corregidor Ursainqui and Lupa themselves in 1773, set up an overall amount of 6,748 pesos. Therefore, the Indians had offered the royal treasury a tribute increase of 3,162 pesos — that is, a 46.9 percent raise with respect to the census elaborated just three years earlier.

The increase must have struck a sensitive chord in the minds of treasury officials. During the previous years an independent judge had produced a raise of similar magnitude for the communities of Chayanta, Aymaya, and Panacachi. As opposition from rural authorities had precluded him from continuing his task, the population count was completed by corregidor Nicolás Ursainqui between 1773 and 1775. In contrast to the 68.65 increment achieved by Pereira de Castro, Ursainqui produced an increase of barely 10 percent.[99] For the crown representatives, this did nothing but reinforce entrenched beliefs in the corregidores' engagement in blatant fiscal embezzlement. With their travel to Potosí, the Pocoatas could tie the defense of their social values to the economic interests of the Spanish crown. In effect, while regional Spanish officials had until then adopted a rather cautious stance toward the Indian protest, an immediate and unmistakable change of attitude took place after the new peasant initiative. In late August, foreseeing the Pocoatas's travel to the mining center, Ursainqui had sent to the royal treasurers of Potosí an order of capture for the leaders Caypa and Ancona. Three weeks afterward, far from arresting the Pocoatas, the Potosí officials formally appointed Pedro Caypa and Francisco Ancona as tribute collectors. The corregidor's petition to imprison the Pocoata leaders was dismissed on the basis that it "is considered to have been made just to hide Lupa's crime, the plundering of royal money." Furthermore, the royal treasurers commanded Ursainqui to support the new collectors, to confiscate Lupa's assets, and to send him to Potosí under custody. Treasury magistrates already identified Lupa as the "deposed cacique." The Indians were authorized to return to Potosí in November to complete the tribute payments, because it was feared that the corregidor could use this money to cancel debts from his own forced sales of goods. If the Indians were to accomplish that, instead of deserving imprisonment "they would make themselves worthy not only of having their previous mistakes overlooked, but as faithful subjects, they should be awarded a prize to complement such distinguished services."[100]

The Pocoata Indians would accomplish the promised increase. At the end of 1776 they returned to Potosí to complete the tribute payments. On December 6 the treasury officials certified that, added to the money delivered earlier, Francisco Ancona and Pedro Caypa had submitted 5,155 pesos, an amount that proved the accuracy of the population records they had exhibited in September.[101]

The Andean peasants' appeal to the most basic principle of the political economy of the Spanish tributary state met approval beyond the realm of the royal treasury bureaucracy. The Charcas court also ratified the appointment of Caypa and Ancona as tribute collectors. Audiencia attorney Joseph de Castilla expressed no doubts about the existence of financial fraud, as well as the personal complicity of corregidor Ursainqui in it, because "this complicity explains his constant alliance and collusion with Lupa and his stubborn propensity to hinder the collection by the same Indians who provoked the disturbances in the first place . . . in order to uncover the accomplices in this thievery; for how long this usurpation has been taking place, and how much his Majesty has been defrauded, *it is necessary that this court call upon [Ursainqui] to appear, not as he pleases, but in person, to answer all the charges that will be made.*"[102]

Besides confirming the leaders of the protest as new ethnic chiefs, the audiencia ordered a new official recount of the Pocoata population. Significantly, the appointment fell on Pedro Pereira de Castro, the same official who had provoked outrageous reactions from corregidores and caciques because of the increase in the population records he had produced in the late 1760s.[103]

It is crucial to note that the Pocoatas's rejection of the state's disciplining policies represented by the enthronement of Florencio Lupa as a multiethnic lord did not mean a conservative defense of the tradition. The Indians rejected the new ways without showing any attachment to the old ones. Once Lupa was deposed, the Pocoatas successfully demanded that the leaders of the movement against him, not the previous caciques, become the new ethnic lords. The fierce opposition to the return of the descendants of the ancient noble lineage of the Ayra Chinchi expressed the repeal of a traditional model of government that had underwritten a process of land concentration and increasing interethnic agrarian strife. Even in the heat of the battles against Lupa, some Pocoatas had acknowledged at least one positive aspect of his government: in contrast to previous ethnic authorities, he addressed the disputes among members of the group, redistributed fields to those who needed them, made the parties ask pardon of each other, and left them "in friendship."[104] Thus, in asking the audiencia for the confirmation of Pedro Caypa as new cacique, the Pocoatas argued that, even though the Ayras alone possessed real hereditary rights, Caypa treated the Indians "with love and fairness, which was not the case with previous caciques. For this reason, the people have remained this time peaceful and quiet without the revolutions and turmoil that caciques usually stir."[105] This representative and contractual principle of legitimacy certainly would also infuse peasant assessments of the new caciques. The Pocoatas of Anansaya would later complain that former protest leader Francisco Ancona charged tribute to mita workers and ritual sponsors when their lands provided just for their subsistence, and "besides that many of us do not have enough land allocations." Instead, they emphasized, the ayllus of Urinsaya governed by Pedro Caypa "do not endure such harms and the year that they serve in any of the mentioned posts they are exempted."[106]

Although corregidor Ursainqui tried to obstruct the enforcement of the regional court's rulings, he had to accede to grant Pedro Caypa and Francisco Ancona the title of tribute collectors. In October 1776, according to the public notary, this title was announced before an audience of Spaniards and Indians in the village of Chayala, in a valley where Pocoata ayllus possessed a large number of lands.[107] The ethnic group had thus recovered command over its structures of government. A few months afterward, Pedro Caypa would secure in the audiencia his promotion from tribute collector to cacique in acknowledgment "of his dedication, loyalty, and zeal" to the treasury and the crown. Equally significant, the Charcas court prohibited corregidor Ursainqui from ruling over any kind of civil or criminal litigation in connection with the Pocoata leader. Furthermore, the highest colonial magistrate in the province was openly accused by the audiencia of misappropriating fiscal resources.[108] In April 1777, in the same decree that ordered the publication of Caypa's title of cacique in the village of Pocoata, Ursainqui was warned against "what has been orally exposed by [Caypa] that one of the reasons for having brought to the village of Potosí the money was because [Ursainqui] intended to assign these funds to his repartos, leaving the Indians as tribute debtors. In this way, the collectors are forced to put all their zeal in collecting again the tributes. *This is what we see every day with the corregidores.*"[109]

Ursainqui resisted until his final days in office the formal announcement of Caypa's title of cacique in the Pocoata village. Eventually, as I will show below, he would have to accede to this, too.

THE MACHAS, THE NEW CORREGIDOR, AND AN INDIAN NAMED TOMÁS KATARI

The outcome of the peasant collective protest must have appeared as if the world had turned upside down. If by successfully appealing to regional courts the Pocoatas had sharply undermined the political authority of the northern Potosí ruling groups, by proving the tribute embezzlement they had positioned themselves as the most genuine defenders of the king's interests. The combination of peasant collective mobilization (with its displays of force, legal politics, and tributary strategies) and state policies during the age of Bourbon reformism (with their emphasis on rising revenues and their deep wariness of local government) seemed to create a nourishing environment for outright challenges to the conduct of colonial rule in the Andean rural world. That this process might dramatically reshape local power relations did not go unnoticed by the provincial magistrates. In 1777, shortly before taking office, the incoming corregidor Joaquín Alós wrote to the highest official in the land, Visitador General del Reino Antonio de Areche, that Caypa and Ancona represented no less than "heads" of an "uprising." He pointed out that, instead of punishing them, both audiencia ministers and royal treasury functionaries had awarded the rebels the titles of cacique. Alós bemoaned the fact that the Pocoatas had not been severely punished because of "the indifference with which these affairs are regarded, thwarting with any pretext, with orders and commissioned judges, the corregidores' authority."[110]

It should be noted that in September 1776, as five hundred Pocoatas were camped in Potosí, one of the treasury officials had expressed his confidence that Ursainqui, or any other corregidor for that matter, would seek to build some sort of compromise with the Indians: "He must consider their restless mood, the facility with which they riot, and that the punishment he may inflict could cause a general uprising, perhaps aided by the neighboring provinces."[111] But Alós thought otherwise. He believed that the high courts of Potosí and La Plata were encouraging popular insurgency by undermining Indian subjection to their real rulers: the caciques, the priests, and the corregidores. As Alós remarked to Areche, he was determined to suppress social unrest by enforcing his own authority over the northern Potosí communities regardless of the policies of the high courts.

Oddly enough, both the treasury official and the corregidor proved to be right. Just two weeks after taking office, Alós would have the opportunity to put to use his concept of authority. By the time he was preparing to assume the post, the Machas, following the example of their Pocoata neighbors, had also started their own movement to regain command over the ethnic system of rule. Between May 1777 and March 1778, numerous Macha Indians urged the audiencia and the treasury officials of Potosí to dismiss their cacique, Blas Doria Bernal, whom corregidor Ursainqui had appointed two years ago. Owner of a hacienda and grain mills in the valley of Pitantora, Bernal was accused of embezzling tribute payments, being mestizo ("the most obnoxious ever alive"), misappropriating the yield of common lands (comunes), demanding labor services without retribution, sending an extra mita worker to Potosí for his own benefit, and making his own particular distribution of goods.[112] Not surprisingly, the Machas, too, handed over in Potosí the population record of the Majapicha and Majacollana ayllus under Bernal's rule, "the same one by which the tributes are collected," they said. It added 78 tributaries, more than 40 percent, to the official census.[113] The influence of the Pocoatas, with whom the Machas regularly engaged in ritual battles called tinkus, is beyond doubt. One of the protest leaders, Melchor Espinoza, even recalled that in La Plata a Pocoata Indian who was at the time promoting the appointment of Pedro Caypa as proprietary cacique, "asked him on that occasion for 12 pesos, *telling him that their suit was going well*."[114] In April 1778, Pedro Caypa himself would volunteer as bondsman (*fiador*) for Espinoza so that the latter could be confirmed as tribute collector of Macha.[115]

Among the Machas who exhibited the census in Potosí was Tomás Katari, whose name seems to appear here for the first time in the historical record. Little is known of him beyond the fact that he was about thirty years old, resided in the puna hamlet of Pararani, and belonged to the Majapicha ayllu of the Urinsaya moiety.[116] The person who would evolve into the most prominent insurgent leader in the history of this Andean region could have had very personal motives to become involved in the protest initially. As he would relate later, in the months previous to his first appeal in Potosí, "I experienced a month in jail, as well as whippings, and I had to bear [Bernal's] cruelty just for having defended my small landholdings from an intrusive woman whom he secretly favored and protected. It is not unusual but very frequent and regular that the cacique profits from taking lands away from the Indians and giving them to mestizo and Spanish people."[117] Like the Pocoata leader Pedro Caypa, Katari apparently had no noble ancestry.[118] Although Melchor Espinoza claimed to be grandson, son, and brother of former caciques, Tomás Katari never explicitly appealed to his lineage to legitimate his claim to the chieftainship. Other than vague allusions to his "rights of blood," his aspiration to replace Blas Bernal would always be tied to communal consent.[119] A non-Spanish speaker, Katari might not even have been among the well-off members of the community: in the census delivered in Potosí, his name appears in the category of Indians who paid 5 pesos — that is, those who contributed the lowest amounts because of the fewer or less-fertile lands assigned to them.

If the indigenous economic and political grievances as well as the forms of resistance pertained to a well-established pattern of conflict in this region, the widespread climate of confrontation over the nature of colonial government (recall that just a few years earlier the Machas had also been actively involved in the disputes between communities, civil officials, and church magistrates) would infuse this protest against the cacique with different undertones. For one thing, the Machas were not the only ones learning from the Pocoatas's experiences. Rural power groups, too, were determined to stand their ground at any cost. Thus, when in February 1778 Katari and his peer Isidro Acho brought to Macha a decree from the treasury officials commanding corregidor Ursainqui to place them as tribute collectors and to "forbid the cacique or any other person from disrupting their activities,"[120] Blas Bernal's relatives, according to Katari, "put us in jail, where they took us, with our hands tied and in the most dishonorable manner, to parade through all the streets and the plaza like common criminals, saying that they were making an example of us for those who intended to denounce the misappropriation of tributes, as we had."[121] But the Indians would not easily be deterred. And without a favorable balance of forces in the Andean villages (and strong support in the regional courts), the politics of coercion was a hard path to take. In early March, twelve Machas commoners journeyed to La Plata to present on behalf of their community a new and more detailed list of grievances against their cacique.[122] Moreover, as soon as Katari and Acho escaped from jail they also returned to Potosí, where they reported the punishment received. Both petitions found sympathetic ears. On March 22, the Protector of Indians of Potosí sent a letter to incoming corregidor Alós, advising him to make sure the cacique or any other person would not "place before the plaintiff [Katari] and his peer Isidro Acho the least obstacle in their labors as tax collectors, a duty they perform under orders from the royal officials."[123] Coincidentally, on March 23 the audiencia ordered Alós to investigate the charges against Bernal and, if true, to dismiss him immediately. Regardless of the outcome of this inquiry, the corregidor had to publish edicts for the appointment of a proprietary cacique.[124]

Meanwhile, as the Macha protest movement was gathering strength, Nicolás Ursainqui performed his final acts as Chayanta corregidor. In February 1778, Joaquín Alós had warned that the main reason for the sorry state of affairs was that "heads of an insurrection" like the Pocoatas leaders were rewarded with their appointment as ethnic lords instead of being severely punished. After many years in office, Nicolás Ursainqui came to understand differently the delicate balance of force and compromise that made possible the exercise of authority in the Andes. In compliance with the orders issued by the Charcas court in April 1777, he publicly announced in the Pocoata village that Pedro Caypa "would remain as interim governor of the Urinsaya moiety of Pocoata, bestowing upon him the honors and privileges attached to his office." Ursainqui also acknowledged that all matters concerning the Pocoata cacique were outside his jurisdiction.[125] Needless to say, this public act carried only symbolic meaning: Ursainqui had arrested Caypa several times since the audiencia decree had been issued, and Caypa for all practical matters had by then been exercising the chieftainship for a long time. But the symbolic aspects of power counted for much in the Andean rural world, and the Pocoata Indians had protested several times to the courts that Caypa's title of cacique had never been formally and publicly announced in his town. Now, the decree was finally published as a broadside in the village of Pocoata, so that all the Indians and nonindigenous neighbors knew about it.

This ceremony took place on March 22, 1778, the same day that the Protector of Indians of Potosí was sending to the province a letter in support of Tomás Katari, and one day before the audiencia, at the request of the twelve Macha Indians, commanded again the removal of Blas Doria Bernal. Three days later, Joaquin Alós took charge of the Chayanta government.

Alós's first act as corregidor was handling those orders. As he had warned before assuming office, on receiving in the village of Macha from Tomás Katari and the rest of the Indians the decrees establishing the removal of Blas Doria Bernal, Alós immediately arrested the leader of the protest, confiscated the document, and had him publicly whipped by Bernal himself. Then, as Katari later recalled, the new corregidor "stated before the presence of all the Indians that he was their absolute corregidor and judge [*visitador*], and that there was no Audiencia or Royal Officials, and if they complained again he would hang them from the stirrups of his horse."[126]

Joaquin Alós would learn the hard way, as his predecessor Pablo de Aoíz had done thirty years before him, that the monopoly of the legitimate force in the Andean countryside could never be taken for granted. Within a few months, following new protests before regional courts, Tomás Katari would set out for the distant city of Buenos Aires, seat of the newly created viceregal court, which was one of the major initiatives of the Bourbon crown to curb administrative corruption. There, he secured from the viceroy a ruling for the corregidor to remove the Macha chief. On returning to northern Potosí, the corregidor (and now also the audiencia) refused to comply with the order of this too recent, remote, and intrusive power authority. Thus, Katari and the Macha peasants delivered the tributes in Potosí (as their Pocoata neighbors before them) and carried out mass protests in both the Andean villages and the colonial courts. Less than two and a half years in office, following a bloody battle in the village of Pocoata that left numerous casualties among Spanish rural residents, Alós would have to leave the province for good.

According to rumors at the time, an Indian waved his hat as a sign for the Indians to start their attack on the Spanish militia. This Indian was the cacique of Pocoata who, as a well-established ethnic lord who commanded the respect of the Machas, had been trying to intercede between the Indians and the corregidor. His name was Pedro Caypa.

THE GLOBAL AND THE LOCAL: BOURBON ABSOLUTISM IN THE ANDEAN VILLAGES

What distinguished from past conflicts the process of social contention that led to the 1780 general peasant rebellion? What were the distinctive historical trends that contributed to such a massive process of political radicalization? Certainly, open social dissension over agrarian resources was nothing new in northern Potosí. Historical records, as we have observed, suggest that it was by the 1740s, coinciding with region-wide economic and demographic trends, that peasant villages started to witness a long series of battles over land boundaries, native chieftainships, tribute obligations, mita workers' rights, corregidores' demands, and the like. The routine of peasant contention — Indian collective appeals to Spanish justice to protest abuses from rural overlords — belongs to even deeper structures of colonialism in the Andes: the general model of rule set up by Viceroy Toledo in the 1570s. The colonial state and the Indian community remained the major actors of this system; state agents, rather than landowners or private entrepreneurs, were by and large the main targets of grievances; and the deployment of the power granted by the crown and the church was the central motif in most of the conflicts.

The basic sources of socioeconomic tensions and the general mechanism of Indian protest are perhaps better explained, then, by reference to mid-term and long-term historical developments. I would claim that it was the implementation of Enlightenment ideas of government and social order that offers a more precise short-term frame of analysis for understanding the crisis of colonial power structures during the years prior to the events of the early 1780s. Bourbon politics of centralized rule, social disciplining, and fiscal efficiency nurtured the kind of political dislocation that set the stage for general challenges to colonial hegemony. And it did so by inflaming, as never before in the eighteenth century, conflicts between local and regional agencies of government, between civil and ecclesiastical magistrates, and between Indian communities and rural power groups. In other words, whereas imperial transformations added new strains in peasant society by bolstering state interference in everyday life and raising economic demands, they also opened up new avenues of collective protest. Further, they offered new opportunities for the development of insurrectionary practices and discourses. The great rebellion of 1780, as I will show in the next chapter, would make exceedingly clear that intraelite strife provided Andean peasants with a platform from which to mount radical assaults on the structure of local colonial authority. In this Andean region, anticolonialism initially sprang from the appropriation, rather than the dismissal, of official discourses of civility.

Court records from the period immediately preceding the mass insurrection reveal the increasing success of legal strategies as the highest colonial courts began to offer more receptivity and more tolerance to collective complaints against local civil and religious authorities. This success rested on finding a common ground with crown authorities, particularly Bourbon administrators' strivings to restrain the power of the rural parish priests and to undermine provincial magistrates' misappropriation of Indian tributes. In so doing, Bourbon reforms represented not only a cause of economic hardship but, paradoxically, a source of political expectations and opportunities as well. And this paradoxical situation progressively nourished a political crisis of colonial legitimacy as peasant collective actions increasingly put in jeopardy social stability in the Andean villages, and as rural ruling groups started to resist more openly and forcefully the aggressive intervention of the highest colonial authorities in the local business of government. Thus, the ideal of "fixed rules" and obedience "without interpretation" gave rise to fierce disputes over the meaning of norms;

disciplining social models helped to probe the profound embeddedness of local customary arrangements; and the new hegemonic project of political centralization, when translated into concrete discourse and practices of rule, resulted in widespread power struggles, both horizontal and vertical. It was this process of social mobilization from below and imperial transformation from above that created, from the beginning of the 1770s, the climate in which the mass Indian challenges to Spanish colonialism analyzed in the next chapter gradually took root.

4

Disputed

Images of

Colonialism:

Spanish Rule

and

Indian

Subversion,

1777–1780

AT THE BEGINNING OF JUNE 1780, a large group of Indians from the ethnic group of Macha traveled to the city of La Plata to denounce their Spanish and ethnic local authorities. Collective pilgrimages to colonial tribunals, as I have shown, had been a common occurrence in northern Potosí. More generally, both Andean and Mexican peasant communities had long gained the fame of being litigious for flooding Spanish courts with complaints that involved abuses in village government. Nevertheless, the circumstances surrounding these Macha Indians were rather extraordinary.

Over the three years previous, the Macha communities had carried out an exceptionally tenacious legal struggle. Juridical battles included several appeals to the royal treasury of Potosí, the audiencia of Charcas, and one astonishing journey to Buenos Aires, a distance of sixteen hundred miles from Chayanta, where the Indians brought their case before the highest authority in the land, the viceroy of the Rio de la Plata. Local power groups responded by repeatedly attacking the indigenous communities and several times imprisoning their leader, Tomás Katari. For example, between September 1779 and April 1780, eight months before the collective presentation in La Plata, Katari remained imprisoned in the town of Potosí. Only an armed attack allowed the Indians to liberate their leader as he was being conducted to Chayanta to be formally tried by the corregidor. That this experience did not deter the peasants from continuing the legal protest is certainly remarkable; still more intriguing are the explicit motives of their quest. Warned by the parish priest of Macha that the audiencia would immediately order his arrest, Katari replied that "he was not afraid of being arrested again because he was innocent and wanted to declare his truth and his justice; and for that reason, he was going to place himself at the gates of the audiencia daily, so that all might see him and know of his presence."[1] On June 10, 1780, the Indian leader was quietly led from the gates of the audiencia to the court prison.

In reflecting on the obstacles that the apparent "irrationality" of sixteenth-century popular religious revolts in France posed to historical analysis, Natalie Zemon Davis (1975: 154) has commented that "to bear the sword in the name of a millenarian dream might make some sense, but why get so excited about the Eucharist or saints' relics? It is hard to decipher the social meaning of such an event." The movement led by Tomás Katari, which began as a routine legal protest but became the most profound challenge to colonial rule in the southern Andes since the Spanish conquest, presents a spectacle perhaps no less enigmatic. Unlike the overt anticolonial rebellions led by Túpac Amaru and Túpac Katari in Cuzco and La Paz, the Chayanta upheaval was a gradual process of social unrest that evolved within the bounds of the existing system of justice and government. Throughout the conflict, continuous processes of judicial appeal to the higher Spanish courts, as well as the self-conscious adoption of European rituals of justice and the fulfillment of tribute and mita quotas, did not seem to preclude, but rather to legitimize, massive armed attacks on the networks of colonial power in Upper Peru. It is this pattern of insurrectional violence and juridical strategies that seems to defy our understanding of the political nature of the great Andean rebellions at the end of the eighteenth century. It also challenges conventional wisdom about the ideological function of the Spanish system of justice in the reproduction of colonialism.

My purpose in this chapter is to trace the ideological foundations of peasant politics. At a more general level I try to discern the social meaning contained in such public performances as Katari's voluntary surrender in order to assert what was translated, in the parlance of the time, as "his truth and his justice"; and I study how this form of political awareness could become the language of mass insurrection. By focusing on the jurisdictional disputes within the imperial bureaucracy during the late Bourbon era I examine in the first section the political framework of peasant collective actions. In the following section I analyze how competitive notions of colonial legitimacy among Upper Peruvian regional officials and viceregal magistrates imbued with the ideology of the Bourbon Enlightenment invested the protest movement with opposing patterns of significance. In the third section I seek to situate indigenous demands within the context of northern Potosí peasant society and to show how the Indians' consistent pursuit of limited, "reformist" objectives undermined the political and ideological basis of Spanish authority. The aftermath of this process, the upheaval that took place in the town of Pocoata at the end of August 1780, is addressed in the fourth section. There I trace the transfiguration of traditional rituals of colonial rule into acts of political subversion. While narrowly conceived as a study of the Chayanta movement, the historical relevance of the case under inquiry may permit us to speak to broader analytical issues in the fields of state hegemony and Andean politics and identity.

In recent years, the historical literature has tended to view Spanish justice as a powerful instrument of European hegemony over the native peoples. Some of the finest historical studies have revealed the extent to which indigenous peoples took advantage of their juridical prerogatives and the complex system of Spanish justice to protect their material resources, political autonomy, and principles of social organization.[2] Although legal strategies constituted powerful means of resistance, they also contributed in the long term to a mentality of subordination to the established order. According to Steve Stern (1982: 137), "to the extent that reliance on a juridical system becomes a dominant strategy of protection for an oppressed class or social group, it may undermine the possibility of organizing a more ambitious assault aimed at toppling the exploitative structure itself. When this happens, a functioning system of justice contributes to the hegemony of a ruling class."[3]

Certainly, juridical politics did not prevent indigenous communities from resorting to violence to resolve their conflicts with local elites. The numerous village riots that mushroomed in the eighteenth-century Mexican and Andean rural world demonstrate the Indians' ability to resort to force to defend their perceived interests. The purpose of these local revolts, however, was not to challenge the system of colonial domination itself but to protest particularly abusive authorities, new taxes, and outside encroachment on the political autonomy of the community. As it did with the Indians' legal claims, the colonial state tended to adopt a cautious approach to these local revolts, a calculated mix of repression and negotiation that would allow Indians and local elites alike to resume their daily routines (Taylor 1979: 122–24; Walker 1999: 81–82). Although the final result varied from case to case, the state did manage to create in this way a certain sense of justice. As stated by Friedrich Katz (1988: 79) in his summary of the hegemonic role played by the colonial state in New Spain:

"Most rebellions were directed at local officials, and the Indians mostly remained firmly convinced that the crown, if it only knew, would redress their wrongs."

The great Indian insurrections came to reflect, as in a mirror image, the hegemonic role of this "juridico-discursive representation of power," as Serge Gruzinski (1989: 18) has called it. Unlike legal protests, peasant insurrections rejected institutionalized mechanisms for resolving social conflict. Mass violence was outside the law, and its very emergence was bound up in the failure (and abandonment) of legal strategies. Jürgen Golte (1980) has, for example, divided resistance against the forced distribution of goods into two stages: first, a period when the Andean communities sought, for the most part unsuccessfully, to denounce their corregidores and caciques before superior courts; and, second, a phase marked by the use of force, which eventually led to the great uprisings of 1780–1781.[4] Insurgent violence, in turn, pursued objectives antagonistic to colonial domination. Unlike the limited goals behind local village riots (objectives often absorbed by the colonial regime) peasant insurrections by definition adopted the form of "conspiracies with explicit revolutionary goals," racial wars intended to exterminate or expel the European government and population (Coatsworth 1988: 29–30). In brief, the political nature of large-scale indigenous insurgency is sharply distinguished from the routine forms of negotiation and conflict between native communities and dominant groups.

In the analysis of the Chayanta movement presented here I propose an alternative perspective on the political foundations of Indian insurgency. I argue that mass violence was informed not by symbolic motifs generated from outside colonial ideology but by an appropriation and redefinition of the principles that legitimized European domination over the Andean peoples. While Tomás Katari led the movement until his death in January 1781, the northern Potosí communities did not formulate their expectations of social change in the language of messianic and millennial utopias, as was the case in other centers of insurgency, but rather in terms of colonial juridical discourse itself.[5] It was by reference to this ideological framework that indigenous politics and identity were constructed. In the case of northern Potosí, the adoption of nativist utopias and messianic expectations was the outcome not the origin of mass insurgency. Certainly, Spanish law was not an objective referential system against which participants in the conflict evaluated their and their enemies' actions. The nucleus of the political struggle lay precisely in antagonistic definitions of the set of rights and obligations that should regulate the relations between indigenous communities and the colonial bureaucracy.

To be sure, the analysis of law and legal discourse is one of the critical means for understanding the languages of authority and consensus that cemented colonial society (Poole 1992: 218). Chayanta records, however, suggest that Spanish justice could become, under certain circumstances, a theater not only of resistance but also of counterhegemony. By the late eighteenth century, under the pressure of imperial reforms and Indian protests, the judicial system seems to have turned into a prominent arena of ideological battles over the fundamental political features of Spanish colonialism in the Andes. In this chapter I intend to show how, in the very process of disclosing this contradiction and enforcing their perceived (and legally acknowledged) rights, the northern Potosí communities could constitute themselves as political actors, contest the local elites' claim to rule, and eventually subvert the forms of identity and cultural hierarchy that authorized colonial domination.

INDIAN PROTEST AND INTRAELITE STRIFE

The collective mobilization of the northern Potosí communities evolved, in the course of three and a half years, from a legal protest into a large-scale insurrection, unique in this region in terms of intensity, geographical reach, and political radicalization. To frame the analysis, three major stages in this process may be distinguished. Between mid-1777 and August 1780, the period covered in this chapter, the social struggle was largely limited to the ten ayllus that made up the Macha community, the most populous group in the province along with the Pocoatas and Sacacas.[6] Although Indian resistance against local authorities had become a routine affair, the relentless mobilization of Macha peasants to remove their lords and to obtain the appointment of Tomás Katari led to a growing political confrontation with the regional network of colonial power. This period saw a long sequence of armed clashes with local Spanish and Indian authorities that ended in a massive uprising in the town of Pocoata on August 26, 1780, which allowed peasant communities to expel the corregidor from Chayanta and to force the release of Tomás Katari from prison. The second phase of the conflict (the focus of the next chapter) begins in early September 1780, when Tomás Katari returned to Chayanta as the officially appointed cacique of Macha. Thereafter, the native communities reigned supreme over the rural villages, and mass violence expanded to Moscari, San Pedro de Buena Vista, and Sacaca, among other communities. Indians from nearby provinces also started pilgrimages to Macha, seeking advice on how to redress their grievances. By the end of 1780, despite Katari's consistent efforts to reconstitute relations between the Andean ayllus and the Spanish authorities, it was increasingly apparent that the conflict had reached the point of no return. The seizure and murder of the Aymara leader in January 1781, combined with the expansion of the insurrection led by Túpac Amaru in Cuzco and a successful uprising in the nearby district of Oruro, brought the confrontation to its last and more violent stage. As will be examined in the last chapter, thousands of Aymara peasants, led by Tomás Katari's brothers, Dámaso and Nicolás, assaulted several towns in Chayanta, killed those who had participated in Katari's execution, and, in February 1781, set up a massive, albeit brief, siege of the city of La Plata. These impressive insurgent activities ended with the military defeat of the rebel army and the execution of their leaders in April and May 1781.

The political struggle that took place in Chayanta between 1777 and 1781 did not originate in a straightforward opposition between native peoples and their European rulers. Peasant resistance against longstanding modes of exploitation in the Andean world became inextricably entwined with a larger, ongoing conflict in the colonial bureaucracy over the government of the Indian communities. As described in the previous chapter, the program of Bourbon reforms played a key role in making these two processes of contention collide. Whereas Bourbon policies were a major cause of Indian unrest because of the growing fiscal burden, in the regional scenario of northern Potosí the other major aspect of Bourbon absolutism, the transformation of the traditional patrimonial system into an absolutist bureaucracy, had very different political implications.

Let us first summarize the ideological and jurisdictional disputes that unfolded in Upper Peru as a result of this contentious process of political reorganization. It should be noted, first, that two central actors in the Chayanta rebellion—the corregidor and the audiencia—were in turn prime targets in what John Lynch (1992: 69–81) has aptly described as a transition from "colonial consensus"—a system of bureaucratic compromise—to "imperial control." In the Andes, a fundamental locus of debate and reform was the relationship between those colonial agencies of government and the forced distribution of goods carried out in the Indian villages. The reparto system diminished the royal treasury's ability to collect tribute from the indigenous communities, invested local magistrates with discretionary economic and political powers, and blocked the highest court in the land, the viceregal tribunal of Peru, as a channel of Indian legal protest.

To break the collusion between Lima elites and local magistrates, the crown decided in 1764 to restrict the viceroy of Peru's jurisdiction in Andean social conflicts by permitting the audiencia of Charcas to rule on Indian complaints against corregidores and the reparto (Golte 1980: 135–38). Although explicitly grounded in the assumption that the empowerment of the audiencia would contain abuses in local government, this decision seemed to encourage new types of judicial corruption. It promoted the establishment of informal networks involving audiencia judges and provincial corregidores, whereby legal support was exchanged for a share in the profits from this commercial monopoly. No doubt the informality and changing bases of these alliances made the relationship between corregidores and the regional court unstable and precarious. As a whole, however, the complicity between audiencia and provincial magistrates bred by the policy of granting the audiencia authority over matters related to the forced distribution of goods consistently weakened the high court's ability to redress indigenous grievances.[8]

The transfer of Upper Peru to the jurisdiction of the viceroyalty of the Río de la Plata in 1776 jeopardized the already delicate balance of power between viceregal, regional, and provincial officials. The new viceregal court, one of the cornerstones of the new politics of centralization, was staffed mostly with enlightened, Spanish-born bureaucrats committed to asserting the crown's fiscal and political interests over those of dominant regional oligarchies (Burkholder and Chandler 1977; Socolow 1987). Unlike their counterparts in Lima, moreover, the Buenos Aires functionaries were linked to local commercial groups with no substantial investment in the reparto system. These two factors combined to foster a new pole of power with a distinctive, and broader, political perspective on Andean affairs. It is not surprising that shortly after the outbreak of the Indian rebellions of the 1780s, the viceregal court was instrumental in implementing the abolition of repartos, the elimination of corregidores, and the establishment of the French system of intendencies, all major Bourbon initiatives.

The collective mobilization initiated by the ethnic group of Macha both exacerbated and took its shape from this struggle between corregidores, the judges of the high court of Charcas, and the bureaucracy of the viceregal court of Buenos Aires. The Machas complained, like many other peasants since the 1740s, that their caciques lacked consensus within the community.[9] The Indians revealed that through the traditional practice of concealing the real number of tributaries, the cacique principal of the Urinsaya moiety, Blas Doria Bernal, stole more than one-fourth of the tribute money. According to the Machas, the corregidores supported the illegitimate caciques due to their active involvement in the forced distribution of goods. Actually, Bernal carried out his own distribution of mules, which he personally acquired in Tucumán (present-day northern Argentina), and traded brandy among the Indians.[10] Despite that from 1777 through March 1778, as mentioned in chapter 4, the Indians obtained various decrees from the audiencia and the Potosí treasury officials, the recently assumed corregidor, Joaquín Alós, not only refused to appoint Tomás Katari as tax collector but also had the protest leaders publicly punished by the very same Macha ethnic chiefs. Alós also made exceedingly clear that appeals to high colonial courts would no longer be tolerated. The Machas were not deterred by these threats, but during 1778 Charcas and Potosí magistrates ratified their previous resolutions but took no actual steps to enforce them. It was then that Tomás Katari, along with a peer named Isidro Acho from his ayllu Majapicha, made the unprecedented decision to bring their grievances directly to the new viceregal court of Buenos Aires. Now it was not only the corregidor but also the audiencia of Charcas whose authority was being challenged.

When at the beginning of 1779 Katari arrived in Buenos Aires, his testimony about the corregidor-caciques complicity in diverting tribute payments and about the audiencia's inefficiency in forcing Alós to dismiss the mestizo caciques struck a sensitive chord among the bureaucrats. The reparto was perceived as a prominent source of fiscal and administrative corruption among Upper Peruvian officials and also as the likely trigger of a general Indian insurrection.[11] Therefore, Viceroy Juan José de Vértiz ordered the audiencia to designate a commissioned judge to verify Katari's allegations. Because the indigenous leader was not able to bring the records of the legal proceedings to Buenos Aires (the corregidor had confiscated them), the judge would have to corroborate whether Alós had effectively ignored decrees emanating from the superior courts. In that case Katari would be authorized to collect tributes, and edicts would be issued for the appointment of legitimate native authorities. More important, the audiencia was asked to notify Alós of "the prohibition that thereafter would be imposed upon him for acting against, or bringing to trial, the commissioned judge, the supplicant [Tomás Katari], or any other having knowledge of or an interest or role in this case."[12]

The journey to the viceregal court and the favorable verdict did not bring the immediate redress of the peasant grievances that Katari might have expected. By not resorting to any direct mechanism of coercion and law enforcement, Spanish justice routinely left the resolution of conflicts to local balances of power, and particularly to the claimants' ability to sustain over time a collective mobilization capable of wrenching new verdicts or enforcing legal decisions through force (cf. chapter 1). But viceregal intervention did have a fundamental, albeit unwitting, effect: by pushing the audiencia and the corregidor to close ranks to defend their shared jurisdiction over the Indian villages, it helped render visible and public the contradiction between the concrete modes of the exercise of power and the ideological premises of colonial domination. Whereas over the previous three years Charcas officials had generally supported protests by Pocoatas and Machas against caciques (and, by extension, against corregidores), after Katari returned from Buenos Aires in March 1779 they consistently repudiated the viceregal order to appoint a commissioned judge. The Charcas court ignored its own previous decisions in favor of Macha communities' demands, professing that it no longer held the legal documents in the case. In response to numerous Indian appeals, and against Viceroy Vértiz's explicit instructions, the court recommended that the peasants return to Chayanta "with the assurance that the corregidor [Joaquín Alós] would address their grievances without inflicting on them any harm."[13]

Such action, however, was certainly not ready to be taken by the corregidor and the ethnic authorities. On Katari's return to the province in mid-May 1779, as the Indians were gathered in their valley lands of San Marcos de Miraflores for the maize harvest, more than one hundred Machas from Katari's ayllu of Majapicha (Urinsaya) and from Alapicha (Anansaya) engaged in an armed clash with Blas Doria Bernal, caciques Pablo Chávez (Majacollana) and Francisco Flores (condata), an alcalde of San Marcos, and other authorities.[14] Bernal, and then Alós, arrested Katari, adducing that he handed over a document "with the false signature of the viceroy" and promoted the no payment of tribute. But, beside the fact that the document was authentic, the Machas did not refuse to pay tribute, rather they simply submitted them to Katari and the new hilacatas that he, as new cacique, had appointed. In early May, Katari wrote to these new tribute collectors that they had to "take care of the four comunes . . . with which the mita workers will be maintained, and I bring now new orders from the Sr. viceroy [so that it will] no longer be all robbery as before . . . That this mestizo [Bernal] could no longer do harm [is] because he cannot claim obedience since he was not appointed by the Audiencia nor the treasury [of Potosí]."[15] While local power groups managed to keep the peasant leader in jail for a while, it was plain that Bernal's position had become unsustainable. By late May, to prevent further disturbances, Bernal accorded with corregidor Alós to leave his place as cacique to his brother-in-law Ignacio Burgoa. In June 1779, when Katari asked the corregidor to return the proceedings of the case and to dismiss Burgoa and the rest of the caciques, Alós had him arrested again.

A few weeks later, in order to prove the misappropriation of taxes, Katari, following the example set by the Pocoatas three years earlier, attempted to deliver the tributes from the Macha ayllus to the royal treasury of Potosí. At the corregidor's request, however, the governor of Potosí, Jorge Escobedo, imprisoned the Indian leader as soon as he arrived at the mining center. Even in Potosí, where Katari would remain in jail for several months, the corregidor would subject him to a long interrogation.[16] As noted, in April 1780, as Katari was taken to Chayanta to be tried by Alós, a multitude of Indians ambushed the party in the ravine of Machamacha, near the village of Pocoata, and released their leader. It should be recalled that the primary objective of the viceroy's resolution had been "to prohibit the corregidor to rule on a matter in which I should assume he had personal interests, as he did have."[17]

The audiencia magistrates' decision in June 1780 to arrest Katari, when he placed himself at the gates of the court "so that all might see him and know of his presence," represented the final outcome of the process of collusion between different agencies of regional government. It also triggered an explosion of mass violence. Within a span of three months, native authorities were forced to resign; Joaquín Alós was compelled to leave Chayanta after a bloody battle; and the audiencia was obliged to liberate the peasant leader and grant him the title of cacique. What had begun as limited local conflict suddenly became a critical test of the balance of power between regional officials, enlightened bureaucrats, and Andean peasants. And still, after being expelled from the province, Alós reportedly resided in the house of the president of the audiencia and participated in court sessions. Between September and December of 1780, despite the volatile political situation in Chayanta, the Charcas court appointed new provincial officials; but because of their ostensible association with the former corregidor, the indigenous communities did not allow them to take office.

As the Indian movement began to gain almost complete control over the province and to expand even beyond the limits of northern Potosí, Viceroy Vértiz decided to remove the audiencia of Charcas from the case against the communities of Chayanta. In October 1780, Vértiz appointed the governor of Mojos, Ignacio Flores, as military chief of Charcas, ordering him to report immediately to La Plata. Flores formally became the only judge with jurisdiction over any matters related to the Chayanta conflict. In addition, Vértiz ordered the audiencia to suspend the death penalty until the actual situation in the province was clarified.[18] "In an affair as gravely important as the Chayanta rebellion," the viceroy wrote to Secretary of State for the Indies José de Gálvez, a prominent Bourbon reformer, "we must avoid the intervention of that court."[19] In disregard of Vértiz's orders and Flores's jurisdiction over Chayanta affairs, however, Katari was ambushed and seized by order of the audiencia in December 1780. En route to La Plata, he was finally put to death.

OFFICIAL NARRATIVES OF COLLECTIVE VIOLENCE

The stance of the regional power groups toward Indian protest and Bourbon absolutism determined the type of narrative strategies that could render Indian initiatives politically intelligible. This "prose of counter-insurgency" (Guha 1988: 45–86) consisted of portraying the indigenous movement as an anti-colonial rebellion, and locating its roots in the "ominous consequences" of Vértiz's instructions.[20] The case of Chayanta thus appeared as a paradigm of the political turmoil that would follow if the new viceregal court were allowed to rule on Andean social conflicts. This symbolic strategy competed with alternative accounts of the causes, intents, and significance of Indian mobilization. Although the forms of peasant political consciousness originating from this process will be explored later in this chapter, the representations of power that shaped the narratives of Upper Peruvian officials and Bourbon functionaries should first be addressed. For it was in this disputed field of political discourse that key concepts like legality and violence, authority and insurgency, took on concrete historical meaning.

The corregidor of Chayanta and the judges of the royal audiencia depicted the indigenous movement through three mutually related images. First, the regional elites described collective actions as illegal forms of protest. At the end of June 1780, four caciques from Macha submitted their resignations to Joaquín Alós because, as they stated, "the powerful arm of royal justice that your majesty administers has not been able to contain the sedition and arrogant uprising of this criminal [Tomás Katari] who believes himself to be beyond the reach of the law because of the support he receives from the Indian communities . . . that zealously protect him from royal justice."[21] Alós, for his part, wrote to the audiencia that "the control that Katari exercises over the Indians leaves them so completely enthralled that they no longer obey the law and submit even less to their Caciques."[22] According to regional power groups, peasant violence originated in the misunderstanding and manipulation of imaginary royal orders. "Katari thought nothing less than to carry out [the viceroy's order]," stated audiencia attorney Juan de Pino Manrique. "He reduced everything to seductions, disturbances, and riots, seeking not to employ moderate methods, or at least methods that would ease the shock of his exorbitant ends, but rather the most irregular extremes."[23]

Despite its seemingly conventional use, the notion of lawbreaking (and law enforcement) evoked in these paragraphs took on peculiar and distinctive connotations in regional authorities' discourses. Thus, for example, in a key fragment of the large corpus produced by the Upper Peruvian officials, Joaquín Alós traced the Macha mobilization to "the example of a similar rebellion that took place in Pocoata during my predecessor's administration. It continued until their leaders, Caipa and Ancona, managed to get themselves appointed as governors; an office they still hold because the royal officials of Potosí and your majesty [the audiencia] confirmed them in their positions, instead of having them appropriately punished for their crimes."[24] It is interesting to note how the fact that the Pocoata caciques were, simultaneously, "rebels" and supported by high colonial courts is not taken as a contradiction. As we have seen, Pedro Caypa and Francisco Ancona had actually obtained their titles as caciques because they had proved the embezzlement of tribute payments perpetuated by the previous native authorities. By the same token, the accusation against Katari for misunderstanding the order he drew from the viceroy is misleading. On his return from Buenos Aires, the peasant leader did not go to Macha declaring that the viceroy had directly appointed him as cacique but traveled to La Plata to submit Vértiz's decree to the audiencia. Because the members of the court refused to appoint any of the three commissioned judges suggested in the decree, arguing that they did not possess the previous legal documents, Katari traveled to Potosí to request a copy of the papers. In late April 1779, he declared before the treasury officials that his request "was aimed at ensuring that the commissioned judge the Viceroy ordered to appoint was satisfied with the legal proceedings so far undertaken."[25] A few weeks later, Katari went back to La Plata again to report on the violent clash with cacique Blas Bernal and his entourage. Along with this testimony he delivered the firearms used by the aggressors, "so that the attack be investigated by the same judge responsible for executing the Viceroy's instructions," Katari explained.[26] Audiencia attorney Pino Manrique, however, presented the event of Katari's journey to Potosí in September 1779 to deliver the tributes directly to the royal treasury not as an attempt to prove fiscal fraud but as "a sign of disobedience to the corregidor," a display of Katari's "ambition and seditious nature, whose consequences have been so harmful . . . [as to] threaten [the peace] of this area, to increase tribute debts, and to offer a bad example for other provinces."[27]

The manipulation of legal testimonies and evidences was, of course, an entrenched rule in the colonial bureaucracy.[28] Peasant judicial strategies, however, pushed regional officials explicitly to assert their representation of colonial authority as discretionary and limitless power. In this account of the events, illegal action designated not an attack on colonial institutions but a kind of challenge to the power of local Spanish magistrates. In this account of the events, it was the act of defiance itself, regardless of its juridical legitimacy, that defined an action as subversive.

The second image of the peasant movement articulated by regional power groups refers to the goals behind the Indian mobilization. Just as the initiatives of the northern Potosí communities were attributed to their ignorance of judicial procedures and their manipulation and misunderstanding of legal orders, a similar argument was put forward to explain the goals of the social unrest. The corregidor in effect portrayed the indigenous movement as a protest against tribute and mita. At first, Alós explained that Katari had spread the news that he had received an order from the viceroy to reduce tribute rates by half. As violence mounted, the charge became even more serious: according to Spanish regional authorities, the communities believed that their leader had been empowered to remove completely the state economic exactions. Although the Aymara peasants repeatedly showed their willingness to fulfill their economic obligations, Upper Peruvian magistrates continued to depict the protest as antitribute rebellion.

The pervasiveness of this argument is connected to the central place that tribute and mita occupied in the colonial imagination. In addition to their economic importance for state revenues and silver production, both institutions represented the prominent symbol of the status of native peoples as vassals of the crown. By articulating this account of the conflict, local elites constructed the political nature of the movement as the rupture of that link between the indigenous communities and the king and as the reversal or antithesis of what the Indians explicitly said. From this viewpoint, the peasants aimed not to curb abuses in government (including the divestment of tribute payments to reparto debts) but "to be released from the entire contribution of tributes and mita service."[29]

The third image characterized the peasant movement as an anticolonial conspiracy, one mounted to oust European civilization from the Andean world. As the corregidor stated, the fundamental drive of the indigenous movement was "to live without any subjection whatsoever, as is their natural propensity." "This rabble," wrote a parish priest from the Macha valley district of San Marcos de Miraflores, "has become excessively insolent, and respects neither the King nor the Church."[30] Through this narrative, regional power groups conjured a profound stereotype in what Partha Chatterjee (1993: 18) has called the rule of colonial difference, "a modern regime of power destined never to fulfill its normalizing mission because the premise of its power was the preservation of the alienness of the ruling group." The manipulation and misunderstanding of royal decrees and the attempt to eliminate economic dues to the state came to reactualize the image of Andean peasants as an essentially lawless and savage people, a constant social menace requiring a continuous work of colonization. By depicting the rural communities in terms of entrenched colonial stereotypes, regional magistrates sought to link the peasant mobilization to widespread fears of a general Andean insurrection. In this respect, the audiencia asserted that the Macha ayllus set alliances with other communities "to eliminate the yoke of obedience [and] to occupy these territories, purging them of Spaniards."[31] The peasants' quest, the corregidor summarized, "was to spread to the neighboring provinces the most detestable unrest that [this realm] has known since the era of the conquest. And demanding exemption from the observation of human and divine laws, they have stubbornly refused to acknowledge the resolutions of royal justice or to show obedience to our Monarch."[32]

The description of peasant actions as an anticolonial conspiracy thus posed the fundamental opposition between Andean peoples and judicial mechanisms of social mediation. In so doing, regional authorities vindicated notions of control and disciplinary power over the ideals of rule of law and bureaucratic rationality on which Bourbon enlightened discourse was predicated. Certainly, this is not the first time that we have found this kind of narrative. The basic structure of this counterinsurgency discourse, particularly in regard to the purported refusal of the Andean communities to comply with their tribute and mita obligations, already appeared during the crisis of local authority in the late 1740s (cf. chapter 1). What endowed this ideological representation a unique resonance now was the scale of the peasant mobilization, the number of state agencies involved, and ultimately the extraordinary outcome of the dispute.

Viewed through the prose of the viceregal ministers of Buenos Aires, the conflict in northern Potosí conveyed a completely different structure of meaning. On receiving the copy of the legal proceedings previous to Katari's journey to Buenos Aires, Protector of Indians Juan Gregorio Samudio explained that those records demonstrated the corregidor's initial dismissal of instructions issued by superior regional courts. For Samudio, this policy obstructed the Indians' right to recuse abusive authorities, violated the higher jurisdiction of appellate tribunals, and harmed royal treasury revenues by allowing embezzlement to continue. Consequently, he suggested that Katari, who at that time was imprisoned by the audiencia, be freed immediately and be appointed to the position to which he had originally been assigned.[33]

For his part the crown attorney of the viceroyalty, Jorge Pacheco, proposed that a letter be sent to the audiencia to determine whether the court actually did appoint a commissioned judge, as the viceroy had ordered the year before. Given that Katari's testimony in Buenos Aires "had not contained false information as the corregidor assumes," nor was it "sinister and deceitful" as the audiencia attorney affirmed, the judge should have named Katari tax collector and investigated the corregidor's behavior. Pacheco went as far as to request that if indeed Katari had been arrested after his return from Buenos Aires, then Joaquín de Alós should be punished for "this new act of violence and transgression [and] suspended from the exercise of his functions."[34]

With respect to regional officials' claims that the Macha communities sought a decrease in tributes by alluding to fictitious royal edicts, the viceroy stated that "it is clear that the corregidor's reports attributing the origin of the disturbance to Katari's distortion of my orders do not deserve credit because the corregidor does not prove it and the documents show otherwise . . . *nor is the reason the audiencia alleged for arresting Katari — that he would seek a reduction of tributes — consistent with Katari's proceeding in Potosí to increase them*; thus, we should suspect that they try to disguise their own wrongdoing with the imputation of abuses to such a defenseless person."[35]

The measures taken by the viceroy show that in his judgment the native communities had basically attempted to enforce his resolution. According to the highest authority in the land, then, Katari should be appointed cacique, Alós dismissed from his post, and the audiencia's jurisdiction over the conflict revoked. The cause of mass violence, as Pacheco put it, "was the series of steps taken by the corregidor, commissioned judges, and others to obstruct the implementation of the Viceroy's order . . . and the [corregidor's] writings that convinced the Royal Audiencia of the abuse that Katari had made of the decree . . . [thus the audiencia] did not protect him, disobeying the orders that Your Excellency [the viceroy] had issued to that end . . . If the superior decree had been promptly obeyed, nothing would have happened."[36]

According to this account of the conflict, it was not the Andean communities but the Upper Peruvian magistrates who had transgressed and manipulated law and legal procedures. Certainly, viceregal authorities perceived the menace of Indian mobilization and the space for political contention that their intervention had helped to open up. Still, if Vértiz's policies had brought "ominous consequences," as attorney of the audiencia of Charcas, Pino Manrique, had stated, it was not because the Indians had misunderstood his orders, but because they had been induced to carry out the process of law enforcement by themselves. The threatening point that the conflict reached, Vértiz concluded, was the result of "the apathy and insensibility shown toward affairs so significant that they should have been remedied and precluded through *the exact administration of justice*."[37]

The highly contradictory, politically charged patterns of interpretation that ensnared peasant collective actions can be used to reformulate the underlying analytical dichotomy in most studies of Indian resistance: the opposition between collective violence and legality, between judicial strategies and armed insurrections. To define Indian mobilization as illegal or extralegal action draws an artificial distinction that belies both the actors' perception and the rules of political struggle in colonial society. As interpreted by the viceregal magistrates, the notions of legitimacy that inspired indigenous practices did not originate from a misinterpretation of alleged royal orders or from abstract definitions of the king's will. Instead, the political framework of peasant initiatives was the execution of official decrees and the pursuit of a judicial process. Certainly, what distinguished mass violence from state coercion is not necessarily the ends pursued, but rather that state coercion was exercised in the name of a politically constituted authority. In this sense, one of the common features of eighteenth-century popular revolts in France and England was "the frequent borrowing . . . of the authorities' normal forms of action; the borrowing often amounted to the crowd's almost literally taking the law into its own hands" (Tilly 1981: 161).[38]

Nevertheless, given the ongoing political clash between Bourbon imperial politics and patrimonial bureaucrats, as well as the wide gap between formal jurisdictions and the actual power of coercion, the imposed distinction between state and mass violence tends to obscure rather than to illuminate the politics of domination and resistance in the Andean world. On the one hand, the customary set of colonial legal procedures made the *private* use of force not an anomaly but a structural component of the operation of Spanish justice. On the other hand, the political and ideological cleavages within imperial government made the legitimate, *official* use of force an issue subjected to multiple and contradictory interpretations. Juridical politics was a politics of violence as much as a politics of rights.

The political struggle between the ayllus and regional and viceregal bureaucrats was organized not around the oppositional forces of popular violence and law but around the contradictory definitions of who was formally acting as the authorized agent of the juridical system. For all its mobilizing power, whether or not the Chayanta movement constituted an insurrection — an attack against Spanish rule — was not a shared premise of the conflict but it was a critical point of contention in the ideological struggle. These different representations of legitimacy and violence gave rise to an ethnic movement that, without rejecting Spanish institutions in the name of revolutionary programs, was gradually to subvert the political culture of colonial administration, and eventually the very notion of racial superiority on which European hegemony rested.

THE POLITICS OF INSURRECTION

The overriding logic running through Indian legal documents is at first glance paradoxical. By denouncing the misappropriation of tributes, the Macha ayllus committed themselves to increasing the amount of money delivered to the royal treasury. Likewise, the revelation of the double census unmasked one of the traditional means of peasant resistance. It is well known that hiding Indians from the official population records constituted a longstanding peasant strategy to diminish state economic demands, especially tribute and mita. Certainly, it must be considered whether judicial appeals were calculated strategies of acqui-escence — that is, tactical devices meant to meet the expectations of the colonial authorities to whom legal claims were addressed.

As we have seen, Upper Peruvian officials stated that regardless of the In-dians' pledges, they refused to meet their fiscal obligations, manipulated the meaning of legal procedures, and eventually mounted a conspiracy to bring down colonial government. The historical literature has also treated the Cha-yanta rebellion as basically a protest against state levies. Whereas at first the Indians' goals were restricted to replacing the mestizo caciques and curtailing the forced distribution of goods, the movement supposedly evolved into a protest against tributes and the Potosí mita (O'Phelan Godoy 1988: 258–59; Campbell 1987: 114). It is this assault on the structural foundations of the colonial regime that seemingly accounts for the notable support that the Cha-yanta rebellion enjoyed among the Indian communities of the southern Andes. From this perspective, the significance of peasant judicial politics is to disguise, not to disclose, the real purpose of collective mobilization.

My argument is that mass violence and juridical strategies were inextricably entwined and cannot be understood in isolation. To dissociate both social prac-tices confuses the logic of peasant politics with the logic of its colonial represen-tation. Indian legal writing was highly consistent with peasant collective actions in the Andean villages — an arena in which gestures of submission toward Span-ish local authorities were steadily vanishing.[39] Contrasted with regional oligar-chies' narrative of the conflict, peasant initiatives were predicated neither on the rejection of state economic obligations nor on the manipulation of imaginary royal orders. Indigenous mobilization pursued profound changes in the inte-gration of Andean communities into colonial society, but these changes did not target, until the final stages of the conflict, the institutional structure of Spanish rule. The insurrectional quality of the Chayanta movement emerged out of a contentious process through which Andean concepts of colonial legitimacy were successfully backed by force in the local setting as well as consistently asserted in the public, highly institutionalized realm of Spanish imperial ad-ministration. It was the articulation, not the disengagement, of mass violence and juridical strategies that made Indian mobilization a radically subversive movement.[40]

To understand the material and symbolic rationality behind indigenous judi-cial claims, we must place the denunciation of fiscal fraud in the context of the internal dynamics of the indigenous society of Chayanta. The Machas complained that the caciques appropriated for themselves the profits resulting from the collective work of the ayllus on communal lands, rented to outsiders ethnic territories, and violated customary Andean norms regulating the operation of the tributary system within peasant society. Rural authorities, on the other hand, transferred debts from tributes to reparto payments. In so doing, they not only personally profited from peasant taxes but also overlapped and confused two materially and symbolically competitve modes of economic exploitation. Whereas the ayllus consistently proved their willingness to deliver tributes and mita, they denounced the abuses emanating from the reparto and eventually asked for its complete elimination.[41] The association between corregidores and caciques thus transformed the mechanism of double empadronamiento from a strategy of collective resistance into a symbol of the disruption of the peasant moral economy. Although the strong emphasis on tax embezzlement in Indian writing must be in part regarded as a legal strategy, this claim took on meanings far beyond its instrumental function. As past indigenous protest had made apparent this charge came to synthesize and fuse the violation of the two sources on which the caciques' legitimacy rested. By appropriating ayllu services to the state, the caciques undermined their role as fiscal agents of the crown; by disrupting the networks of reciprocity and redistribution within peasant society, they relinquished their function as native lords.[42] The workings of the tribute system thus represented the battlefield of a larger struggle over the command of communal economic assets and the articulation of highland communities with the structures of political and mercantile colonialism.

At a more general level, the collective mobilization expressed a larger political strife to define the meaning of colonial rule. As did many other ethnic groups in northern Potosí earlier, Macha communities attempted to revitalize an ideal "pact of reciprocity" with the state. In exchange for bringing to light the misappropriation of tributes and for confirming their allegiance to the crown, the peasants expected colonial authorities to recognize and enforce their rights to political autonomy.[43] What this autonomy signified in concrete terms had become apparent since the 1740s, when Andean peoples began to articulate contractual notions of legitimacy that challenged the discretional appointment of caciques by the provincial magistrates and hereditary succession rights, a practice that had underwritten a protracted process of social differentiation. Although this conception of ethnic authority and the set of social relations it meant to protect were firmly rooted in the fabric of the Andean ayllu, the general outlook of a state/community pact was not incompatible with the juridical formulation of colonial government as it had been established since the late sixteenth century. The "pact of reciprocity" might have indeed constituted the symbolic transformation of coercive power relationships into the language of asymmetrical exchange.[44] Yet it would be misleading to conceptualize the idea of Indian/state reciprocity as the mere ideological mystification of the realities of colonial exploitation. State economic dues, as well as Spanish justice, represented both modes of material and symbolic violence *and* sources of political rights. The day-to-day experience of colonial hegemony — after the traumatic events of Spanish conquest gave way to an integrated, longterm common history — rested not on the dominance of alien institutions itself but on the power of defining the social meaning of such institutions, the specific links that would bind Spaniards and Andean peoples to the colonial order.[45] The analysis of peasant actions seems precisely to reveal how political subversiveness could emerge in a process through which the Andean communities successfully used both law and force to contest that power — that is, a process to enforce their perceived corporative prerogatives and to make colonial authorities accountable for their policies.

The three months that passed between the audiencia's imprisonment of Katari in June 1780 and the battle of Pocoata in late August witnessed, as a corregidor's assistant put it, "the largest disturbance experienced in the governing of this province in many years."[46] The popular violence, however, was anything but random. Although unable to bring about the appointment of a commissioned judge, the Andean communities made full use of the means of coercion at their disposal to enforce the decrees gained in Potosí, Charcas, and Buenos Aires. As peasant practices and discourses show, the Indians assumed the right to expel their caciques and to overlook the corregidor's authority. During this period, the mestizo caciques and their allies in rural society were so completely overwhelmed by the Indian mobilization that their position as brokers between the colonial state and the communities collapsed. Two main leaders, Pascual Chura of Anansaya and Salvador Torres of Urinsaya, emerged during these clashes, most of which took place in the valleys where the Indians gathered during the winter months for the crop harvest. In accordance with the superior courts' decisions, the Macha ayllus did not allow the caciques to continue collecting tribute, selecting the mita contingent, and raising money for debts from the reparto.

Thus, for example, after chasing him for two days, the Machas warned the mestizo cacique from the Anansaya moiety, Norberto Osinaga, to stop collecting tribute. The Indians told him that "among them each one would go to the royal treasury to deliver the tribute."[47] In June 1780, approximately forty Indians attacked one *jilacata* (tribute collector) of Macha, "warning him to suspend the collection of money from the reparto until Doctor Ormaechea arrives to inform the corregidor of the instructions concerning this matter issued by the Royal Audience."[48] Juan Ormaechea had been one of the three lawyers recommended by the viceroy to act as the commissioned judge in the trial of the mestizo caciques. The corregidor's main assistant, Lieutenant Luis Núñez, stated that within the communities, word had gone out "not to pay the tributes and repartos to Spaniards or mestizos until further notice."[49] A mestizo testified that in early June in Chimbona he had met "a large number of Indians." When he asked what was the purpose of the gathering, two Indians replied that the community had designated them captain of the mita and cacique of the ayllu Majapicha, respectively, "and all the people had come together to select mitayos, which was what they had just done."[50]

Indians from Urinsaya dragged their cacique, Francisco Flores, out of his house by force and tied him to a mule. Wrapped in a blanket and badly hurt, he was brought to a hacienda, where some in the crowd persuaded the others to treat him with mercy because he was an Indian like them. After demanding that Flores hand over the money he was carrying with him, the cacique was told "not to dare collect tribute and repartos, and no longer to consider [himself] cacique."[51] The alcalde mayor of San Marcos de Miraflores, an Indian named Dionisio Chura, who later (in early 1781) would be taken from inside the Macha church and executed, reported that over one hundred Indians, men and women, forced him out of the parish house where he was hiding. The Indians took away his *bastón* (wooden staff of authority) "saying [he] was the greatest thief . . . and that had [he] been the Lieutenant [Luis Núñez], [he] would have been stoned to death by the entire community, men as well as women."[52]

Peasant communities exerted a strict control over the circulation of letters and people within the province. Thus, Anansaya cacique Roque Sánchez Morato declared that he could not send letters to the corregidor "because all the roads are blocked, and there is no way to dispatch a letter without it being intercepted by the Indians who register all the people going to see the corregidor."[53] Blas Bernal's brother in law, Antonio Ribota, saw two Indians handling a paper, which turned out to be an order issued by Alós for the mestizo caciques to present themselves to him in order to give testimony against the Macha communities.[54] A priest stated that all the mail received had been opened, and that "the Indians who have risen against our corregidor keep gathering at the crossroads to check all the correspondence to see if it contains information about their disturbances."[55] One alcalde from Macha said that nobody wrote messages to Alós because they were afraid of being discovered by the Indians.[56] A mestizo stated that as he was coming back from Potosí to

Macha, he found the Indians distributed in groups controlling the access roads to the province. Each person arriving in Chayanta was asked "who he was, where he was from, which papers he carried, what he went to Chayanta for, and to which town he was heading." Then the Indians checked the traveler's clothes and baggage.[57]

Collective violence was not aimed only at removing the caciques from office, but also at compelling them to retract their previous statements against the Macha communities and their leader. The ayllus knew that the caciques' denunciations against Katari—accusing him of pretending to possess viceregal orders to reduce tribute quotas—had contributed to his indictment by the authorities. The peasant communities attempted to reverse this legal process. In the weeks preceding the battle of Pocoata, collective actions showed a consistent pattern of behavior: after harassing mestizo caciques and forcing them to resign, the Andean peasants accused them of Katari's arrest. Then they either pressured the caciques to persuade the corregidor to release Katari, or threatened to bring them to La Plata to have them declare Katari's innocence before the audiencia. Thus, during the night seventy Indians attacked Francisco Flores and Pablo Chávez, caciques of the ayllus Condata and Majacollana of Urinsaya, and forced them to write a letter requesting Katari's liberation. Flores and Chávez were also obliged to hand over the money necessary for sending the letter to Alós.[58] In mid-June 1780, Antonio Ribota was arrested and beaten up. Bernal had previously told one of the assailants "that due to Ribota he [Bernal] is suffering the persecution of the rebellious Indians who want to kill him . . . that his brother-in-law has the Catari's [Katari's] papers . . . [and] that he [Bernal] had done nothing wrong for the Indians to want to arrest him and take him to Chuquisaca."[59] In mid-July about two hundred Indians assaulted Anansaya cacique Roque Sánchez Morato as he was trying to elect the mita team. Although Sánchez Morato somehow managed to escape and put himself under the protection of a non-Indian neighbor, the communities, "who in anticipation had set spies in place," broke in and threatened to burn the house to the ground if Morato did not surrender. The conditions that the Indians imposed on the cacique for not taking him prisoner were, in his words, that "I was no longer Governor and had no rights as cacique whatsoever, [and] if I did not obtain Katari's release within eight days, my protector would hand me over to the Indians so that they might do with me as they wished."[60] A mestizo from Macha heard the Indians proclaim "that they recognized no Corregidor, but only the Royal Audiencia, who ordered them to bring all the caciques and Alcaldes Mayores to the city of La Plata."[61]

In the months preceding the Pocoata battle, corregidor Joaquín Alós also faced intense harassment. In June, Alós accused the Indians of plotting to reduce tribute payments and to assassinate him during his annual visit to the valleys of Chayanta.[62] One of his informants, the alcalde mayor of San Marcos de Miraflores, Dionisio Chura, said that all the Indians from the ayllus of Collana and Majapicha were going to kill the corregidor, "for whose execution all have been called forth under the banners of Katari."[63] Alós informed the audiencia that the Macha peasants were "traveling in groups and provoking tumults, threatening to assault my person and those close to me."[64] Four days later, Indians from the Urinsaya moiety led by Salvador Torres journeyed to Moscari to talk to the corregidor. Their purpose, however, sharply differed from Alós's claims. When the Indians met him they presented a decree issued by the audiencia two weeks earlier. According to the decree, the corregidor was to take testimonies about the caciques' abuses, "and if the mentioned caciques were temporary and failed to be accepted by their respective communities, [Alós] would have to issue edicts for the appointment of permanent caciques in both moieties [*parcialidades*] [and] to consider all candidates who might present themselves for the post."[65]

The corregidor did initiate the inquiry, but the only question he posed was related to the charges against Katari for supposedly having turned the communities against colonial institutions. This trial relied on accusations made by the same caciques that the decree handled by the Machas ordered to dismiss. The Indians responded unanimously that they were not responsible for the disturbances, "and once Katari's freedom [could] be secured, and he could be seen in the village of Macha, the Indians would become peaceful and quiet."[66] As the questions had been only about Katari's behavior, the peasants made their way back into the corregidor's room and shouted at him that Salvador Torres had to be appointed cacique immediately, so that he could conduct the next tribute collection and dispatch the mita. Despite "the great insistence with which this demand was made," Alós dismissed the request by arguing that they should bring their case back to the audiencia. The peasants, who had traveled several times to La Plata during the previous weeks, responded so wildly and recklessly that neither the corregidor nor the Protector of Indians could understand their words. But a witness at the scene stated that as the Indians "left the said room, they continued to yell at him that if Torres were not appointed governor, they would continue the war or revolt they had begun."[67]

The revolt announced by the Indians materialized a few days later. On July 22, the corregidor accompanied by around 120 soldiers headed to the valley where the Macha communities had agricultural lands.[68] Not surprisingly, Alós sought support in the traditional allies of Spanish provincial officials within the indigenous society, prominently the ethnic lord of Moscari, Florencio Lupa. In Moscari, effectively, the corregidor instructed the cacique "that in case of emergency, upon receiving a notice from me, he comes to my help with all the people he could gather, as he did before in such cases."[69] Yet, Alós's attempt to round up Indians to strengthen the troop was a failure, because "no Indian wished to serve the Corregidor, not even for money; only a few chiefs came but did nothing."[70] When the militia arrived in the valley of Guanoma, a large crowd of peasants from both Macha moieties covering the hillsides began to throw and sling stones to the cry of "Thieves!" As the corregidor ordered the troops to stay quiet not shoot, the Indians halted their attack. Two priests sent as mediators managed to convince the Indians to come down and talk to the corregidor, although, in the atmosphere of mistrust and confrontation, they only agreed to talk after two Spanish hostages were sent to the Indian camp. Once the Indians came down to deliberate with Alós, he invited them to abandon their positions and go to a nearby hacienda, where justice, the corregidor vowed, would be promptly administered. In spite of their military superiority, the Indians eagerly accepted this proposition and asked the corregidor for his pardon. However, that pardon did not mean repentance would become exceedingly clear hours later.

In ensuring that Joaquín Alós kept his promise, over two hundred peasants gathered in the hacienda of Comoro that afternoon. The corregidor tried to divert the interrogatory to other topics, but a new round of threats and shouting forced him to name Pascual Chura and Salvador Torres as caciques of Anansaya and Urinsaya, respectively. Having promised Visitador General del Reino Antonio de Areche before assuming office that he would put an end to the practice of rewarding "heads of uprisings," Alós now had to accept the replacement of all the native authorities of Macha by the protest leaders. In addition, Alós was forced to submit the audiencia the decrees that Katari had obtained in Potosí and La Plata — decrees that would serve as the basis for the investigation ordered by the viceroy in 1779. It is significant that while rural authorities denied that the reparto was a motive of complaint (rather it was tribute, according to official accounts), what the corregidor was indeed impelled to promise in this context of open confrontation was to reduce the repartos during the forthcoming annual meeting at Pocoata. (Later, the Indians would make sure that the corregidor made good on this promise.)[71] Regarding Katari's freedom, however, Alós only offered to give the peasants a letter recommending that the audiencia release their leader. According to a witness, "the Indians rejected the proposal and persisted with their demand [to obtain Katari's release], continuing to make threats, until the corregidor finally offered that at the time of the dispatch of mitayos scheduled for August 30, he would do as much as possible to ensure the release of Katari, which finally calmed the group down."[72] Before withdrawing, the communities demanded that the corregidor again grant them pardon. That this ceremony did not involve an admission of guilt is reflected in the account of two witnesses of the event, who later related that "[the Indians] withdrew, but with cries that if Tomás Katari were not handed over, there would always be war."[73]

There would be war at the time of the annual meeting in the village of Pocoata for the dispatch of the mita workers, but before that the Machas undertook an exceptional measure in the context of northern Potosí: they killed their former cacique, Blas Doria Bernal. Although in the months to come instances of extreme violence would become almost routine, this was the first time that one of the Indians' foes was executed. Apart from the old motives of resentment against their former cacique, the Machas held Bernal personally responsible for their leader's repeated imprisonment, particularly because of his role in the armed clash in May 1779.[74] During the revolts in the valleys, the former cacique had managed to divert Indian outrage toward his brother-in-law. On August 8, however, a large group of Machas of Majacollana (Urinsaya) along with some Anansaya ayllus — three hundred Indians according to a witness, "all inebriated, armed with slings, and shouting insolent things" — dragged Bernal from his house while beating him up. The Machas exclaimed that Bernal "was the cause that they were now engaged in fighting with all the caciques, the corregidor, and the lieutenant [Luis Núñez]."[75] The former cacique was taken to the Altos of Ayoma, a Macha hamlet southwest of the village of Macha. One week later, despite the repeated pleas of the priests, Bernal was killed. His relatives were unable to recover his body.[76]

Matching the steady escalation of collective violence during this period was a parallel increase in juridical appeals to higher colonial courts. In the course of two months, the northern Potosí peasants journeyed back three times to La Plata and presented six claims to the audiencia and to the viceroy of Buenos Aires. Although regional Spanish authorities did their best to confine the conflict within the province, peasant legal politics successfully brought the dispute to several settings simultaneously, thereby bridging the physical and political gaps that under colonial administration isolated the realm of law production from the realm of law enforcement. The Machas conveyed the viceroy's orders to the audiencia, the Charcas court's decisions to the corregidor, the corregidor's actions to the audiencia, and the audiencia's measures to the viceroy. By enforcing juridical resolutions, the communities had seized from local authorities the legitimate use of force. The circulation of information generated by their actions in turn transformed Spanish justice from a potential means of redressing grievances into the very target of the political struggle. The native communities no longer restricted themselves to reporting abuses by the corregidor and caciques; they began to dispute the legitimacy of the corregidores in general, as well as the legality of the audiencia's policies and the viceroy's ability to exercise power.

Legal writing, needless to say, was penned by lawyers and scribes. What matters here, consequently, are not the legal technicalities but the overall framing of the conflict, particularly because the general notions of justice articulated before the colonial courts were highly consistent with collective actions in the rural villages and other types of testimonies.[77] Thus, the Indians declared that Tomás Katari had been arrested by the audiencia and "had been treated as a criminal without our knowing why he had not been permitted to take office, as we expected . . . [For] there is no other person who would be more scrupulous and vigilant in the collection of tributes and would give us the good treatment so recommended in the laws so that we do not experience even the slightest harm or abuse."[78] In one of the presentations before the audiencia, Katari declared that he had been informed that the court "has ordered Joaquín Alós to conduct my trial and to find evidence of the charges against me. In this particular," continued Katari, "I must say to your Highness that the said corregidor has been and is my mortal enemy, and as such has tyrannically persecuted me throughout that province . . . As I could not bear his violent methods anymore, I came to this court in order to continue my claims; it is also apparent that if I were the type of criminal [I'm alleged to be], I would have never come to seek the justice that the well-known mercy of your Highness administers."[79]

As well known as the audiencia's mercy might have been, it was again challenged in a petition that Katari and several Indians sent to the viceroy. The Aymara leader, the letter stated, had spent over two months in jail, having committed "no other crime or fault than to have gone to that Higher Court [of Buenos Aires] to testify on behalf of the interests of the Royal Hacienda and the miserable Indians." The Machas petitioned Vértiz to appoint a new Protector of Indians in Chayanta "because the corregidor has named his secretary Juan Antonio Castañares, [who] is the corregidor's associate and domestic, and is not instructed in our languages, [something that] is indispensable if his functions are to remain independent from those of the Corregidor." Finally, the Indians not only recused Joaquin Alós but also pleaded for the viceroy "to protect us with a decree that would serve as an example for other corregidores, and [another decree] against Blas Bernal for being a criminal and thief of royal tributes." "On both matters," the Machas concluded, "Your Majesty has indisputable jurisdiction."[80]

The armed battles for the enforcement of the law thus corresponded to an ideological struggle over the meaning of the legal structures (rights, jurisdictions, and juridical procedures) that framed the conflict. As Pierre Bourdieu (1987: 818–24) has pointed out, the practical content — the real significance — of the law is not enclosed in the juridical canon itself. It emerges out of disputes over its interpretation. The appropriation of the "symbolic power" contained in legal texts "is the prize to be won in interpretive struggles." If the symbolic power of the law lies in its capacity to designate certain actions as juridical acts and others as arbitrary violence, then the peasants' legal politics broke the "chain of legitimization" that bound the exercise of political authority to the juridical canon. In the process, the Aymara peasants were able to turn the official narratives of the conflict upside down: Indian collective violence now appeared as juridical acts, and the actions of political authorities as forms of arbitrary violence.

Peasant politics transformed a conflict that had originated from a restricted set of grievances into a general struggle over the role of different institutions and social groups in colonial society. In peasant discourses, the corregidor and caciques had no legitimate claim to rule whatsoever; the audiencia colluded with the corregidor in defrauding the royal treasury and disavowing juridical structures of authority; and the viceroy had to exercise his jurisdiction forcefully if the crown's interests and the native communities' legal prerogatives were to be served, "since all the province — as one of Katari's legal writings claimed — lacks the Royal Protection that by Right and Justice we deserve."[81]

Indigenous strategies thus led to a profound disruption of the political culture of the colonial regime. "If politics is defined as the process by which competing claims and policies are transformed into authoritative definitions of the general good," as Keith Baker (1987: 209) has argued about the political culture of ancient régime France, "then absolutist politics occurs, in ideal terms, only in the mind and person of the king." If we substitute for the image of the king that of the crown's representatives in Spanish America, this statement could be applied to the absolutist colonial state.[82] And just as in eighteenth-century France, the juridical protests against seignorial rights nurtured a process of "politicization of the village" (Chartier 1991: 144),[83] the direct effect of the peasant mobilization was to place into a public arena, to make visible, the relationship between formal and informal mechanisms of power imposed on Andean ayllus.

Neither the "parish pump," the peasant microcosm, nor "(conceptually) the human race" or the universe — the usual framework of peasant revolts and millennial movements, respectively (Hobsbawm 1973: 8) — constituted the unit of the collective actions; that unit was the space in between, the domain of colonial allocation of political and economic resources. The "theology of the administration," which by definition had to be contained within the realm of the Spanish bureaucracy, began to be subjected to scrutiny and challenge in the "public transcript of power relations." In seizing that critical power, the Indians ceased to function as passive recipients of colonial justice, as "legal minors." They transformed themselves into autonomous political actors, capable not only of asserting their rights but also of defining the means by which the delegates of the crown should exercise their authority.

AMBIVALENT RITUALS OF JUSTICE

The long process of contestation initiated by the Macha ayllus in 1777 concluded in a bloody upheaval that took place on August 26, 1780, in the village of Pocoata. During the customary annual meeting, at which the Chayanta communities delivered tributes and presented the mita team to the corregidor, the Indians undertook a massive assault on the Spanish militia. Andean communities from throughout the province convened in Pocoata to demand the liberation of Tomás Katari, and perhaps the reduction of repartos the corregidor had promised during the preceding clashes in the valleys. In anticipation of the battle, Alós had mobilized nearly a hundred soldiers from several rural areas, including the mining center of Aullagas and the valleys of Pitantora and Moromoro, zones of concentration of private haciendas. After failed talks between the corregidor and some rebel leaders — Dámaso Katari (Tomás's brother), Pocoata cacique Pedro Caypa, and Tomás Acho, the Indian who had accompanied Tomás to Buenos Aires — the Andean communities stormed into the town launching rocks with their slings. About thirty soldiers were killed and the rest were compelled to take shelter in the village church. Only the exhortations of the Pocoata priest who ventured out of the church carrying an image of Christ seemed to deter the Indians from invading the building. Alós himself was captured and taken hostage. In a display of public humiliation and a reversal of social hierarchies, the corregidor was forced to walk barefoot and chew coca as he was conducted to a hill near the Macha village. Over the course of the days following, the Indians allowed the soldiers to leave Pocoata with the condition that they surrender their weapons to the priest. Yet some of the Indians' foes, such as the corregidor lieutenant Luis Núñez or the beleaguered former cacique of Macha, Norberto Osinaga, could only save their lives by escaping during the night and traveling in disguises. The episode came to a close the first week of September when the Machas exchanged the corregidor for the imprisoned Tomás Katari.[84]

This revolt has been compared with the opening move of the Tupamarista rebellion. According to Leon Campbell (1979: 9), the capture of Joaquín Alós in Chayanta and that of Antonio de Arriaga in Tinta present some common characteristics. Jan Szeminski has maintained that both leaders alluded to royal decrees to legitimate an outright assault on colonial institutions. Túpac Amaru, certainly, evoked fictitious royal orders to try to publicly execute the corregidor Antonio de Arriaga in Tinta's central square. Whatever its ideological justification, this action marked the beginning of an insurrection in which Túpac Amaru proclaimed himself the new Inca king (Flores Galindo 1987: 117). Did the northern Potosí rebels follow a similar political pattern? For the purpose of my argument, three specific moments immediately before and after the Pocoata revolt are crucial: the dispatch of the mita, the negotiations conducted by the parish priest of Chayrapata to obtain the release of the corregidor, and the culminating encounter between Katari and Alós in the village of Macha.

As part of his general prediction that the Indian people would seek "to cast off the yoke of royal subjection," the corregidor expected Indian violence to erupt by the time the mita was scheduled to be delivered. On August 25, some two hundred soldiers took up strategic positions while Alós, escorted by twelve armed men, went to perform the traditional ceremony of reviewing the mita team. About two thousand Indians were gathered in the outskirts of Pocoata, when the corregidor and his small party arrived. Despite the corregidor's repeated warning that the peasants sought to be released from their duties to the state, the dispatch of the mita did not provoke a single act of defiance. In the context of a well-prepared confrontation, the uneventful dispatch of the mita quota to Potosí was not a matter of chance but rather a calculated performance, carrying a definite political message.

By deferring the battle for a few hours, the communities seemed to be proving that it was not their compliance with state economic obligations that was at stake in the conflict.[85] An incident that occurred during the ceremony reinforced this message. When, for unclear reasons, Alós attempted to seize a mine laborer, the peasants immediately came to the worker's rescue and wrested him away from his captor. Amid threats and mockery, the communities warned the corregidor that the Indian "was mitayo [*cédula*] and so could not be arrested" (*Comisión* 1971: 238). Centuries of Spanish government should have taught the Andean peasants that corregidores had no jurisdiction over mitayos. Yet in the context of an intense political struggle over the position of Indian peoples and Spanish authorities regarding colonial polity, those gestures and utterances carried a broader ideological point. The mining mita, far from being a target of mass violence, emerged as a crucial symbol of the privileged relationship linking the Andean ayllus and the king. From this perspective, the mita was an institution that empowered Andean communities to challenge and overlook local political authority. In the Indians' eyes, what rendered the corregidor's power illegitimate was not that he embodied colonial rule, as Alós had repeatedly argued, but that he no longer did.

The negotiations to obtain the liberation of corregidor Alós after the battle on August 26 underscore the fact that the rebels' stance toward the mita was consistent with their position toward the tribute. Two days after the bloody clash in Pocoata, the priest of the highland Macha district of Chayrapata, Miguel de Arazdum, arrived at the village of Macha to arrange for Alós's release. The priest then journeyed to La Plata to report to the audiencia about the settlement he had reached with the communities. On August 29, Arzadum said that the Indians had promised to permit the corregidor to leave the province in exchange for the immediate appointment of Katari as cacique of Macha. The Charcas magistrates immediately asked him if "the Indians resisted or had resisted the payment of tributes." The priest replied that when queried about their conditions for setting Alós free the Indians responded that they wanted the liberation of their leader and a reduction in the reparto de mercancías. As described earlier, this was exactly what they had demanded of Alós during the previous confrontations in the valleys. And, during his brief captivity, the corregidor would in fact be forced to issue a decree lowering the repartos.[86] The communities made no other request, Arzadum said. He recalled, "having warned them that as for the tributes it would not be possible to grant them that [same] reduction because it did not depend upon the corregidor, but upon our Sovereign Monarch, they replied that of course this was so, and that they did not seek a reduction of tributes."[87] That very night, the audiencia decided to grant Katari the title of cacique, "in order for his compatriots to remain calm and for him and them to comply with their promises." When Katari was informed of the decision, he replied "that of course he would deliver the entire amount of tribute, with the increase he had promised, which he guaranteed with his head."[88]

The encounter between Tomás Katari and Joaquín Alós that followed the Aymara leader's release represented a crucial moment in the history of Andean resistance against colonial authority. Like the public execution of the corregidor of Tinta two months later, it also staged a remarkable ritual of justice. Yet, Katari's assumption of the position of cacique and Alós's dismissal as corregidor illustrate the striking contrasts in ideology and strategy that distinguished the Chayanta movement from that of Cuzco. To highlight its social meaning, this juridical ceremony should be set against the background of Katari's arrest in Macha almost two years before, at the beginning of the collective protest. In March 1778, as Katari was delivering to the corregidor the decrees he had obtained in Potosí and Charcas, Alós arrested him, had him publicly whipped by a mestizo cacique, and then confiscated the documents, thereby depriving Katari of written evidence in his subsequent appeal before the viceroy. Katari's recollection of the incident is worth quoting again. He describes that as he was being punished, "the corregidor stated before the presence of all the Indians that he was their absolute Corregidor and Visitador, and that there were no Audiencia or Royal Officials, and if they complained again [before these courts], he would hang them from the stirrups of his horse."[89]

At the beginning of September 1780, as soon as Katari reached the village of Macha, he had the decree appointing him cacique read out loud. He asked the hundreds of peasants gathered to celebrate his release to obey the decisions of the audiencia. Then he went to the house where the corregidor was being held and, according to Alós's own account, "accompanied by innumerable Indians from all groups and even from other provinces, Katari and the others made the ceremony of asking for my pardon."[90] We know by now that for the communities pardon meant a formal recognition of gains, not forgiveness of guilt. After prostrating himself "at the feet of the corregidor with the most profound submission I must have for Royal Justice," the Aymara leader ordered that a decree commanding Alós to appear before the audiencia also be read out loud.[91]

Before Katari had left La Plata, the court had assured him that the corregidor and his lieutenant "would never return to the province and a [new] Justicia Mayor who looks upon the Indians with love and charity would be appointed."[92] In vivid contrast to his previous threats before and after assuming office, Joaquín Alós was asked to voice his compliance to the royal decree. In past years, the Indians often had been deprived of the favorable ruling they drew from the courts of appeal. Now, once the corregidor publicly accepted his legal removal before the large crowd of peasants, Katari requested that the edict be returned to him to keep "for his protection."

Spanish domination was reproduced, writes Thomas Abercrombie (1991: 202–3), "in many forms of public theater and rituals through which the Andean people had to publicly express their submission to colonial rule (and in this manner civilize themselves)." Doubtless the administration of the king's justice in the Indian towns stands out as one of the fundamental forms of public theater. Paradoxically, however, political insurgency in northern Potosí was expressed through the mimicry, rather than the dismissal, of such rituals. But mimicry was neither a disguise for anticolonial conspiracy nor a display of ideological submission. As shown by the events in the Pocoata village, the encounter between Katari and the corregidor was simultaneously a formal administration of justice and an act of political subversion. On the one hand, it featured a carefully arranged sequence of judicial procedures through which authentic royal decrees were enforced. On the other hand, its extraordinary performative context divested this juridical ceremony of its prescribed meaning as a ritual of colonial authority, recasting it as a mimic act, something that is both the same as and different from what it duplicates.[93]

On the public stage of colonial political theater, the Andean ayllus met their obligations to the state and respected the jurisdiction of the Spanish courts. The drama they performed, however, no longer represented the ayllus's submission to European rulers but something that went against the very ideological core of colonial domination: the fulfillment of native ideas of legitimacy and the superior coercive power of indigenous peoples.

The founding premise of colonialism, the notion of European cultural and military superiority, was thus opened to contestation. The acute process of political radicalization that emerged in the aftermath of the mass violence was vividly exemplified in a letter that the corregidor was forced to send to the audiencia before leaving the province. First, the communities reiterated their commitment to fulfill all their economic obligations. Then they asked the audiencia to support Katari; to appoint a new, impartial corregidor; and to recognize a reduction of the forced distribution of goods, which they had obliged Alós to grant. While these demands were essentially similar to previous ones, their political framework was not. As Alós explained, "I have tried to erase their impression that Your Highness may wish to send a great number of soldiers, in which case, *these miserable Indians say that all the Kingdom will tremble [since] their number is overwhelmingly larger than that of the Spaniards; and everything could be avoided by not disturbing them.*"[94]

As with all legal writing, the Indians were speaking through a language not their own, but even with such writing their rhetoric was not empty. When, in January 1781, the Aymara leader was captured and killed, the threatening message the Andean communities had sent came true. A few weeks later, thousands of peasants from several southern Andes provinces covered the hillsides of La Plata, threatening to kill the entire Spanish population.

The analysis presented in this chapter demonstrates that the mobilization of northern Potosí communities was a truly subversive movement long before news of Túpac Amaru's uprising started to reach the region at the end of 1780. The key interpretative problem lies in how to define political subversion in this historical context. Certainly, Chayanta peasants did not seem to pursue what we would call economic and political structural transformations, the kind of goals that historians have identified behind every large-scale insurrection in colonial times. Rebellion in northern Potosí, the process of mass mobilization whereby Andean peasants gradually divested institutions of local government of legitimacy and power, was not led against the two fundamental means of exploitation over native peoples, tribute and mita, and it certainly was not intended to expel the Spanish population and institutions.

As interpreted by most historical accounts, the insurrection of Cuzco led by Túpac Amaru and Túpac Katari, by contrast, aimed to reestablish pre-Hispanic polities. Although a more thorough comparison between the centers of Andean insurrection will be presented later, suffice to say here that Túpac Amaru was seen as a messiah, and the social transformation he championed was viewed as part of a broader cosmological cataclysm. Under the leadership of Túpac Katari in the La Paz region, what began as an anticolonial rebellion ultimately came close to a total race war (Campbell 1979: 11). My argument is that in the insurrection of Chayanta, nativist utopias, revolutionary programs, and binary identities were neither the origin of the struggle nor the driving force behind much of the conflict. Given the Indians' socioeconomic objectives, the Macha uprising clearly belongs to the cycle of local revolts and judicial protest that had mushroomed in Upper Peru since the 1750s. Like earlier episodes of litigation and Indian violence, the uprising led by Tomás Katari sought to regain control over community social and economic resources by attacking the most abusive aspects of village government.

Historians may have underestimated the insurrectional potential of local grievances against particular caciques, tribute collectors, parish priests, or corregidores. These demands may seem to refer to "reformist" goals, but for the peasant communities they represented issues vital enough to put lives, property, and social standing at risk. And regional power groups shared this view. It took a three-year mass mobilization and the most violent armed revolt the northern Potosí region had ever experienced for the corregidor to dismiss illegitimate caciques and to reduce the reparto, and for the audiencia to allow Tomás Katari to rule the Macha ayllus.

Nevertheless, it is crucial to note that the indigenous challenge to colonial domination lay not so much in the aims of peasant mobilization as in the process of political confrontation itself. As much as the Indian demands disrupted the ongoing modes of exploitation in the Andean world, they did so within the margins of the existing legal framework. Juridical records reveal that the removal of Macha native authorities should have taken place almost immediately after the Macha communities' first appeal in mid-1777; this, as argued earlier, was also the judgment of the higher authority in the land, the viceroy of the Río de la Plata. Not only did the Chayanta peasants believe that they had the law on their side (and then take it into their own hands), but what counterinsurgency narratives sought to conceal is that the Indians were mostly right. The paradox of this movement is that the peasants' continual reference to colonial legality and institutions did not inhibit but instead unleashed and legitimated mass violence. Peasant political consciousness grew out of the symbolic articulation of discursive battles in colonial courts and armed battles in the Andean villages.

It was the sustained collective exploration of the contradictions between power and law and truth and justice in Andean society that gradually undermined the consensual and coercive foundations of colonial authority. As distinguished from previous isolated and short-lived outbursts of violence, as well as long but usually unsuccessful legal protests, this collective effort also empowered Indian communities to nurture broad links of solidarity and political awareness.

The Chayanta movement, therefore, presented a case of "radical subversiveness" not only for attempting "to seize existing authority" but also for challenging "the principle upon which authority was based" (Greenblatt 1981: 41). The political premise that inspired the protest was that of a pact between the ayllus and the colonial state whereby the Indians' fulfillment of their economic obligations was linked to the state's assurance of their social and political autonomy. Whereas Indian communities from the Cuzco and La Paz region manipulated imperial Inca memories of the Tawantinsuyu, the Aymara peasants from northern Potosí seemed to resort to a traditional pattern of incorporation into both Inca and Spanish state structures. The political struggle to transform this ideal model into concrete power relationships gradually enabled the Andean communities to question the Spanish authorities' claim to a monopoly of legitimate force, to redefine the legal modes of rule in colonial administration, and to turn time-honored judicial rituals of domination into manifestations of the communities' own ideological and military success.

The process through which the Andean communities appropriated the physical and symbolic power to redefine political legitimacy led, finally, to a complete disarticulation of the modes of colonial subjectivity, the way both the colonizers and the colonized recognized themselves and recognized others.[95] What should be stressed, in my opinion, is that northern Potosí peasants did not construct their collective identity by negating the idea of civilization imposed by European domination. Insofar as the European concept of humanity was bound to Indian subordination to Spanish institutions and laws, as well as to the fulfillment of their economic obligations as the king's vassals, it was in the regional power groups' interests to portray indigenous practices as a regression to the precolonial stage of barbarism and paganism (Dillon and Abercrombie 1988: 67). The description of peasant mobilization as a protest against tribute, the king, and the church represented an attempt to subsume indigenous communities under cultural stereotypes that justified colonial authority. "To live without any subjection whatsoever," as the corregidor worded it, "is their natural propensity." It is in the opposition of savagery and submission that colonial discourse represented native peoples and legitimized its civilizing mission.

The unintended outcome of collective mobilization in Chayanta was precisely to dislodge this opposition, to disavow any attempt to locate Andean communities' actions at either extreme. Civilization or savagism were the terms through which power groups cast the events. But the movement's political subversiveness should be sought not in what the Spanish rulers said but in what colonial discourse suppressed. If the European colonial project required the construction of a "reformed, recognizable Other, as a subject of a difference that is almost the same but not quite" (Bhabha 1984: 126), the Chayanta insurrection emerged from the pursuit of the concept of equality, such as defined in the juridical theory of the two Republics.[96] Peasant discourses and actions did not deny or seek to deny difference *itself* but rather difference as a signifier of cultural isolation and inferiority. Peasant strategies pushed to the limit what Jacques Rancière would describe as the consequences of their full participation in the category of human beings; or, more specifically in this case, in the category of the crown's free subjects.[97] The Spanish authorities were thus forced to cope not with the denial of the European concept of civilization but with the disarticulation of cultural and racial hierarchies that this concept was meant to produce.

The strangeness of Katari's voluntary surrender to the audiencia in order to declare "his truth and his justice" lies in the way this act exceeded the Indians' established role as objects of colonial knowledge and control. What in normal times constituted gestures of obedience and consent (Katari surrenders himself to colonial courts, the Indians obeyed juridical decisions, the mining labor was dispatched, and the tributes were collected) became, in this particular context, fragments of a larger insurrectional script. Those practices radically undermined the prescribed meaning of the categories of civilization and savagism through which Spanish authority and Indian rebellion could be understood. Therefore, counterinsurgency accounts of the events dissociated those acts from the flux of mass violence by depicting peasant judicial politics as the result of the Indians' inherent inability to understand law and legal procedures or, when that interpretation was already unsustainable, as the surface of a secret anticolonial conspiracy. But Tomás Katari and the Andean communities from northern Potosí did not conform to the role they were assumed and pushed to play. Thus, indigenous practices and discourses not only challenged entrenched relations of economic and political power in the Andean world; they also subverted the historical experience of colonial identities: the function of the Spaniards as legitimate agents of colonial institutions, the collective violence of native peoples as a symptom of savagery inscribed in nature and history, and, in the end, the justification of European rule as an *endless* civilizing process.

THE RETURN OF TOMÁS KATARI TO CHAYANTA in late August 1780 marked the beginning of a historically unique period of self-rule among the northern Potosí indigenous communities. However precarious and short-lived, this political experience allowed the native peoples to gain almost complete control over the rural villages. Not since the Spanish conquest, and indeed not until the insurrection led by Zarate Wilka a century later, would the Indians enjoy a situation of such freedom from outside powers. The particular type of insurgent politics that unfolded during this period of self-rule was somehow prefigured by the assumption of Katari as cacique of Macha and the removal of Joaquín Alós from his post. The exchange had, as noted in chapter 4, the appearances of a juridical act. It had been formally sanctioned by the audiencia and was also in tune with Viceroy Juan José de Vértiz's instructions. It remained, of course, that this ruling had not been voluntary but the result of a successful indigenous uprising. The inherent ambivalence of this momentous event would epitomize the relationship between the Andean peoples and the state in the turbulent months to come. The predicament in which the peasant communities would find themselves is that if they mostly thought of their claims as part of an ongoing process of negotiation with the colonial administration (and many of their petitions were actually not unlike those of past protest movements), the consolidation of their power position rendered such a negotiation increasingly unfeasible. Whereas the Spanish government could eventually absorb some of the indigenous socioeconomic grievances, it could not possibly tolerate the upset of colonial hierarchies represented by the intensifying challenges to its authority and its monopoly over legitimate force.

The political undercurrents informing Indian insurgency during the period between the arrival of the Aymara leader in Chayanta and his murder four months later are the focus of this chapter. In it I show how the Andean communities tried to reestablish their bonds with the Spanish government by undertaking a series of initiatives such as demanding a "general pardon" or amnesty, delivering tribute monies, and sending a large number of letters to various state agencies. At the same time, the Indians were determined to hold on to, and expand, their newly gained command over the political and economic institutions shaping their daily lives. Not coincidentally, corregidor Alós heard before leaving the province "that the Indians had called upon twenty-five or thirty thousand Indians from neighboring provinces in the event attempts are made to correct their abuses and punish their crimes."[1] A much more sympathetic witness, Macha priest Gregorio Joseph de Merlos, also reported that "thousands of Indians from several provinces are on notice to be ready to help if the royal audiencia sends soldiers, as the Indians expect will happen."[2] In the weeks ahead, vows of acquiescence to colonial domination were accompanied by widespread collective attacks on rural overlords, from Andean chiefs and parish priests to Spanish and mestizo town-dwellers. Likewise, indigenous petitions for the appointment of a new corregidor to replace Joaquín de Alós were followed by an active resistance to those candidates who did not fit their expectations. Between these two poles, the dilemmas of self-rule created by the sweeping demise of colonial power in the countryside would be played out.

A DISMEMBERED CORPSE

An elderly Spanish resident of Chayanta once remarked that the process leading to the battle of Pocoata on August 26, 1780, was set in motion with the rise of the Moscari cacique Florencio Lupa to the chieftainship of Pocoata eight years earlier.[3] It could also be argued that the process leading to the final collapse of colonial domination in the region began with his murder barely ten days after that battle. On September 5, the Indians of Moscari killed their native lord, dismembered his body, and then placed his heart in one of the hills surrounding the city of La Plata. No other event until the death of Tomás Katari early the next year would have a deeper impact on the estrangement of state/community relations than the execution of the hitherto powerful cacique. Moreover, no other event would bring into focus so clearly the intricacies of peasant politics. City residents and state officials both thought of the assassination of Lupa as part of a larger insurrection plot designed by Tomás Katari. But this was not the case. If the event disclosed the radicalization of indigenous political practices underway, it revealed, too, the narrow limits of Katari's authority. Indeed, the cacique had been killed despite the opposition of the Aymara leader. Where colonial authorities tended to see a general conspiracy, there was in fact a local dispute rooted in a long-term accumulation of grievances.

Already in July 1780, a large group of hacienda tenants of Moscari had refused to deliver the tribute to the cacique, took away the bastón of his tax collectors, and insulted and physically harassed them. One of the ethnic authorities was told that his life was saved only because he was an Indian; had Florencio Lupa been in his place the result would have been different.[4] The warning materialized two months later. In early September, about three hundred peasants, many of whom had had an active involvement in the previous incident, stormed Lupa's house in the village of Moscari and assaulted the Indians guarding his house and his family. Barefoot and wounded, the cacique was conducted to Macha, where Katari found him when he returned from escorting the deposed corregidor on his way to La Plata.[5] Certainly, the Moscari peasants were not the only ones waiting for Katari; other communities had brought their native chiefs to Macha as well. But whereas most Indians abided by the request of Katari and the Macha priest Gregorio Joseph de Merlos to turn over their caciques, the Moscari Indians did not. At one point Katari seemed to persuade them, but as Lupa was being taken to the house of the Macha priest, "all the [Moscari] Indians started to throw so many stones at us that had we not returned Lupa to them, we all would have died."[6]

Lupa was decapitated during the night. Even among the Moscari peasants themselves there appeared to have been disagreements about Lupa's fate. One of the participants in the killing narrated that "many were opposed [to murdering Lupa], arguing that it was better to bring him alive to this city [La Plata] to submit him to the audiencia. And although many agreed to this at the time, they changed their mind during the night and in the midst of confusion, shouting, and uproar, they cut his head off. In the morning, there was a meeting in which . . . they resolved to bring [Lupa's head] to this city and put it during the night on a cross called Quirpinchaca, as they did between one and two o'clock in the night, and then they came back to Moscari without making stops."[7]

As shown by historians Jan Szeminski (1987: 169–70) and Jorge Hidalgo

Lehuede (1983: 125), in the Andean system of cultural beliefs heart extraction and beheading are intended to make sure that the dead, by not being buried, would not be reborn. This ritual rendered the deceased person as beastly, as a "nonhuman human." If this were the case, there could be no doubt that the placement of Lupa's head in the outskirts of La Plata was aimed at showing the devilish nature of the Moscari cacique to those who had supported and protected him in life.

Early in the morning, as the Spanish residents, officials, clergy, and common people learned the news, they thought that the end of the world was imminent. Rumors quickly spread that insurgent Indians were about to invade the city (see chapter 2). Although the initial fears of an immediate Indian assault gradually receded, colonial authorities took two important measures. First, the killing of Lupa launched the audiencia into preparations for an all-out armed conflict. The court immediately began to organize a militia in the city, asked for the dispatch of military reinforcements from other areas, and commanded provincial magistrates in the southern Andes to raise their own troops. The first military movements of what eventually would become, following the uprising of Túpac Amaru in early November, the largest mobilization of colonial armies in the Andes since the sixteenth century was thus set in motion. Second, as soon as the incident became known, the Charcas officials released the Indians imprisoned since 1774 for the killing of Lupa's peers, the Condocondo caciques Gregorio and Andrés Llanquipacha.[8] The Condocondo Indians possessed land in several areas of Chayanta, including Macha territories, and Tomás Katari had often asked for their liberation. Spanish officials might have believed in the existence of a large-scale anticolonial conspiracy, but at the verge of disaster, in a desperate move to appease peasant unrest, they instinctively looked at the concrete, longstanding sources of discontent.

Back in northern Potosí, the mobilization of troops in La Plata and in nearby cities and villages confirmed the rebel peasants' worst fears that an army would be dispatched to the province to punish them for the bloody assault on the provincial militias in the village of Pocoata. This belief only enhanced the scale and strength of the cooperation among Andean communities. Since early September, in an effort to thwart punitive expeditions, indigenous communities stored maize, dry-salted meat, coca leaves, and slings in caches scattered through the northern Potosí hamlets. Cattle were moved to the valleys or even to lands outside the province in case of invasion.[9] The Indians checked the people traveling through the province,[10] and Spanish residents complained that their correspondence was routinely intercepted. Moreover, *cañaris* (messengers) were sent to neighboring provinces to coordinate military assistance. It was widely reported that the Indians of Condocondo (Paria) and Tinquipaya (Porco) were also patroling the area.[11] The buffer zone between northern Potosí and the Charcas region, an area comprising Ocurí and the valleys of Pitantora, Guaycoma, and San Marcos de Miraflores, became a major center of rebel activity. All the ravines and main passageways connecting the province of Chayanta and La Plata were under close surveillance by the Andean communities that gathered along the area armed with slings, clubs, and sticks.[12] On September 10, numerous Machas and Pocoatas invaded the village of Poroma, in Yamparáez province, because soldiers had been dispatched from there to La Plata the previous week. Some days later, Indians covering the nearby ravine of Cruz Casa could still be seen from the village's central square.[13] Peasants were heard boasting that if troops were to be dispatched from La Plata, two forces of fifteen hundred people each would be waiting for them in Pitantora and Guañoma, a hamlet located a few miles to the north.[14] Summing up the state of affairs in the region, a mestizo resident of Chayanta reported that northern Potosí Indians contended that they were ready to "fight and drive back" the Spanish troops, should the opportunity arise.[15]

The opportunity would not arise in the immediate future, however, for the audiencia, in large part because of the very scale of the peasant mobilization, eventually decided to change its strategy and pursue the suppression of rural insurgency by other means. It was this mass mobilization and political consciousness, in any case, that provides the backdrop for what followed: a sweeping demise of colonial social hierarchies throughout the province. Now that the corregidor had been definitively expelled; that Florencio Lupa, the most ostensible symbol of the state's intrusion in indigenous affairs, was dead; and that rebel Indians reigned supreme over the countryside, the Indians set out to assert their command over the institutions of local government.

THE DEMISE OF VILLAGE SOCIAL HIERARCHIES

When the ministers of the audiencia of Charcas decided to set free the Indians of Condocondo in response to the exhibition of Florencio Lupa's head in the outskirts of the city, they tacitly recognized a fundamental tenet of rebellion in northern Potosí: even at the peak of mass violence, social unrest was focused on the institutions and practices that represented longstanding motives of disaffection. In this sense, Andean peasants did not perceive the expelling of corregidor Alós, or the murder of Blas Bernal and Florencio Lupa, as initial acts of a larger revolutionary plot—as clearly was, for instance, the execution of the Tinta corregidor by Túpac Amaru. Rather, these acts represented sheer expressions of the primary ideological drive of peasant insurgency. What collapsed during this period was the structure of rural authority; the all-out repudiation of Spanish rule came later.

Among the motives of peasant mobilization, regaining control of the ethnic structures of government unquestionably remained the prime driving force. On September 6, a few days after the ousting of corregidor Alós, Tomás Katari communicated to the audiencia that many Indians were at the time gathering in Macha and that only the removal of the caciques "would calm down these Indians from the daily and continuous uprisings that are very detrimental to your Majesty because they are occupied and perverted with these revolutions."[16] Successful revolts in Macha and Moscari (and Pocoata before them) were followed by a persecution of illegitimate native lords, whether of noble lineage or appointed by the corregidores, in virtually all the communities, including Laymi-Puraca, Chayantaca, Sicoya, Sacaca, San Pedro de Buena Vista, Moromoro, and Pitantora.

Struggles over the control of native chieftainships, on the other hand, not only expanded spatially but also socially. Conflicts between communities and caciques soon escalated into violent clashes with the other traditional claimants of peasant resources: nonindigenous town-dwellers and, above all, the Catholic priesthood. The entire structure of rural authority thus began to crumble. Although Spanish and mestizo residents were not the focal point of contention, the private landowners, tax collectors, and associates in the reparto (often related by kin and economic partnership to the native elite), who encroached on community lands and agricultural surpluses and played an important role as formal or informal agents of social control, were greatly affected by the complete demise of indigenous political subjection. The role of the clergymen during these months, on the other hand, was crucial. As the power of state officials and former ethnic chiefs vanished, in the aftermath of the battle of Pocoata parish priests became the highest Spanish authority figures in the villages. As elsewhere in the Andes, church magistrates commanded in principle a great deal of respect. Insurgent Indians certainly continued to value their service in religious celebrations. Yet while in Cuzco considerable sectors of the priesthood seemed to sympathize with the Túpac Amaru movement, this was not the case in northern Potosí, with the prominent exception of the Macha priest Gregorio Joseph de Merlos.[17] Nor was the priesthood spared of peasant violence, as seemingly occurred in the neighboring communities of Paria (Abercrombie 1998: 299). Most of the rural clergy fled to La Plata, leaving their assistants in charge of the parishes, and many experienced physical assault and public humiliation. Not surprisingly, among them was Dionisio Cortés, the hitherto powerful priest of the highland parish of Aymaya who had been the object of peasant protests during the 1770s.[18] The reason for the attack on the clergy is twofold. First, the vast majority of parish priests openly sided with state and ethnic rulers, especially caciques and nonindigenous town-dwellers. Second, there was a longstanding source of social contention with its roots far beyond this conjuncture of war: the dispute over the compliance with the new arancel that unfolded during the 1770s would regain center stage in this context of mass insurgency. As I will show in chapter 6, as the confrontation deepened what would be at stake was the institutional role of the church in local society as mediator between the Catholic God and the native peoples.

It is useful here to examine some of the major instances of peasant uprising. One of the first occurrences of collective violence in the wake of the battle of Pocoata took place in the area of Pitantora and its vice-parish of Ocurí. In this zone, which as already noted became a focus of insurgency because of its strategic location, the revolt against the native chiefs became inextricably linked to attacks on mestizo and Spanish residents. As the seat of several private landed estates, including the hacienda and grain mills owned by the murdered Macha cacique Blas Doria Bernal, Pitantora's elite town-dwellers had been actively involved in the repression of revolts against the Macha chiefs and the corregidor between June and August. On August 21, a large group of Pitantora residents marched to the village of Pocoata to join the Spanish militia; they came back one week later, defeated. Two days before the battle of Pocoata, several Indians warned the priest Josef Miguel Salazar y Solís in the cemetery adjacent to the Pitantora church "that the grievances and hardships of the natives were not heard because they were voiceless, and thus they wanted to defend themselves with their hands."[19] Little wonder that shortly after returning from Pocoata, the elite town-dwellers reported that they had to hide in the woods and ravines because the Indians were about to invade the village. In fact, in mid-September, Macha peasants led by the three main ethnic authorities of both Anansaya and Urinsaya entered the town of Pitantora and compelled the public announcement of a decree — probably the one signed by corregidor Alós while being held hostage — stipulating a reduction of the reparto, and the realization of a cash collect (*derrama*) to allay the expenses imposed by the conflict.[20] The Machas also demanded that the Pitantora parish priest hand over those responsible for past punitive actions,[21] and in this context, the ethnic chiefs, themselves private landowners, were assaulted. In early September, the cacique of Ocurí, Ignacio Salguero, was prevented from collecting tributes, and was harassed and even assaulted with a knife. Ignacio Salguero eventually managed to flee to La Plata, but the Indians expropriated his grain and other goods.[22] The Pitantora Indians also warned their cacique, Anselmo Bernal, that they wanted to be returned to them the tribute monies he had collected for the last Navidad quota.[23] Significantly, Anselmo Bernal was among the town-dwellers who demanded of the Charcas officials military reinforcements, the punishment of Indian leaders, and the erection of two gallows in the village of Pitantora so that local peasants would be deterred from joining their Macha neighbors.[24]

In the northern part of Chayanta province, the prominent caciques of the ethnic group of Sacaca, Manuel and Phelipe Ayaviri Cuisara, were also victims of peasant violence. The Ayaviris were descendants of an ancient sixteenth-century lineage of Andean lords and, like Florencio Lupa, they were private hacendados and mestizos.[25] In the wake of the battle of Pocoata, Manuel Ayaviri, cacique of Urinsaya, took refuge in the chapel of the village of Acasio, where the Sacacas had their valley lands. Hundreds of Indians (two thousand according to the Acasio priest) gathered in the village armed with stones, slings, clubs, and a red flag. After throwing stones and threatening to tie the priest with a rope and set the building on fire, the Sacacas finally captured their cacique. The Indians took Manuel to Macha, but perhaps because he was very sick at the time (it was said that he was even shrouded), they eventually let him go.[26] Phelipe Ayaviri, cacique of Anansaya, decided in turn to leave for the neighboring province of Cochabamba on failing to deter the ayllu authorities of Sacaca and Acasio from joining the rebellion. In mid-September, the Indians invaded his house in Sacaca and took possession of his hacienda, livestock, and grain mills, whose revenue they thereafter began to collect.[27] In his estate, the Indians captured Phelipe's son, Ambrocio Ayaviri, and a tribute collector, whom they submitted to Katari in Macha. Then, the Sacacas headed for Cochabamba in pursuit of Phelipe himself. Four hundred Indians, according to some estimates, arrived in Colcha and Arque, the main passageways from the Andean highlands to the central valleys and one of the Cochabamba areas most densely populated by indigenous people (Larson 1997: 185). The Sacacas scrutinized the entire town of Arque, but Phelipe Ayaviri managed to escape to the village of Cochabamba two hours before the Indians arrived.[28] Eventually, the corregidor of Cochabamba dispatched one hundred soldiers to the area to prevent the Chayanta Indians from "infecting" the neighboring communities, but the strong links between the Sacacas and the peasants of Arque and Colcha made repression very difficult.[29] The Indians would actually return to Cochabamba in search of Phelipe Ayaviri during the feast of San Francisco in early October. They inspected once more the haciendas and the towns of Colcha and Arque, where frightened village officials even allowed them to look inside the church.[30]

It is worth noting that despite the massiveness of the invasions, the Sacacas displayed great restraint while in Cochabamba during this period. As even the Cochabamba corregidor conceded, they conducted a thorough search for their cacique but without "doing major extortion."[31] When in their homeland, however, they behaved quite differently. After returning to the village of Sacaca from their second failed venture into Cochabamba, the peasants dragged the priest's assistant, Antonio Dorado, from the church because he was believed to have helped Phelipe Ayaviri run away. Then, they tied him up and publicly humiliated him by crowning him with thorns. The Indians attacked people in the village as well: it was reported that the peasants forced some Spanish residents to dress as Indians and insult other non-Indians and throw stones at their houses.[32]

For all this extraordinary display of collective violence and defiance, peasant mobilization was driven by longstanding grievances against the caciques. In Macha, the Sacacas of Urinsaya contended that Manuel Ayaviri "did not assist the mitayos as he should as Main Cacique," and in his collecting of tithes, veintenas, alcabalas, and primicias "he inflicted a lot of harm on us for he put in prison the Indians, gave them whips [*azotes*], and made other punishments in order to collect those taxes, which were demanded prior to the royal tribute because those were more profitable for him."[33] The Sacacas of Anansaya, in turn, claimed that Phelipe used the income of a grain mill that was owned by the community "to help the Indians to meet their obligations for his own particular benefit, leaving the people overloaded with burdens." In asking for the appointment of two Indians, Diego Pari and Diego Grande, Katari urged the audiencia "to remove all the Spanish and mestizo caciques that remain in power for only then will peace be reached and the royal interests of Your Catholic Highness augmented."[34]

The most visible expression of how disputes between communities and native lords turned into clashes over the broader mechanisms of colonial domination in the Andes occurred in the valley of San Pedro de Buena Vista. In late September, several ethnic groups openly confronted the most prestigious ecclesiastical official in the province, the priest and vicar of San Pedro de Buena Vista, Isidro Joseph de Herrera; assaulted the Spanish people and caciques sheltered inside the church; and then went on to challenge private-land property rights.[35] San Pedro was a multiethnic valley inhabited by two purely lowland groups, the Cayanas and Auquimarcas, and by indigenous families belonging to the highland communities of Sicoya and Chayantaca (Chayanta repartimiento). It shared its border to the north with the valley of Acasio, inhabited by the riotous Sacaca ayllus, and to the south with Moscari and Micani (a valley district occupied by Chullpas, Laymis, Carachas, and Pocoatas). As one of the most fertile agricultural areas in the region, San Pedro hosted many of the private haciendas in the province. Individuals wary of indigenous assaults in their own villages sought refuge among its relatively large Spanish and mestizo population. During the first week of September, the widow and daughter of Florencio Lupa, Pedro Yavira, the cacique of Caracha, and several other caciques gathered in San Pedro with their wives and children. While those arrested by rebel Indians ended up in Macha, those who managed to escape persecution ended up in the church of San Pedro. Little wonder, then, that this area immediately turned into one of the main sites of political turmoil, and, in March of 1781, it would become the location of the most violent indigenous onslaught during the entire insurrectionary period.

Open confrontations first erupted in early September in the sanctuary of the Pitunisa, five miles from the town of San Pedro. As priest Isidro Herrera was scheduled to celebrate a religious feast in the sanctuary, most caciques and their families preferred to follow him instead of staying behind inside the San Pedro church.[36] On September 11, however, the sanctuary was surrounded by a large group of Indians who demanded Herrera hand over their native chiefs. They stoned the chapel and, during the night, camped in the cemetery adjacent to the church. Eventually, most of the clergymen and the caciques managed to return to the village of San Pedro after talks between the assailants and the priest, but the Indians showed great reluctance to quit the assault and uttered threats as they left the sanctuary. Meanwhile, in San Pedro, the conflict had also engulfed elite town-dwellers, who tried to keep the peasants at a distance from the village. In fact, two Indians who had chased one of their caciques' assistants inside the church were captured and placed in the stocks.[37] Because about three hundred Indians threatened to attack the village, the two prisoners eventually had to be released. The tensions exploded on Sunday, September 17. When Herrera was celebrating mass, hundreds of Indians on the hills surrounding San Pedro and the lower part of the village began to launch stones at the church. Cayanas and Auquimarcas were mentioned as being most active in the attack because they were eager to take hold of their caciques Hilario Caguaciri and Manuel Puma, respectively. As in the sanctuary of Pitunisa, Herrera's emissaries managed to convince the Indians to halt the assault and come down to talk to the priest. Although little is known of the content of this conversation, it seems clear that the Indians wanted not only the delivery of their caciques but also the acknowledgment of a reduction in ecclesiastical fees. Although on this occasion they decided to withdraw, the next Sunday, September 24, an even larger crowd of more than a thousand peasants deploying their arms and blowing their horns would return to demand that the priest keep his promise.

This second attack was led by a Sicoya Indian named Simón Castillo, who would become the most prominent insurgent leader in northern Potosí after Tomás Katari and his brothers.[38] Castillo had just returned from Macha, where he had handed over the Sicoya cacique Nicolás Guaguari to Tomás Katari.[39] One week before, the Sicoyas had caught their native chief near the sanctuary of Pitunisa as he attempted to escape in the company of the parish priest of Acacio.[40] The exchange that took place reflects the linkage between the different causes of peasant outrage. When the clergy resisted submitting the cacique, the Indians threw stones at him, seized some of his possessions, and threatened to kill him.[41] When the priest told the Sicoyas that they were excommunicated, the Indians replied that "their tasa was only 1 peso and that even this they will not pay because the King did not receive even half a real from this, and that *they will pay for fiestas only 12 pesos for the main ones, for weeding 2 pesos, and not even half a real for* holy oils [*oleos*]."[42]

The clash on September 24 began, by all accounts, when after mass Simón Castillo, who spoke Spanish, publicly confronted Isidro Herrera for not having published the official tariff list of church fees, as done in other parts of the province.[43] It was also said that Castillo contended that the Indians did not have to pay tithes and veintenas to the church, an issue that had also raised peasant discontent over the previous decades.[44] These allegations made the hitherto restrained priest loose his composure. Enraged, he slapped and arrested the Sicoya leader, which prompted a violent response from the Indians. Spanish residents fired their arms against the crowd gathered outside the church, wounding at least seven Indians. The Indians at first retreated about two blocks, but they soon resumed the attack by launching rocks and using their clubs. The neighbors were then forced to lock themselves inside the church.[45] For many hours, until Simón Castillo was finally set free, the peasants continued to surround the church, whose iron fence was destroyed. Sicoyas, Cayanas, Auquimarcas, and according to some versions, Indians from Moscari and Pocoata as well, wielded complete control of the village, sacking the empty houses of the Spanish residents.[46] Violence slowly began to recede after the beginning of a new round of talks between the Indians and Herrera. One of the mestizos locked inside the church at the time later recalled that the priest finally vowed to reduce the church fees, "which was by then the aspiration of the Indians."[47]

This promise may account for an odd ceremony that took place the following Sunday when a multitude of Sicoyas, Cayanas, and Auquimarcas descended for a third time on the town. After a public procession with an image of Nuestra Señora del Rosario, Isidro Herrera was met in the village central square by some of the older Indians of the communities and by Simón Castillo and two other indigenous leaders. Although only the priest's version is available, the rendering of the dialogue that then took place shows the ideological undertones of the movement. Confronted by the Indians about his refusal to lower church fees, Herrera claims that he said

> that all the fees had been reduced according to the arancel. They, then, displayed a copy of the arancel that the good Castillo had brought. I sent someone for another copy. Then, as all the Indians who knew how to read stood there, they with their copy and I with mine, we started to compare item by item . . . It is hard to convey the noise, turmoil, and confusion they made while we were waiting for the exemplar of the arancel I ordered to be brought from my house, so much so that I thought I was lost because they were poised to destroy the town.[48]

The priest of San Pedro presented the exchange as a defeat for the Indians; he reported that they quietly, "without saying a word," left the town afterward. The intense struggles over the public recognition of the new tariff list during the 1770s, and especially the fierce confrontations over the last two weeks that had made the ceremony possible, indicates otherwise. One Auquimarca rebel leader later recalled that as a result of these disturbances the communities indeed diminished their contributions for feasts and withdrew their labor services (*pongos* and *mitanis*) to the church.[49] A week after the events, several of the Auquimarcas directly involved in the battles argued before Tomás Katari that the Indians would not have perpetrated these acts, "had the clergy not convoked the Spaniards to kill us with shotguns only to avoid exhibiting the Real Arancel, so that the tyranny with which we have been so far treated could be put to an end once the community was instructed on the content of the arancel." The linkage between the conflicts with the church and the native chiefs was also pointed out. In the past, little could be done to suppress Herrera's tyrannies, "because of the collusion that our priest has had with corregidor [Joaquín de Alós] and with our [Auquimarca] governor Manuel Puma, who fled to avoid paying for his wrongdoings."[50] When looking back to these occurrences, Simón Castillo also recalled that after these incidents "although there was this or that grievance in the communities they were not major things, and they lived in peace because the priest [Isidro Herrera] accepting their petitions made a reduction in the church fees."[51]

The same crisis of domination that empowered the Indians to remove caciques, enforce the arancel, and assault rural elites prompted them to challenge land property rights. In fact, a few days after the clashes in San Pedro, the Indians invaded a hacienda in a hamlet named Colcha in the valley of San Pedro and murdered the hacienda owners, Matías and Martín Coca.[52] We know that between the 1740s and the 1770s, a man named Faustino de Coca, the owner of a hacienda and grain mills in Colcha, had been involved in a lengthy confrontation over some lands of the Chayantaca community. Coca claimed that he had inherited the fields by virtue of his marriage to the daughter of a former cacique of this group. Considering the mounting population pressures, the loss of communal farming lands must have represented for the Indians not only a matter of principle but also of economic necessity. By this time, the Auquimarcas, too, were engaged in disputes over property rights with a Spanish hacendado in three valley sites: Coconoma, Tarca, and Cinto.[53] Already in the late 1740s, Faustino de Coca and his wife had been warned that they "would never have the right of enjoying these fields peacefully."[54] The killing of Martín and Matías Coca, in any case, could have involved more sweeping agrarian claims. Indians in San Pedro were at the time reportedly "seizing lands and all the haciendas in this valley under the specious rumors spread by their promoters that the landowners possessed the lands in bad faith, and that the lands are theirs."[55] Likewise, the priest of Macha noted that an Indian from San Pedro "published some decree establishing that the owners of the haciendas of that district had to go away and turn over the lands to the Indians of the community."[56]

Disturbances soon moved from the valley of San Pedro de Buena Vista to the highland district around the village of Chayanta. There, unlike the violent clashes in San Pedro, Pitunisa, Sacaca, and Acasio, the priests sheltered no caciques by early October. Some of the native lords of the Chayanta repartimiento had been already taken to Macha or had fled the area. The most prominent case was the Laymi-Puraca cacique Marcos Soto who was conducted to Macha at the same time that the Moscari cacique Florencio Lupa was being held there. Soto, a Laymi cacique appointed as Puraca chief sometime in the 1760s and a close ally of Florencio Lupa, had been among the native chiefs of the Chayanta repartimiento and of Aymaya and Panacachi who had denounced before the corregidor the Andean tributary customs in September 1770.[57] Ten years later, in early September 1780, it was the Laymi and Puraca commoners who denounced Soto's transgression of Andean norms regulating tribute collection, the mita system, religious festivals, and the use of common lands (comunes).[58] They did not appeal to Spanish officials, however, but to Tomás Katari. In Macha, they complained that in the course of his twenty-two years in office, "[Soto] had amassed a larger fortune than any of the gentlemen devoted to commerce (caballero de comercio)" and had dispatched part of the money he usurped "to the towns and cities to pay for lawyers, which makes him very arrogant."[59] Their demand for the replacement of Soto by an Indian named

Diego Chico reflected the egalitarian undertones of the movement. "We no longer want as our governor someone from whom we experienced so much mistreatment and levies," the Laymis contended, *we want instead someone who is from our own class and is chosen by the community*."[60]

Despite the fact that Soto and other caciques had already been removed, attacks on the Chayanta priest still occurred. On Sunday, October 8, a multitude of Indians, Diego Chico and Simón Castillo among them, confronted the priest of the Laymi parish, Vicente Berecochea, to demand the return of the tribute he had received from the former caciques. It was then publicly announced in the village that "nobody had to pay repartos, and those who had already done it could seek compensation from the corregidor's and his collectors' possessions; [the Indians] had also to go to the city [of La Plata] for the money of the Censos."[61] Later in the day, after a drinking spree, the Indians returned to the church and asked for a copy of the arancel so that it could be published. It must be noted that the highland parish of Chayanta had been one of the focal points of the wave of protests over church fees in the early 1770s.[62] Facing outright violence, Berecochea was forced to hand over the arancel, but as he himself acknowledged, he refused to promise compliance. According to one version of the story, he locked himself in his house and, speaking from a window, tried to calm down the Indians. In response, the Indians defiantly shouted, "curita . . . why don't you come down to lend obedience to your governor?"[63]

During the following week rebel Indians traveled through the hamlets alerting their peers from all the ethnic groups (Sicoya, Caracha, Chayantaca, Laymi, Puraca, and Chullpa) to the events of the following Sunday, when "great announcements" would be made. The Laymi priest was warned that next Sunday he was going to have to abide by the publication of the arancel, as his colleague from San Pedro de Buena Vista had just done. The Indians vowed to chase down Berecochea "even in the most hidden places."[64] Compensation for the forced distribution of goods was also expected. Juan Bautista Murillo, an associate of Joaquín Alós taken to Macha along with Marcos Soto in early September, had already written to the former corregidor that the Indians had arrested him and he had returned the reparto already collected.[65] Now, two other Chayanta residents linked to the forced sale of goods were also under close surveillance.[66] During the course of the week, Berecochea wrote in despair to a friend that the Indians wanted to seize "your effects, those of the corregidor, ours, and those of the rest of the Spaniards."[67] Eventually, fearing for his life, Berecochea managed to leave town before the weekend and ask asylum in Oruro. His departure was instrumental in preventing a major clash. On Sunday, October 15, a large gathering of Indians took place in the village and people blew horns, but no incidents occurred. Rather, Berecochea's assistant was compelled in the presence of the Indians to dispatch to the priest his personal belongings in order to reassure them that Berecochea would not return. Then, he wrote to the priest not to return.[68]

The reaction of the rural elites to the sweeping subversion of village power relations was vividly summed up in a letter that the parish priest of Sacaca, Idelfonso de Mina y Escobar, sent to Tomás Katari, whom local elites personally blamed, in large part wrongly so, for all the episodes related above. Having contended that parish priests were right in refusing to publish the arancel because they had already done so, the priest went on, saying: "Fall all the plagues upon you, for you are the cause of [all the trouble], as all the Indians are voicing it; the Indians, who are already more than four thousand, invaded this town and inside the church took away from my own hands, in the presence of Our Lord Transubstantiated, [Sacaca] governor Manuel Ayaviri, who was sick and suffering. Look at what they do! Be afraid of God! That you are mortal and when you expect it the less, God will throw you to hell for all the eternity."[69]

The Sacaca priest warned that these disturbances and the murder of Moscari cacique Florencio Lupa and others only called for vengeance, and concluded with a sarcasm that epitomizes all the anxieties brought about by the abrupt demise of colonial social hierarchies in the Andean villages: "Let me know how I must henceforth address you, because I want to exchange letters with you, if as Majesty, as Excellency, as Your Lord, so that I do not err since I ignore everything, and I only suffer in your name, all we suffer in our parish, and the priests of the valleys in theirs. So, I wait for your answer because it would be against reason that a man of such high qualities does not answer."[70]

INTERNAL DISSENSION

The notion that the assaults on the church and elite town-dwellers followed directives from the peasant leader was largely a misrepresentation. If the brief period under Tomás Katari's rule saw the collapse of colonial authority, it also revealed the limits of peasant political solidarity. This stemmed in part from the very evolution of the movement, which began as a routine judicial protest, turned into collective violence in the course of the battles for obtaining Katari's release, and then slid into a region-wide rebellion as numerous Andean communities rose up in revolt against rural overlords. Transitions from one stage to another made for a fluid and often ambiguous political situation, and the nature of Katari's leadership was not conducive to a more cohesive organization. After his death, he seemed to have been the object of religious devotion, but during his lifetime his power was both limited and contested. Although he commanded great prestige and, perhaps, growing messianic expectations, Katari did not, and could not, like Túpac Amaru, claim to be the reincarnation of the ancient Inca kings, or appear as a military chief of a full-fledge Indian army like Túpac Katari. Tomás Katari's aura and reputation far exceeded the boundaries of his community (and the province of Chayanta, for that matter), but his actual command over village political affairs outside Macha was shaky at best.

The calculated mix of disapproval and vindication with which Tomás Katari responded to the events in San Pedro de Buena Vista, Sacaca, or Chayanta is indicative of the conflicting internal dynamics of insurgent politics. Against contemporary official accounts, he strongly disavowed some of the actions. It seems evident that the massive attack on the priests and Spanish residents, as with the murder of Florencio Lupa earlier, put the conflict in a path to a situation that Katari was unwilling to embrace: a forthright confrontation with the colonial authorities. In reference to some of the disturbances, one of his letters stated: "What I know is that there are many Cataris [Kataris] to perform the greatest wrongdoings, and there is no reason why I must be responsible for somebody else's crimes."[71] Because the organizers of the assault on San Pedro de Buena Vista's church proclaimed that they had received instructions from Katari to carry out this action, he sent a missive to the Indians stating that he had not. He even denounced Sicoya leader Simón Castillo to the audiencia as a forastero "without occupation and of extremely bad behavior."[72] Manuel Ortuño, one of the closest associates of Castillo, received a special warning for having used a "false staff of authority [*bastón*]" to commit "serious offenses" against the priests and Spanish people.[73] While one can see the hand of Gregorio de Merlos behind these expressions, Katari's proclamations were not empty ones.[74] Nicolás Guaguari, the Sicoya cacique arrested in Macha, was released so that the Indians would restore to him his possessions. Katari told the audiencia that he had ordered the arrest of both Simón Castillo and Manuel Ortuño. Although it is not entirely clear whether the former was imprisoned, Ortuño was.[75] In a remarkable initiative given the political context, he dispatched the Sicoya Indian arrested to La Plata.[76]

The genuineness of Katari's opposition to the most exalted forms of collective violence against the priesthood is confirmed by the fact that, while he rejected the means, he made exceedingly clear that social outrage was entirely justified. Echoing past struggles, he wrote to the audiencia that the Indians "could not bear the yoke of the exaction of parish dues." For all his condemnation of Simón Castillo, Katari recognized that the Sicoya Indian had just been beaten because he had petitioned the publication of the arancel. Isidro Joseph de Herrera was indeed depicted as "friend, advisor, and director of Joaquín Alós."[77] Vicente Berecochea and Dionsio Córtes had fled their parishes of Laymi and Aymaya just for refusing to recognize the arancel. The Sacacas's violence against the priest's assistant, Antonio Dorado, had also stemmed from his "tyranny."[78] In more general terms, Katari wrote to the archbishop that "all the parish priests defend the corregidor and just want to persecute us and to bury our justice."[79] If Gregorio de Merlos encouraged Katari to condemn the assaults on the clergy, he himself had to abide by the indigenous demands. Just as in October 1771 the Machas had demanded the immediate publication of the arancel because several fiestas were forthcoming in their parish, now, in October 1780, Merlos was compelled to read out loud the arancel before mass.[80] A copy of it was fixed on the front door of the Macha church so that the Indians would be aware of its content.[81] Further, the Machas refused to fund two fiestas whose sponsors already had been selected a year earlier.[82]

Strife over political strategy became entangled with traditional sources of village factionalism. Even during insurgency times, engrained tensions between neighboring ethnic groups and moieties continued to shape peasant political behavior. The relationship between the Machas and Pocoatas and the behavior of Pocoata cacique Pedro Caypa during these months are cases in point. As analyzed in chapter 3, the rise of Caypa had provided a model of collective action for his Macha neighbors. The Pocoatas, including his cacique, were then actively involved in the revolt in the village of Pocoata on August 26, 1780.[83] Machas and Pocoatas routinely engaged in tinkus, Andean forms of ceremonial warfare meant to work out social tensions by reestablishing equilibrium and harmonic relations between neighboring groups.[84] Fears that ritual battles between both groups could be directed, under such exceptional political circumstances, against a common enemy were exposed by Manuel Alvarez Villarroel, the chief of the militia of Aullagas, a mining town at the heart of Macha and Pocoata ethnic territories. He reported that there were rumors that on September 29, during the feast of the archangel San Miguel (the patron saint of Aullagas village), Indians would assault the village, taking advantage of the fact "that they always come to [the feast] to perform the custom they have that that day the Indians of the towns of Macha and Pocoata stone each other, [but] getting together on this occasion they will finish off all the Spanish and mestizo people who opposed their insolence."[85]

Notwithstanding the actual and potential bases of cooperation between both communities, Pedro Caypa and the Pocoatas in general were in a uniquely delicate predicament. If as the leader of a protest movement akin to that of the Machas and many other Andean communities he remained a respected figure (at a time when native lords were widely persecuted, not a single complaint against Pedro Caypa surfaced), he seemed also reluctant to risk his hard-won standing as a well-established cacique by appearing to be involved in a mass upheaval. Thus, barely one week after the Pocoata battle, Caypa asked the Protector of Indians of Chayanta to receive testimonies that showed the supposed lack of involvement of the Pocoatas in the disturbances.[86] To prove that, he personally journeyed to La Plata one week later.[87] But his gestures of cooperation evoked no sympathy from the Spanish magistrates: Caypa was arrested as soon as he set foot in the city. As the Pocoatas began to show signs of distress with the arrest of their cacique, one of Alós's successors, Juan Antonio de Acuña, tried to use village factionalism for his own ends.[88] After speaking with Caypa through the jail bars he urged the court to release him, arguing that the cacique could serve as counterweight to Tomás Katari.[89] Although the audiencia rejected the proposal, Acuña's maneuver might have paid off anyway. Later on, when the official entered the valley village of Carasi where a group of Macha Indians seemed determined to physically attack him, "seeing this, a principal Indian of Pocoata told them that if they did not restrain themselves, the Machas and Pocoatas would have to step aside because the war would be between them; at which they calmed down."[90] Interethnic tension did not result in violence this time, but eventually it would. Following the failed assault on the city of La Plata in February 1781, the Pocoatas would submit dozens of Macha rebels to the Charcas officials.

As for Pedro Caypa, finding himself in an impossible predicament between increasingly rebellious Indians and hostile Spanish rulers he appealed in the end to what had proved so effective in past years: the logic of the tributary state. In November 1780, he sent from prison to Viceroy Vértiz the entire record of his successful undertakings to augment tribute monies between 1776 and 1778, and he offered to produce even more increases if allowed to escort an impartial official in a general recount of the province.[91] Yet, as other tribute-abiding rebel Indians would learn, in times of insurgency the pact of reciprocity with the state no longer applied. For all his past economic services to the crown, his spontaneous travel to La Plata to probe his lack of involvement in the disturbances, and his ensuing vows of political loyalty, Pedro Caypa would remain in jail. And then, once the rebellion was effectively suppressed, he would be publicly executed.[92]

Internal fault lines within the Andean society were felt even more severely within the very ethnic group of Macha. Ironically, whereas Tomás Katari's reputation was steadily expanding, his leadership role was disputed within his own community. There, disputes over issues of political solidarity seemingly stemmed from traditional rivalries between Anansaya and Urinsaya. As we have seen, in obtaining the replacement of their native authorities by Pascual Chura (Anansaya) and Salvador Torres (Urinsaya), Machas from both moieties had mobilized together between June and August 1780. Nonetheless, as the moieties had separate ethnic chiefs, the extraordinary prominence achieved by Tomás Katari bred political strife. Thus, in the first week of September when the audiencia's decree appointing Tomás Katari as cacique principal was read out loud in the village of Macha, Indians from Anansaya refused to recognize it, shouting that they wanted Pascual Chura, not an Indian of Urinsaya, as their ethnic chief.[93] The priest tried to mediate by organizing a meeting in his house between Pascual Chura, Tomás Katari, and Salvador Torres, but the result was only a heated exchange of insults and threats.[94] On September 9, Pascual Chura and eight Indians principales of Anansaya wrote to the audiencia, wondering "how could it be, Sir, that pertaining the chieftanship [*cacicazgo*] to us by heritage, a foreign Indian from a different ayllu could pretend to govern us?"[95] Having one single ruler, the Anansaya principales added a week later, was unacceptable because the ayllus were greatly scattered and "disputes and issues among us are daily and continuous, especially over the distribution of lands."[96]

Colonial authorities were able to take full advantage of internal rivalries within the peasant society. In early September, following audiencia attorney Juan del Pino Manrique's request to find out "if among them [the Indian rebels] and their parcialidades there is any kind of disunion or disagreement that could be fomented, because once divided they could be more easily subjected," Aullagas miner Manuel Alvarez Villarroel stated that the current strife between both Macha moieties could serve well these ends.[97] He was right; thus, Pascual Chura, although hitherto one of the main insurgent leaders, told Alvarez Villarroel and Macha priest Gregorio Merlos that he was ready to mobilize the Anansaya Indians to defend the mining town in case of attacks.[98] Then, in early October, Pascual Chura, with the support of the Aullagas's priest, Roque Burgoa, and Alvarez Villarroel, confronted Tomás Katari as Indians from both moieties met at the Rosario, a mine and refinery within the Macha territory owned by Alvarez Villarroel. While information on the incident is contradictory, it is clear that Katari's political legitimacy was publicly called into question.[99] In consolidating their alliance with Spanish authorities, some Anansaya Indians also offered protection for one of the corregidores appointed by the audiencia at the time, Domingo Anglés.[100] In mid-October, Anansaya's segunda persona, Juan Pirapi, traveled to La Plata to demand the appointment of Chura and himself as ethnic chiefs. He contended that Tomás Katari "has infected the private province by proclaiming that he alone is the true governor because he has a title from this royal audiencia, and he alone deserves this distinction, with which artifice he tries to attract those who remain indifferent. Since this argument had made a strong impression, most Indians had decided to follow Katari adamantly."[101] As expected, the audiencia did not hesitate to issue immediately the title of cacique to Pascual Chura.[102] The title was publicly read in the village of Macha on October 29. This time, it was the Indians loyal to Katari, and the peasant leader himself, who expressed their dissatisfaction and uttered threats directed at the Anansaya chief.[103]

The extraordinarily menacing tone that the Aymara leader adopted when referring to these episodes speaks to the perceived gravity of internal dissension. He urged the archbishop of Charcas to dismiss the Aullaga priest on the basis that Burgoa exposed himself to an assault, "because it is very apparent the daring of some Indians, who I would not say live in a state of outrage, but are very sensitive at being offended."[104] In reference to the clashes with the Anansaya's caciques, Katari warned the audiencia that if the court did not prevent the Indians from being provoked "with threats and challenges . . . *the Kingdom will be lost.*"[105] Hostility would eventually translate into violence. Pascual Chura suggested that if colonial authorities provided assistance to both the Anansaya Indians of Macha and those of Pocoata, they could "bring arrested [to La Plata] the intruder Indian Tomás Katari, who keep correspondence with Indians of other provinces, where pillages, violence, and loss of respect to the priests are conducted in his name."[106] This was more than mere rhetoric. In December, when Tomás Katari was arrested, ethnic chiefs from the Anansaya ayllus of Macha and from Pocoata would be called on to defend Aullagas, where the Aymara leader was being held. A few weeks afterward, Pascual Chura himself would pay with his life for his collaboration with the Spanish rulers.

THE COLONIAL PACT REASSESSED:
A JOURNEY THROUGH THE CHAYANTA VALLEYS

By the time Túpac Amaru was launching his rebellion in the town of Tinta in early November 1781, the northern Potosí communities were two months into a unique experience in self-rule prompted by the expelling of the corregidor. The wave of protest that swept away the power of the former corregidor and illegitimate Andean chiefs swept with it the political and social preeminence of parish priests and Spanish elite town-dwellers. Yet, as much as the Andean peasants worked to overthrow the institutions of local government and prepared themselves against a possible punitive expedition, they never cut off their links with the colonial state. Katari and other Indians sent more than forty letters to the audiencia magistrates, the archbishop of Charcas, treasury officials, the governor of Potosí, the viceroy of Buenos Aires, and even the Spanish king. Also flowing from the insurgent-controlled territories were peasants wanting to testify before the audiencia and petitions for the issuance of a general pardon. Moreover, at least one particularly unruly Indian was arrested and sent to the La Plata court jail. Equally significant, even though the structure of authority in the countryside had completely vanished, rebel communities expressed no resistance to dispatch the tribute. On September 28 Katari, along with the other authorities of Anansaya and Urinsaya, Pascual Chura and Salvador Torres, sent to the audiencia 2,595 pesos, 339 pesos more than the current official assessment.[107] Therefore, even at the height of mass rebellion, as Katari had repeatedly promised, the Macha communities increased the tributes. By mid-October, Diego Chico, the rebel leader of Laymi-Puraca who had replaced Marcos Soto, also delivered 1,566 pesos 5 reales,[108] and so did the Moscari peasants, who were responsible for the most obvious act of defiance thus far.[109] The new cacique, Diego Yugra, one of the participants in Florencio Lupa's murder, then asked the audiencia the official validation of his title: while lacking, as he put it, the "qualities" (i.e., noble lineage) of the deceased cacique, the community had chosen him and, as the delivering of tribute showed, he was a crown's loyal vassal.[110]

By October 1780 the Charcas authorities began to change their counterinsurgency policies. Even a stanch supporter of the audiencia's jurisdiction (and therefore a sharp opponent of the viceroy's envoy, Ignacio Flores), such as audiencia attorney Juan del Pino Manrique, argued that he had hitherto supported the suppression of the insurrection through military force, thereby endorsing the policies advocated by corregidor Alós and other audiencia ministers, just because "he had not seen what was behind all these machinations." He had realized his mistake "now that we have seen the [Indians'] demand of pardon . . . that the Indians had effectively delivered the tribute and that they will likely unify themselves and act with desperation when seen surrounded by armed men."[111] No doubt the sheer breath and scale of the Indian uprising must have also reassessed the feasibility of a military solution. In any event, following the guidelines laid out by Manrique (whom rebel Indians would later call the "fiscal king"), the court called off plans to send out soldiers to the province. It was imperative to arrest "the heads of the riot," whatever they might say or do to show subordination, but this had to be conducted "without noise and fanfare."[112]

The man entrusted with implementing this policy was Juan Antonio de Acuña, who owned a hacienda in the valley of Guaycoma, near Macha territories, and who was a former corregidor of the neighboring province of Yamparáez. He was the first Spanish provincial magistrate to reside in Chayanta after the expulsion of Joaquín de Alós. Two previous corregidores had refused to assume the post because of indigenous opposition. One of them, Domingo Anglés, had traveled to the province but decided to return to La Plata as soon as he saw the mood of the Indians who were waiting for him in the village of Ocurí.[113] Acuña was certainly an unlikely candidate for the post. He had participated in the repression of the Machas before the Pocoata battle, and shortly after the battle, a multitude of Indians — "hungry wolves," he dubbed them — surrounded his estate, suspicious that soldiers were being hidden there. When notified of his appointment, Tomás Katari claimed that Acuña was unacceptable because "he is a decided enemy of the Indians and Alós's close friend"; his appointment, he warned, "made us think that our Father and Lord the King has abandoned us."[114]

As a landowner in an overwhelmingly indigenous area and as a former corregidor, Acuña was keenly sensitive to established forms of deference, honor, and social hierarchy. During moments of great political turmoil, before and shortly after the battle of Pocoata, he had taken pains in noting that the Indians showed him due respect and "did not dare to insult me, from what they have not spared even their priests."[115] His brief tenure would teach him how weeks of mass unrest had radically transformed the relations between rulers and ruled in the Andean villages.

It should be noted that in reasserting some measure of state control in the countryside, Acuña would not be able to resort to any display of force. Despite that he had asked for a large retinue, the audiencia compelled him to travel to the province escorted by just five soldiers, and to be dressed in civilian clothes so as to not further agitate the already voluble demeanor of the Indians.[116] Acuña had at his disposal one political resource alone: the public announcement of the much-demanded edict establishing a general pardon for the rebel Indians. Certainly, neither the audiencia magistrates (who secretly instructed Acuña to seek a means of arresting Tomás Katari and his associates) nor the Indians believed in the sincerity of the amnesty. Nonetheless, in the political culture of the Andean colonial world public ceremony was an indispensable vehicle through which colonizers and colonized recognized their standing in the social order and their relation with the symbolic guarantors of that order, the king and the Christian God. As is so often the case in times of insurgency, symbolic actions that might appear perfunctory or uneventful in normal times are suddenly invested with great political significance.[117] Furthermore, as we learned from past clashes, a pardon for the northern Potosí peasants meant something radically different from Spanish notions: it did not imply admission of guilt but rather recognition of gains—economic, political, and otherwise. The need for this public ritual, the lack of trust of it, and, further, its deeply ambiguous significance would all be acted out in the interactions of the Indians with Antonio Acuña, the last corregidor before colonial ceremonies, and the social order underneath them, no longer mattered.

In mid-November Acuña undertook a journey through the Chayanta valleys where the peasants resided at this time of the year for the sowing of grain. The justicia mayor began his journey in the valley of Guaycoma, where on November 5 he issued for the first time a general pardon from the audiencia.[118] Three days later, from his hacienda, he sent a letter to his "dear son, don Tomás Katari." There he assured the rebel leader that he wanted to be a "father" for the Indians, as compared to the "military envoys who, because they are trained for war, commit violence and look for immediate solutions regardless of the damage that violence engenders." Paternalism notwithstanding, he took pains in reminding Katari that the crimes being pardoned by the audiencia were "enormous."[119] Acuña could not possibly foresee at the time that in less than two months he and Katari would be killed together, the peasant leader at his own hands, he at the hands of the Indian crowd. But their mutual distrust became evident from their first encounter: the peasant leader came to the meeting, which took place in Carasi, a multiethnic valley inhabited by Machas, Pocoatas, Laymis, and Puracas—accompanied by a multitude of Indians even though Acuña had asked him to attend the meeting with no more than twelve men. The justicia mayor reported that he told Katari that he could not continue receiving Indians from other provinces who came to "lend him their obedience as if he were the sovereign."[120] Yet, knowing that his letters would be widely read by different factions within the colonial administration, he remained silent as to what the Indians had to say in response. In any event, we know that after a round of talks in the morning, the general pardon was publicly announced. Then, the Indians returned some goods from the former corregidor, and a *misa de gracias* (mass of gratitude) was celebrated with "much pomp" in the church of the Carasi village.

As far as the Andean communities were concerned, however, this event was not the end of the ceremony. In Guancarani, a hamlet in route to the village of Micani, Acuña's next destination, more than one hundred peasants armed with their slings met the justicia mayor and his five-man guard. Acuña argued that he had prevented a massacre by advancing alone toward the crowd and commanding his escorts not to fire their guns under any circumstances; however, the Indians did not intend to kill him but rather compel the full implementation of the pardon, such as they understood it. Katari invited Acuña to sit down, then he handed him "petitions from several Indians, which they wanted me to approve right away," the justicia mayor recalled. These petitions, as we can infer from the rest of Acuña's tour, must have dealt with the appointment of new ethnic authorities, the enforcement of tribute exemptions, and perhaps the lowering of the repartos that former corregidor Alós had been compelled to issue when arrested in Macha. After their claims were addressed, the Indians offered chicha to Acuña and his soldiers, a gesture aimed at showing the demise of social hierarchies (chicha was a consumption culturally associated with the Andean people) and symbolically reaffirming Acuña's commitment to his rulings.[121] This offering, on the other hand, was matched by a symbolic gesture of a very different order: while the crowd was surrounding Acuña, some Indians made the point of seizing a shotgun and a sword from the soldiers. Yet, they offered no resistance when the justicia mayor asked them to return the weapons.

At the beginning of his tour, Acuña had warned the Indians to stop carrying slings and clubs, and to cease gathering in the highways and registering travelers. Groups of about two hundred Indians, nevertheless, watched from the hills as the justicia mayor and his retinue walked to Micani. He also discovered by then that Simón Castillo and other rebels had registered some luggage he had dispatched from La Plata, and they only returned it when they assured that no arms were being transported. To Acuña's dismay, neither the priest nor his assistants came to receive him when he arrived in Micani. Rather, he was met by two Indians, who were not precisely in a deferential mood. They "turned out to be even worse than Katari," he commented. Indeed, the peasants demanded at once to be appointed as caciques, and they handed him written petitions from their respective communities (Micani was populated by Pocoatas, Chullpas, Laymis, and Carachas). Although Acuña did not say what his response was, there is little doubt that he conceded.[122]

In Micani, Acuña would also have to concede a reduction of tributes, but this concession had nothing to do with the version put forward by former corregidor Alós and other authorities—namely, that Katari made the Indians believe that he had received a decree from the viceroy establishing a decrease of the tasas (head tax). Acuña reported that after listening to the reading of the general pardon in the village of Micani, the Indians refused to relinquish their belief in a reduction of tribute. The next Sunday, however, it became clear that their belief was not related to a decrease in the tasas, and that the decree supporting it was not related to Katari's deception. After mass, a huge crowd of Indians (yet surely smaller than the four thousand natives Acuña estimated) handed him a copy of a decree issued by Viceroy Conde de la Monclova in 1692 freeing mita workers from tribute payments. The Indians told the justicia mayor that the mitayos did not pay tribute in the past, but one of the caciques whom they had just removed had started demanding it seven years ago. Although northern Potosí peasants had in fact begun to voice this grievance since at least the late 1750s, it was in the early 1770s when, in the context of general assaults on Andean tribute practices, the caciques of some of the groups inhabiting the Micani valley explicitly stated the need to uproot this tax exemption.[123] Coincidentally, just a few weeks earlier while bringing their cacique, Marcos Soto, to Macha, the Laymis had complained that he charged 10 pesos to the "unhappy mitayos . . . when elsewhere the mitayos do not pay tributes during his yearly turn in Potosí. [Soto] has introduced this custom, which did not exist with his antecessors."[124]

At first, Acuña resisted proclaiming the validity of the 1692 decree, but he had again to acquiesce to indigenous demands. Later in the day, as he described,

> in view of the demeanor of the Indians who were inclined to kill me and my retinue, I decided right away to climb to the top of an oven for baking bread — which was the most elevated spot in this plaza — and tell them from there: "the order of his Excellency [Viceroy Conde de la Monclova] must be obeyed." And I also said, "Long Live the King," which all the people repeated with much rejoicing. The Indians, then, carried me in their arms from the oven to my room, kissing my hands and feet, and hugging me. After that, they left me alone.[125]

This episode encapsulates remarkably the politics of insurgency in this Andean region. At a formal level, it featured once more less an inversion of colonial power — the Indians taking on the role of the rulers, "the world turned upside down," as did many other instances of peasant rebellion in other places and times — than it did mimicry: the Indians forcing a Spanish official to exercise his authority on their own terms (Hill 1972; Guha 1983: chap. 2). And as for the content of the claims, despite the repeated allegations of regional elite groups, after this odd ceremony of colonial power took place the Indians vowed "to deliver promptly the tribute they still owed and to be subordinated and obedient to the royal justice, returning the possessions they had seized from the Spanish residents and the caciques they had deposed."[126] The importance of the exemption of mitayos and ritual sponsors for the Andean communities, as opposed to the reduction of the tasas, was underlined by the same justicia mayor, who warned the audiencia that, whether or not the 1692 ruling was still valid, this demand needed to be addressed. Otherwise, brute force would be the sole available resource to restore order.

San Pedro de Buena Vista was the last village reached by Acuña. What the justicia mayor found there was even more dismal. When he arrived in San Pedro during the last week of November, many Spanish residents were lodged in the church or in the house of the priest, Isidro Joseph de Herrera. One of the deposed native chiefs under the priest's protection, Esteban Callisaya of the group Sicoya, recalled that he had expected that the justicia mayor would restore some "respect" for authority and release the peasants "from their blind faith in the thief Indian Tomás Katari."[127] None of this materialized. In fact, a harsh exchange of missives between Acuña and Simón Castillo, the main rebel leader in this area, took place even before the justicia mayor and the Sicoya Indian met. As soon as Acuña arrived in San Pedro, Castillo communicated to him that "all the [Spanish] neighbors [of San Pedro de Buena Vista] are in arms against the royal treasury, and if this is so we thus cannot receive your justice because all this [affair] has to be meanness; excuse my impertinence, and I wait for your answer."[128] Acuña wrote him back stating, "I'm not a man with two faces" (i.e., a "father" and "military envoy"), and he invited the Sicoya Indian to come to talk to him "and I will be very glad to address all the matters of justice."[129] This, Simón Castillo was ready to accept. Accompanied by two hundred Indians, he met the justicia mayor in the village. Reflecting the state of affairs in the area, Acuña seems not even to have tried to resist indigenous demands or even to pretend to have done it. He just noted that in order to appease the Indians he needed to appoint caciques at their wish and to issue "other rulings." We know what those other unspecified rulings were: an expansion of what the ethnic groups inhabiting the valley of Micani had already forced him to sanction. The justicia mayor, in effect, was compelled publicly to proclaim that "three tribute quotas must be returned to the Indians [mitayos] who went to Potosí and the mayordomos of the Church." This, of course, did not make things any easier for the already battered former native lords. As a result of this ruling, "all the Indians have stirred up even more violently, crying out that all the former caciques of this province must return to the Indians all the money they have unjustly collected and stolen in the course of their tenures."[130] Esteban Callisaya, not surprisingly, did not share Acuña's portrayal of the success of his mission. He laconically remarked that, against his expectations, the arrival of the justica mayor had in fact "left matters in even worse shape."[131]

Although the Indians had hardly displayed any sign of repentance for their actions, or even deference for the justicia mayor's public persona, Acuña reportedly proceeded to pardon and honor Castillo and his peers as he did with the rest of the peasants. The rebels then returned some expropriated goods, and both Indians and Spaniards made the gesture of pardoning each other. The profound ambivalence of the event was punctuated by still another element: Isidro Joseph de Herrera, the priest whom the Indians had violently confronted some weeks earlier, was asked by Castillo to witness the ceremony in which indigenous claims were sanctioned and pardon was declared.[132] But the next time that Castillo and Herrera would appear together in the historical record the circumstances, and the outcome, would be very different: the most massive massacre in the history of this Andean valley counted Herrera among its first victims.

A LOST KINGDOM

Having experienced what the institutions of government had been reduced to, Juan Antonio de Acuña spent most of the remaining weeks of 1780 in the mining center of Aullagas, the main Spanish stronghold within the province. As news from the great insurrection in Cuzco began to reach the southern Andes, the situation must have looked more and more ominous. In late November, Acuña stated his belief that all the provinces of the viceroyalty would eventually rise up together. He might have been alluding to a connection with Túpac Amaru or to the most obvious fact that indigenous agitation, when not outright revolt, was mushrooming across the neighboring provinces. In either case, the likelihood that Tomás Katari would turn from mediator between the Indians and the state into an alternative source of sovereignty—whatever form this presumed political development might have assumed—was tangible. In the wake of the Pocoata battle, Indians from the Paria communities of Condocondo, Toledo, Challacollo, and Challapata rose up against their ethnic lords.[133] Most of these communities had members residing in haciendas or in the ayllu lands of Chayanta, and they had traveled to Macha to consult with Tomás Katari. Paria corregidor Bodega y Llano, who in early 1781 would be killed by the Indians, argued that "[Tomás Katari] is the oracle whom the natives of these provinces consult on their doubts and questions."[134] In the province of Porco, an ayllu of the Tinquipaya community, located in the boundary markers (*mojones*) with Macha, was the first to assault the cacique.[135] Indians from the Porco community of Coroma, following Katari's recommendation, replaced their cacique with one "of their entire confidence," and then proceeded to deliver the tributes directly to the royal treasury, as the Machas had done before. When the new Coroma chief was arrested in Potosí, he explained that they lent obedience to a cacique of another province because "among the Indians it is known that Katari had brought some rulings that benefited them, especially regarding repartos; and for this reason everybody respects him and views him as superior."[136] Not in vain, then, Acuña warned Tomás Katari that to receive "Indians from other provinces who come to the town of Macha to pay him obedience as if he was sovereign . . . was an extremely grave crime because it amounted to usurping the right to the Sovereign."[137] The peasant leader, in turn, addressed Spanish officials, including the viceroy of the Río de la Plata and the Spanish king, as his humble vassal but also as de facto governor of this Andean region. If the Spanish rulers failed to recognize the legitimacy of the Indians' demands, he warned, "the Kingdom will be lost."

And the kingdom eventually was lost. In mid-December, despite the proclamation of the general pardon, the chief of the Aullagas militia, Manuel Alvarez Villarroel, arrested Tomás Katari as he was collecting tributes around the area of the Rosario mine. His *amanuense* (clerk), Isidro Serrano, was seized as well. Although no official order of capture had been issued, Alvarez Villarroel followed the secret instructions of the audiencia, which were unknown even to Ignacio Flores who supposedly held exclusive jurisdiction over such matters. The fact that at this time of the year most of the Indians were working their valley lands may explain why just a small retinue accompanied Katari when he was captured, and why no immediate attempts at releasing him occurred other than several petitions to Acuña to set him free. Knowing that a massive assault on the town was just a matter of time, Alvarez Villarroel summoned to Aullagas the potential foes of Tomás Katari within the Andean society, the Machas from the Anansaya moiety and the Pocoatas. However, his success was partial at best: only Pascual Chura, his assistants, and some native authorities from Pocoata answered his call. Although Alvarez Villarroel seemingly believed that the reason for the low response was that the peasants were in the valleys, it would soon become apparent that internal rivalries did not nearly suffice to counter the mass outrage unleashed by the arrest of the Indian leader.[138]

In the first week of January 1781 Juan Antonio Acuña made the decision to conduct Katari to the city of La Plata. Escorted by a small guard (the Spanish militia, Alvarez Villarroel included, decided to stay in Aullagas to protect the mining center), the justicia mayor tried to avoid Indian attacks by undertaking secondary paths. On January 8, however, in a narrow ravine near the town of Quilaquila in the province of Yamparáez, a multitude of peasants from both Yamparáez and Chayanta, including men, women, and even children, ambushed the small party. After the first skirmish, seeing himself in a hopeless situation, Acuña proceeded to kill both Tomás Katari and Isidro Serrano. The Indians then stoned to death the justicia mayor and his retinue. As in other rebel areas at the time, the Indians took the clothes of the dead Spanish soldiers and left the bodies unburied as a sign of their beastly, devilish nature (Szeminski

1987: 170). They also pierced the eyes of Acuña's corpse "so that they had him taken by the Devils," as one of the assailants put it.[139]

The bodies of Tomás Katari and Isidro Serrano were taken to a hamlet near the village of Quilaquila. During the night, the bodies, with the stocks still on their feet, were mourned in the house of some of the Indians who had taken part in the assault. The Indians drank chicha and conducted Andean rituals that sources succinctly render as "superstitions." The next day the bodies were brought to the village of Quilaquila, where the parish priest gave them a Christian burial in the cemetery of the church (Andrade 1994: 132–33).

A Christian burial it might have been, but what Christianity was supposed to signify in this context would thereafter be fought over in the churches and on the bodies of Catholic priests, their Spanish parishioners, and other Andean peasants' foes. In the wake of the battle of Pocoata, Tomás Katari had vowed that if the Spanish officials dispatched soldiers to punish them, "we will have to retreat to the land of heretics, not only the Indians from Chayanta but also those from the rest of the provinces of this Kingdom."[140] "The land of heretics," of course, was nothing but a well-understood euphemism for the Indians' willingness to defend to the end their hard-won achievements and to rebuff if not a Christian order then their colonial rulers' version of it. Into this symbolic land of heretics, the southern Andes would indeed turn after Tomás Katari's death.

AFTER THE DEATH OF TOMÁS KATARI, Indian insurrection in Chayanta shifted from attacks on particularly exploitative figures to a generic onslaught on the agents and symbols of colonial power. Led by Tomás's brothers, Dámaso and Nicolás Katari, the Andean peasants wielded complete control over the countryside, established regular communications with rebellious communities in Paria, Porco, and Yamparáez, and marched on the city of La Plata, threatening to kill the entire population. Then, in the valley of San Pedro de Buena Vista, hundreds of Spanish and mestizo residents, including several priests, were massacred inside the church. Only by late March, as repression and internal divisions within the Andean communities deepened, did mass mobilization recede.

No doubt this shift toward anticolonial warfare was linked to developments outside the region. By the time Tomás Katari was murdered, the upheaval led by Túpac Amaru in the Cuzco region was already in full swing. Indigenous forces took control of large areas of southern Peru, from Paucartambo and Quispicanchis to the provinces bordering Lake Titicaca. In early January, rebel troops headed by Túpac Amaru embarked on their most daring military operation: the siege of the city of Cuzco. Peasant communities across the region, often ignoring directives from the insurgent command, assaulted rural villages, Spanish haciendas, and textile mills — targeting white people in general, whether Spanish or creole. The scale of the movement reflected its ideological breath. Túpac Amaru presented himself, and was perceived by his indigenous followers, as a new Inca king. These messianic expectations were accompanied by millennial beliefs that the expelling of white people from the Andes was part of a new cosmological era in which the Catholic God was bound to lose his prominence.[1] By the first weeks of 1781, no Spanish or indigenous person living in the territory of the old viceroyalty of Peru must have remained unaware that a vibrant anticolonial uprising aimed at rebuilding the Tawantinsuyu was sweeping the Andean world.

Whereas the expectations awakened by the emergence of a neo-Inca movement greatly influenced the course of events in northern Potosí, the embracing of messianic expectations was rooted in a discrete history of contention. By early 1781, northern Potosí peoples had exhausted their hopes of transforming the regional structures of political and economic power through the traditional repertoire of violence and compromises. The unwillingness of colonial rulers to recognize the new state of political affairs, epitomized in the arrest and execution of Tomás Katari, must have nurtured the belief that solely through mass upheaval would a lasting social transformation be achieved. What the emergence of a neo-Inca uprising did was to endow Aymara peasants with a seemingly political alternative, with a powerful emblem that could be opposed to a social order in apparent disarray. A native, indigenous king could replace a too-distant, too-powerless Spanish monarch. Ideally, if not practically in any meaningful way, a revolutionary situation of "multiple sovereignty," to borrow Charles Tilly's (1978: chap. 7) definition, took root. When asked why the Indians wanted to seize the city of La Plata under the banner of Túpac Amaru, Dámaso Katari explained that, "as Túpac Amaru was native of this country, he was of the same nature as they are; and as they inhabited these lands from the beginning all have served for [Dámaso] and his partners as an incentive and driving force. They believed that by offering their alliance and by seeing by himself their misery, [Túpac Amaru] would redress their hardships, being also thankful for all their effort in advancing his cause."[2]

This crisis of ideological legitimacy matched a crisis of the perceived coercive capability of the colonial state. If a new political order seemed desirable, it seemed increasingly attainable as well. In the course of the small and large confrontations described in chapters 4 and 5, implicit assumptions of the military superiority of the European rulers began to crumble. Colonial relations, needless to say, invested a great deal of symbolism in the phenomenon of violence. As normalized in routine state rituals and Catholic festivals, the victory of the Spanish invaders was regarded not just as an instrument for imposing alien governmental institutions but as an epiphany of cultural supremacy. In a society whose founding myth was a successful act of war—a military invasion—calling into question the coercive might of the government was, in some fundamental regard, the undoing of the discourse of the conquest. Certainly, despite the crucial symbolic role of violence in this society, in practical terms the colonial regime in the southern Andes never mounted a military force capable of establishing tight control over the peasant communities,[3] and rural insurgency made this visible. Since winter 1780 the Indians faced no major obstacles in controlling the circulation of people and goods within the province, organizing massive gatherings and prevailing in virtually every armed clash with rural ruling groups. A successful uprising allowed Tomás Katari to become the de facto provincial governor. In the ensuing weeks, social unrest expanded from one community to another, within and outside Chayanta, without significant resistance. As the material foundations of the Spanish regime proved fallible, its basic ideological assumptions must have appeared increasingly disputable, too.

In brief, as James Scott (1985: 333) has put it, "the deroutinezation of daily life, in which the normal categories with which social reality is apprehended no longer apply, appears to be as important as material deprivation in creating the social soil for millennial activity." Nicolás Katari explained that the collective decision to confront local authorities first, and the colonial order as a whole afterward, stemmed from the fact that the Indians, "confident in the protection from other summoned provinces, came to believe that they were capable of sustaining their undertakings, achieving many advantages; and as they received at the time information about Túpac Amaru, and that he had been crowned as King, a renewed enthusiasm emerged in recognizing him as such and paying him obedience, without hesitating to live under his domination, with fewer hardships, which could be accomplished if they finished off all the Spaniards."[4]

REBELS INTO WARRIORS

Between the killing of Tomás Katari on January 7, 1781, and the siege of La Plata five weeks later peasant unrest in northern Potosí evolved into anticolonial war. For the Andean communities this transition from rebels to warriors was an exceedingly complex process. Ideally, this process amounted to a shift from actions aimed at reshaping rural power relationships and state policies to actions aimed at uprooting the foundations of the old order. This is precisely what insurgent Andean peasants in the Cuzco region and then in the area of La Paz did by attacking the colonists' economic assets (haciendas, textile mills, rural villages); by killing those who actually or potentially opposed the rebellion (most white people, in practice); and by seeking to destroy the Spanish armies. In northern Potosí, revolutionary nativist projects seemed to coexist, and overlap, with engrained notions that the indigenous communities could gain control over the institutions of local government by drastically reconstituting the colonial pact with the Spanish king and his agents in the Andes. During the weeks prior to the siege of La Plata, collective mobilizations showed a great deal of radicalization in their levels of violence, regional scope, and challenge to religious and political symbols of colonial rule. The nature of the uprising inexorably turned the conflict into an all-or-nothing affair. Northern Potosí peasants, however, never seemed to abandon altogether their own brand of Andean utopianism: the idea that Spanish domination could somehow be refashioned as to conform to the ayllus' moral economy and principles of political legitimacy.

In the wake of Tomás Katari's death, indigenous communities' conscious or tacit engagement in radical revolutionary politics could be followed through two types of initiatives: retaliation and abolition of some colonial exactions. In order to avenge the murder of the Aymara leader, the Indians finally undertook an action that Spanish residents had feared ever since the battle of Pocoata: a massive assault on the mining town of Aullagas, the bulwark of Spanish resistance in the province. During the second week of January hundreds of peasants convened in the place where Tomás Katari had been seized and held prisoner. Most of the Indians from Macha and the neighboring communities of Ocurí and Pitantora were convoked by Nicolás Katari and Sebastián Colque, an Anansaya Indian actively involved in previous initiatives.[5] In other cases, the mobilization was more or less spontaneous, because "it consisted just of a simple notice, as happened with the four hundred from Condo [Paria province] who just came because some Indians who were selling coca leaves told them of the Tomás Katari's imprisonment."[6] Their prime objective was to capture the main person responsible for their leader's death, the chief of the Aullagas militia, Manuel Alvarez Villarroel, and to do this assailant forces would stop at nothing. "The only voice heard," Alvarez Villarroel himself reported in one of his final letters, "has been this: *since our king Catari died, let us all die killing*."[7] The peasants laid siege to the town for about a week and set fire to the house and silver refining facilities owned by Alvarez Villarroel; after fierce battles the Spanish militias and the Indian mining workers (*coyarunas*) were forced to take shelter in the church. Eventually, as the Andean communities threatened to burn down the church, the coyarunas walked out and agreed to turn Villarroel over to the peasants. Andean forms of reciprocity helped to cement the alliance between the mining workers and the peasants: on January 23, after a collective consumption of coca and chicha, the coyarunas took Alvarez Villarroel from his place of captivity in a mine and brought him to a nearby hill named Anconaza. There, in the presence of Nicolás Katari, he was beaten to death. His body, like Florencio Lupa's before, was beheaded, and his possessions, including more than 6,000 pesos, silver, clothes, and coca leaves, were then distributed among the assailants.[8]

As the attack on Aullagas was unfolding, several other acts of retribution took place. In the village of Macha, the Indians captured and murdered the main foe of Tomás Katari within the ethnic group, the Anansaya cacique Pascual Chura. Chura had sought refuge in the church along with the others, but the Andean peasants did not hesitate this time to violate the most prominent symbol of religious authority. On January 20, indigenous men and women stormed into the church, dragged out the Anansaya cacique, and put him to death. One week later, they again invaded the church, this time to arrest the wife of Santos Cárdenas, "who the Indians loathed because he was an alcabala collector," as well as a prominent Indian of Anansaya, Dionisio Chura, who had been the target of collective violence during the confrontations in the valley between June and August 1780.[9] Both individuals were then executed. Meanwhile, Indians persecuted two other former native lords of Macha: Pablo Chávez of the ayllu Majacollana (Urinsaya) and Roque Sánchez Morato, a former cacique of the ayllu Alapicha (Anansaya) to which most of the residents in the Macha district of Chayrapata, including Nicolás Katari, belonged.[10] Both men had been harassed and compelled to resign in winter 1780, and both were now accused of having promoted the arrest of Tomás Katari. In the case of Sánchez Morato, the Indians killed his wife and his brother-in-law in the church cemetery of the Chayrapata village.[11] In turn, the Indians of Moromoro, a valley district in southwestern Chayanta, beheaded their cacique Blas Aguilar (who had already experienced harassment in October 1780) and his brother.[12] Led by their cacique lieutenant, they also sacked Moromoro village, most of whose Spanish residents had lent military assistance to corregidor Alós for the battle of Pocoata.[13] Shortly afterward, the Moromoro Indians would join the rebel force led by Dámaso Katari, which was laying siege to La Plata. In Pitantora and Ocurí, whose territories bordered with Nicolás Katari's ayllu, Indians confiscated the assets (mules, cattle, lambs, and horses) of two caciques, Ignacio Salguero and Anselmo Bernal, who had also been the object of attacks in October 1780.[14] The pitantora Indians reportedly ate Salguero's food and destroyed his property, saying that "Governor Salguero owed them much and that they could steal from him in compensation for his many wrongdoings."[15]

Just as retribution for Tomás Katari's fate gave rise to extraordinary displays of collective violence (executions, assault on Spanish militias, and violation of churches), so the enforcement of economic changes took on novel meanings. Spanish officials repeatedly charged rebel leaders with issuing orders to abolish all the colonial levies. Indeed, edicts dealing with peasant economic exactions circulated among the Indians, and the Kataris looked to no other source of authority than themselves. Nonetheless, the edicts were far more discriminating than was reflected in counterinsurgency narratives, which were always prone to render peasant consciousness as the outright negation of colonial institutions. One of those edicts issued by Nicolás Katari, barely ten days before the siege of La Plata, presents a subtler picture. Penned by his personal scribe, a mestizo from Chayrapata, the complete document reads as follows:

> In the town of Santa Lucía de Pitantora, today, February 4, 1781, I leave this in favor of all the tributary Indians. I, their governor don Nicolás Catari, [declare] that the said tributary Indians who paid veintenas and primicias will be freed and none of them will have to pay veintenas or primicias of livestock, such as calves, lambs (Carneros de Castilla), donkeys, colts, nor those of wheat, potatoes, onions, and maize. Neither single men and women nor households have to pay as it used to be . . . I warn all the Spaniards, who are very fond of buying the collection of veintenas and primicias, no longer to try to buy the said veintenas, because those who serve in this post would be warned that their lives will be in danger . . . and all [the Spaniards] must be notified, because it is clearly established by law that there are not veintenas and primicias for the tribute payers . . . [signed] Governador Principal Nicolás Catari.[16]

This ruling underscores the complexity of the politics of insurgency in northern Potosí, the notion that a new social order could somehow be built within the constraints of the old one. On the one hand, it tackles a specific colonial exaction, as opposed to the elimination of tributes and state charges at large. In fact, the edict draws on the idea that the tributaries should be exempted from veintenas and primicias precisely because of their status as tribute payers; a notion akin to time-honored claims that paying tribute while serving as a mita worker or ritual sponsor transgressed the morally acceptable economic burden that the Andean household should bear.[17] Moreover, as mentioned in chapter 1, the collection of veintenas and primicias was a longstanding peasant grievance.

While colonial ordinances on this tax provided an intricate (and contested) set of norms as to which persons, lands, and agricultural produce were to be charged, Indians in northern Potosí and elsewhere had often asked for their exemption. Nicolás Katari's edict reflects this traditional claim, yet, it did so in an entirely untraditional fashion. Tax collectors who persisted in the old ways would be killed. Mestizo and Spanish rural town-dwellers, typically the tax collectors, would have to find other ways to make a living.[18] Equally significant, although the proclamation mentioned that this measure conformed to existing laws, no actual decrees were backing it. In the past, as we have seen, Andean communities had appealed to such official documents as the order eliminating repartos that Joaquin Alós was impelled to write in the aftermath of the Pocoata battle; the state tariff list of church fees (arancel); or the seventeenth-century royal edict exempting mitayos from tribute. Now, legitimizing the pronouncement as its source and guarantor, stood Nicolás Katari the *gobernador principal*.

This radical edge of the movement weighed more heavily as the stakes of the conflict escalated. Toward the end of January, the imminence of a full-fledged armed conflict precipitated either by an indigenous attack on La Plata (whose preparation was already underway) or by a Spanish attack on the province loomed large. In some documents, Dámaso and Nicolás Katari began to identify themselves with political titles that echoed the emergence of notions of universal indigenous political solidarity, such as "Capitán Mayor de la provincia de Charcas" and "Gobernador y Apoderado de todas las comunidades."[19] Accordingly, both leaders were said to have appointed rebels to authority positions at the request of several communities of Chayanta and of neighboring provinces.[20] These appointments, moreover, were not restricted to cacique posts, as had been the case during previous months, but encompassed titles like alcalde, capitán, or cacique lieutenant (segunda). It is possible that an incipient militarylike insurgent command, which never fully blossomed, began to appear. And whatever the extent of the conscious commitment to revolutionary nativist projects, rebels were in practice turning into warriors. Hence, in late January, Nicolás Katari warned the communities of Yocalla and Tarapaya, located in the surroundings of the mining town of Potosí, that

> soldiers are being dispatched from all the big towns such as Chuquisaca, Potosí, and other places, and for this reason *I write to you because we the Indios Originarios from all the corregimientos are subjected to the works first for God and our Lord the King and the other governors*, and considering this you must put all your effort into not allowing the soldiers to pass because if the soldiers pass they will attack us and do whatever they want with us. And we

in all the provinces of communities on this side are holding on so as not to be defeated . . . and I warn you that if you do not strive to resist, you will see the works that will be imposed on us in the future; and thus my brothers I ask you to be watchful of the soldiers that will be sent from Potosí, and I hope you warn the same to the people of Puna and Timabi who are part of the tributary people. Let God preserve you many years, [signed] Macha, January 28, 1781. Your servants who want to serve you, I Nicolás Katari and the Communities.[21]

The communities near Potosí did mobilize against possible military attacks. Two weeks later, through a priest, Indians from Yocalla warned the governor of Potosí, Jorge Escobedo, that if soldiers were sent and the Indians were not fully pardoned, "all the neighboring provinces were ready and in arms to defend themselves." They added that, "rumors had that Your Majesty has gone out with soldiers to Tarapaya, and if they want to fight with [the Indians] they can come to the boundary marker of the Tres Cruces and just name the day and [the Indians] would be ready."[22]

Nicolás Katari, on the other hand, was right when he described that "communities on this side" were ready to engage the Spanish army. Under his command, northern Potosí Indians traveled approximately eleven days through the rural hamlets in the southeastern frontier border of Chayanta and Charcas gathering people and foodstuffs. The cacique lieutenant of the valley community of Caracara later recounted the journey: starting in Ocurí they headed for Caracara, Guayllas, Pitantora, Acharaca, Tarara, and Cachipata, then returning to Caracara, Chajaca, and Ocurí.[23] In the multiethnic valley of Carasi, around forty Indians stormed into the village and, as the town was by then almost empty, sacked the houses of the Spanish and mestizo residents. One of the Machas involved in this action was told that in the town of Poroma (Yamparáez province), soldiers were being enlisted "to slaughter them, and therefore it was necessary to summon Indians to defend themselves."[24] The increasing polarization of the conflict is also illustrated by the execution of at least six mestizo and Spanish residents in several Pitantora hamlets.[25] In accounting for these acts, one of the participants said that "when they rose up and gathered in gangs it was with the spirit of looting and killing those who crossed their way, as long as they were Spaniards, because this was the word that has run among the Indians, and they were informed and determined to do it every time that the occasion arose."[26] Another Pitantora Indian argued that "as they were offered freedom in tributes, tithes, and primicias, as well as interests on the lands of the Spaniards, the latter were seen as an obstacle to fulfill these ends."[27] Northeast of Pitantora, in the valley of Guaycoma, a group of insurgent Indians issued an edict from Dámaso and Nicolás. According to one of them, a hacienda tenant named Antonio Cruz, "in the presence of all the Indians in the square of the village of Guaycoma and Guaca Plaza we said that in those letters Dámaso and Nicolás commanded not to pay primicias and veintenas, and that everybody marched to La Punilla, under penalty of death, the Thursday of this week, so that they participated in the war against the Spanish."[28] For the war against the Spaniards, rebel Indians had managed to mobilize in this valley around one thousand men and women.

War against the Spaniards would be waged, indeed. But it would be a peculiar kind of war, one that mirrored the ideological intricacies of the process leading to it. In early February, for instance, a multitude of peasants surrounded the village of Ocurí, forcing Spanish and mestizo residents to lock themselves inside the church. But for all this display of violence, what they impelled the clergy to do was to write an edict "prohibiting the Spaniards from labeling the Indians as insurgents, under penalty of death, and to place this [edict] on the church's doors, all of which [the priest] did because of the terror induced by the Indian mob."[29] Even in this situation, one can see traces of the expectation that the existing political order might eventually accommodate the deeply subverted state of social affairs. This complex transition from rebellion to warfare and the political underpinnings of it were nowhere more apparent than in the paramount expression of armed insurgency in northern Potosí: the siege of the city of La Plata.

THE ASSAULT ON LA PLATA

In the course of 1781, native peoples lay siege to three of the most important urban centers in the Andean world: Cuzco, the old Inca capital, in early January; La Plata, at the time the seat of the only audiencia in Upper Peru, in February; and the city of La Paz, the fastest-growing commercial center in the area, from March through September. The siege of La Paz was by far the most successful of these military movements. The altiplano Aymara communities led by Túpac Katari managed to sustain the siege for six months and effectively prevent supplies and foodstuffs from getting into the city for 109 consecutive days, thereby starving to death scores of residents (Thurner 1991, 99). Túpac Amaru's forces, which moved on Cuzco before regular troops from Lima arrived, outnumbered so badly the local militia that Spanish officials had little doubts that an all-out advance could not have been stopped (Campbell 1978: 127). The attack on La Plata by thousands of Indians from several surrounding provinces represented the most serious threat ever experienced by the residents of the city, the oldest and most prestigious European settlement in the southern Andes. Eventually, however, none of the Andean armies would launch a massive and sustained assault. The Cuzco, La Paz, and Charcas Indians were defeated in the outskirts of the cities—the sanctuary of Las Peñas, Picchu, and La Punilla, respectively.[30] Issues of military strategy, native conceptions of warfare, and political calculations accounting for this phenomenon have been the object of much historiographical discussion, but the rebel forces led by Túpac Amaru and Túpac Katari seemed determined to occupy the cities either through some kind of armed action, war of attrition, or negotiation.[31] It is this political resolve that appears less certain in the case of the northern Potosí indigenous army.

No doubt questions of organization and leadership in part account for this relative lack of political determination. The decision to march on La Plata was taken sometime in early February, barely ten days before the Indians camped in La Punilla, a hill near the city. This meant that rebel forces in Guaycoma, Macha, Ocurí, and Pitantora did not have time to move on La Plata because news of the defeat found them in the process of preparation. It appears, moreover, that none of the two organizational forms that proved effective in Cuzco and La Paz could fully develop here. In Cuzco, Indians mobilized along traditional communal hierarchies under the powerful symbolic banner of the new Inca king: Túpac Katari's movement relied on new community-elected officials, at the bottom, and the formation of a sort of centralized military command, at the top. In northern Potosí, the caciques, segundas, and hilacatas who emerged from the numerous local revolts that swept the province of Chayanta since September 1780 were instrumental in directing assaults on rural villages, but they did not collide into a unified insurrectionary force.[32] Dámaso Katari, on the other hand, could not appeal to his Inca lineage or build a hierarchical structure of military command. These factors might explain a striking phenomenon: the Indians from some of the main rebel centers—San Pedro de Buena Vista, Sacaca, and Moscari—were reportedly not present at the siege of La Plata as a group. It should be noted that in an area where Andean insurgents had no access to firearms an overwhelming numerical superiority was needed to have a real chance of military success. Spanish weapons were hardly effective, but the extraordinarily high ratio of indigenous casualties in battle, even those battles clearly favorable to them, underscores the sharp disadvantage resulting from the clash between bullets and rocks.[33]

These organizational obstacles were compounded by a more fundamental element: the ambivalent political aims that stemmed from the fusion of local experiences of contention and overarching messianic expectations. On the one hand, hopes of epochal social change unquestionably underpinned the assault. The decision to march on La Plata was made by Dámaso Katari while meeting with Indians of Chayanta and adjacent provinces in the Yamparáez village of Quilaquila. Andean peoples began to congregate there to honor the memory of his brother,[34] because it was said that Tomás's resurrection was expected.[35] Indians of Paria, all along closely linked to the events in northern Potosí, had just defeated Spanish militias and hanged the corregidor in the square of the Challapata village. News of the Túpac Amaru uprising must also have been known through the usual communication channels: indigenous merchants, muleteers, mita workers, and mestizo informants were familiar with rumors circulating in the cities. Significantly, the date of the assault was set by the time of the celebration of carnival (*carnestolendas*), a key moment in the Andean ritual and agricultural calendar.[36] Carnival, which roughly coincides with the beginning of the harvest and the end of the rainy season, symbolically split the year into two, marking the beginning of a time of celebration in which the devils were to be sent to the world of the dead.[37] Dámaso Katari summarized this ideological side of the movement in his final interrogation. What the Andean communities wanted, he contended, was to take over the city and wait for the arrival of Túpac Amaru. In Dámaso's words,

> [they expected] a thorough change in the government . . . [which] should be equitable, benign, free of pensions; and in retribution for the good they expected as well as for having a native King, they wanted to wait for him by conquering a city and putting it under his feet with the obedience of all the Indians that should inhabit it; and with his arrival they expected to be free from tributes, taxes, repartos, tithes, and primicias, and to live without the worry that these contributions bring, making themselves lords of their lands and the fruits that these produce, with peace and quiet.[38]

And yet, rebel forces did not make an actual move to accomplish this objective, either by force or otherwise. While there is no doubt about the existence of radical nativist projects, the ideological certitudes at the time of the siege might have been less solid than that on which the Aymara leader reflected retrospectively. The success of the Oruro rebellion, an event that contributed to bridge the gap between Cuzco and Chayanta by providing a visible proof of the pan-Andean dimension of the upheaval, became known only after the defeat of the siege. Although actively involved in defensive military preparations, Nicolás Katari himself, the second most important leader in the region, considered the advance on the city a grave mistake.[39] Nicolás received four letters from Dámaso asking him to bring the communities from Chayrapata to La Punilla, but he refused to do it. To the last of these letters, Nicolás responded that he "neither could nor wanted to organize the people, because he had wife, children, and a King, to whom he had paid his tributes for nineteen years."[40] When Dámaso returned to Macha from La Punilla, the brothers had a heated confrontation over this lack of collaboration.[41]

Nicolás Katari's behavior was not a mere matter of personal opinion. The exchange of messages between the Indians and the Charcas officials before and during the siege discloses that along with the allegiance to Túpac Amaru alluded to by Dámaso during his final confession there was a far more circumscribed agenda; one that resonated with the local roots of the confrontation. Thus, on February 11, while still in Quilaquila, Dámaso Katari sent two missives to the Charcas officials, threatening to assault the city if their requests were not met. But what the ultimatum demanded was the papers taken from Tomás Katari after his death, and, further, the release of the Quilaquila Indians imprisoned in La Plata for the murder of Juan Antonio Acuña. The language was indeed far more defiant than the explicit demands: if the Spanish authorities failed to meet their petitions, the Indians would "drink *aloja* in the [audiencia ministers'] skulls."[42] When colonial authorities publicly hanged in La Plata four Quilaquila Indians on February 12, two thousand men and women, according to Dámaso (seven thousand, according to Spanish sources) moved on the city the following day.[43] Significantly, the audiencia immediately declared the abolition of the repartos de mercancías (Lewin 1957: 554). Yet, even from La Punilla the tenor of the messages did not change much. Insurgent leaders added some new conditions to lift the siege, and promised that the wife of the audiencia president would be taken to Macha to serve as Dámaso's cook were these petitions disregarded, but gave no signals of trying to negotiate the terms for the occupation of the city, as did Túpac Amaru in his brief move on Cuzco and Túpac Katari in his much more prolonged assault on La Paz.[44] On February 17, as their letters continued to go unanswered, a new ultimatum was issued that the city would be invaded within eight days if the audiencia failed to address their requests. In response, Spanish forces carried out the next day a disorganized and failed attempt at forcefully dislodging the Indians from La Punilla.[45] On February 18, in the face of the military failure, Spanish authorities finally sent two clergies to La Punilla with a copy of the decrees that Tomás Katari had obtained in Buenos Aires and an offer for a "general pardon" or amnesty.[46]

The rebels' reaction to this offer reveals the deep strains within the indigenous movement. For one thing, these documents were not the ones asked for by the Indians: they wanted all the records that Juan Antonio Acuña had confiscated from the peasant leader, and, reportedly, they expected the documents to contain a release from tribute and other exactions.[47] More important, however, these papers must now have appeared completely inadequate. While Dámaso himself had a special investment in recovering his brother's papers, for most Indians what was at issue was not some specific economic and political grievances but the fate of an entire civilization. As Dámaso later recounted, "the repugnance and resistance of many Indians to accept any deal was so strong that, afraid to lose [any] life, [I] was forced to remain in the place and to disregard the emissaries' reasons." Dámaso added that he himself was prone to accept the proposal "but the warning of the women, who were more than forty, stopped him, threatening to kill him; and crying, shouting, and full of rage asked him not to show cowardice and to abandon the place."[48] Thus, on receiving the offer conveyed by the two priests, the Indian leader sent a missive to the audiencia saying that the court had responded to his previous letters by "waging war on us . . . and now I cannot accept any truce. I am with all my people here in La Punilla and all the outskirts of the city are covered by two thousand soldiers who I am maintaining, and the Community does not admit now any peace because as my brother was deceived until he was finally murdered, the same would happen to me."[49] He added that those who brought food into the city would be killed.

And even then, the ambivalence regarding the purpose of the assault did not completely vanish. Dámaso repeated in his letter that the community "waits for the papers with the concessions that my brother drew from the Viceroy, and my Lord, which included the papers dealing with the Arancels, and the repartos and alcabalas that had been abolished, and for these motives my brother was killed." "I warn you," the Indian leader concluded, "that we are tributaries of Our Lord the King."[50] Ambivalence was not just a matter of words. At least one group of Indians, the members of the Moromoro community—who had mobilized on La Punilla after killing their cacique and assaulting the Spanish residents—did accept the authorities' offer: in response to the issuance of the general pardon, they collectively withdrew from La Punilla.[51]

Vacillation proved in the end to be disastrous. On February 20, led by Ignacio Flores, three columns of around 750 Spanish soldiers moved on La Punilla and other positions occupied by the Andean peasants. The Indians resisted the attack as long as they could. Yet, as described by a Spanish witness, "after they realized that their deluge of rocks was impotent to stop the advance . . . they tried to save their lives by running away; so that as a herd of sheep they scattered all over the hill looking for hidden places in caves and ravines, where our [people] beheaded all those who failed to flee, even staining their weapons with the blood of the hapless women. More than three hundred Indians lay dead, besides the many wounded who passed away in the surroundings afterward" ("Relacion" 1900: 169).

Commitment to radical insurgency still survived this military debacle. This resulted in part from the fact that, in the wake of the battle of La Punilla, resisting the Spanish troops became a matter of subsistence. At one point when Dámaso Katari was on his way to Macha, some Indians "begged him to make efforts to resist with as many people as possible because it was likely that the soldiers would soon move forward against everybody, killing them and consuming all their cattle and possessions."[52] In preventing an invasion, in fact, Indians from Sacaca and other communities confronted a Cochabamba provincial army in the town of Arque, the same place they had invaded the previous September when chasing their cacique Phelipe Ayaviri Cuisara. On February 24, in the ravine of Colcha and Larrano, Indians and Spanish soldiers engaged in open battles that ended in the Indian's defeat, with more than seventy Indians dead.[53]

Furthermore, it was at this time that the rebellion in Oruro led by creole Jacinto Rodríguez became known: news of it, in fact, found La Plata residents celebrating their own victory over the Indians.[54] On February 23, three days after the battle of La Punilla, an Indian named Tiburcio Ríos along with other Indians from the groups Chullpa and Caracha (Chayanta repartimiento) traveled to Oruro. There they obtained a copy of an edict issued by Túpac Amaru himself, proclaiming that people "must not be aggrieved in any way and must live in brotherhood as vassals of mine, and that the Europeans have no commerce or entrance in our Kingdom for they have possessed it for so many years."[55] This was quite possibly the first edict from Túpac Amaru to reach northern Potosí. Several peasants from Paria also told Dámaso that "Indians and creoles together had killed all the Spaniards [chapetones] of Oruro. They were waiting for Túpac Amaru, who was about to arrive with eight thousand creoles and six thousand Indians who had executed all the European Spaniards that they found in their way." Dámaso recalled that a piece of paper from Túpac Amaru had circulated "from hand to hand," and that "in conference with the principal Indians of Macha and in gratefulness for their new King, the community agreed to send a missive to Túpac Amaru offering him their obedience and their persons."[56] By early March, Indians from several neighboring provinces journeyed to Chayanta looking for information and instructions; and the Aymara leader sent messages to insurgent indigenous communities as far as Yura, Tomave, and Tacobamba in the province of Porco, Tupiza in the province of Lipez, and several communities in the province of Paria, warning them to be ready to march to war.[57] This new scenario of pan-Andean insurrectionary politics might have finally allowed northern Potosí Indians to view their own history of contention in a different perspective. Dámaso Katari was now reportedly told that "the decrees of [tax] reductions he had talked about no longer applied because they would have immunity with their new king, and they would not pay tasas or church fees."[58]

Although peasant upheavals would effectively occur across the area, projects to foster a rebel army in coordination with the ongoing Tupamarista upheavals in Oruro and southern Peru did not prosper after all. In Oruro the creole-Indian alliance rapidly fell apart, and Jacinto Rodríguez abandoned his allegiance to the neo-Inca movement. Rumors of the advance of Túpac Amaru were, of course, inaccurate. By the time the upheaval in the La Paz area led by Túpac Katari gained momentum, the opportunity for a new insurrection in northern Potosí had largely vanished. But as the efforts to build a unified force failed, insurgent activities returned to their local roots. It was in the northern Potosí villages where the last and fiercest outburst of resistance to Spanish rule flared up. And some of these disturbances disclosed, as perhaps no other occurrences before, the extent to which months of overt confrontation between colonizers and colonized had eroded the foundations of Spanish domination in the Andean world.

WARRIORS INTO APOSTATES

The Catholic Church constituted, metaphorically and literally, the last refuge of Spanish colonialism in the northern Potosí peasant villages. While scores of Spanish and mestizo people, including many clergymen, fled the countryside following the outbreak of mass violence in late August 1780, the only places with some measure of protection for those who stayed were the rural churches, sanctuaries, and chapels. Ideologically, the attachment to Christian rituals proved more resilient than the allegiance to secular political authority. Northern Potosí communities continued to celebrate Catholic festivals while engaged in forthright confrontations with Spanish people and government. Historians have shown that elements from Christian theology were firmly embedded in a larger system of religious beliefs and practices that encompassed worship of ancestors, sacred places, and Andean deities. As underscored by previous conflicts with the clergy in the early 1770s, or by contemporary centers of rebellion elsewhere in the Andes, such as the Túpac Katari movement where the indigenous army laying siege to La Paz conducted mass and feasts, Indians conceived the performance of Catholic rituals as their right as much as their duty. Even during the attack on La Plata, native communities proved to be keen in distinguishing the cultural value of some of the social institutions that had long shaped their daily life from the legitimacy of the Spanish government: rebels made a point of excluding the archbishop, the nuns, and the clergy from their prospective list of victims.[59]

It is safe to affirm that the central place of Catholicism in Andean society ended up bolstering rather than precluding assaults on the church in the rural world. Insofar as the church was crucial for the symbolic life of the native communities, and the behavior of the clergy failed to meet peasant political and economic expectations, the standing of the priesthood became increasingly unattainable. In the context of northern Potosí, as analyzed in chapter 5, parish priests had by no means been spared of collective violence. During the second half of 1780 Indians in San Pedro de Buena Vista, Sacaca, Acasio, and Chayanta assaulted and publicly humiliated priests and their assistants when, as often, the former had fled their parishes. These actions were not initially meant to eliminate the clergymen but rather to gain control of the role of priests in local life. Economically, there was a long-term struggle over church fees and festivals; politically, the struggle was over the protection that ecclesiastical ministers and places of worship offered to rural power groups. In the wake of Tomás Katari's death, the clashes with the clergy underwent a process of radicalization that matched the radicalization of insurgency at large. As expectations of effectively dictating the behavior of the rural clergy receded, and hopes of an epochal social transformation associated with the Kataris and Túpac Amaru gained momentum, a more fundamental ideological challenge to the persons and symbols associated with the Catholic religion emerged. Attacks on the human and material embodiments of the Christian God were this time more than instrumental violence: they seemed to defy their place in society.

Indeed, the profound deterioration of the relationship between the clergy and the Indians became plain even before the siege of La Plata. Paradoxically, perhaps the first sign of trouble surfaced in the parish of Macha, one of the few places where the communities had kept an amenable relation with their priests, thanks largely to the active collaboration of Gregorio Joseph de Merlos and Tomás Katari. As noted earlier, in chasing the Anansaya cacique Pascual Chura, a multitude of Indians not only rocked the church and physically assaulted the priest, as other communities had done in previous months, but also stormed into the building. Women reportedly were among the main participants of this attack. According to one account, as the priest's assistant, Mariano Vega (an Aymara-speaking clergyman in charge of the parish after the departure of Merlos to La Plata in late 1780) tried to calm down the Indians outside the church by exhibiting sacred images and appealing to Indians' piety, an Indian named Tomasina Silvestre, "said aloud that only the women should enter the church to capture the refugees because the men would be excommunicated, and so she headed the invasion with a sling in her hands, shaking it as if she were in the countryside; and she uttered these formal words: 'why are you worshiping this piece of tortilla when the sacristan makes it with flour of the valley; if it were God it would not have allowed our God and King Catari [Katari] to have been killed. Come on priest, ask me now the prayer as you use to do!' "[60]

New blasphemous utterances and acts of religious irreverence occurred one week later when the Indians gathered again to invade the church in order to seize other refugees. Mariano Vega went to the front doors to display an image of Christ but he could do nothing to deter the Indians, both women and men, from breaking in. It was said that this time Tomasina "ordered the organ to stop, warning that if the player continued to make noise with the instrument he would be hung up from the choir."[61] The Indians found Dionisio Chura, a former alcalde, near the altar, and he and the wife of an alcabala collector were dragged outside and killed.

This time Gregorio Joseph de Merlos himself was not spared harassment during his brief return to the province from La Plata, where he had stayed since the previous December.[62] Sent by the audiencia and Ignacio Flores as a desperate attempt at deterring the Indians from marching on La Plata, Merlos arrived in the village of Macha on January 27, less than a week after the incidents described above. As his assistant and some mestizo residents were still reluctant to leave the church, he met open hostility as well.[63] During the feast of the Purificación de Nuestra Señora (the Candlemas festival), Merlos tried to gain the favor of the community by conducting "the most solemn memorial" to Tomás Katari and inviting the peasants for food. The Indians showed no resistance to attending this Catholic celebration, but shortly afterward the priest was compelled to leave town because of threats that he and all of his assistants would be killed. Some Machas, particularly from Pascual Chura's moiety, showed some repentance, but Merlos acknowledged that "they were too few to defend me and the contrary party more numerous . . . and moreover their loyalty was dubious or null."[64]

Acts of defiance toward the church were by no means limited to the Macha village. In late January the priest's assistant of the Chayrapata village, Miguel de Cabrera, was brutally stoned and beaten for trying to protect some former native authorities. Cabrera was in Potosí recovering from the wounds more than four months later.[65] Chayrapata priest Miguel de Arzadum, who was at the time in La Plata, informed the archbishop that he could not possibly return to his parish because of "the complete risk and peril in which his life would be."[66]

The priests of San Marcos de Miraflores, Micani, Moscari, and Carasi, some of whom had fled to La Plata as early as August 1780, also refused to come back to their villages.[67] In late January, the Indians launched stones and physically assaulted the Ocurí priest's assistant, Manuel Parraga, inside the church, where the elite town-dwellers were sheltered at the time. It was reported that this priest, "in view of the outrage of the mob, carried the Holy Sacrament in his hands for his protection, and the most exalted among [the Indians] tried by force to take the Holy Sacrament away from him, breaking the sunbeams."[68] The fact that churches no longer represented safe havens was made plain by the Pitantora priest, who explained that several of his parishioners had recently fled to La Plata because "they have been threatened by the Indians, who vowed to wall up the doors of that church and put them to death with their knives."[69]

In the aftermath of the battle of La Punilla those ominous warnings would come true. It comes as no surprise that the first execution of a priest in northern Potosí should take place in the highland town of Aymaya. The victim was the most visible emblem of the abuses of church ministers in the rural villages, Dionisio Cortés, the once-powerful priest whose quarrels with his indigenous parishioners traced back to the early 1770s (cf. chapter 3). His killing made apparent the link between the longstanding local grievances and the current challenges to the colonial order. We know that the Aymaya priest had already been confronted during the celebration of Navidad over the contribution for feasts. In the hamlet of Chaylloma, the Jukumani cacique Joseph Roque, the Bellos (a Jukumani family that had long been engaged in litigation against Dionisio Cortés), and other Indians challenged him. The Indians asked the priest, "Why did he charge for alferazgos [standard-bearers] and mayordomías [stewards] sometimes 50 pesos, sometimes much more? Then, they instructed the main Alférez to submit only 12 pesos for the [Navidad] feast. And the priest remained silent all along and said yes to all of this."[70] Let us remember that less than three years earlier, Indians who defied Cortés' practices were dragged along the streets of the village, forced to flagellate themselves, and underwent other punishments and forms of public humiliation. During the course of Candlemas, in early February, Cortés was said to have faced another round of provocations in the central plaza of Aymaya.[71] It is clear that by this time collective defiance of the priest took a larger pattern of conflict. Edicts from Dámaso and Nicolás Katari abolishing veintenas circulated among the Aymaya Indians. Contacts with the Oruro rebels were reportedly attempted. Rumors had it that the tribute quota of Navidad due in early April would not be paid.[72]

Then, during the first Sunday of Lent (Domingo de la Tentación), the Aymayas and specially the Jukumanis, the two ethnic groups that comprised the

Aymaya repartimiento, descended in mass on the town. The Indians, who had been seen with their horns and banners the night before, were summoned by their ethnic authorities, including the caciques of Jukumani, Joseph Roque, and Aymaya, Pedro Nolasco Gallego, as well as by several members of the Bello family.[73] The clash began in the morning when the Indians took the church keys from the sacristan, thus preventing the celebration of mass. Later in the afternoon, they went to Cortés's house "to provoke him, and as he did not go out, the four caciques broke into his home, saying: 'leave room for the thief priest that for you we are naked.'"[74] Shortly afterward, the Aymaya priest was taken to the cemetery where he was beaten to death. His livestock and silver money were then distributed among the Indians. Reflecting on the causes of the killing of Cortés, one of the perpetrators argued that "Domingo Bello always demanded that the priest display the arancel, and this originated the resentment and bad blood between him and the Indians."[75] The importance of this and other economic grievances is beyond doubt. But the execution of Cortés must have required a broader rationale: "Killing priests," one of the Bellos was heard saying, "is not a sin."[76]

That fact would soon be known to the elite residents of the valley of San Pedro de Buena Vista. One week after the disturbances in Aymaya, the center of rebel activity moved to the village of San Pedro de Buena Vista, the site of the most violent attacks on the church during 1780. In early March, by the second week of Lent, a multitude of Indians from Auquimarca, Cayana, and Sicoya surrounded the village, as they had done before in September and October of the previous year. This time, however, the Indians did not hesitate to storm the church where the elite town-dwellers were sheltered. Inside the church, the Andean peasant conducted a massive carnage. According to two Indian leaders, between one hundred and two hundred people were killed, but two months afterward a Spanish official, while in San Pedro de Buena Vista punishing those responsible for the act, counted 1,037 dead.[77] Women and children of all ages were, for the most part, executed along with male adults,[78] and the clergy also was not spared: the priest and vicar of San Pedro, Isidro Joseph de Herrera, who had played such a prominent role during the previous year's confrontations, was taken to the cemetery and beaten to death. At least four other priests were executed as well. The killing of hundreds of people inside the church was accompanied by symbolic gestures that underscored the radical rejection of what the church represented both spiritually and politically. One of the rebel leaders, the cacique of Auquimarca, Pascual Tola, related that "after having triumphed, they entered into the church dancing with horns and drums, and there they drank until getting inebriated and they did whatever iniquity their resentment pushed them to do."[79] Spanish sources asserted that the Indians made a point of using the *vasos sagrados* (holy vessels) for their libation of chicha; destroyed and profaned some sacred images; made banners and clothes out of the clergy vestments; "began to dance the dances of carnival [*Carnestolendas*] over that pond of blood in which the beheaded corpses swam"; and then looted silver cups and other objects.[80] Many corpses were moved to the plaza across from the church where, as happened with other victims of indigenous violence at the time, they were left unburied as a sign of their devilish nature. One of the participants said that after the assault some Indians even proposed to demolish the church; its roof and some of the walls had been destroyed by several days of sustained attacks, anyway.[81]

The attack on San Pedro, like the murder of Dionisio Cortés before, bridged the gap between past and present events in ways that the siege of La Plata could not. Auquimarca cacique Pascual Tola did not hesitate to trace the origins of the mass violence to the confrontation led by Sicoya leader Simón Castillo in September of the previous year. Violence started escalating again when one of the priests refused to lower the Sicoyas's fees for Candlemas, the same celebration that had ignited tensions in Macha and Aymaya.[82] Drawing on his previous experience, and emboldened perhaps by the recent indigenous defeat in La Punilla, Isidro Joseph de Herrera decided this time to suppress the gestures of defiance at the outset. He accorded with Francisco Arsiniega — the same hacendado who the previous year had stirred violence by wounding some Indians with his firearm — to organize a militia that ended up killing some Indians.[83] It proved to be a terrible miscalculation: This punitive measure did nothing but provide the trigger for the final onslaught on the village. Simón Castillo did not participate personally in the battle of San Pedro, but he was instrumental in organizing Indians for the attack. Moreover, he was involved in a subsequent assault on the priest of the Sicoyas in the highland village of Chayanta, which had also been a target of collective violence during 1780.

The spontaneous release of collective outrage and ritual violence that occurred in San Pedro de Buena Vista, as historian Jorge Hidalgo Lehuede (1983: 127) has argued, reminds us of the "phase of excesses" that take place in most millenarian movements, a moment in which there is a complete rupture with the traditional moral values before "the instituting of the new age." The assault was still a well-organized operation. The leaders were the ethnic authorities who had emerged from previous protests, particularly those of the two lowland communities that inhabited the valley of San Pedro: Pascual Tola of the group Auquimarca and an Indian named Guacachara of the group Cayanas. The hilacatas and alcaldes of these two communities, as well as those of Sicoya, were also actively involved in all the stages of action, from the mobilization of forces to the distribution of the booty.[84] The highly structured nature of the movement along traditional ethnic lines is stressed by the participation of their neighbors in Moscari. Facing difficulties in overcoming the resistance of the Spanish residents, the Auquimarcas's and Cayanas's chiefs asked the Moscari Indians, who also owned some lands within the district of San Pedro, to lend them military assistance. Headed by Marcos Colque, the cacique who had replaced Florencio Lupa, the Moscari peasants arrived on the second Thursday of Lent in mass to the assault. Their presence hastened, by all accounts, the surrendering of the town and the ensuing carnage inside the church the following day.[85] After the battle, there was a "banquet" in a hill near the town in which Pascual Tola and Guachacara offered chicha, coca leaves, and food to the Moscari Indians.[86] In normal times, this traditional Andean ritual of reciprocity was performed for economic services of a different kind. Its significance here as a means of cementing military cooperation between whole communities was reinforced by the words that Marcos Colque reportedly said: "That he offered this aid with his people so that when the Spanish troops went to Moscari, they [Tola and Guacachara] also helped him with all their people, a matter on which the three of them were in agreement."[87] Although no major confrontation occurred in Moscari, the Indians would in fact conduct an assault on the town during Easter, blowing their *pututus* (bugles made from a bull's horn), surrendering the church, and setting fire to several houses belonging to hacendados (Andrade 1994: 206–7).

The scale of the killings indicates that rural elite members were not exterminated for who they were as individuals but for what they represented. This is not to deny that many Indians might have had personal motives of resentment or tried to settle old scores. Besides priest Isidro Joseph de Herrera, who was one of the first to be executed, Manuel Puma, the cacique of Auquimarca who had already sought refuge in the church during the previous year's disturbances, lost his life, as did Apolonia Hinojosa, Florencio Lupa's widow.[88] Naturally enough, the mestizo and Spanish residents who were killed and then left unburied inside the church and on the plaza across from it were not anonymous enemies but the same landowners, merchants, tax collectors, and various officials with whom the Indians regularly interacted. For instance, a Yanacona Indian of Moscari said that he personally killed his master, Antonio Carabajal, inside the church.[89] Nonetheless, personal animosities appeared now to be articulated in a broader challenge to the colonial order. That challenge was embodied by the distant but symbolically powerful figure of Túpac Amaru. Tiburcio Ríos, the Chullpa Indian who had obtained the edict of Túpac Amaru in Oruro, was associated with Simón Castillo and other instigators of the attack. Castillo contended that rumors from Oruro had it that Túpac Amaru would arrive in the area in March. A letter he sent reveals the broad political underpinnings of the attack on San Pedro de Buena Vista, as follows:

> Be this note dispatch to Moscari and all the towns and parishes of this province. This is, by orders of señor don Grabriel Tupacmaro [*sic*], to help the people of the community for the war and defense of the community of this town of San Pedro de Buena Vista. Don Francisco de Arsiniega has been appointed captain of the Spaniards and it has been published that Our King has deserted us and we will be finished off, and that only God protects us and has mercy on us, and his Holy Mother with her piety does not leave us, we hapless sinners. And thus all the governors and Alcaldes Mayores or ordinarios dispatch all the people without exception [blank space] all, but Caracara, are sheltered inside the church, more than two hundred soldiers, and so would it not be the case that they finish us off, we must unite among us as they do . . . The big column of soldiers is also coming, and thus you try to get this done as soon as possible, and God bring good to all of you. [signed] Your servant, Simón Castillo.[90]

A final glimpse into the demise of the colonial hegemony associated with the attack on the church of San Pedro de Buena Vista is offered in the images described below.

In San Pedro an Indian published an edict commanding "the owners of the haciendas in this district to leave the place and turn over their lands to the Indians of the community."[91] In fact, the possessions of elite town-dwellers were expropriated and some of their houses burned down after the assault.

Auquimarca cacique Pascual Tola ordered one of the captains of a rebel force of three hundred Indians gathered in Torotoro, a few miles northwest of San Pedro, to confront a Spanish column from the province of Mizque. Although no battle occurred, during Easter some of these Indians assaulted the village of Cuchira, a hamlet near the Mizque border, where they killed around thirty nonindigenous residents to prevent them from joining the Spanish soldiers.[92]

After the events in San Pedro, Cayana cacique Guacachara traveled to the nearby mining town of Toracari, a place that had also experienced indigenous disturbances over the previous weeks. There, he set out to mobilize "all the people to go chase the Spaniards in the hamlet of Poncani and the rest of the surrounding hamlets with the spirit and the order that the same governor [Guacachara] gave that all the Spaniards they found be killed."[93]

When the peasants stormed the house of priest Isidro Joseph de Herrera, it was reported that as the Indians were killing a pregnant mestizo woman, "from the wound in her belly the baby began to cry, and they wrench the baby from her body and smashed him against the floor, saying: what would traces of the cholos be left for?"[94]

A DIVIDED KINGDOM

For all their radicalism, mass participation, adherence to pan-Andean revolutionary projects, and region-wide defensive preparations against Spanish columns coming from Cochabamba, Mizque, or Yamparáez, insurgent activities ultimately rested on loose coordination and uncertain political goals. The leadership of Dámaso and Nicolás Katari appeared to have been more firm, at least nominally, outside the province of Chayanta than within it. If they had never mustered the political power of Túpac Amaru or Túpac Katari, their influence on village mobilization largely vanished after the defeat of the siege on La Plata. Some of the leaders of the attacks on San Pedro de Buena Vista, Moscari, or Aymaya said that they personally did not know Tomás Katari's brothers, nor did they follow their orders. The shift of political expectations from developments inside the province to occurrences in Oruro and Cuzco undoubtedly weakened the movement. The link of northern Potosí peasants with these distant and complex political events was too tenuous to hold together a movement of this magnitude. In the face of expanding levels of violence that left no room for expectations of clemency in case of defeat, this weak sense of strategic purpose proved fatal.

In the end, the demise of insurgency in northern Potosí took on the form of an implosion rather than outside military repression. Wary of the consequences of some of the extreme acts of violence, some Indians took in their own hands the punishment of the main rebel leaders immediately after the events. Thus, several peasants who had personally participated in the assault on the church of San Pedro de Buena Vista then killed one Indian because he boasted of having personally beaten priest Isidro Joseph de Herrera to death.[95] The Jukumani Indians Phelipe, Manuel, and Domingo Bello were executed by some of their own peers a few days after the killing of Dionisio Cortés.[96] Most often, however, the persecution took place once the prospects of success of the rebellion had vanished. The vast majority of the rebel leaders would in fact be seized and brought to the audiencia by members of the Andean communities. The much-anticipated entrance of Spanish troops in northern Potosí occurred only after the main insurgents had been turned over by the same Indians. By the end of April, audiencia attorney Juan del Pino Manrique noted that it was difficult to keep up with legal formalities because the court jail was filled with Indian felons.[97] Despite rampant unrest in some of the neighboring provinces as well as the new major focus of insurgency that emerged in the La Paz area by March 1781, it is clear that radical projects of social transformation had lost their appeal for important segments of northern Potosí society. It was this shift in political expectations that in large part sealed the fate of the insurrection.

This turn of events had diverse origins. Switching sides in the face of defeat was not, of course, an occurrence peculiar to northern Potosí. Given the fact that sedentary peasant families conducted the insurrection, the battlefield was the place where they lived and drew their source of livelihood, and given that they had thus neither the inclination nor the possibility to flee, this behavior represented their only chance of survival. Political loyalty was a luxury that peasants could not afford. Even in La Paz, where insurgency had assumed the form of full-blown anticolonial warfare, many Andean peasants rapidly turned against their leaders when debacle appeared imminent (Thomson 1996: 316). As William Taylor (1979: 123) summarizes in his explanation of the Mexican peasants' conciliatory spirit and desire for a rapid return to settle village life in the aftermath of the eighteenth-century rural revolts, "the villagers had lands to farm, families to feed, and a sense of community that was not easily destroyed at one blow."

From a larger historical standpoint, northern Potosí communities reproduced, in a nutshell, a pattern of behavior apparent during the Spanish invasion of the area in the sixteenth century. The Charka and Karakara Aymara kingdoms fiercely resisted the European invaders and their native allies in the valley of Cochabamba. Yet, as defeat seemed inexorable, the different ethnic groups began to offer to collaborate with the new lords of the land — a fact that they would repeatedly evoke in the year to come when asking for certain privileges and economic exemptions from the crown. Tristan Platt (1987c: 104) has suggested that the efforts to transform a situation created by extreme violence (*ch'axwa*) into a new state of harmony (*muxsa*) reflected the modes through which Aymara groups had historically sought to secure certain margins of political and economic autonomy in the face of the harsh realities of warfare and domination. This applied to the relationship of the ethnic groups with the authorities of the ancient Aymara confederations and kingdoms, as much as to the articulation of rural communities with large imperial polities, the Inca first and then the Spanish. If between 1780 and 1781 rebellious Andean communities had challenged the very foundations of European colonialism — the racial hierarchies shaping everyday life, the assumptions of European superior military might, the rules of deference toward religious authorities and symbols, the state monopoly over economic policies — their defeat in some regards reenacted the discourse of the conquest. As one Indian succinctly put it to account for the seeming contradiction of having participated in the killing of hundreds of people in the church of San Pedro de Buena Vista and enlisting himself with the Spaniards shortly afterward, "this was [his] way of apologizing."[98]

In a sense, the struggle between indigenous captors and the captured was less a struggle over whether to make peace with the Spanish rulers but rather over the terms on which to do so. Significantly, the main rebel leaders also began to explore ways out of the predicament on which the military defeat had placed them. They did it in their own way, however. On March 4, Dámaso and Nicolás Katari and several Indians, in the name of all the Chayanta communities, urged the main official and the priest of Aullagas to ask in La Plata for the issuance of a general pardon. But, besides the fact that connections with Túpac Amaru and other rebel centers were still in the works, the petition showed little submissiveness because it consisted of a rather generic expression of repentance for their "mistakes" as well as a promise of allowing the free circulation of people within the province and future "subordination" to the king and their ministers of justice, "as we have practiced before."[99] By contrast, the following day two Pocoata principals, in the name of their community, submitted to the same Aullagas authorities a document that displayed a very different understanding of the basis on which peace had to be pursued. It argued that since last August the Kataris had been falsely affirming that Tomás "had gained a reduction of the royal tributes and repartos from the viceroy of Buenos Aires, with which they have disturbed the peace and tranquility of us, the miserable Indians." The Pocoatas also promised to exhibit an order signed by Nicolás Katari commanding the Indians not to pay the Navidad tribute quota.[100] Finally, on March 11, Macha insurgent leaders responded to this statement by sending a letter to the audiencia that, while formally asking for the pardon for their recent actions, was evidently intended to set the historical record straight. It stated that

> [we] have been for a long time without anybody to look up to only because we were informed of and have seen a copy of some decrees that our deceased main cacique Tomás Catari [Katari] had received from the hands of the Viceroy of the great city of Buenos Aires, and we have seen and understood said copy with the dates and seals of the very Sr. Viceroy because said copy is in our hands; and now we want to obtain as well similar or the same decrees from the merciful hands of Your Lordship [the audiencia acting president] for the same reasons, which are in our favor as poor miserable and defenseless [people].[101]

True as it might be, the time for this kind of political compromise had long passed. In mid-March, the audiencia offered complete amnesty and other symbolic and monetary rewards to those who captured the peasant ringleaders. Andean peasants involved in some way or another in the battles since the previous August (the vast majority), realized that this represented the only way back to the routine of village life. And they seized on the opportunity.

The Pocoatas set in motion this process by capturing the most visible symbol of the insurrection, Dámaso Katari. As discussed in the previous chapter, the Pocoata communities had shown a great deal of political ambivalence after Tomás Katari's return to Chayanta. From January through March of 1781, small groups of Pocoatas were reportedly seen in some of the assaults, but a Spanish source estimated that, on balance, "the Indians of the town of Pocoata had been neutral witnesses of the uprisings and maneuvers of the Cataris [Kataris] without getting involved in them."[102] In the aftermath of the defeat of La Punilla, neutrality turned into active opposition. Six hundred Pocoatas took Dámaso and twenty-eight other rebels to La Plata in late March ("Relación" 1900: 182). The impact of this event is illustrated by the three hundred Indians camped in the area of Torotoro, who waited for the arrival of the Spanish troops from Mizque, "until with the news they received that the rest of the captains had been conducted to the city of La Plata, they dispersed in all directions."[103]

While the Pocoatas were the main organizers in taking rebel leaders to the audiencia jail, many other Indians joined in this endeavor. Groups of Machas, including members of Tomás Katari's ayllu of Majapicha, the main rebel leader of Urinsaya, Salvador Torres, and one of the heads of the assault on Aullagas, Anansaya Indian Sebastián Colque, had an active participation in the arrest of Dámaso and Nicolás Katari. In addition, Simón Castillo and Tiburcio Ríos were captured by their peers of Sicoya and Caracha, and Jukumani cacique Joseph Roque, who had reportedly been personally involved in the killing of priest Dionisio Cortés, boasted that he had sent to La Plata fourteen arrested Indians from Aymaya.[104] To be sure, some rejected this movement. As Indians were trying to capture first Dámaso Katari and then Nicolás Katari, they met some resistance from people who remained loyal to their leaders.[105] In the end, nonetheless, the number of Indians willing to turn over insurgent leaders to the authorities was too overwhelming. Along with the two Kataris and Castillo and Ríos, many others were taken to La Plata by northern Potosí Indians, including Pascual Tola and some of the peasants involved in the assault on San Pedro de Buena Vista; the Moscari Indians who had executed Florencio Lupa; some of the Machas who had attacked the mining town of Aullagas and the churches of Macha and Chayrapata to revenge the death of Tomás Katari; Indians of Ocurí and Pitantora where the edicts abolishing primicias and veintenas had been first published; Indians who had joined the siege of La Plata or had intended to join it; and those who brought to Chayanta news of the rebellion in Oruro and the edicts of Túpac Amaru.

In recognition for their contribution to the restoration of subordination to the Spanish crown, in formal ceremony the audiencia granted medals to the principal Indians who handed over the insurgents.[106] Certainly, when confessions were taken, colonial officials realized that many of the Indian conductors had been more deeply involved in insurgent activities than those whom they had conducted. Some rebel Indians even mixed in with the hundreds of Indians bringing the peasant leaders to La Plata in the hope of passing as captors.[107] As the contingent arrived in La Plata, who was bringing whom was not always entirely evident. "Having asked [Nicolás] Catari [Katari], during his final interrogation, who accompanied him in his looting and atrocious deeds," a contemporary source remarked, "he replied with great integrity: the same ones who brought him in arrested" ("Relación" 1900: 183). But then, once more, this behavior did not differ much from the way the Spanish conquest had consolidated three centuries earlier, it was the last line of defense of the Andean social fabric in the face of the harsh realities of warfare and domination.

For those whose hopes of personal survival had all but disappeared, "integrity" might have represented the last line of defense indeed. On April 1, as Dámaso Katari, along with his wife and many other prisoners, made their entrance into the city, the populace of La Plata filled the streets, the balconies, and the plaza to watch the procession. The Aymara leader walked the streets wearing a crown of feathers and holding a horn for a scepter, which the soldiers had given to him as a sign of humiliation. Echoing the racial hatred and, more significantly, the anxieties of the colonial glance in the aftermath of mass insurgency, a contemporary account noted that, "neither his person nor his attire conveyed any authority whatsoever to warrant obedience, and on the contrary it provoked derision and mockery for being a disgusting and ragged Indian who did not stand out from even the most ridiculous pongo [domestic servant]."[108] And yet another source sheds a different light on the attitude of the prisoners as they met the derision of the people in whose skulls they had promised to drink chicha two month earlier: "it provoked admiration to observe [Dámaso Katari's] impassive demeanor and his great dignity looking at the balconies without showing any sign of fear, so that once he was inside the jail he asked [oidor] Cernadas for something good to eat and something to drink because he was thirsty."[109]

The confessions of the main leaders bear witness to their efforts, under extraordinary pressures and often under torture, to articulate their own vision of the events and the rationale of their acts. This does not need to be confused with martyrdom: the responsibility of their peers in the events was pointed out and facts were manipulated in order to incriminate their personal foes, especially those who had brought them to La Plata. Yet, as already shown by the letter sent from Macha on March 4, discriminating what they had done from what they had not, and why, was a matter of great significance. However, this was not a simple task because the inquisitors wanted to see a conspiracy aimed at overthrowing the colonial order from the outset. These attempts to subsume insurgent consciousness to its final incarnation met stubborn resistance. Whereas indigenous followers of Túpac Amaru and Túpac Katari in Cuzco and La Paz might have revolted against the colonial rule from the start, northern Potosí rebels did not. In laying claim to their own agency, the last thing they could lay claim to, they needed to show the process that had brought them there. Thus, Nicolás Katari admitted to have ordered the assaults on Aullagas, Chayrapata, and Pitantora but insisted he had refused to join the siege of La Plata because he had just considered it a mistake. In answering a question about whether his brother, Tomás, had deceived the Indians upon his return from Buenos Aires by saying that he had received an order reducing the tributes, Nicolás argued that Tomás had been arrested for demanding the removal of Blas Doria Bernal in exchange for a promise to increase tribute monies; when Tomás returned from Buenos Aires he told Nicolás that "he brought an order to be enforced for [one] of three [Spanish] individuals dealing with the removal of Bernal for the said abuses and also with the increase of tribute" (which was what Viceroy Vértiz's order indeed was about).[110]

For trying to get this decree enforced, Tomás had been arrested several times thereafter; and for trying to get corregidor Joaquín de Alós to make good on his promise of releasing Tomás, the Indians had revolted in Pocoata. Simón Castillo, in turn, recognized that in February and March 1781 he had sought to mobilize the communities against the Spaniards in the name of Túpac Amaru, but he also remarked that his initial involvement in the insurrection was "the desire to remedy the works of the Indians by alleviating them from church fees and other hardships."[111] Dámaso and Nicolás had little sympathy for Macha priest Gregorio Joseph de Merlos (the community, it was argued, knew "he was a wicked priest for he had had trouble everywhere").[112] Still, before being executed, both men were willing to declare for the record that the priest had never induced the Indians to revolt, of which he was being accused. Merlos, after all, was the Spanish authority who had most forcefully defended Tomás

Katari's behavior in life and his memory after his death. Dámaso Katari said that he meant what he had promised in La Punilla that he would behead all the Spanish people with the exception of those in the priesthood. And then, if they also refused to recognize Túpac Amaru, his new Inca king would know what to do with them. But, he added, his brother would never have promised a reduction of tributes, and things might have never reached this point, "if right from the beginning [Tomás Katari's] petition had been met. He would not have been stigmatized as a rebel and troublemaker, nor would he have been persecuted by his enemies until tragically losing his life, leaving as inheritance to his brothers these agonies."[113]

The execution of the rebel leaders reflected, with all its ritualized display of state violence, the reassertion of the king's sovereignty over his seditious subjects typical of the ancient régime in the European metropolis and of overseas colonies alike. Dámaso Katari, for example, was condemned "to be taken out from the public jail to let people see him dragged by a big animal to the gallows that will be placed in the Plaza. He will be hung until he is dead and then his head will be cut off and his body split into four parts in order to exhibit them in public places. His head can be dispatched, if necessary, to the place where he resided, to be shown there."[114] A similar fate would befall his brother Nicolás, Simón Castillo, the Auquimarca cacique Pascual Tola, Tomasina Silvestre (the woman who broke into the Macha church), and the Bellos family of Jukumani, among others. More than fifty Indians were executed in La Plata and hundreds more suffered punishments ranging from mutilations to forced services. When Spanish troops finally entered the province in the weeks ahead, new rounds of executions were performed in the rural villages.

Facing their fate, free at last from the only choice left for the vanquished, condemning their past and their peers as the sole means of survival, insurgent peasants could be true to themselves and to what they had stood for. "It was very noticeable," a Spanish chronicler said, "the cool demeanor with which these hapless people stepped up to the gallows, more worried about earthly than heavenly things. It is motive of much pity and confusion for us who profess the Catholic religion to see these miserable people walking to their death chewing coca, others refusing to take off their hats [*monteras*] or put down their coca sacks [*chuspas*], and others getting upset at the priests' exhortations, telling them to go scold someone else" ("Relación" 1900: 185). In other words, they met the wrath that the Spanish king and Christian God reserved for the criminals and the sinners, not as sinners and criminals but as Andean warriors of a world that could not be; showing in the end, as our chronicler noted in dismay, "no sign of regret for their faults."

Conclusion:

Andean

Political

Imagination

in Times

of

Insurgency

TO DISCERN THE HISTORICAL SIGNIFICANCE of insurgency in northern Potosí, the process needs to be located within the larger scenario of pan-Andean rebellion. A brief comparison of the movement led by Túpac Amaru in Cuzco and that by Túpac Katari in La Paz affords a general overview of the extraordinary cycle of Andean insurrection as well as a better appreciation of the contrasts and similarities between the centers of rebel activity. Historical investigations have shown that anticolonial consciousness presented significant regional variances both in ideological content and formation. By way of conclusion I focus here on how insurgent practices expressed disparate historical patterns of Indian/white relations, political worldviews, and structures of leadership.

In the Cuzco area, interracial relations were shaped by a distinctive feature: the continued recognition of the Inca past and the high social standing of the Indian aristocracy. During the eighteenth century, Inca imagery and Andean cultural motifs gained increasing visibility in elite and popular artistic expressions, as well as in public ceremony in which most Cuzco social groups took part as performers or spectators. John Rowe (1954) and Alberto Flores Galindo (1987), among others, have demonstrated that a renaissance of Inca culture took shape in canvas and mural painting, textile design, clothes, *queros* (drinking verses), public representation, dance, and the wide circulation of works like Garcilaso de la Vega's *Comentarios Reales*.[1] By the eighteenth century, it was fashionable for Andean lords to have themselves portrayed in Inca garb and insignia of power. Even Christian deities, according to the bishop of Cuzco, were dressed in Inca costumes during the celebration of Corpus Christi and Santiago the Apostle. Leon Campbell (1987: 116–17) notes that "an active cult of Inca antiquity had flourished in Cuzco from at least mid-century, carried on both by creoles who adopted Inca dress and furnishings, and by caciques who proudly exhibited the ancient symbol of the Sun God and of the Incas in public ceremonies." The colonial government greatly contributed to maintaining the vibrancy and meaningfulness of precolonial memories by continuing to endow the Indian aristocracy with privileges and by teaching them the "Incaic tradition" in the *colegios de caciques*, such as the college of San Francisco de Borja in Cuzco whose walls were covered, in the course of the eighteenth century, with images of Inca figures.[2] Although little is known of the impact of this process of cultural renewal on ordinary members of the Andean communities, their active participation in those dramatic representations along with noble Indians and white elites is beyond doubt. It has even been suggested that for the indigenous people theater began to replace ritual as the main vehicle of community identity (Flores Galindo 1987: 69).

Accordingly, in Cuzco society the Indian aristocracy enjoyed high social standing among both indigenous peoples and white settlers. The shared celebration of pre-Columbian heritage was indeed part of a larger pattern of cultural and economic interaction between the Andean nobility and creole groups. Most indigenous lords were bilingual, literate mestizos, and they developed social and kinship networks with regional elites. Some caciques owned private haciendas and mines and engaged in commercial and financial ventures with Spanish officials and entrepreneurs as partners rather than as subordinate agents (Flores Galindo 1987: 137–42; O'Phelan Godoy 1986: 53–72). Several prestigious Cuzco noble families even had some of their members admitted into the priesthood (O'Phelan Godoy 1995: 47–68). At the same time, in sharp contrast to other regions, Indians of noble birth remained in control of most native chieftainships. These hereditary ethnic lords exerted a relatively undisputed authority within their rural towns, at least they did so judging by the low levels of overt indigenous dissension (Stavig 1999: 229–33). Taken as a whole, the Cuzco native lords enjoyed a degree of social prestige unknown elsewhere in the Andes.[3]

The strain underlying the public recognition of Inca historical legacies and the full integration of the indigenous nobility into the colonial society was manifested in several layers of tension shaping insurgent practices and discourses. First, the notion of Inca restoration was infused with millennial and messianic beliefs, including cyclical visions of history, circulation of prophesies announcing imminent cosmological and social cataclysms, and myths about the resurrection of the last Inca emperor.[4] Yet Túpac Amaru could also translate his political aspiration into the language of the ancient Spanish *pactismo* — that is, the reconstitution of the balanced relation between the king and the political communities or kingdoms that comprised the monarchy.[5] It is debatable whether this traditional claim was ultimately meant to redefine the terms of the colonial pact or to terminate it altogether, but in either case, Túpac Amaru did not define this Andean political community as merely indigenous but as composed by diverse American social groups.[6] This initial appeal to both Indian and white people born in Peru may point to the incipient formation of a discrete interracial "imagined community." Although unrelated to later liberal concepts of nationhood, this notion of political community underscored Andean elites' and creoles' sense of cross-cultural identity as Americans rather than merely as members of the Republic of Spaniards or the Republic of Indians.[7] Bourbon absolutism must have played a major role in subordinating racial antagonisms to a broader clash between imperial projects and local interests. Sharp tax increases and the exclusion of creoles from government — that is, Bourbon strivings for transforming overseas possessions into full-fledged colonies — provided a cross-section of local society with a common source of resentment and, for a short while at least, a sense of common destiny as well (O'Phelan Godoy 1988: 175–294; Fisher, Kuethe, and McFarlane 1990). To be sure, Andean leaders and creoles held divergent understandings of the aims of the movement: the former might have expected nonindigenous peoples to recognize the new balance of power emerging in the wake of Inca political revival; and the latter might have hoped to manipulate Indian unrest to halt the ongoing program of reforms. Still, the spontaneous, albeit short-lived, support of some creole groups for a social upheaval of this magnitude suggests that Túpac Amaru's appeal to the Inca heritage was a language they understood and shared. In fact, creoles and mestizos staffed the highest ranks of the insurgent command, and the revolt appeared to have initially gained the sympathy of numerous members of the clergy.[8]

Ideological ambivalence also pervaded peasant-cacique relations. On the one hand, the strength of the ascendancy of Andean lords over their communities passed the test of widespread political unrest: unlike in other centers of rebel activity, Indian commoners tended to abide by their ethnic chiefs' decision either to support or to oppose the Túpac Amaru insurrection. And yet, those commoners who joined the upheaval understood their endeavor in an entirely different light than did the indigenous aristocracy. Rank-and-file rebels saw the uprising as an opportunity to redress longstanding economic grievances against colonial officials, haciendas, textile mills, and white overlords in general. Collective mobilization was structured along traditional community lines, but from the peasants' standpoint the distinction traced by the Indian leaders between Europeans and creoles appeared pointless and vain.

In northern Potosí, we have found a different dynamic in terms of the role of ethnic lords, the implications of state policies, the process of political radicalization, and the meaning of neo-Inca claims. The single most contentious issue during the process leading to the outburst of mass violence was the control of native chieftainships. The protest grew out of intense battles over illegitimate ethnic chiefs, regardless of whether they belonged to noble lineages or were mestizo, or both. The movement was therefore much less hierarchical and much more organized from the bottom up than in Cuzco. On the other hand, as social conflicts revolved around customary modes of exploitation by rural overlords, Bourbon absolutism appeared to Indian communities less as a motive of discontent than as a political resource to be manipulated for their own ends. The language of contention evolved from the enforcement of specific corporate privileges and the fair administration of justice to a redefinition of the power relations between the king, the rural colonial rulers, and the peasant communities. Such a redefinition of power relations was the local version of the Andean utopia. Entailing the reorganization of engrained systems of colonial and ethnic power, it proved to be as radical as any other utopia. Distinctions between creoles and peninsular Spaniards were notoriously lacking from the concerns of leaders and common peasants alike. The basic antagonism here was located between indigenous and nonindigenous people within the rural world, rather than between local interests and imperial policies.

Because local deities and rituals with little Inca undertone supported ethnic identities in northern Potosí, the path to subversion differed from that in southern Peru. The articulation of a common language of indigenous corporate rights and the formation of regional webs of political solidarity were the very outcome of a protracted process of political awareness. Rebellion in the Cuzco area was set in motion by an insurrection plot that caught the authorities by complete surprise: the capture and public execution of the Tinta corregidor by a purported descendant of the last Inca. Although Túpac Amaru claimed to follow the king's instructions to purge the kingdom from corrupt rulers, the seditious nature of this action would have escaped no one.[9] Widespread peasant uprisings thus ensued. As Flores Galindo (1987: 146) has noted, the general mechanism of expansion of the movement was less that of the advance of a rebel army than the establishment of contacts in the rural areas in order to encourage local revolts. Mobilization in northern Potosí ran in the opposite direction: anticolonial radicalism stemmed from a gradual process of contention. Collective violence escalated progressively and every open confrontation between authorities and Indians was foreseen and announced in advance: from the small clashes provoked by Tomás Katari's several arrests (March 1778 and June 1780) and the bloody battle of Pocoata (August 1780), to the mass killings following the leader's murder in late 1780. In short, for Cuzco rebels, the outright challenge to the colonial order represented the starting point; for their peers in northern Potosí it was the closing one.

In addition, northern Potosí Indians' allegiance to Túpac Amaru in late 1780 had nothing to do with the restructuring of the relation between the Spanish monarchy and the kingdom of Peru but rather with the embracing of an alternative source of sovereignty. Túpac Amaru came to occupy the vacuum left by the profound legitimacy crisis of the Spanish government in the region. Whereas in Cuzco the ideological strains lay in the variety of outlooks and expectations brought to the movement by their different participants — the native nobility, the creoles, and the peasant masses — here the main source of tension derived from the extraordinary trajectory of the conflict. The final engagement in nativist anticolonial projects coexisted in a rather difficult way with the much more modest initial agenda of the protest: the tension between the original motivation and the outcome of the movement was always there, and it surfaced in a divided and weak leadership and contradictory set of goals during the last stage of the conflict.

The case of La Paz presents several contrasts with its counterparts in the Charcas and Cuzco regions. First, the rebellion led by Túpac Katari was not the result of endogenous political mobilization, nor was it a neo-Inca uprising turned into massive upheaval (Cuzco) or a gradual process of radicalization (northern Potosí). It was born out of a full-scale revolutionary situation both south and north of Lake Titicaca. Insurgent activities began in late February 1781, when mass mobilization was well under way in Cuzco, Charcas, and Oruro. The fact that La Paz was the last region to rise up does not mean that it had remained unaffected by the widespread social unrest prior to 1780. On the contrary, Aymara communities in the altiplano provinces had an unparalleled record of collective violence and open resistance, especially against provincial magistrates (two were killed in Pacajes and Sicasica in the early 1770s), illegitimate caciques, and the forced distribution of commodities. The city of La Paz itself had witnessed one of the most notorious tax revolts against the establishment of a customs house for the collection of the alcabala.

The egalitarian ideas forged in the course of this historical experience help to explain the distinctive meaning that La Paz peasants attributed to the pan-Andean upheaval. In exploring several social conflicts in the altiplano provinces starting from the 1740s, historian Sinclair Thomson (1999: 294) has identified a series of defined radical ideological motifs. These "anti-colonial political options," unrelated to notions of Inca restoration, consisted of "radical elimination of the colonial enemy; regional Indian autonomy that did not necessarily challenge the legitimacy of the Spanish Crown; and racial/ethnic integration under Indian hegemony." Clearly the neo-Inca projects that were sweeping the Andes served as the trigger of the Túpac Katari upheaval, but the specific way that Aymara peasants engaged and experienced the pan-Andean insurrection was linked to those discrete forms of political thought. From its inception, the movement adopted a radical racial agenda. There were no illusions about cross-racial alliances against imperial policies, as in Cuzco, or about the reenactment of an ideal ayllu-state reciprocity pact against rural overlords, as in northern Potosí. Moreover, the organization and leadership of the movement did not present the traditional community power structure of the Cuzco rebellion. Nor did it evidence the kind of informal and loose quality—that is, a social protest turned into anticolonial war—of the northern Potosí uprising. The Paceño leadership had a definite military style, at least at the top. Túpac Katari and his assistants exerted firm control over the Indian troops and had the will and power to discipline hostile peasants and competitors for the rebel command, especially members of the Túpac Amaru entourage. Unlike its counterpart in Cuzco, communities in the La Paz area conducted a caste war that left no room for republican elites' future historical constructions as a protoindependence movement (Thomson 1996; Valle de Siles 1990).

While insurrectionary experiences greatly varied, the general roots of Indian rebellion could be found, in my opinion, in a long-term process of cultural and political empowerment of the Andean peoples. This common trend also presents, as should be expected, regional variances. An argument could be made that the Cuzco of the years preceding the Túpac Amaru rebellion represents the moment in the history of Peru with the highest level of equivalence ever achieved between the Andean nobility and white elites, in terms of social standing, economic power, and cultural prestige. Alberto Flores Galindo's (1987: 136) assertion that by the eighteenth century "an [indigenous] Cuzqueño aristocrat . . . was considered as honorable as a Spanish aristocrat" could be something of a hyperbole. It may be pointing yet to an extraordinary historical trend in the patterns of interracial relations in the Andean world that the political cataclysm of 1780 (and then the defeat of the Pumacahua rebellion of 1814–1815) turned into archeological ruins. In effect, in contrast to nineteenth-century Peruvian creole nationalism (or creole readings of the ancient Meso-american civilizations in colonial Mexico), the celebration of the Tawantinsuyu was not meant to function as the mirror image of the irredeemable backwardness of contemporary Andean peoples. Nor was it a paternalist discourse imposed on the natives, like twentieth-century indigenismo.[10] Cuzco colonial society, unlike postindependence caudillos such as Agustín Gamarra or Andrés Santa Cruz who also invoked the memories of the Incas, recognized tangible continuities, both cultural and political, between past and present. Unlike the indigenismo, the Indian peoples themselves were directly involved in the growing prestige and visibility of Andean traditions. Flores Galindo (1987: 136–37) has aptly summarized this growing sense of cultural and economic self-reliance: "In the plastic arts, as in any other field, indigenous culture is not despised; it is respected. . . . Thus the power of the Incaic aristocracy is not a mere gift from the Spaniards for their role as local authorities, but derives in part from the fortunes that they themselves managed to accumulate through involvement in trade, as in the case of Túpac Amaru, and the ownership and management of agricultural and mining enterprises, as in the cases of the kurakas [caciques] of Acos, Acomayo or Tinta."

It needs to be stressed that the commemoration of the Inca past and the symbolic prestige and economic success of the Andean lords was by no means bound to evolve into nativist utopias. The celebration of native traditions was a hybrid and ambiguous device providing a type of historical narrative to which disparate members of colonial society could relate. Memories of the Tawantinsuyu were not automatically associated with a questioning of the legitimacy of the European conquest, nor were public dramatizations of the capture of Juan Santos Atahualpa and the Spanish conquest necessarily interpreted as a celebration of the fall of native imperial traditions. They must have simply reminded people of the mixed origins of the civilization emerging out of the colonial encounter.[11] Actually, the majority of caciques and communities in the Cuzco area remained royalist during the rebellion. Ideas and representations of the Inca past were not radical per se, the fact that they seem destined to produce neo-Inca sovereignty claims is indeed one of the outcomes of the revolution itself. The larger point, however, is that an engrained sense of cultural pride and social prestige, rather than deprivation and marginality, bred the growing radicalization of important sectors of Cuzco's indigenous aristocracy. As Andean cultural traditions became vested with swelling symbolic power, they ceased to function as marks of subalternity. By unwittingly undermining notions of racial inferiority, this process made the envisioning and diffusion of radical utopias possible. The astonishing readiness with which thousands of Andean peasants in southern Peru followed the leadership of Túpac Amaru (whether they dreamed of an egalitarian society instead of a hierarchical imperial system, and of a *pachacuti*, a complete reversal of the existing order, rather than of a coalition with creoles and other power groups) can only be understood through this unique historical process of cultural empowerment.[12]

This trend was matched by equally significant changes in the relations of political subordination. The increasing number of popular riots in cities and rural villages throughout the Andean region nurtured a climate of contention and unrest that proved the feasibility of outright assaults on colonial government. Antifiscal movements in cities like La Paz, Arequipa, Cochabamba, and Cuzco; Juan Santos Atahualpa's millennial upheaval in central Peru; abortive conspiracies in Huarochiri and Cuzco in 1750 and 1780; and the spreading of rural revolts across the Andean world must have demonstrated the vulnerability of colonial rule. Ward Stavig (1999: 215) has rightly noted that although the large number of local protests could create a statistical mirage because each individual area tended to experience just a few episodes of political violence, the multiplication of these episodes produced "a climate in which violent protests were more likely to occur." Compliance to authority, in other words, should have no longer appeared as a fact of life.

This process of political empowerment is particularly noticeable in the case of northern Potosí. As discussed in chapter 3, the movement led by Tomás Katari was preceded by an exceptional conjuncture of defiance to provincial magistrates, parish priests, and ethnic chiefs. While village revolts elsewhere in the Andes tended to fail during these years, the northern Potosí upheaval grew out of successful processes of indigenous mobilization, most notably the Pocoatas's ousting of the Moscari cacique Florencio Lupa in 1776. Although the cultural and social trends found in Cuzco were mostly lacking in northern Potosí, the distinct dynamic of those political struggles goes a long way in accounting for the unique role of this region as the first, and largely autonomous, focus of insurgency. Mass rebellion, in brief, was not a desperate response to failure, rather it was the result of successful previous challenges to rural power relations. For reasons distinct from those of the Cuzco Indian nobility, northern Potosí peasants also had motives for defiance and self-confidence.

The undermining of notions of racial and cultural superiority on which European claims to rule were predicated was at the heart of Indian insurgency once mass mobilization gathered strength. The socioeconomic goals of the rebellion are peripheral (if historically significant in many other respects) to what made Indian collective actions so deeply subversive.[13] Túpac Amaru could have proposed socioeconomic reforms broad enough to lay the foundations for cross-racial alliances and could have articulated notions of colonial legitimacy that bore resemblance to previous creole conspiracies in Peru or to the contemporary rebellion of the Comuneros in New Granada (Phelan 1978: 39–186). Nevertheless, once colonial hierarchies were dismantled, considerations of the insurgent economic programs and the political projects (whether separatist or royalist, exclusively indigenous or "Peruvian") became, for all practical matters, utterly irrelevant. As is well known, the vast majority of creoles and members of the clergy withdrew their overt or tacit support of Túpac Amaru within the first weeks of confrontation.

The case of Oruro is in this sense particularly instructive. Oruro was the only rebel territory where creole groups held a firm command of the insurgent movement and Andean peasants lent explicit support to a cross-racial coalition. Led by Jacinto Rodriguez, city dwellers (creoles, mestizo, and others) joined Indian communities to rise up against the authorities, peninsular Spaniards in general, in the name of Túpac Amaru. Unlike other areas, insurgent Indians here made a conscious effort to distinguish creoles from Europeans, while Oruro elites treated Indian communities as formal allies. Despite these auspicious circumstances, interracial alliances could be sustained for less than a week. Andean peasants undertook a series of autonomous initiatives, from forcing all Oruro residents to dress as Indians and demanding the execution of the Europeans, to asking for a redistribution of lands. The creoles first tried to negotiate but then compelled the withdrawal of the Indians from the city. Eventually, the creoles would ally themselves with the Europeans and abandon their allegiance to Túpac Amaru altogether. As did nonindigenous groups elsewhere, the Oruro elites found out that no interracial cooperation could be sustained once the marks of social distinction and deference—which in a colonial society were based upon caste hierarchy—collapsed.[14]

The measures implemented by the Spanish government once the suppression of the risings was secured are further indications of the kind of peasant claims that could be contained and those that could not. Thus, in the aftermath of the Túpac Amaru rebellion, the colonial administration was able to address some of its main explicit objectives, prominently the abolition of repartos, the elimination of corregidores, the reduction of tax pressure, and the establishment of a new audiencia in Cuzco.[15] The historical forces that had quietly contributed to blur the signs of Indian subalternity had instead to be rooted out: in the Cuzco area hereditary chieftainships were suppressed, the paintings of Inca emperors removed from public view, and the use of old Andean dresses forbidden. Visitor General Antonio de Areche made a point of banning theatrical representations of the Inca past and the conquest and even outlawed the use of native languages. In retrospect, Cuzco's Bishop Juan Manuel de Moscoso considered that allowing the display of such "gentile" practices and symbols had been a "capital error."[16]

In deterring the repetition of the political process that had bred widespread peasant defiance, Charcas authorities needed to strike a different kind of political balance. In contrast to Cuzco, colonial magistrates in northern Potosí advocated the maintenance of hereditary or at least consensual caciques, instead of the mestizo or arbitrarily appointed authorities who staffed the native chieftainships before the uprising. While the Cuzco nobility was regarded as a serious political menace, here legitimate native chiefs reminded native communities of their subordination of the king. Interestingly, too, whereas in the aftermath of the rebellion colonial authorities in the viceroyalty of Peru sought to appease the region by commuting one year of tribute, this measure was not enforced in the district of the audiencia of Charcas (Sala i Vila 1996: 25–28). According to Ignacio Flores, the creole president of the audiencia of Charcas from 1781, who had firsthand experience in the repression of the rebellion, the Andean peasants could even be persuaded to pay a moderately higher tribute as long as they were assured that "the benefit from the abolition of the reparto [de mercancías] and the decrease in parish contributions . . . exceeds handsomely the rise in the tasa (head tax)."[17] In preventing new eruptions of violence, Flores contended that the colonial administration had to project an image of strength that deterred "anarchy" (i.e., the empowerment of indigenous peoples), but peasant claims "needed not to be disregarded when they represent the public convenience" (i.e., preventing the growth of moral outrage).[18] To make this possible, the crown needed to set up an administrative career so that only officials with recognized probity and knowledgeable about local peoples and customs were promoted to high courts, as opposed to the traditional oidores whose alliances with "wealthy persons" allowed justice to be bought off. Likewise, future audiencia presidents had to be obligated to travel through the rural villages once a year in order to punish power abuses expeditiously. Evoking the recent indigenous insurgency, Flores remarked that if the audiencia president, "instead of addressing the best service to the King, devotes himself to personal business and takes gifts, he must be beheaded in Buenos Aires in a golden scaffold erected for this end."[19]

If Andean insurgency should be understood for its capacity to upset exiting relations of power, it should also be acknowledged for its challenges to engrained structures of knowledge. One of the crucial aspects of the age of the Andean insurrection was the way it defied official representations of the natives either as passive bearers of inherently subordinate (and ultimately inert) traditions, or as unruly savages and barbarians. The impossibility of representing indigenous agency outside those colonial stereotypes is twofold. First, and more obvious, official renderings of rebel activities tended to overlook any culturally oriented pattern in collective actions. Warfare practices, collective rituals, the integration of Christian and Andean deities, and the supernatural power attributed to Indian leaders all appear in elite accounts as deprived of social meaning, as emerging out of a state of nature rather than out of a distinctive Andean system of beliefs. Even those who justified the socioeconomic causes of the uprising did not hesitate to depict rebellious Indians as irrational creatures and their actions as the release of murderous instincts.[20] While in normal times Andean ritual life and social practices had been widely tolerated, evoking at best the invincible resilience of Indian customs and mental structures, in the context of a general challenge to European superiority, they confronted Spanish elites with the absolute limits of the colonial enterprise. In this radically altered political context, colonial rulers could not afford to recognize the continuous existence of a distinctive set of cultural norms. They assumed instead the crudest version of the discourse of the conquest: in the place of recognizing cultural difference, they asserted the natives' ability to have none.

Second, Spanish accounts of the conflict reflect the difficulties of portraying the way in which European notions of justice, property rights, Catholicism, and monarchical legitimacy informed peasant insurgency. Túpac Amaru's explicit allegiance to Charles III, Tomás Katari's appeal to the very principles of Spanish justice, and Túpac Katari's Christian convictions all were reduced to mockery, ignorance, or deceitfulness.[21] If those elements in peasant actions and discourses related to Andean cultural traditions and worldviews were deprived of meaning, those elements that did speak to European ideology and institutions were denied authenticity. These elements, however, genuinely partook of Indian consciousness. After more than two centuries of colonial rule, Catholic religious beliefs, market economies, and European political imaginaries and statecraft ultimately became part of the cultural repertoire and identity of the native communities. Jan Szeminski (1987), for instance, has convincingly shown that rebels considered themselves true Catholics and true vassals of the Spanish king. In the mid-sixteenth century, the Taki Ongos and the Manco Inca's followers might have still radically rejected any contact with the new rulers of the land and their cultural artifacts. But by the late eighteenth century, anticolonialism bore a disparate meaning: Andean insurgents everywhere rejected Spanish government not by rejecting colonial institutions altogether, but by claiming them as their own.

To be sure, Andean understanding of Spanish political legitimacy, Indian rights, Inca sovereignty, and Catholicism differed in very important ways from those of the colonial rulers. But, then, heterodox religious practices and Andean conceptions of political legitimacy had been an accepted component of the colonial world in the first place. It was in response to a mass challenge to their claim to rule that Spanish elites needed now to draw a line distinguishing civilization from savagism, to establish a normative conception of colonial values. What the 1780 rebellions questioned was, precisely, this symbolic monopoly over the meaning of colonial institutions: What did it mean to be a Catholic vassal of the king? What was the set of rights that the Indians possessed as tributary subjects, and what were the practical consequences of this? The most disturbing ideological underpinning of the movement was not what was portrayed in counterinsurgency discourses (namely, the downright rejection of European institutions and values) but rather what was not portrayed: the deployment of intercultural notions of corporative rights, Catholic religious beliefs, and Inca imperial traditions in order to challenge Spanish rule and colonial racial hierarchies. Therefore, the mass upheavals of 1780 not only put Spanish elites face to face with the failure of their civilizing project—with what European domination was unable to transform in the Andean ways of life and thinking after more than two centuries of rule—it also confronted them with that which European rule did accomplish and with the implications of that accomplishment; that is, with the native peoples' own understanding of colonial rights and values.

In the final analysis, Andean insurgency challenged not only official images of the Other but also colonial rulers' self-image—the stories that ruling European people told about themselves and about their role in the New World. It offered an unsettling image, to return to the words of Philip Corrigan and Derek Sayer quoted in chapter 1, of the "messages of domination" underlying the administrative, economic, and political practices that the Spanish government performed and commanded others to perform. Peasant insurgency rendered visible and public, in ways that made them no longer possible to disregard, fundamental aspects of Spanish colonialism in the Andes, such as the structural flaws of the system of justice, the flagrant collusion of private mercantile interests and administrative functions, and the indifference of ecclesiastical ministers toward the religious indoctrination of their Indian parishioners.[22] As the era of Spanish rule was drawing to a close, the massive upheaval of the Andean peoples forced government officials and white settlers in general to face the vacuity of official discourses of civility and evangelization and the naked image of the colonial project as sheer exploitation. Viewed through the eyes of an enlightened official typical of the Bourbon era, such as audiencia President Ignacio Flores, for instance, the Spanish government conjured up nothing but irremediable moral decadence. Writing about the audiencia magistrates, with whom since the days of the Indian rebellion he had a longstanding feud, Flores said in 1783 that, "the ministers of this court will always be a bad example for America because being ordinarily devoid of moral virtues and a liberal education they do not resist the precious bounties of Peru . . . the interest unites them, and then separates them, and each day they represent a ridiculous force . . . so that the King does not possess a more hollow and despicable kingdom."[23]

In the aftermath of the great Andean insurrection, Minister of the Indies José de Gálvez had similar remarks to offer. When looking back to the events of 1780–1781, the most prominent political figure in eighteenth-century Spanish America ruminated that "in Peru, the sole occupation was drawing from the hapless Indians as much material benefits as possible, without inculcating in them religion, customs, utility, knowledge, nor obedience and love to the King. As they had not seen [anyone] but tyrannical corregidores and priests, and the same for all those who had dealings with them, they became mean to an extent impossible to fathom."[24] The portrayal here of what the colonial regime had supposedly made of the Andean peoples is undoubtedly misleading. To recognize that the Indians rose up not out of ignorance but out of their own understanding of the meaning of Catholicism and loyalty to the king would have amounted to a disavowal of the entire colonial enterprise. Thus, with a view of the Indians as innocent victims of despotic rulers, the statement firmly attached them to a condition of inferiority as their place in the natural order of things. Yet, if the description of the natives is deceptive, the account of the path leading to it is worth noting. The spectacle of mass insurgency might not have taught the great Bourbon reformer much about the people he ruled, but what it did teach about his own flock is still revealing.

Introduction

All translations are mine unless otherwise indicated. Note that the peso was the standard monetary unit for ordinary transactions. It was a silver coin weighing one ounce and was subdivided into eight reales.

1   See, for instance, Platt 1982a and 1986; Godoy 1990; Rivera 1992; Pacheco Balanza and Guerrero Peñaranda 1994; Harris 1986 and 2000 (collection of previously published essays). On northern Potosí communities' opposition to liberal policies and intervention in national conflicts in the nineteenth and twentieth centuries, see Grieshaber 1977; Platt 1982b and 1987a; Rivera Cusicanqui 1984; Langer 1990; Irurozqui 2000.

2   For recent studies of different aspects of the northern Potosí rebellion, see Andrade 1994; Adrián 1993 and 1995; Arze 1991; Penry 1996. The first thorough studies of this movement are in Lewin 1957, chaps. 12–13, 21; and Fisher 1966: chaps. 3–4.

3   The need to study Indian unrest from this perspective has been highlighted in surveys on Andean rebellion made by Campbell (1979) and, especially, Stern (1987a and 1987b).

4   As Coatsworth (1988: 49) has noted, whereas village uprisings in Mexico mostly resulted from purely local grievances, in the Andes rural unrest responded to general economic conditions and public policy.

5   See Joseph and Nugent 1994; Mallon 1995; Thurner 1997.

6   See Ossio 1973; Hidalgo Lehuede 1983; Szeminski 1984; Flores Galindo 1987; Campbell 1987; Burga 1988; Stavig 1999.

7   On continuities and discontinuities between precolonial and colonial times in the southern Andes, see Saignes 1991; Bouysse Cassagne 1987; Del Río 1995.

8   It is useful here to add a note about the terminology used in this book. The terms "ethnic groups" (following the anthropological literature on northern Potosí) and "communities" refer to polities such as Caracha or Jukumani (see table 1). Accordingly, multiethnic units such as Chayanta (repartimiento) or Carasi (parish/town district) are not designated here as "communities." It

will be clear from the context when I refer to Macha or Pocoata as rural villages or as non-nucleated ethnic groups. When Andean peoples identified themselves as "Macha" or "Pocoata," they typically meant their ethnic affiliation rather than the pueblo de reducción (when they needed to identify their place of residence, their rural hamlets were mentioned). The term *ayllu* (following common usage in eighteenth-century sources) refers to minor ayllus (Collana, Sullacata, Pari, etc.) composing the ethnic groups. I also refer to the Andean ayllu in generic terms as a distinctive type of peasant community. Because northern Potosí Indians were primarily Aymara speakers (at present they are mostly Quechua speakers), I employ Aymara communities, Aymara leader, etc. in generic terms. Of course, this does not presuppose at all the existence of an Aymara identity as such.

9 The reforms implemented by the Republican state in the nineteenth century did not alter significantly this organization (Platt 1987a: 287–92).

10 There were two other repartimientos on the southeastern part of the province: Moromoro and Pitantatora-Arecacha-Caracara, areas of several Spanish haciendas. It must be noted that Pocoata had also valley lands in Chayala and Surumi, in the vice-parish of San Marcos, and in the Machas in Guycoma. Paria communities of Condocondo and Challapata also rented fields in several places in the province.

11 For fiscal purposes, valley districts were called *anejos* (annex). Multiethnic valleys like Carasi or Micani were therefore anejos of several puna-based groups. For instance, in the 1770s Carasi and Micani appeared in the repartimiento of Chayanta (where several of their ethnic groups possessed lands) (see "Planilla receta" of 1772 and 1780, in Archivo General de la Nación de Buenos Aires (hereafter AGN) XIII, 23-3-1, and AGN, XIII, 18-10-4, Leg. 84, Libro 1). Yet, Indians residing in Carasi and Micani are also included in the repartimiento of Pocoata y Sus Anejos. In fact, a Pocoata census carried out in June 1778 was realized in the very village of Carasi, and the Pocoata caciques identified themselves as "caciques del pueblo de Pocoata, Micani y Carasi" (AGN, IX, Interior, Leg. 4, Exp. 7, ff. 13–14). The Carasi priest noted in 1771 that all the Indians residing there were *originarios* (in its double meaning of ethnic ascription and fiscal status) of Pocoata, Macha, and Chayanta (repartimiento) (Archivo Nacional de Bolivia [hereafter ANB] EC, 1772, 120, ff. 56–57). Note that there was no contradiction in this because the different puna caciques were not claiming jurisdiction over these two valley towns but only over the lands and Indians of their respective ethnic groups. Political conflicts did emerge when two ethnic groups were lumped together — such as Macha and Pocoatas in the late sixteenth century (Platt 1978: 102–3; Del Río 1995: 3–47) — or when caciques claimed authority over other ethnic groups (cf. chapter 2 and 3, this volume). As a provincial magistrate put it in 1784, in denying the claim of the Cayana cacique to the chieftainship of Auquimarca, "it is well known that these two are different parcialidades [communities], like others [parcialidades] encompassed by the rest of the towns, and as such they have been ruled by two caciques" (ANB, SGI, 1784, 63, f. 61). On the multiethnic nature of valley districts and the crucial role of the intervention of puna authorities in valley parishes for the maintenance of ecological complementarity during late eighteenth and nineteenth centuries, see Platt 1982b: 33–34, 47–52, and 1987b; Cangiano 1987; Adrián 1995. For an interpretation of valley towns as sites of new social identities, politically independent from puna caciques, see Penry 1996.

12 Note that these are not precolonial polities but groups that emerged from the fragmentation of those polities. Ethnographic studies have demonstrated the continuous role of ethnic identities

and ecological complementarity in Macha and Pocoata (Platt 1982a and 1986; Pacheco Balanza and Guerrero Peñaranda 1994), Laymi-Puraca (Harris 1986 and 2000), and Jukumani (Godoy 1990). While ethnic authorities increasingly became elective and rotative, they continued to extend jurisdiction over distant puna and valley households (a synthesis of this process is given in Rivera Cusicanqui 1992: 75–121).

13 For the southern Andes, see Saignes 1991: 108.

14 For instance, in 1778 the valley parish of San Marcos de Miraflores (inhabited by several Macha ayllus and some Pocoata and Condocondo families) reportedly had a permanent population of 1,400, which rose to 7,000 during the harvest season (ANB, EC, 1779, 23, f. 20). Puna Indians celebrated festivals while working on their valley fields. Adrián (1997: 85–92 n.22, and 1995: 21–35) has pointed out that the breaking up of parishes during the eighteenth century (Macha/ Chayrapata, San Marcos/Surumi, and Pocoata/Chayala), which was promoted by new state policies and demographic growth, did not affect significantly existing "ethnic relations" among puna and valley households. In brief, new independent parishes did not imply new actual polities, it implied new burdens (festivals and labor prestations) that the Indians, particularly in the case of Macha, strongly resisted. Adrián has also noted (1995: 32) that the priests tried to accommodate the Andean organization of space by sending their assistants to outside parishes following their parishioners' migratory patterns.

15 Cangiano 1987: 9–24. On common lands in present-day northern Potosí, see Godoy 1990: 42–45.

16 For new approaches to Indian intervention in colonial markets, see Larson and Harris with Tandeter 1995.

17 Northern Potosí's chronology matches Thomson's (1996: 89–90) research on the La Paz region, where the proliferation of political conflicts in the 1740s (some of which, as in our case, lasted for several decades) amounted to a full-fledged crisis.

18 See Golte 1980; O'Phelan Godoy 1988; Larson 1997: 127; Thomson 1996: chap. 6.

19 See Moreno Cebrián 1977; Tord Nicolini 1974; Haitin 1983.

20 The increase between the 1770s and the 1780s is partly the result that the latter *revisitas*, carried out after the establishment of the *intendencia* system, were conducted with much greater zeal than former counts.

21 See Glave and Remy 1983; O'Phelan Godoy 1983; Larson 1997; Stavig 1999 and 2000.

22 In 1786, Chayanta authorities sanctioned this link between land and taxation by placing former originarios (9 pesos per year) without sufficient lands into the category of "forasteros con algunas tierras de 7 pesos" and creating a new category (5 pesos) for those who had fewer lands or rented outside parcels (called "forasteros sin tierras"). Hence, the 1786 census increased the overall tribute monies by 10,149 pesos, while diminishing the number of originarios (AGN, XIII, 18-10-3, "Cuaderno de . . . Francisco de Arias," ff. 102–12). Certainly, in other Andean regions the term forastero continued to carry its literal meaning. For the cases of Cochabamba, Cuzco, and Quito, see Larson 1997: 139; Wightman 1990: 45–73; Powers 1995: 107–32.

23 Rivera Cusicanqui (1992: 96) has noted that in modern times the ayllu members could in the course of their lives move from originarios to forasteros and vice versa. For an interpretation of the growth of forasteros in nineteenth-century northern Potosí as a migratory phenomenon, see Godoy 1990: 34; Klein 1992: 129–32.

24 AGN, XIII, 18–9–2.

25 Corregidor Navarro to Viceroy Amat, AGN, XIII, 18–9–5. It is worth noting that since the seventeenth century several colonial officials had been warning about the negative consequences of the process of land privatization (see Larson 1997: 105–6; Wightman 1990: 136).

26 Corregidor Nicolás Ursainqui's request is from 1773 (AGN, XIII, 18–10–3, ff. 116v–117r). On this proposal, see Adrián 1996: 104–7.

27 On mining production, see Tandeter 1992; Fisher 1977. On agricultural production, see Larson 1997; Glave and Remy 1983; Tandeter and Wachtel 1989.

28 On the increase of tribute income in the audiencia of Charcas district, see Klein 1992: 72–74.

29 See, for instance, Cahill 1990; O'Phelan Godoy 1988: 175–221.

30 On mining production in Mexico, see Brading 1975; on Potosí, see Tandeter 1992.

1 Political Legitimacy in Mid-Eighteenth Century Andean Villages

1 ANB, EC, 1772, 98.

2 The list specified Indians from several minor ayllus of Chullpa (ANB, EC, 1772, 98).

3 Allegedly, Portugal had quit his position due to his old age, yet his name is among those caciques having difficulties collecting tribute because of the social turmoil (ANB, EC, 1750, 20, ff. 104–9; ANB, TI, 1772, 118, f. 4).

4 ANB, EC, 1753, 104.

5 ANB, EC, 1748, 19. It must be noted that during this time of the year most of the Indians resided in the valleys for the grain harvest.

6 The term *routines of contention* is borrowed from Tilly's (1989: 27–28) analysis of seventeenth-century French peasantry.

7 The Jukumanis, Panacachis, Sicoyas, Laymis, and Chullpas were the only groups that maintained the precolonial divisions into minor ayllus (Rivera Cusicanqui 1992: 76–77).

8 On the persistence of economic ecological complementarity and ethnic identity between valley and puna Laymi (including Puraca) households during the twentieth century, see Harris 2000: 77–137.

9 Juan del Pino Manrique, "Descripción de la villa de Potosí y de los partidos sujetos a su intendencia" [1787], in de Angelis 1971: 40–41.

10 Harris (2000: 108) has noted that Chayanta, like the towns of Macha, Sacaca, and Pocoata, were already important centers before becoming pueblos de reducción.

11 On northern Potosí agrarian structure, see Platt 1982a; Harris 2000; Godoy 1990; Rivera Cusicanqui 1992.

12 See Sala i Vila 1996: 68. On the differences in economic resources and institutionalization of confraternities (*cofradías*) in Upper Peru vis-à-vis Lower Peru and Mexico, see Platt 1987b; Thomson 1996: 76–79. On the ascent of the alcaldes' authority in late-eighteenth-century southern Peru, see Hunefeldt 1982; O'Phelan Godoy, 1988: 41–52; Walker 1999; Thurner 1997. On cofradías in Peru, see Celestino and Meyers 1981. A review of this topic is in Larson 1997: 353–59.

13 An example of religious-civil town posts as part of a larger Andean cargo system is in ANB, TI, 1772, 98, ff. 78–82. In pointing out the need not to subsume ayllu identities into confraternities, Platt (1987b: 168) has maintained that "rural confraternities in the Southern Andes were tailored in such a way as to take account of Andean seasonal migrations and the ethnic organization of ecological complementarities . . . It is clear that, by the 18th century, the social reproduction of

the system [of confraternities] had fallen entirely into the hands of the ayllus, who have maintained it—with important modifications—until today" (cf. also this volume's introduction). For the provinces in the La Paz region, Thomson (1996: 51, 76–79, 342–43) has noted that community-based challenges to caciques' power did not stem from the fiesta-cargo system (religious posts were by no means the determining factor in legitimizing authority) but from the quest for empowering traditional local ayllu authorities without town jurisdiction such as hilacatas (tribute collectors), principales, elders, and so forth. Roger Rasnake (1988: 136) has shown that by the 1750s the Yuras and other communities in the Porco province lost their links with their "ecological outliers" so that ethnic authority and identities were reoriented around the pueblos de reducción. This fragmentation also gave rise to the multiplication of local ayllu caciques. Abercrombie (1998: 291–96) and Penry (1996) have found a similar process of fragmentation for the indigenous communities in the Paria province, but in this case the system of authority did shift from the caciques to the reducción-based fiesta-cargo system. Penry offers this interpretation for eighteenth-century Chayanta province as well. The rise of town-based religious-civil officeholders seems to have encompassed the crisis of the cacicazgo as an institution, the emergence of new polities, and the demise of traditional Andean forms of verticality. For instance, Penry argues that "it was in the valley land such as Carasi, Micani, or Chayala that parishes of mixed 'ethnicities' were forming towns increasingly independent of any cacicazgo" (290); "these [ethnic] rivalries were 'ethnic' only in the sense that the doctrina/town had come to be the primary source of identification and in that manner, an 'ethnic group'" (349). While I do not agree with this conclusion for the case of Chayanta and with the reading of the documents used to support it, how the existence of a rotative, elective system of religious-civil hierarchies could have contributed to erode hereditary principles of caciques' legitimacy is, in my opinion, an issue that merits attention.

14 On the Ayaviri and Ayra Chinchi, see Arze and Mendinaceli 1991; Saignes 1987: 147–48; Platt 1978: 108–9; Sánchez-Albornoz 1978: 132–34; Serulnikov 2000. On the Lupa, cf. chapter 2, this volume.

15 On the crisis of hereditary lords in Upper Peru prior to the 1780–1781 insurrections (which contrasts with the prestige of Andean caciques in the Cuzco area), see Rasnake 1988; Thomson 1996; Penry 1996; Abercrombie 1998.

16 For two concrete examples of the role of the caciques as intermediaries in corregidores' repartos during this period, see corregidor Pablo de Aoíz and Pocoata cacique Blas Cori in 1753, ANB, EC, 1753, 140, and corregidor Nicolás Ursainqui and Sicoya cacique Nicolás Guaguari (Chayanta repartimiento) in 1779, ANB, EC, 1779, 257.

17 ANB, EC, 1750, 60.

18 ANB, EC, 1750, 20.

19 ANB, EC, 1772, 58.

20 On the case of Tapacarí, Cochabamba, see Larson 1997: 159–67. Puracas and Chullpas exhibited, between 1747 and 1750, at least four lists of tribute payers, some of which detailed the hamlets, minor ayllus, and number of cabildo officeholders and ritual sponsors (ANB, EC, 1750, 20; ANB, EC, 1750, 60; ANB, EC, 1772, 58).

21 ANB, EC, 1750, 20.

22 On the Policarios, see Serulnikov 2003.

23 On the applicability of the concept of moral economy to Andean communities, see Larson 1989; Stavig 1988.

24 In the 1760s, the Bombo leases were reportedly used for sustaining the church's singers and covering tributes (ANB, EC, 1762, 63). In 1835, these fields continued to be rented for 300 pesos (Platt 1982b: 44–46).

25 ANB, EC, 1762, 63. Bernabé Choque had reportedly spread the word that "the Royal Audiencia had ordered the rented lands to be 'divided' among the Indians."

26 ANB, TI, 1775, 54.

27 ANB, TI, 1775, 54.

28 ANB, Minas, 127, XIII, 1757, 1151. Vilca's successor, Pedro Yavira, said the caciques spent much money in salaries "for the judges who are asked to settle conflicts over land demarcations, which are almost every year called into question by the dwellers" (ANB, EC, 1762, 63).

29 ANB, TI, 1758, 3.

30 ANB, TI, 1758, 3.

31 The Chullpas explained that land invasions had taken place "in the boundary [mojón] of Acarani, bordering with the community of Carachas. The other boundary is named Villa Apacheta and borders with the Chayantacas and Sicoyas. The other one, Chinchifalla, also borders with the Sicoyas" (ANB, TI, 1772, 98, f. 94). On land conflicts within the Pocoata group, see Serulnikov 2000.

32 Colqueruna payments could have first represented a way of raising money to compensate the mining entrepreneurs for shortcomings in the number of mitayos, or to commute labor services by cash (Cole 1985: 36–45; Bakewell 1984: 123–24). Toward the late seventeenth century, the caciques seemed to begin to use this practice as a way of exempting well-off Indians (Tandeter 1992: 77–79).

33 ANB, Minas, 127, XIV, 1757, 1153.

34 ANB, Minas, 127, XII, 1757, 1151.

35 ANB, TI, 1772, 98.

36 Tandeter 1992: 74–75. Cangiano (1987: 13–14) has calculated, for the case of the Auquimarcas, that approximately 18 percent of the maize produced in communal lands was used for the mitayos' maintenance.

37 August 1758, ANB, TI, 1758, 3.

38 Ibid. On the Puraca cacique's failure to provide for the mitayos, see the testimonies of the seven mitayos appearing before Potosí governor Santelices in ANB, Minas, 127, XIV, 1757, 1153.

39 ANB, TI, 1761, 30. In order to access these funds, caciques needed the authorization of corregidores and priests.

40 ANB, Minas, 152, X, 1759–1779.

41 ANB, TI, 1761, 30. In 1762, the Caracha cacique said that the Chullpas "have influenced the mita Indians and alfereces about not paying [tribute] under the promise that they would defend them" (ANB, EC, 1762, 63).

42 It must be noted that the disclosure of concealed tributaries did not imply in principle tax increases for peasant families. It just meant that caciques had to submit to the state a larger part of the overall tribute collected from the community.

43 See also Rivera Cusicanqui 1992: 97–99.

44 March 1761, ANB, TI, 1761, 30.

45 See Choque 1978; Barragán Romano 1985; Cangiano 1987; Zulawski 1987; Stern 1995; Rivera Cusicanqui 1978; Saignes 1987; Glave 1989: 279–304.

46 August 1757, ANB, Minas, 127, XIV, 1757–58, 1153.

47 ANB, TI, 1761, 30.

48 March 1762, ANB, TI, 1761, 30.

49 See Stern 1995: 73–99; Rivera Cusicanqui 1978; Saignes 1987: 156.

50 On the concrete workings of the colonial justice system in Mexico and Peru, see Borah 1983: 237–47; Stern 1982: chap. 5; Walker 1999: 69–83.

51 April 1750, ANB, EC, 1772, 98.

52 March 1748, ANB, EC, 1750, 20. It was said that one of the judges took testimonies from "mestizos, forasteros, compadres, and nephews of Tococari and my priest . . . [they] declared against God's name what they do not know" (January 1749, ANB, EC, 1750, 20).

53 ANB, EC, 1750, 20.

54 May 1748, ANB, EC, 1750, 20.

55 ANB, EC, 1753, 104.

56 Isidro Policario to Alcalde Francisco Ignacio and Alguacil Pedro Chira, September 1752, ANB, EC, 1753, 140.

57 ANB, EC, 1750, 20.

58 ANB, EC, 1762, 63.

59 Ignacio Bohorquez, ANB, EC, 1750, 20.

60 Florencio Gallo y Veles, ANB, EC, 1750, 20.

61 ANB, EC, 1750, 20.

62 José Ignacio Virto to corregidor Vargas, March 1748, ANB, EC, 1750, 20.

63 José Ignacio Virto, August 1748. ANB, EC, 1750, 20. Two years later, Chullpa Indians complained that during Lent cacique Gregorio Jorge de Medina had demanded 2 reales for church reparations: "We think that most of this he has kept for himself because the expenses of the monument are not that high, and even if they were, we should not be forced to contribute what should be voluntary" (ANB, EC, 1772, 98).

64 The date of the Chayantacas's cabildo is mentioned in a nineteenth-century document cited in Platt 1987a: 289.

65 In June, the authorities managed to produce a writing in which the Puracas declared that since Tococari had been removed, "we desist from, cease, and put aside the lawsuit and proceedings that we initiated against him" (Andrés, Asencio, and Sebastián Auca, ANB, EC, 1750, 20).

66 A 1754 census of San Pedro de Buena Vista shows that Arsiniega owned the hacienda Chacoma (AGN, XIII, 18–9–2).

67 In 1780–1781, Arsiniega led the San Pedro militia in the bloody clashes with rebel forces. His hacienda was looted (AGN, IX, Criminales, Leg. 18, Exp. 3).

68 ANB, EC, 1750, 20 (italics mine).

69 Ibid.

70 Ibid.

71 Ibid.

72 Ibid.

73 Ibid.

74 Ibid.

75 Choque to Domingo de Toledo, March 1750, ANB, EC, 1750, 20. This letter indicates some complicity between the priest and the Indians. By contrast, in Chayanta town, the main center of agitation, the priests firmly defended the beleaguered caciques.

76 April 1748, ANB, EC, 1750, 20.

77 Letters of José Ignacio Virto and Nicolás Virto to corregidor Vargas. March and April 1748, ANB, EC, 1750, 20.

78 See, for instance, testimonies of Dalmacio Nina, Luis Pomar de Medina, and Florencio Gallo y Veles, April 1748, ANB, EC, 1750, 20.

79 Manuel Chico, Gregorio Jorge de Medina, Marcos Tococari, Juan de la Cruz Portugal, Gregorio Mamani, Pedro Yavira, Pedro Choque, Gaspar Soto, Diego Flores, Sebastián Senteno, Cruz Chico, Mathias Ventura, Cristobal Torocari, Matheo Torocari, and Francisco Guarachi to corregidor Vargas, April 1748, ANB, EC, 1750, 20.

80 The Pocoata cacique (Anansaya moiety) Blas Cori appears here under the name of Blas Quispe. The Macha caciques of Anansaya and Urinsaya were Francisco Porcel, Nicolás Flores, Lorenzo Mamani, and Blas Centeno, April 1748, ANB, EC, 1750, 20.

81 ANB, EC, 1750, 20.

82 ANB, EC, 1750, 20.

83 ANB, EC, 1750, 20.

84 Report of Gómez García, May 1748, ANB, EC, 1750, 20. Information on Gómez García is given in Burkholder and Chandler 1982: 140.

85 July 1749, ANB, EC, 1750, 20.

86 May 1749, ANB, EC, 1750, 20.

87 March 1749, ANB, EC, 1750, 20.

88 ANB, EC, 1750, 20.

89 On Landaeta's family, see Cornblit 1995: chap. 7.

90 Sebastián Auca, April 1750, ANB, EC 1750, 60.

91 Indian families completed the Navidad quota in June and July during festivities in the valleys, where they resided for the maize harvest (Platt 1987a: 289–90). The Puraca cacique said that, "he had not collected the whole amount because some of the Indians were in their valley lands and others dispersed within and outside this Province" (ANB, EC, 1750, 20).

92 ANB, EC, 1750, 60.

93 Imprisoned Indians, some of them in handcuffs, paid Landaeta 67 pesos. Asencio Auca, Sebastián's father, had all his goods confiscated (ANB, EC, 1750, 20).

94 ANB, EC, 1750, 20.

95 Two alcaldes reported that on March 21 Francisco Choque climbed the walls of the prison and ran away with another Indian prisoner ANB, EC, 1750, 20.

96 ANB, EC, 1750, 20 (italics mine).

97 ANB, EC, 1750, 60.

98 Ibid. See also Marcos Condori's testimony.

99 López Lisperguer's arguments are from a report of April 12, 1750 (ANB, EC, 1750, 20) and a report of April 17 (ANB, EC, 1750, 60). López Lisperguer and Gómez García considered the repression of the Jukumanis absolutely unjustified (April 12, 1750, ANB, EC, 1750, 20; April 20, 1750, ANB, EC, 1750, 60).

100 Audiencia's edict, May 1750, ANB, EC, 1750, 60. Puraca's recount in Aoíz's edict, August 1750, ANB, EC, 1750, 60. The census produced an increase of thirty-nine Indians and 234 pesos per year. The recount of Chullpa Aoíz's edict is in July 1750, ANB, TI, 1772, 98.

101 ANB, TI, 1772, 98.

102 December 1750, ANB, EC, 1750, 60.

103 On Chayanta, see ANB, EC, 1753, 104; on Bombo, see ANB, EC, 1754, 103. For a thorough

analysis of conflicts over diezmos and veintenas, including the case of Bombo, see Barragán and Thomson 1993.

104 ANB, TI, 1753, 140. On this inquiry, see Serulnikov 2003.

105 Policarios to audiencia, ANB, EC, 1755, 63.

106 While Caracara alluded to a seventeenth-century cacique, his claim clearly rested on the active peasants' support, as well as his involvement in the denunciations leading to the demise of Dionisio Choque and Gregorio Jorge de Medina in the 1740s (ANB, TI, 1772, 98).

107 AGN, IX, Criminales, Leg. 18, Exp. 3, f. 153. In February 1781, one of the main insurgent leaders, a Sicoya Indian named Simón Castillo, wrote to other rebel Indians that Caracara was the only cacique who had not sought refuge inside the church of the San Pedro de Buena Vista (ff. 138–39).

108 July 1757, ANB, TI, 1758, 3. He added that all the charges against the caciques were false, with the exception of being drunkards, "which all the Indians are."

109 November 1757, ANB, Minas, 127, XIV, 1757, 1153. During his tenure, Santelices took several measures to protect mita workers from abuses that were sharply opposed by elite groups (Tandeter 1992: 55, 63, 72, 129–34).

110 For examples of punitive measures, see Pedro Pisgua to Santelices, and several Puracas to Potosí's Protector of Indians, October 1757, ANB, Minas, 127, XIV, 1757, 1153.

111 The new Chayantaca cacique was arrested, among other times, during the celebration of San Francisco (October 4, 1758), All Souls Day (November 1, 1758), the Exaltation of the Cross (November 1758), and Candlemas (February 3, 1759) (ANB, EC, 1759, 163). On Espinoza, see ANB, TI, 1772, 118.

112 The census is in AGN, XIII, 18-7-3.

113 See the 1786 census in AGN, XIII, 18-10-3. In the 1790s, Puraca and Laymi had again different caciques and segundas (Cangiano 1987: 35). In the nineteenth century, Puraca and Laymi continued as two distinct ethnic groups (Platt 1987a: 288, 308). Harris (1986: 262–63) has noted that present-day Laymis's and Puracas's territories are intermingled, while the social (and spatial) identity of the other four groups of the town of Chayanta is clearly differentiated.

114 ANB, Minas, 127, XIV, 1757, 1153.

2 From a Multiethnic Community to a Multiethnic Chieftainship

1 Benito Carrión de la Piedra, ANB, SGI, 1781, 83.

2 Lorenzo Delgadillo, ibid.

3 Audiencia's edict, ibid.

4 ANB, SGI, 1781, 83.

5 Francisco Arias, ANB, SGI, 1781, 83.

6 A 1624 census still included the Moscari community within the Chayanta repartimiento, although it was given as an independent *pueblo* instead of as a *parcialidad*, the designation given to the other ethnic groups (AGN, XIII, 18-7-1). On Moscari, see also Penry 1996: 152–61.

7 Some documents refer to the Moscari community as having eight ayllus instead of four (AGN, IX, Interior, Leg. 8, Exp. 1, ff. 163–66; ANB, SGI, 1784, 112).

8 Manrique quoted in de Angelis 1971: 43.

9 On Indian labor in haciendas in various Andean regions, see Macera 1971; Polo Laborda 1981; Stern 1982; chap. 6; Glave and Remy 1983; Larson 1997; Stavig 1999: 133–38.

10 AGN, XIII, 18–9–2.

11 By the mid-1760s, twenty-five Moscari families lived in the hamlets of Hipira and Consata, and ten in Coropoya (AGN, XIII, 18–9–5).

12 Martín Cochini and Francisco Catusiri, ANB, TI, 1773, 34.

13 Martín Cochini, Pedro Gonzalo, and Ambrosio Guango, ibid.

14 ANB, SGI, 1784, 112.

15 In the late 1770s, Ramirez reportedly was in the service of corregidor Joaquín Alós, Lupa's close ally (ANB, SGI, 1784, 112). In October 1780, Pedro Velazco was among the Indians testifying in the audiencia in favor of the murdered cacique (AGN, IX, Interior, Leg. 8, Exp. 8). It must be noted, however, that, in the late 1760s, Ramírez defended Moscari priest Josef de Osa Palacio against charges that Lupa had brought against him (Penry 1996: 203–4).

16 Larson 1979: 214. On Fernández Guarachi, see Rivera Cusicanqui 1978.

17 AGN, IX, Interior, Leg. 1, ff. 123–24; AGN, IX, Interior, Leg. 10, Exp. 1, ff. 213–14.

18 ANB, SGI, 1784, 112.

19 Testimonies of Marcos Colque and Marcelino Lupa, Ibid. On Marcos Colque's leadership role in the rebellion, cf. chapter 6.

20 Francisco Arias, ANB, SGI, 1781, 160.

21 Juan Lupa appears as cacique in 1614 and 1624 censuses (AGN, XIII, 18–7–1). The 1645 document is in AGN, XIII, 18–9–5.

22 ANB, EC, 1697, 47.

23 "Recibos de salarios de los caciques," AGN, XIII, 18–9–2. Forty-eight-year-old Martín Lupa figures as cacique in a 1725 census (AGN, XIII, 18–8–4). It is unclear whether he was the same cacique of 1697. As discussed in chapter 1, he was involved in the conflicts of the 1740s.

24 AGN, IX, Interior, Leg. 8, Exp. 1, f. 123–24.

25 AGN, IX, Interior, Leg. 8, Exp. 14 (italics mine).

26 ANB, TI, 1773, 34.

27 This exaction continued well into the nineteenth and twentieth centuries (Platt 1987a: 291; Rivera Cusicanqui 1992: 101).

28 Matheo Estevan, ANB, TI, 1773, 34.

29 Martin Cochini, ibid.

30 Pascual Alejo, ibid.

31 Pascual Mamani, ibid.

32 Matheo Estevan, ibid.

33 Francisco de la Torre, ibid.

34 Lopez Vázquez, ibid.

35 Marcelino Lupa, December 1781, ANB, SGI, 1784, 112.

36 Marcelino Lupa, July 1784, ANB, SGI, 1784, 112. It was reported that most of the Moscari haciendas' value came from the mills rather than land (AGN, XIII, 18–9–5, ff. 6–7). On the economic function of grain mills in Cochabamba, see Larson 1997: 185–86.

37 As an audiencia minister remarked in 1779, "by not allowing the Indians to make flour from the grains, and then selling them, they are deprived of all the benefit" (AGN, IX, Interior, Leg. 8, Exp. 14, ff. 23–24).

38 Moscari hilacatas Bartolomé Quispe, Pedro Flores, and Lazaro Chipata, ANB, TI, 1773, 34.

39 ANB, TI, 1773, 34, ff. 44–45.

40 Francisco de la Torre, ibid.

41 On the formation of a class of hacendados among native elite, see Rivera Cusicanqui 1978; Larson 1997: 152–70; Pease 1992: 154–69.

42 ANB, TI, 1773, 34, ff. 45–47.

43 ANB, EC, 1776, 77, ff. 39–47.

44 This litigation is in ANB, TI, 1773, 34. Ten years older than Florencio, Pedro was also Martín Lupa's grandson (AGN, XIII, 18–8–4). Because both before and after the Spanish conquest hereditary rights were not ruled by rigid European criteria of primogeniture, successions were potentially always open to contestation. See Rasnake 1988: 116–17; Rostworowski 1961: 58–62. Florencio forced his cousin to live outside Moscari. Pedro died in La Plata in the late 1760s (AGN, XIII, 18–9–5).

45 The sentence is of September 1760 (ANB, TI, 1773, 34).

46 Matheo Jorge, March 1770, ANB, TI, 1773, 34; and fiscal head Castilla, ANB, EC, 1776, 77.

47 AGN, IX, Interior, Leg. 8, Exp. 14, ff. 23–24.

48 "Representación hecha al rey por D. Tomás Catari," October 13, 1780, in de Angelis 1971: 662–63.

49 See Sánchez-Albornoz 1978: 35–67; Larson 1997: 97–101; Wightman 1990.

50 See Spalding 1974: 61–87; Assadourian 1982: 314; Sánchez-Albornoz 1978: 43.

51 See Zulawski 1987: 159–92; Saignes 1983: 27–75, and 1995; Powers 1995.

52 AGN, XIII, 18–7–3.

53 In 1786, the subdelegado of Chayanta noted that it was customary for tenants and Indians with few land allocations to pay 5 pesos (AGN, XIII, 18–10–3, ff. 103–4). The crown established this tax in 1734 (Klein 1993: 11), but until 1786 Chayanta had only two official taxes, 9 pesos 6 reales (originarios) and 7 pesos (forasteros and agregados).

54 AGN, IX, Interior, Leg. 10, Exp. 1, ff. 110–14; and AGN, IX, Interior, Leg. 8, Exp. 1, ff. 163–66.

55 ANB, TI, 1773, 34.

56 Corregidor Navarro, "Autos obrados por Juan Francisco Navarro, Corregidor de Chayanta, sobre la numeración de Indios de Moscari," AGN, XIII, 18–9–5. On this process, see also Adrián 1996: 106–7.

57 AGN, XIII, 18–9–5.

58 On January 1765, the justicia mayor also composed a new census that registered 107 households (AGN, XIII, 18–9–5).

59 Among other forms of fiscal fraud, Navarro reported that Urtizberea requested 200 to 400 pesos from the native lords "in exchange for their right to grant exemption to whomever they wished, saying that in the long term this would be much more profitable for them." As evidence, Navarro sent to Viceroy Amat an original blank receipt issued by Urtizberea that read: "The Indian [blank space] is over fifty years of age and therefore he is tax exempt and no governor from now on can demand from him tribute payments or mita service." The receipt was signed by Urtizberea and dated in the Chayanta village, February 28, 1765 (AGN, XIII, 18–9–5).

60 Edict of Navarro, AGN, XIII, 18–9–5.

61 Lupa to Navarro, ibid.

62 Navarro to Amat, ibid.

63 AGN, XIII, 18–9–5.

64 Report of Lima's Contador de Retazas, AGN, XIII, 18–9–5.

65 See Larson 1997: 92–108; Stern 1982: chap. 6; Assadourian 1979.

66 AGN, XIII, 18–9–5. This figure is consistent with 1614 and 1624 censuses, which listed 93 and 81 tributaries, respectively (AGN, XIII, 18–7–1).

67 Navarro to Amat, AGN, XIII, 18–9–5, ff. 1–7.

68 Ibid., ff. 87–91.

69 See also Platt 1982a: 33.

70 AGN, XIII, 18–9–5.

71 Navarro to Amat, ibid.

72 AGN, XIII, 18–9–5.

73 This litigation is in ANB, TI, 1773, 34.

74 Basilio Catuziri, July 1760, ANB, TI, 1773, 34; Bartolomé Quispe, Pedro Flores, and Lazaro Chipata, July 1760, ANB, TI, 1773, 34. Matheo Jorge, Manuel Baleriana, Tomás Chipara, and Matheo Caysari, June 1769, ANB, TI, 1773, 34. On Matheo Jorge, see 1754 census of Moscari (AGN, XIII, 18–9–2).

75 ANB, TI, 1773, 34, ff. 3–4. A detailed analysis of the disputes between Osa Palacios and Lupa is in Penry 1996: 194–213.

76 ANB, TI, 1773, 3y.

77 ANB, TI, 1773, 34 ff. 3–4, 87–88, 109.

78 On the forced distribution of goods, see ANB, TI, 1773, 34, f. 1–2; on the haciendas, see Penry 1996: 207, 211–12. In addition, Osa Palacios on occasion refused to bless Lupa at the end of Mass and once slapped him in the plaza of Moscari (Penry 1996: 196, 200).

79 A Chayanta priest wrote in 1748 to corregidor Vargas that "the good Lupa (whom your majesty knows very well)" was responsible for inciting the Indians against their caciques (ANB, EC, 1750, 20).

80 ANB, TI, 1772, 98. A Carasi priest reported that having asked the protesters "who dictated their writings, they finally declared that the governor of the Moscari parish, don Florencio Lupa, had done it" (ANB, EC, 1720, 120, f. 53). The conflict between Lupa and Osa Palacios in the late 1760s was one of the antecedents for the issuance of church tariff lists in the Charcas district (Adrián 1995: 18–19). As I show in the next chapter, however, the widespread protests against church levies during the 1770s could not be exclusively attributed to Lupa.

81 AGN, IX, Interior, Leg. 10, Exp. 1, ff. 110–114.

82 Katari quoted in de Angelis 1971: 662–63. To be sure, Katari and the Moscari Indians' remarks against Lupa should not be taken as a token of their approval of the priests' behavior or of church economic demands. During the rebellion of 1780, Katari would note the priests' resistance to lower ecclesiastical fees as one of the chief motives of Indian outrage. A few months after killing Lupa, the Moscari Indians were involved in a massacre of priests and other people inside the church of the town of San Pedro de Buena Vista (cf. chapters 5 and 6).

83 In the context of the revolt of hacienda tenants in August 1780, Lupa singled out the owners of the hacienda Chirocari, Yarquivirique, Lipichicayme, and Pisaca for stirring indigenous violence (AGN, IX, Interior, Leg. 10, Exp. 1, ff. 110–14). Sandoval also had links with the Moscari's priest (Penry 1996: 278).

84 ANB, TI, 1773, 34, ff. 70–72, 135–36. Ten years later, after killing Florencio Lupa, Moscari rebels tried to capture two persons in particular: Juan Lupa, Florencio's son, and a man named Donoso Estévez (AGN, IX, Interior, Leg. 10, Exp. 1, ff. 213–14).

85 ANB, TI, 1773, 34, ff. 12–13.

86 Ibid., ff. 117–26.

87 Ibid., f. 83.

88 Ibid., ff. 21–22.

89 Ibid., ff. 17–20. Ursainqui handed over the report to Lupa during the meeting for the collection of tribute in Macha on August 29. Lupa then sent it to the audiencia.

90 ANB, TI, 1773, 34, ff. 11–11v.

91 Jorge to Escobar, March 1770, ANB, TI, 1773, 34, f. 136. Jorge later said that Ursainqui was Lupa's "compadre and dinner guest" and observed that all of La Plata's lawyers had refused to represent the Indians (f. 137).

92 Jorge to the audiencia, March 1770, ANB, TI, 1773, 34, f. 137.

93 ANB, TI, 1773, 34, ff. 141–50.

94 Information on Lupa's appointment as cacique of Panacachi and Pocoata is in AGN, IX, Interior, Leg. 4, Exp. 7.

95 Other than the twelve families leasing lands in a Moscari hacienda, the Pocoatas did not share valley lands with Moscari ayllus. Before the Spanish conquest, Moscari territory was encompassed by the Charcas confederation, whereas Pocoata belonged to the Karakara confederation.

96 AGN, XIII, 18–9–2. The ayllus belonging to Anansaya were Collana, Pisaca, Chacaya, Carigua, and Pari; the Urinsaya ayllus were Capac, Sulcavi, Hilata, Chanca, Hilave, and Sullcata. For a demographic and agrarian analysis of eighteenth-century Pocoata, see Serulnikov 2000.

97 Serulnikov 2000. At least one Pocoata ayllu, Capac, was noted as favoring the appointment of Lupa as a way of improving their members' standing in these land disputes.

98 Lupa stressed that many Pocoatas named Ayra refused "to give up the excessive lands they occupy, for during their term as tribute collectors they monopolized for themselves and their relatives the best of the community lands. Hence, everyone regards himself as a hacendado and makes use of the lands as he wishes, entirely contradicting royal ordinances" (ANB, EC, 1776, 12, f. 18). Diego Ayra, one of the Pocoata caciques (Urinsaya) replaced by Lupa, owned for instance a hacienda in Chayala, a valley populated by two Urinsaya ayllus. The hacienda accommodated several Indian families and at least two Spanish and mestizo residents (ANB, EC, 1776, 57, ff. 72–73, and 108).

99 AGN, IX, Interior, Leg. 4, Exp. 7.

100 Escobar's report, August 1772, ibid.

101 Audiencia's edict, November 1772, ibid.

102 Juan José de Saavedra to audiencia, October 1772, ibid.

103 Escobar's report, October 5, 1772, ibid.

104 Escobar to audiencia, October 8, 1772, ibid.

105 AGN, XIII, 23–3–1, Cuaderno 1.

106 Esteban Baldivieso, May 1781, ANB, SGI, 1781, 160. (Note that as an ally of the Ayras, the former Pocoata caciques, Baldivieso had also personal motives to recall this event. See ANB, TI, 1775, 111.)

3 Customs and Rules

1 Karen Spalding (1984: 216) has observed that the original model for village government was mainly drawn "from Renaissance plans for ideal states."

2 See, for instance, Saignes 1983; Wightman 1990; Burkholder and Chandler 1977; Burga 1988.

3　See Pietschmann 1987; MacLachlan 1988; Lynch 1992; Voekel 1992.

4　See Joseph and Nugent 1994, Mollen 1995.

5　See, for example, Fisher, Kuethe, and McFarlane 1990: 1–16; O'Phelan Godoy 1988: 175–221.

6　Reforms encompassed, with varying degrees of success, a precise regulation of corregidores' forced distribution of commodities, a greater control over the church, a removal of creoles from government, and the setting up of more efficient tax collection systems, such as the elimination of tax farming or the erection of customhouses to secure the collection of the alcabala.

7　Edict of corregidor Hereña, May 5, 1772, ANB, EC, 1776, 57.

8　Ibid.

9　During 1774, all the corregidores confirmed the reception of this order (ANB, Minas, 127, XXII, 1773, 1161).

10　Marcos Soto (Laymi-Puraca), Alejandro Yavira y Ayavirí (Caracha), Manuel Ninavia (Chullpa), Esteban Callisaya (Sicoya), Andrés Villegas (Chayantacas), Esteban Sicara (Panacachi), Leonardo Umacaya (Jukumani), and Pedro Gallego (Aymaya) to Ursainqui, September 1770, AGN, XIII, 18–10–2, Libro 2.

11　On Pereira de Castro's population count, see AGN, XIII, 18–10–2, Libro 2; ANB, TI, 1776, 77; ANB, TI, 1779, 76.

12　The agregados paid variable taxes of 2 pesos 4 reales, 2 pesos, or 1 peso 4 reales, none of which corresponded to state rates (AGN, XIII, 18–10–2, Libro 2). On sixteenth-century tribute exemption of Indians serving civil and church offices, see Spalding 1984: 218–19.

13　A thorough discussion of the revisita process is in Stern 1982: 121–28; Salomon 1994: 1–34.

14　Luis Lojo, ANB, TI, 1773, 34.

15　Andrés Cala, ibid.

16　Twenty-one Indians submitted 10 pesos, ten Indians 3 pesos, and thirty-eight Indians 5 pesos (AGN, IX, Interior, Leg. 5, Exp. 2).

17　ANB, EC, 1750, 20.

18　AGN, XIII, 18–9–2. The extraordinarily large number of ritual sponsors, and the fact that the posts were rotating, explains that most Indians involved in collective protest against caciques, priests, or corregidores were (or had been in the past) part of the fiesta-cargo system.

19　ANB, TI, 1772, 14.

20　AGN, IX, Interior, Leg. 4, Exp. 7.

21　ANB, TI, 1775, 111.

22　ANB, TI, 1779, 195, ff. 27–28.

23　Commenting on peasant responses to the transformations during the European ancient régime, Levi (1988: xv) observed that "a rationality specific to the peasant world . . . not only [found] its expression in resistance to the spread of the new society, but it was also actively engaged in transforming and utilizing both the social and natural world. This is the sense in which I have used the word 'strategy.'"

24　AGN, IX, Interior, Leg. 4, Exp. 7.

25　ANB, TI, 1779, 195, ff. 47–49.

26　It was said that "there are other Indians who can be Governors without demanding these new taxes and allowing Indians to keep their old customs to which they are so attached" (ANB, TI, 1779, 195, f. 67).

27　AGN, IX, Tribunales, Leg. 65, Exp. 54, ff. 1–3.

28 Melchor Espinoza, AGN, IX, Tribunales, Leg. 181, Exp. 29.

29 AGN, IX, Tribunales, Leg. 65, Exp. 54, ff. 1–3.

30 ANB, EC, 1776, 57, ff. 31–32.

31 ANB, Minas, 127, XXII, 1773, 1161.

32 See Farriss 1968; Cahill 1984; Taylor 1996; Ramos 1994.

33 Given the dispersed patterns of settlement, however, the clergy's control over peasant life should not be exaggerated. For instance, referring to the Pocoatas, Lupa said that the Indians kept unlawful spouses and "have their children receive the sacrament of the Baptism only when they [go] to the village for some annual feasts, leaving their sons without the oil until the age of ten or twelve years" (ANB, TI, 1775, 111, f. 3).

34 By the mid-eighteenth century the fourteen Indian parishes of Chayanta claimed nearly 40 percent of the overall tribute dues (AGN, XIII, 18–9–2). Parish fees might have produced even higher revenues. A comparison of Hunacavelica and Caranga shows that direct payments from the parishioners produced a higher yield than did synods (O'Phelan Godoy 1988: 133–34; Cahill 1984: 261). On feasts and conflicts over church fees in colonial northern Potosí, see Adrián 1995 and 1996; Penry 1996: 219–67.

35 Archivo de La Paz, UMSA, Intendencia Justicia Año 1795 (I am grateful to Tristan Platt for providing me his notes on this document). On the indigenous obligations for feast days in eighteenth-century Upper Peru, see Cangiano 1987: 25–43; Platt 1987b; Adrián 1995; Penry 1996: 219–67; Serulnikov 1999: 253–60. On the southern Andes, see Santamaría 1983; Abercrombie 1998: 291–94.

36 In the case of the valley parish of Carasi, the corpus ricuchicu included a fat cow, a pig, a flask of wine, a *fanega* of flour, a *carga* of potatoes, a peso of cakes, a peso of bread, a dozen of hen, a gift of 8 pesos and 2 reales for spices, oil, and vinegar, a box of sweets, two platters of *chocachoca*, two bowls of *chuño* (freeze-dried potatoes), two bowls of peeled maize, a real of *ají* (dried chilis), a real of green peppers, a real of tomatoes, a real of cabbage, a real of little squashes, a real of eggs, an olla of lard, and a pound of beeswax. The corpus alfereces also offered the priest a leg and the tongue of a cow they slaughtered especially for the festivities (ANB, EC, 1772, 120, ff. 1–3).

37 The priests of the Carasi and Chayantaca parishes explained, for example, that ritual sponsors were assigned more plots and other Indians helped them to sow and harvest their fields. The standard-bearers responsible for paying major feasts (over 100 pesos) received even further land and labor allocations (ANB, EC, 1772, 120, f. 55, 76–78).

38 In the 1790s, the intendant of Potosí explained that the Indians served as alfereces "a cuenta de la mita" (on account of the mita) (Cangiano 1987: 30). Cangiano's study provides examples of the system of turns between mita and ritual sponsorships for the Chayanta communities. The participation of the alferazgos into an integrated system of forced labor rotation was also pointed out by the Chayanta priest in 1771 (ANB, EC, 1772, 120, ff. 76–78).

39 The cacique lieutenants from Pocoata, Macha, and Laymi said the Carasi priest did not participate in the appointment of ritual sponsors because "it is a tradition that [the cacique lieutenants] wait for the arrival of their caciques, which usually is by [the feast of] San Juan [in June], and each governor gets together with his segunda and his people, and chooses the alfereces of each ayllu in such a way that very often the priest does not know who they will be, and only finds out the very day of the feast" (ANB, EC, 1772, 120 ff. 16–17). On the involvement of puna caciques of Macha in affairs in the valley parishes of San Marcos de Miraflores and Surumi, see ANB, SGI,

1782, 10. On the case of San Marcos de Miraflores and Micani, see Platt 1987b: 184; Cangiano 1987. The stronger role of the caciques vis-à-vis the priests in the election of ritual sponsors has also been pointed out for the case of the La Paz region in Thomson 1996: 62–65.

40 ANB, EC, 1772, 120, f. 55.

41 On the 1767 arancel in New Spain, see Taylor 1996: 425–47; on the Andes, see O'Phelan Godoy 1995: 314; on Chayanta, see Adrián 1995: 15–22.

42 ANB, EC, 1772, 120, f. 31. The 1770 arancel was meant to moderate and replace two previous tariff lists issued in 1628 and 1653 (Santamaría 1983: 9).

43 ANB, EC, 1772, 120, ff. 31–33.

44 For firsthand accounts of ancestor cults and rituals during feast days in eighteenth-century northern Potosí, see ANB, EC, 1750, 20, ff. 62–65, and Archbishop San Alberto's description of the All Saints' Day feast in Buechler 1981: 215. See also Platt 1987b: 144. For ethnographic studies, see, for instance, Abercrombie 1998: chap. 8; Rasnake 1988: 165–229; Pacheco Balanza and Guerrero Peñaranda 1994: 113–49; Platt 1983: 50–62; Harris 2000: 27–50.

45 The banner remains today the prime focus of "ritual attention" in the feasts celebrated in the southern Andes (Rasnake 1988: 158–59).

46 Note that Andean peasants defended customary ritual celebrations (thereby implicitly or explicitly disavowing Bourbon polices of rationalization and secularization) at the same time that they strove to curtail the large amount of agrarian surpluses appropriated by the rural parishes.

47 ANB, EC, 1772, 120, ff. 44–46. It must be stressed that structural antagonisms between caciques/corregidores versus priests/ritual sponsors does not seem to account for the struggles over political power and economic resources in Chayanta. Despite the ongoing conflicts between the archbishopric of Charcas and the corregidores over repartos (O'Phelan Godoy 1988: 168), neither the archbishop nor the rural priests complained about the Chayanta corregidor, Carlos de Hereña, or his justicia mayor and successor, Nicolás Ursainqui. One of the accused priests even urged the audiencia to consult Ursainqui about how riotous his Indian parishioners were at the time (ANB, EC, 1772, 120, f. 76–78). By contrast, some Indians explicitly requested the audiencia not to place the corregidor in charge of publishing the arancel "because they were convinced that he would do nothing" (ANB, EC, 1772, 120 f. 81). As suggested below, Ursainqui acted in collusion with the beleaguered Aymaya priest Dionisio Cortés. The caciques did not have direct participation either, and with the exception of Florencio Lupa (Moscari), Alejandro Yavira (Caracha), and, more indirectly, Manuel Ninavia (Chullpa), Indians and priests did not mention them as promoting the protests. Interestingly, while Lupa did enjoy the corregidores' strong support and had a longstanding feud with some of the priests (cf. chapter 2), Ninavia and Yavira were removed from their posts by this time. Furthermore, ritual sponsors were clearly among the protesters against church levies. Chapter 5 shows that exactly the same grievances (including the publication of the arancel) would resurface during the insurrection, when the power of caciques like Lupa and corregidores had entirely vanished. Then, in the 1790s, commoner Indians, even in the context of rejecting a state proposal to commute church services by new mining mita assignments, voiced their sharp dissatisfaction with the monetary charges associated with Catholic festivals (Cangiano 1987: 31–33).

48 ANB, EC, 1772, 120 ff. 34–36 (italics mine).

49 Ibid., ff. 36–38.

50 Ibid., ff. 39–40.

51 Ibid., f. 61.

52 Ibid., ff. 32–34.

53 Ibid., f. 49.

54 Ibid., f. 76.

55 ANB, TI, 1778, 48, ff. 55–56.

56 ANB, EC, 1772, 120, ff. 78–79.

57 Ibid., ff. 76–78.

58 Ibid., ff. 78–79.

59 ANB, TI, 1772, 194 (italics mine). Macha Indians had previously attested that the priests committed acts of extortion "so that just because a chicken was not given to them they suspended one feast." And if they reacted in this way over one chicken, they insisted, "it would be even worse over interests and money, especially now that [the Feast of] San Sebastián is approaching. Seven alfereces have been appointed for this feast, and each one has to contribute 35 pesos, besides the obligation of the ricuchicu and other offerings" (ANB, EC, 1772, 120, f. 111).

60 ANB, EC, 1772, 120, f. 81.

61 Ibid., ff. 87–92 (italics mine).

62 See also Scott 1985: 306–7.

63 ANB, EC, 1772, 120, ff. 87–92 (italics mine).

64 Ibid., f. 98.

65 Ibid., ff. 111–12.

66 ANB, TI, 1778, 48, ff. 56–57.

67 Ibid., f. 51.

68 Ibid., f. 54.

69 AGN, XIII, 23–3–1. The previous Jukumani cacique was named Leonardo Umacaya.

70 Cutting the hair of those who resisted marriage was mentioned among the punishments (ANB, TI, 1778, 48, ff. 15–16, 21–22).

71 On sirvignacuy, see Stavig 1999: 38.

72 ANB, TI, 1778, 48, ff. 21–22.

73 Ibid., ff. 1–2. Colque's alleged mistress reportedly passed away while in jail (ff. 25–27). A discussion of polygyny in seventeenth-century Sacaca and Acacio is in Tandeter 1997.

74 ANB, TI, 1778, 48, ff. 73–74.

75 Ibid., ff. 21–22.

76 ANB, TI, 1778, 48, ff. 15–27.

77 Ibid., f. 70 (Joseph Roque spoke Spanish). Note that Roque was under strong pressure to excuse himself for his participation in this protest.

78 Ibid., f. 80.

79 On chullpas and mojones, see Abercrombie 1998: 181–82, and 288–89; Rasnake 1988: 250–59.

80 ANB, TI, 1778, 48, ff. 15–16. This Indian, Matheo Choque, had been involved in the conflicts of 1771–1772.

81 AGN, IX, Criminales, Leg. 18, Exp. 3, ff. 140–41.

82 ANB, EC, 1776, 57, ff. 31–32. A detailed examination of this process is in Serulnikov 1998: chap. 6; Penry 1996: 286–309. It must be noted that the Pocoatas reassumed their protest against Lupa (there had already been complaints following his appointment in 1772) shortly after the killing of the Condodondo caciques, the Llanquipachas, in 1774. This community had strong links with several Chayanta communities. (A thorough analysis of the Condocondo is in Penry 1996: 21–146.)

83 ANB, EC, 1776, 57, f. 3.

84 ANB, EC, 1776, 57, f. 3.

85 ANB, EC, 1776, 12, f. 39.

86 ANB, EC, 1776, 57, f. 26.

87 Ibid., ff. 38–39.

88 Blas Ayra, Pedro Caypa, Juan Herrera, Pedro Mamani, Manuel Yavira, Manuel Tupuri, Santos Phelipe, Andrés Lisacay, and Andrés Pacara to audiencia, November 1775, ANB, EC, 1776, 57, ff. 21–22.

89 ANB, TI, 1779, 195, ff. 66–67. Note that the ritual sponsors' tribute status is not necessarily associated with attacks on the church (the Indians did not demand here a decrease in religious sponsors' levies but rather their tribute exemption while in service). As discussed above, both caciques and Indians alluded to this issue in the context of a larger strife over Andean tributary customs. During this period, the Pocoata Indians included ritual sponsors in detailed lists of singles, mita workers, and others who were now forced to submit their tribute (ANB, EC, 1776, 57, ff. 57–59).

90 ANB, EC, 1776, 57, f. 23.

91 Ibid., ff. 56–59. On the feast of La Cruz, see Platt 1984: 14–15.

92 ANB, EC, 1776, 57, f. 53.

93 Ibid., ff. 62–63.

94 Ibid., ff. 97–98.

95 AGN, IX, Interior, Leg. 4, Exp. 7.

96 ANB, TI, 1779, 5, f. 17.

97 AGN, IX, Interior, Leg. 4, Exp. 7.

98 ANB, EC, 1776, 57, ff. 62–63 (italics mine).

99 AGN, XIII, 23–3–1, Cuaderno Cuarto.

100 ANB, EC, 1776, 77, f. 36.

101 AGN, IX, Interior, Leg. 9, Exp. 2, ff. 2–3.

102 ANB, TI, 1776, 77, f. 62 (italics mine).

103 Ibid., f. 65. Because of opposition within Chayanta, Pereira de Castro could not undertake new censuses (ANB, TI, 1776, 77; ANB, TI, 1779, 76; ANB, EC, 1785, 144; AGN, IX, Interior, Leg. 4, Exp. 7).

104 ANB, TI, 1779, 195, ff. 5–6.

105 AGN, IX, Interior, Leg. 9, Exp. 2, ff. 11–14.

106 ANB, Minas, 152, X, 1759–1779, ff. 52–53, 55.

107 ANB, TI, 1776, 77, ff. 36–37.

108 AGN, IX, Interior, Leg. 9, Exp. 2, ff. 16–17.

109 AGN, IX, Interior, Leg. 9, Exp. 2, ff. 16–17.

110 AGN, XIII, 18–10–2.

111 ANB, TI, 1776, 77, f. 36.

112 AGN, IX, Tribunales, Leg. 181, Exp. 29, ff. 34–35; AGN, IX, Tribunales, Leg. 65, Exp. 54, ff. 1–3. Two Indians in favor of Bernal recognized that the cacique traveled to Tucumán and Moquegua to buy mules and brandy (AGN, IX, Tribunales, Leg. 65, Exp. 54, ff. 5–6). On Bernal's hacienda, see AGN, IX, Interior, Leg. 10, Exp. 1, f. 248.

113 AGN, IX, Interior, Leg. 5, Exp. 2.

114 AGN, IX, Tribunales, Leg. 181, Exp. 29, ff. 40–41 (italics mine).

115 Ibid., f. 39.

116 In January 1780, Katari explained that the Majapicha ayllu's Indians supported him because they belonged "to the same ayllu as he does, and he has defended them as much as he could so that they did not have anything to complain about" (AGN, IX, Interior, Leg. 10, Exp. 1, ff. 21–22).

117 Katari to Vértiz, January 1779, in Lewin 1957: 803. These personal motives were reiterated in August 1780, AGN, IX, Interior, Leg. 10, Exp. 1, ff. 130–37; the confession of Nicolás Katari is in de Angelis 1971: 717.

118 Only in 1759 did an Andrés Katari appear holding one of the five chieftainships of Macha, but not in the Majapicha ayllu. Andrés Catari appears as Macha cacique along with Nicolás Flores, Phelipe Tamayo, Lucas Pirapi, and Juan de Espinoza (Melchor's brother) (ANB, TI, 1774, 252). Tomás Katari never mentioned Andrés as his relative.

119 In his petition in the viceregal court of Buenos Aires in 1779, Katari did not defend hereditary principles of legitimacy (he mentioned his "blood right" in passing and exhibited no documents demonstrating his noble lineage). Consider, for instance, the case of a Panacachi Indian named Asencio Isidro Sicara Florgain who in early October 1780 (at the height of mass uprising) traveled to Buenos Aires to seek the removal of an illegitimate cacique, as Katari had done two years before. Asencio, who was a relative of the Panacachi cacique, Esteban Sicara, replaced by Lupa in the early 1770s, produced before the viceregal magistrates documents from 1696 and 1705 accrediting his hereditary rights (ANB, IX, Interior, Leg. 8, Exp. 17). Colonial ordinances, Asencio pointed out, established that caciques "must succeed one another only by blood rights," a proposition that rebel peasants, albeit fiercely opposed to corregidores' discretionary appointments, would certainly dispute. It is significant that unlike most of the Indians looking for the removal of their caciques, Asencio did not seek support from Tomás Katari. Rather, one Sicara of Panacachi appeared among the several members of the native elite who needed to seek refuge in the church of San Pedro de Buena Vista.

120 AGN, IX, Interior, Leg. 5, Exp. 2.

121 AGN, IX, Tribunales, Leg. 181, Exp. 29, f. 38.

122 AGN, IX, Tribunales, Leg. 65, Exp. 54, ff. 1–3.

123 AGN, IX, Tribunales, Leg. 181, Exp. 29, ff. 38–39.

124 AGN, IX, Tribunales, Leg. 65, Exp. 54, ff. 3–4.

125 AGN, IX, Interior, Leg. 9, Exp. 2, ff. 18–19.

126 AGN, IX, Interior, Leg. 10, Exp. 1, ff. 130–37.

4   Disputed Images of Colonialism

1 AGN, IX, Interior, Leg. 10, Exp. 1, ff. 130–37.

2 See, for example, Stern 1982: chap. 5; Borah 1983; Walker 1999: chap. 3.

3 See also Taylor 1985: 151–57.

4 For a critique of Golte's emphasis on the reparto system as a general cause of Indian unrest, see Flores Galindo 1981.

5 See Hidalgo Lehuede 1983: 117–38; Szeminski 1984 and 1987; Flores Galindo 1987: 127–57.

6 The five ayllus of Anansaya were Alacollana, Alapicha, Tapunata, Guaracuata, and Sullcavi. The five Urinsaya ayllus were Majacollana, Majapicha, Guacoata, Condoata, and Sullcata. The Machas's territory stretched from the highland districts of Macha, Chayrapata, and Aullagas to

the valleys of San Marcos de Miraflores, Surumi, Carasi, and Guaycoma. According to official receipts of 1780, Macha had 120 originarios and 502 forasteros (AGN, XIII, 18–10–1, Leg. 84, Libro 1). This organization exists still today (Platt 1986: 230–31).

7 See Golte 1980; Moreno Cebrián 1977; Larson 1997: 126–32; Stein 1981: 2–28.

8 Audiencia fiscal Juan del Pino Manrique said, for instance, that Alós gave to the president of the audiencia 60,000 pesos at the time he took office. Oidores Lorenzo Blanco Ciceron and Pedro Cernadas Bermudez were also Alós's unconditional allies (Lewin 1957: 241).

9 Besides Blas Doria Bernal (Urinsaya), the caciques under attack were Norberto Osinaga (Alacollana), Roque Sanchez Morato (Alapicha), Pablo Chávez (Majacellana), and Francisco Flores (Condata).

10 AGN, IX, Tribunales, Leg. 65, Exp. 54.

11 Commenting on the 1764 royal edict endowing the audiencia of Charcas with jurisdiction over reparto disputes, Viceroy Pedro de Ceballos reported to the king in 1778 that although the audiencia had suspended many corregidores from their posts, "it is also well known that all were absolved, and from this resulted deaths, insurrections, and other serious disturbances" (quoted in Golte 1980: 139). On conflicts over repartos, see O'Phelan Godoy, 1988: 149–73; Thomson 1999.

12 Audiencia quoted in Lewin 1957: 354.

13 AGN, IX, Tribunales, Leg. 181, Exp. 29, ff. 82–83.

14 Tomás Katari submitted to the audiencia the firearms used by the cacique and offered a report of his version of the episode (see Lewin 1957: 806–8). Bernal reported that Katari "revolted all the people so that I got into great trouble to appease them" (AGN, IX, Interior, Leg. 10, Exp. 1, f. 1).

15 Cited in Lewin 1957: 357. A Macha cacique also reported that Katari "appointed a lieutenant and hilacatas by arguing that he is the governor and that the tributes have to be delivered into the royal treasury [of Potosí]. Because of this, none of the Indians obey me" (AGN, IX, Interior, Leg. 10, Exp. 1, ff. 10–11).

16 An analysis of this interrogation is in Serulnikov 1988.

17 Resolution quoted in De Angelis 1971: 667.

18 AGN, IX, Interior, Leg. 11, Exp. 8, ff. 68–71.

19 Vértiz quoted in Lewin 1957: 843–44.

20 AGN, IX, Interior, Leg. 8, Exp. 8, ff. 85–93.

21 Norberto Osinaga, Roque Sanchez Morato, Pablo Chávez, and Francisco Flores, AGN, IX, Interior, Leg. 10, Exp. 1, ff. 38–39.

22 AGN, IX, Interior, Leg. 10, Exp. 1, ff. 39–40.

23 AGN, IX, Interior, Leg. 8, Exp. 8, f. 89.

24 AGN, IX, Interior, Leg. 10, Exp. 1, ff. 54–55.

25 AGN, IX, Interior, Leg. 5, Exp. 2.

26 Katari quoted in Lewin 1957: 806–8.

27 AGN, IX, Interior, Leg. 8, Exp. 8, f. 86.

28 As Horst Pietschmann (1987: 427–47) has aptly pointed out, because the value system of colonial social groups did not conform to the structure of legal norms, Spanish elites' and Indians' attachment to the law was, by definition, a strategy rather than a rule. The Bourbon reforms represented the first consistent, albeit unsuccessful, effort to impose a normative conception of law based on the universal application of legal norms.

29 AGN, IX, Interior, Leg. 10, Exp. 1, f. 103.

30 Ibid., f. 84.

31 AGN, IX, Interior, Leg. 11, Exp. 8, f. 44.

32 AGN, IX, Interior, Leg. 10, Exp. 1, f. 141.

33 AGN, IX, Interior, Leg. 11, Exp. 8, ff. 39–40.

34 Ibid., ff. 58–67.

35 In de Angelis 1971: 669 (italics mine).

36 AGN, IX, Interior, Leg. 11, Exp. 8, f. 62.

37 Vértiz quoted in de Angelis 1971: 669 (italics mine).

38 See also Brewer and Styles 1983: 17–18.

39 All the written documents that Aymara-speaking Chayanta peasants produced were written by Spanish clerks. Analyses of these kinds of discourses have to be cautious, yet it is worth noting some features of the corpus at hand. First, there is a long series of documents produced in very different power situations. This allows us to distinguish between legal formalities and substantive notions of justice. Second, the Indians of Chayanta demonstrated considerable control over the content of their writings. For instance, when Tomás Katari was in Buenos Aires, he asked to be able to give a new declaration because his first testimony registered by the Protector of Indians did not fully represent what he wanted to say (AGN, IX, Interior, Leg. 11, Exp. 8, f. 2). Third, written language was probably perceived by peasants as a symbol of order and legitimacy rather than as a means of cultural domination. For examples of the use of lawyers and legal writing in radical insurrectionary activities in nineteenth- and twentieth-century northern Potosí, see Platt 1987a: 316–18; Langer 1990: 227–53. For a theoretical critique of a rigid ascription of writing to the sphere of power and hegemony in illiterate popular cultures, see LaCapra 1985: 51–54.

40 Indian legal writings, to be sure, participated in what James Scott (1990: 87) has called "the official transcript of power relations." Nevertheless, should we follow Scott's methodological approach, we would not seek out in this sphere "explicit displays of insubordination . . . [because] the official transcript is a sphere in which power appears naturalized because that is what elites exert their influence to produce and because it ordinarily serves the immediate interest of subordinates to avoid discrediting these appearances [of consent and unanimity]."

41 For a more extensive analysis of peasant grievances, see Serulnikov 1989.

42 On the double legitimacy of Andean caciques as state fiscal agents and native lords, see Larson 1979; Rivera Cusicanqui 1978; Saignes 1987; Spalding 1984: 228.

43 On the role of juridical rituals, the tribute system, and colonial land titles in the legitimization of Indian uprisings in nineteenth- and twentieth-century Bolivia, see Rivera Cusicanqui 1984: 42–52; Lehn 1987; Langer 1990; Platt 1982b: 73–111.

44 Platt 1987c: 99. About the merging of Andean political thought and the Spanish juridical tradition, see Salomon 1987: 162–64.

45 See Comaroff and Comaroff 1991 and de Certeau 1984: xiii for discussion on processes of anticolonial resistance not based on "the simple negation or exclusion of the 'content' of an other culture [but as] the effect of an ambivalence produced within the rules of recognition of dominating discourses" (Bhabha 1985: 153).

46 AGN, IX, Interior, Leg. 10, Exp. 1, f. 40.

47 Ibid., ff. 68–70.

48 Ibid., f. 42.

49 Ibid., f. 40.

50 Ibid., f. 61.

51 Ibid., ff. 115–17.

52 Ibid., ff. 84–85.

53 Ibid., ff. 80–81.

54 Ibid., f. 64.

55 Ibid., f. 79.

56 Ibid., f. 117.

57 Ibid., ff. 119–20.

58 Ibid., f. 101.

59 Ibid., ff. 49–51.

60 Ibid., f. 80.

61 Ibid., ff. 117–18.

62 Ibid., f. 54.

63 Ibid., ff. 37–38.

64 Ibid., f. 54.

65 AGN, IX, Tribunales, Leg. 181, Exp. 29, ff. 76–77.

66 AGN, IX, Interior, Leg. 10, Exp. 1, ff. 70–71.

67 Ibid., f. 75.

68 "Diario del General Juan Gelly (21 de junio–26 de agosto de 1780)," cited in Lamas 1849: 359–71.

69 AGN, IX, Interior, Leg. 10, Exp. 1, ff. 81–83.

70 "Diario," cited in Lamas 1849: 362.

71 It must be noted that regarding the reparto Alós seems just to have continued customary practices. He even commuted effects of little use such as clothes and increased instead the number of mules — he sold 2,900 mules at the customary price of 25 pesos instead of the 2,000 peso price established in the arancel (ANB, SGI, 1780, 43, ff. 66–67). A basket of coca leaves, however, was sold at 14 pesos, 5 more than the price established in the official tariff (AGN, IX, Interior, Leg. 5, Exp. 3, ff. 1–2). As a whole, however, Alós might have just become the focal point of a deep-rooted indigenous opposition to this commercial monopoly, in particular to the prices and mechanisms of the cancellation of debts.

72 AGN, IX, Interior, Leg. 10, Exp. 1, ff. 186–92.

73 "Diario," cited in Lamas 1849: 363.

74 In June 1780, while imprisoned, Tomás Katari recalled that despite that the Indians had exhibited the weapons to the audiencia, he was accused of "rioter and head of a revolt . . . so that the corregidor began a litigation against [Katari] when it should have been against [Bernal and his relatives] for aggression . . . Hence, following the plan they had to prevent my recourses [and] my prison was ordered" (AGN, IX, Tribunales, Leg. 181, Exp. 29, ff. 71–73).

75 AGN, IX, Interior, Leg. 10, Exp. 1, ff. 117–18.

76 Ibid., 107–8, 118.

77 See, for instance, the two long interrogations of Tomás Katari in December 1779 and August 1780 in Serulnikov 1988. Katari's missive to other Machas is in Lewin 1957: 357. Two La Plata residents, Fabian Lucero and Marcos Gutierrez de Ceballos, prepared most of the Machas's writings during this period.

78 Forty-eight Machas to audiencia, AGN, IX, Tribunales, Leg. 181, Exp. 29, f. 81.

79 AGN, IX, Interior, Leg. 10, Exp. 1, ff. 53–54.

80 Katari and fifteen Machas to Vértiz, AGN, IX, Interior, Leg. 11, Exp. 8, ff. 34–37. These Indians were the same ones leading the confrontations in Chayanta.

81 AGN, IX, Interior, Leg. 11, Exp. 8, ff. 37–38.

82 For economic and political analyses of the eighteenth-century colonial administration in terms of an absolutist state, see Coatsworth 1982: 25–41; Lynch 1992.

83 See also Root 1987: 155–204.

84 According to Tomás Katari, three hundred Indians died during the battle. Accounts of this battle are in Lewin 1957: 365–69; Fisher 1966: 58–62. See also "Diario," cited in Lamas 1849: 364–71; AGN, Interior, Leg. 10, Exp. 1, ff. 186–92; "Relación" 1900: 145–51.

85 Tomás Katari stated later that "it is true that many Spaniards and Indians died in Pocoata, but this is not reason [enough] to say that the Indians rose up, because before the confrontation the mita was dispatched and the corregidor was told that the Indians were ready to pay the tributes in the village of Macha as is customary" (cited in de Angelis 1971: 658).

86 Alós's decree established that "the reparto is to be lowered as follows: mules to 12 pesos; clothes to 4 reales; sacks [*costales*] to 4 reales" (cited in Lewin 1957: 375).

87 AGN, Interior, Leg. 10, Exp. 1, ff. 138–39.

88 Ibid., ff. 139–40.

89 Ibid., ff. 130–37.

90 Katari quoted in Lamas 1849: 369.

91 AGN, IX, Interior, Leg. 10, Exp. 1, ff. 148–49.

92 Cited in de Angelis 1971: 671.

93 On the concept of mimicry, see Young 1990: 147–48; Bhabha 1984: 125–33.

94 AGN, IX, Interior, Leg. 10, Exp. 1, ff. 151–52. Alós sent this letter while imprisoned in Macha (italics mine).

95 The assumption is that colonial rule was not only a means of economic and political domination but also a subject-constituting process. Michel Foucault (1982: 212) has defined this form of power as one "which categorizes the individual, marks him by his own individuality, attaches him to his own identity, imposes a law of truth on him which he must recognize and which others have to recognize in him. It is a form of power which makes individuals subjects. There are two meanings of the word *subject*: subject to someone else by control and dependence, and tied to his own identity by a conscience or self-knowledge. Both meanings suggest a form of power which subjugates and makes subject to."

96 As Phelan (1967: 213) has pointed out, the most egalitarian aspect of the colonial justice system "was that the members of every corporation had free access to the courts in order to protect what they thought were their privileges and obligations, however substantial or modest those rights might be."

97 According to Rancière (1992: 60), "The logical schema of social protest, generally speaking, may be summed up as follows: Do we or do we not belong to the category of men or citizens or human beings, and what follows from this? The universality is not enclosed in *citizen* or *human being*; it is involved in the 'what follows', in its discursive and practical enactment . . . The construction of such cases of equality is not the act of an identity, nor is it the demonstration of the values specific to a group. It is a process of subjectivation."

1   Quoted in Lamas 1849: 370.

2   AGN, IX, Interior, Leg. 10, Exp. 1, ff. 192–93.

3   Esteban Baldivieso to Ignacio Flores, May 1781, ANB, SGI, 1781, 160.

4   AGN, IX, Interior, Leg. 10, Exp. 1, ff. 110–13.

5   Lupa's allies (tribute collectors, alcaldes, etc.), his widow (Apolonia Hinojosa), and his daugh-
    ter (Teodora Lupa) claimed that the Indians of the ayllu Sunichito (possibly a section of the
    ayllu Chito, Anansaya, residing in the highest areas of Moscari) and the hacienda tenants were
    responsible for the murder (AGN, IX, Interior, Leg. 8, Exp. 8, ff. 38–39; AGN, IX, Interior, Leg
    8, Exp. 1, f. 123–24, 163).

6   AGN, IX, Interior, Leg. 8, Exp. 1, ff. 10–12.

7   AGN, IX, Criminales, Leg. 18, Exp. 3, ff. 139–40. Nicolás Katari confirmed that after returning
    from La Plata the Moscari Indians did not stop in Macha (cited in de Angelis 1971: 721).

8   ANB, SGI, 1781, 83. A thorough analysis of the Condocondo uprising of 1774 and its repercus-
    sions are in Penry 1996: 21–146. See also Abercrombie 1998: 294–96.

9   AGN, IX, Interior, Leg. 8, Exp. 1, ff. 60–61.

10 An audiencia's spy reported that the peasants prevented people from crossing the Río Grande
    toward the province (AGN, IX, Interior, Leg. 10, Exp. 1, ff. 225–28).

11 AGN, IX, Interior, Leg. 8, Exp. 1, ff. 38, 60–61, 97–98.

12 Ibid., ff. 71–72, 85–87.

13 AGN, IX, Interior, Leg. 10, Exp. 1, ff. 225–28.

14 Ibid., ff. 219–21.

15 Ibid., ff. 221–22.

16 AGN, IX, Interior, Leg. 8, Exp. 1, ff. 12–13.

17 It is worth noting that the extent of the involvement of the priests in the Cuzco insurrection has
    been questioned (Garzón Heredia 1995). The role of rural clergymen in the Mexican peasant
    insurrections of the second decade of the nineteenth century is also under review. Eric Van
    Young (2001: 201–23) has recently argued that despite the leadership position of Miguel
    Hidalgo and José María Morelos the overwhelming majority in the priesthood remained loyal.
    On Merlos, see Adrián 1993.

18 AGN, XI, Interior, Leg. 8, Exp. 1, ff. 169–71.

19 AGN, XI, Interior, Leg. 8, Exp. 1, ff. 27–28. Solís seemed to have played a temporizing role at the
    beginning of the uprising, but by early 1781 he fled to La Plata and refused to return to Pitantora
    (AGN, IX, Criminales, Leg. 21, Exp. 17, ff. 13–15).

20 AGN, XI, Interior, Leg. 8, Exp. 1, ff. 85–87.

21 AGN, IX, Interior, Leg. 10, Exp. 1, ff. 246–48.

22 AGN, IX, Interior, Leg. 8, Exp. 1, ff. 61–62.

23 AGN, IX, Interior, Leg. 10, Exp. 1, ff. 246–48. Ignacio Salguero appears as cacique of Ocurí and
    Anselmo Bernal as cacique of Pitantora in the tribute receipts from 1780 (AGN, XIII, 18–10–1,
    Libro 84, Leg. 84). Salazar y Solís's letter mentioned Bernal as Salguero's lieutenant (segunda
    persona).

24 AGN, IX, Interior, Leg. 8, Exp. 1, ff. 85–87.

25 On the Ayaviris, see Arze and Mendinaceli 1991.

26 AGN, IX, Interior, Leg. 8, Exp. 1, ff. 106–7, 125–27.

27 Ibid., ff. 128–29.

28 AGN, IX, Interior, Leg. 8, Exp. 1, ff. 125–27.

29 Ibid., ff. 89–90, 143–44. The Cochabamba Indians were from the towns of Sayari, Quinquiavi, and Totora (ff. 88–89).

30 AGN, IX, Interior, Leg. 8, Exp. 1, ff. 128–29. It was reported that some Indians of Pocoata, Panacachi, and Macha joined the Sacacas on this occasion.

31 AGN, IX, Interior, Leg. 8, Exp. 1, ff. 143–44.

32 Ibid., ff. 128–29.

33 Ibid., ff. 65–66.

34 AGN, IX, Interior, Leg. 8, Exp. 1, ff. 65–66.

35 In 1777, the archbishop of Charcas, Francisco Ramón de Herboso y Figueroa, appointed Herrera as *visitador general* Visitor-General of all the parishes (and vice-parishes) in the province. This inspection served as a basis for the creation of new independent parishes, one of the most ambitious (and most resisted by the Indians) ecclesiastical initiatives at the time (ANB, EC, 1779, 23). (On the division of parishes, see also Adrián 1995 and 1997; Penry 1996: 249.) In addition to being priest of San Pedro de Buena Vista, Herrera was "abogado de la audiencia de La Plata, Teólogo Real, consultor del Concilio Provincial Platense y examinador sinodal del Arzobispado" (attorney of the Charcas audiencia, Crown Theologian, Councilor of the Provincial Council of La Plata, and Synodal Examiner of the Archbishopric).

36 AGN, IX, Criminales, Leg. 18, Exp. 3, ff. 120–23. The account of these events is in Isidro Herrera to the archbishop, September 24, 1780, AGN, IX, Interior, Leg. 8, Exp. 1.

37 AGN, IX, Interior, Leg. 8, Exp. 1, ff. 102–4.

38 It was reported that Castillo lived in a hamlet four leagues from the village of San Pedro de Buena Vista (AGN, IX, Criminales, Leg. 18, Exp. 3, ff. 114–20).

39 In 1779, Castillo had helped Nicolás Guaguari to rebuff charges from former corregidor Ursainqui for supposed debts from the reparto. In a letter to the audiencia, Castillo urged the court not to permit caciques to "serve the tyrannical repartos of the corregidor for our total ruin." He even sent a detail list of twenty-one Indians who had made undue payments in cash and kind to Guaguari (AGN, IX, Interior, Leg. 8, Exp. 1, ff. 64–65). On the conflict between Ursainqui and Guaguari/Castillo, see ANB, EC, 1779, 257. On disputes in 1779 between former corregidor Ursainqui and corregidor Alós over the collection of Ursainqui's reparto debts, see AGN, IX, Interior, Leg. 8, Exp. 14.

40 In April 1781, Nicolás Guaguari recalled that the Sicoyas had taken him to Macha with the aim of "beheading" him. Priest Merlos managed to place Guaguari under his protection along with the arrested ethnic authorities of Laymi and Sacaca (AGN, IX, Interior, Leg. 30, Exp. 31). Esteban Callisaya, another cacique principal of Sicoya, was sheltered inside the church of San Pedro. Tribute receipts from 1774 mentioned both Esteban Callisaya and Nicolás Guaguari as caciques (AGN, XIII, 23–3–1, Cuaderno Primero). In a 1779 document, Nicolás Guaguari is identified as cacique of the town of San Pedro de Buena Vista, group [*parcialidad*] Sicoya (ANB, SGI, 1779, 257).

41 AGN, IX, Interior, Leg. 8, Exp. 1, ff. 106–7.

42 AGN, IX, Interior, Leg. 8, Exp. 1, ff. 106–7 (italics mine).

43 AGN, IX, Interior, Leg. 8, Exp. 1, ff. 174–75.

44 AGN, IX, Criminales, Leg. 18, Exp. 3, ff. 120–23. On veintenas, cf. chapter 1.

45 AGN, IX, Interior, Leg. 8, Exp. 1, ff. 107–110.

46 AGN, IX, Interior, Leg. 8, Exp. 1, ff. 107–10. AGN, IX, Interior, Leg. 8, Exp. 1, ff. 156–59.

47 AGN, IX, Criminales, Leg. 18, Exp. 3, ff. 120–23.

48 AGN, IX, Interior, Leg. 8, Exp. 8, ff. 24–26.

49 AGN, IX, Criminales, Leg. 18, Exp. 3, ff. 114–20.

50 AGN, IX, Interior, Leg. 8, Exp. 1, ff. 174–75.

51 AGN, IX, Criminales, Leg. 18, Exp. 3, ff. 134–39. During the feast of San Francisco, on October 4, the Indians again entered the village central square to ask for the handover of their caciques. The much sought-after Cayana cacique, Hilario Caguaciri, found his way to La Plata dressed as a woman.

52 AGN, IX, Interior, Leg. 8, Exp. 1, ff. 149–50.

53 ANB, TI, 1775, 54.

54 ANB, TI, 1772, 118. In February 1772, an audiencia minister lamented that that mestizo people like Coca usually took advantage of kin relations, and corregidores' complicity, to seize Andean communities' landholdings ANB, TI, 1772, 118.

55 Callisaya to Alós, December 1780, AGN, XIII, 18–10–2, Libro 2.

56 AGN, IX, Criminales, Leg. 21, Exp. 7.

57 On the relationship between Laymis and Puracas, cf. chapter 1. On the collaboration between Lupa and Soto, and the denunciation of 1770, cf. chapter 3. Marcos Soto's son, Francisco, was married to Catalina Felix Llanquipacha, a relative of the Condocondo caciques killed by rebel Indians in 1774 (ANB, XIII, 18–10–4).

58 AGN, IX, Interior, Leg. 8, Exp. 1, ff. 8–10.

59 AGN, IX, Interior, Leg. 8, Exp. 1, ff. 8–10.

60 AGN, IX, Interior, Leg. 8, Exp. 1, ff. 8–10 (italics mine). On September 6, the Macha leader submitted this petition to the audiencia AGN, IX, Interior, Leg. 8, Exp. 1, f. 10. Marcos Soto himself was forced to send a letter to the audiencia, on September 17, asking for the appointment of Diego Chico (ff. 35–36).

61 AGN, IX, Interior, Leg. 8, Exp. 8, ff. 60–62. Protests over the misappropriation of the Caja de Censos had already appeared in this area in the 1750s (cf. chapter 1).

62 A mestizo dweller lamented that Castillo's endeavors to publish the arancel and to get reimbursement for the repartos gained him, "a great veneration [on the part of Indians], so there is nothing he says that is not taken as gospel" (AGN, IX, Interior, Leg. 8, Exp. 1, ff. 149–50).

63 Ibid., ff. 150–51.

64 Ibid., ff. 149–50.

65 AGN, IX, Interior, Leg. 10, Exp. 1, f. 161. Later, Murillo, who served also as alcabala collector, attributed his arrest to Indians' belief that the king had eliminated the alcabalas (ANB, SGI, 1781, 160).

66 The residents were Theresa Alvarez, the daughter of Aullagas's miner Manuel Alvarez Villarroel, and Valerio Marino, an assistant of Berecochea who had in the past testified before corregidor Alós against the Indians (AGN, XI, Interior, Leg. 8, Exp. 1, ff. 149–50, 152–53).

67 Ibid., f. 148.

68 Ibid., f. 63.

69 AGN, XI, Interior, Leg. 8, Exp. 8, ff. 74–75. Mina added that "[Katari's] counselor and fomenter, [who] is well known and his deeds show it to the whole world," will also go to hell. It is not clear whether Mina refers to Merlos or to Katari's personal *amanuense* (clerk), Isidro Serrano. In April 1781, during Merlos's trial, Mina sharply defended the Macha priest's behavior during these months (AGN, IX, Interior, Leg. 11, Exp. 6). Moreover, a letter from Chayanta

priest Berecochea on October 17 noted that Katari's edicts on church fees had been written by his scribble, presumably Isidro Serrano (AGN, XI, Interior, Leg. 8, Exp. 8).

70 AGN, XI, Interior, Leg. 8, Exp. 8, ff. 74–75.

71 AGN, Interior, Leg. 8, Exp. 1, ff. 169–71.

72 AGN, IX, Interior, Leg. 8, Exp. 8, ff. 48–49.

73 AGN, XI, Interior, Leg. 8, Exp. 1, ff. 167–68. Ortuño was likely thought to be responsible for the murder of San Pedro's hacendados Martín and Matías Coca.

74 The priest also sent a letter condemning these actions (AGN, IX, Interior, Leg. 8, Exp. 1, ff. 168–69).

75 In a letter to the audiencia on October 19, Katari said "Castillo has been arrested by orders I gave so that he can be put at your disposition" (AGN, XI, Interior, Leg. 8, Exp. 8).

76 On November 11, the audiencia attorney confirmed that Manuel Ortuño was being held in the court jail (AGN, XI, Interior, Leg. 8, Exp. 1, ff. 169–71).

77 AGN, XI, Interior, Leg. 8, Exp. 8, ff. 52–53.

78 AGN, XI, Interior, Leg. 8, Exp. 1, ff. 169–71.

79 AGN, XI, Interior, Leg. 8, Exp. 8, f. 78.

80 Ibid., ff. 73–74. October 15 is the feast of Señor Sacramentado; October 23 is the feast of Nuestra Señora del Rosario (cf. chapter 3).

81 Several months afterward, a Spanish resident recalled witnessing this ceremony (ANB, SGI, 1781, 160, f. 8).

82 ANB, IX, Interior, Leg. 8, Exp. 8, ff. 73–74. The Machas also complained about the creation, in 1779, of an independent highland parish of Chayrapata separated from Macha, and of a valley parish of Surumi separated from San Marcos de Miraflores. On this process and on Merlos's reduction of fees, see Adrián 1985: 21–35, and 1996: 103–4.

83 Alós reportedly asked Caypa to prevent the Pocoatas from joining the Machas, but when the Pocoata cacique left the house he made a sign with his hat that set off the Indians' assault on the village (AGN, IX, Interior, Leg. 10, Exp. 1, ff. 186–92).

84 It is worth observing here that tinkus could also be conducted between two moieties of an ethnic group and between minor ayllus of the same moiety (Platt 1987c: 83–84).

85 The feast was eventually suspended. Villarroel added that oidor Manuel García de la Plata was aware of this tinku because, having been in Aullagas by September 1779, he had personally traveled to the place of the ritual battle (AGN, XI, Interior, Leg. 8, Exp. 1, ff. 68–70). See also Abercrombie 1998: 300.

86 AGN, XI, Interior, Leg. 9, Exp. 2, ff. 1–2.

87 AGN, XI, Interior, Leg. 8, Exp. 1, ff. 25–26. Caypa's duplicity was denounced by Katari himself (AGN, IX, Tribunales, Leg. 124, Exp. 3, ff. 117–21).

88 On the Pocoatas's threats to a previously appointed justicia mayor, Domingo Anglés, see AGN, XI, Interior, Leg. 8, Exp. 8, ff. 28–30. Four Pocoatas took the risk of traveling to La Plata to ask for the release of their cacique (ff. 59–61).

89 AGN, IX, Interior, Leg. 8, Exp. 8, ff. 71–72. Alvarez Villarroel, in contrast, considered Caypa one of the main culprits of the uprising and did not recommend his liberation (AGN, XI, Interior, Leg. 10, Exp. 1, ff. 242–46).

90 AGN, Interior, Leg. 10, Exp. 1, ff. 257–62.

91 He pointed out, rightly so, that a subsequent census of Pocoata conducted by corregidor Alós had even diminished the number of tribute payers he had proven to exist. He blamed the reparto

de mercancías for this entrenched corruption (AGN, XI, Interior, Leg. 9, Exp. 2, ff. 21–24). By contrast, on September 18 in a previous interrogation, shortly after Caypa was imprisoned, carried out by Alos's close ally oidor Lorenzo Blanco Ciseron, the cacique denys that Alós had made excessive repartos and that rural authorities embezzled tributes. The testimony then proceeded to repeat the standard version of causes of the rebellion proposed by the corregidor (Katari had said that he had met "the King," who had promised reduction of tributes) (AGN, IX, Interior, Leg. 10, Exp. 1, ff. 222–25).

92 This allusion to the *suplicio* of execution of Pedro Caypa is in ANB, SGI, 1781, 142. Fisher (1976: 90–91) and Penry (1996: 403–4) mention that Caypa was released and imprisoned again because of his involvement in a new insurrection plot. He was executed in August 1781.

93 AGN, XI, Interior, Leg. 8, Exp. 1, ff. 32–33, 43–44. Nicolás Katari attributed this confrontation to Chura's attempt "to rule all the moieties" (cited in de Angelis 1971: 724).

94 Various versions of this meeting are given in Merlos to audiencia, AGN, XI, Interior, Leg. 8, Exp. 1, ff. 32–35, 43–44.

95 Ibid., ff. 14–18.

96 Ibid., ff. 34–35. Over the next few weeks Chura delivered the tribute of his moiety and kept his own correspondence with the audiencia and treasury officials of Potosí (AGN, XIII, 18–10–1, Libro 8, Leg. 84).

97 AGN, IX, Interior, Leg. 10, Exp. 1, ff. 180–83.

98 AGN, XI, Interior, Leg. 8, Exp. 1, f. 81.

99 Alvarez Villarroel himself acknowledged that all the Urinsaya Indians and "many of the [moiety] of Chura" continued to lend allegiance to Katari (AGN, XI, Interior, Leg. 10, Exp. 1, ff. 242–46). Villarroel and Chura said Katari was challenged to produce the edict establishing the reduction of tributes, which he naturally failed to do. Yet, Villarroel's own account of the reaction of the Indians to the incident seems to indicate that the putative royal decree was not the issue at stake. Tomás Katari's version is in AGN, Interior, Leg. 8, Exp. 8, ff. 63–66.

100 This offer was of no use because Anglés stayed in Chayanta for a few hours (AGN, Interior, Leg. 8, Exp. 8, ff. 78–79). Shortly afterward, in La Plata, Anansaya's segunda persona, Juan Pirapi, handed over to Anglés some possessions he had left behind (f. 31).

101 AGN, Interior, Leg. 8, Exp. 8, ff. 43–46. A "noble Indian of Anansaya" follower of Tomás Katari confirmed this dispute over political prominence by explaining that Pascual Chura, "under the influence of some gentlemen in the town of Aullagas," was seeking his appointment as cacique when the Machas were already contented with the titled bested by the audiencia on Tomás Katari (ff. 66–67). Katari himself warned the court not to attend Pirapi's petition (ff. 52–53).

102 AGN, Interior, Leg. 8, Exp. 8, ff. 46–47. Drawing on his firsthand experience, Domingo Anglés keenly supported this decision (ff. 31–34).

103 AGN, Interior, Leg. 8, Exp. 8, ff. 78–82; AGN, IX, Interior, Leg. 8, Exp. 1, ff. 169–71.

104 AGN, IX, Interior, Leg. 8, Exp. 1.

105 AGN, Interior, Leg. 8, Exp. 8, ff. 63–66 (italics mine).

106 Ibid., ff. 78–79.

107 The number of correspondents to Anansaya was 1,358, and to Urinsaya 1,237 (AGN, XIII, 18–10–1, Leg. 84, Libro 8). Macha owed 2,256 pesos for the 1780 San Juan quota.

108 AGN, XIII, 18–10–1. Katari said that Chico wanted to know the tribute dues so that he could cancel them.

109   As in the case of the Laymi, the Indians ignored the official dues but the 1,593 pesos they submitted came only 35 pesos short of the official figures.

110   AGN, IX, Interior, Leg. 8, Exp. 1, ff. 112–13. On Yugra's participation in Lupa's murder, see ff. 163–66.

111   AGN, IX, Interior, Leg. 8, Exp. 8, ff. 34–37.

112   AGN, IX, Interior, Leg. 8, Exp. 8, ff. 34–37.

113   AGN, XI, Interior, Leg. 8, Exp. 8, ff. 28–33. Before departing from La Plata, Anglés had an edict published in the northern Potosí villages saying that "all the Indians of [Chayanta] involved in gatherings and meetings in whatever sites and places must split and withdraw to their homes so they can continue with the work of farming and other occupations which they are subject to" (AGN, IX, Justicia, Leg. 10, Exp. 190, ff. 1–2). When Anglés saw the crowd gathered in Ocurí, the gateway to the province, he immediately returned to La Plata.

114   AGN, XI, Interior, Leg. 8, Exp. 8, ff. 68–70. It is worth noting that Katari's Urinsaya ayllu of Majapicha possessed lands in the valley of Guaycoma, where Acuña owned his hacienda (see 1786 census in AGN, XIII, 18-10-4). By contrast, when the audiencia had appointed in early September a La Plata dweller named Manuel de Valenzuela—who stated in letters to the authorities as well as to Chayanta's caciques and priests that he intended to collect tribute and administer justice but not to demand reparto debts—Katari wrote to the audiencia that "today, I have sent mules for our Justicia Mayor [Valenzuela], to whom, as I said, we pay total obedience, and the facts will prove it" (AGN, IX, Interior, Leg. 8, Exp. 1). Yet, Valenzuela's policy provoked Alós and his allies in the audiencia to effect Valenzuela's immediate replacement by Domingo Angles (see Lewin 1957: 369–71; de Angelis 1971: 673–74). In November Valenzuela, who was lieutenant colonel of cavalry, complained to the viceroy that he had been deposed despite having received positive responses to his letters from caciques and priests (AGN, IX, Tribunales, Leg. 124, Exp. 3, f. 123).

115   AGN, IX, Interior, Leg. 10, Exp. 1, ff. 58–59; see also AGN, IX, Interior, Leg. 8, Exp. 1, f. 38.

116   AGN, IX, Interior, Leg. 8, Exp. 8, ff. 55–59.

117   This is borrowed from Hunt's (1984: 15) analysis of the French Revolution, where she states that "the investment of symbolic actions with political significance gave specific policies, individuals, and organizations greater impact than they would have had in nonrevolutionary times."

118   AGN, IX, Interior, Leg. 10, Exp. 1, ff. 255–56.

119   Ibid., ff. 264–65.

120   Information on these events is drawn from Acuña's report to the audiencia on November 24, 1780, AGN, IX, Interior, Leg. 10, Exp. 1, ff. 257–62.

121   In explaining the cultural meaning of offering and accepting chicha, the rebel leader Antonio Cruz related that as he was traveling through the province a priest offered him chicha in exchange for not joining the rebels, but "he did not want to accept the offering because he considered that by drinking he would betray the trust bestowed on him" (*agraviaba la confianza que de él se hacía*) (AGN, IX, Criminales, Leg. 18, Exp. 3, ff. 99, 101) (italics mine).

122   Other sources, for instance, reported that Acuña appointed (or at least confirmed in his post) an Aymaya cacique at the Indians' request (ANB, SGI, 1781, 19). Acuña did not mention this in his reports.

123   On the conflict in the 1750s, cf. chapter 1; on the caciques' explicit opposition to Andean tributary customs, cf. chapter 3. Adrián (1996: 105–6) has suggested that the belief in tax decreases might also have been associated with corregidor Ursainqui's proposal in the 1770s

that the tasas of the originarios lacking adequate land had to be lowered. Unlike the demand for the exemption of mitayos and ritual sponsors, Tomás Katari or other rebel Indians apparently did not explicitly mention this issue. It is interesting to note, however, that like the criteria of tribute exemption this expectation would have also entailed an attempt to conform state taxes to Andean tributary practices, which established a direct relationship between tribute and landholding. As I note in the introduction, since 1786 the state in fact established a connection between tribute liabilities and land tenure.

124 AGN, IX, Interior, Leg. 8, Exp. 1, ff. 8–10.

125 AGN, IX, Interior, Leg. 10, Exp. 1, ff. 257–62. On Conde de la Monclova's policies, see Wightman 1990: 34–36.

126 AGN, IX, Interior, Leg. 10, Exp. 1, ff. 257–62.

127 AGN, XIII, 18–10–2, Libro 2.

128 AGN, IX, Interior, Leg. 10, Exp. 1, f. 256.

129 Ibid., f. 257.

130 The quotes from two letters that Callisaya wrote to Joaquín Alós and his son "Chepe" are from San Pedro de Buena Vista, December 16, 1780 (AGN, XIII, 18–10–2, Libro 2).

131 AGN, XIII, 18–10–2, Libro 2.

132 AGN, IX, Interior, Leg. 10, Exp. 1, ff. 257–62.

133 Condocondo cacique Lucas Llanquipacha reported that the mitayos and church servants, like their peers in Chayanta, refused to pay tribute. Unable to leave the village of Condocondo, he asked the Paria corregidor to accept his resignation (AGN, IX, Interior, Leg. 8, Exp. 1, ff. 183–85). After being pardoned by the audiencia, the Indians allegedly responsible for the murder of Lucas's predecessors visited Macha (f. 134). Challapata's highland territories bordered with Aymaya and Laymi. As seen in chapter 2, ten Challapata families rented lands in Moscari's haciendas. Incidents in several Paria communities are in ff. 179–192.

134 AGN, IX, Interior, Leg. 8, Exp. 1, ff. 189–91.

135 On the Tinquipaya's ayllu Casia and exchanges between Tomás Katari and Tinquipaya, see AGN, IX, Interior, Leg. 8, Exp. 1, ff. 116–17, 130–33; AGN, IX, Justicia, Leg. 10, Exp. 205. On the Tinquipayas, see Pacheco Balanza and Guerrero Peñaranda 1994: 36; Del Río 1995: 3–47.

136 Antonio Guarachi to Potosí Governor Escobedo, November 22, 1780, AGN, IX, Interior, Leg. 10, Exp. 1, ff. 253–54. Letter from Katari to the Coroma Indians is in Lewin 1957: 372–73. Adrián (1997: 90–91) has pointed out the fact that Macha priest Merlos had in the past served as Coroma priest.

137 ANB, SGI, 1780, 207 (also quoted in Andrade 1994: 101).

138 ANB, SGI, 1781, 53.

139 Quoted in Andrade 1994: 129. The documents covering the murder of Tomás Katari and its immediate aftermath are missing from the ANB. The most complete rendering of this event is in Andrade's book.

140 AGN, IX, Interior, Leg. 8, Exp. 1, ff. 130–33.

6 *In the Land of Heretics*

1 See Szeminski 1984; Flores Galindo 1987; Hidalgo Lehuede 1983.

2 Confession of Dámaso Catari [Katari], in de Angelis 1971: 713–14 (hereafter cited as "Confession of Dámaso Catari").

3   On the colonial military in Peru, see Stern 1987b; Campbell 1978.

4   Confession of Nicolás Catari [Katari], in de Angelis 1971: 731 (hereafter cited as "Confession of Nicolás Catari").

5   Nicolás Katari resided in the hamlet of Lurucachi, north of Chayrapata village (AGN, IX, Criminales, Leg. 18, Exp. 3, ff. 75). Most of the Machas came from the hamlets of Chayrapata, Lurucachi, and Guadalupe. On the previous role of Colque, see AGN, IX, Tribunales, Leg. 181, Exp. 29, ff. 80–82.

6   AGN, IX, Criminales, Leg. 18, Exp. 3, ff. 36–42.

7   Villarroel to Ignacio Flores, ANB, SGI, 1781, 53 (italics mine).

8   The distribution followed established rules regarding the amount that corresponded to community members, coyarunas, women, and so forth (ANB, SGI, 1781, 194; "Confession of Nicolás Catari," 713–14). Reflecting the specific aims of the attack, the Indians apparently refrained from taking money and goods from other miners (AGN, IX, Criminales, Leg. 18, Exp. 3, ff. 30–42; AGN, IX, Criminales, Leg. 21, Exp. 17, ff. 22–23; "Relación" 1900: 162). Dámaso Katari, who arrived in Aullagas two days after the disturbances, also received his share.

9   AGN, IX, Criminales, Leg. 18, Exp. 3, ff. 42–52. María Cardenas, Santo's wife, could have been related to Blas Doria Bernal because his widower's surname was also Cárdenas (AGN, IX, Interior, Leg. 10, Exp. 1, ff. 107–8).

10 Morato appears again as cacique of the ayllu Alapicha in 1783 (AGN, XIII, 18–10–4, Leg. 87, Libro 5). On previous attacks on Morato, cf. chapter 4. The present-day cantón of Chayrapata is inhabited by the Anansaya moiety with the ayllu Alapicha predominating (Pacheco Balanza and Guerrero Peñaranda 1994: 31).

11 "Confession of Nicolás Catari," 729; AGN, IX, Criminales, Leg. 18, Exp. 3, ff. 91–94. Pablo Chávez somehow managed to avoid death (ANB, SGI, 1782, 3). Led by Nicolás, the Machas also expropriated the hacienda of Luis Núñez, former corregidor Alós's main commercial partner and assistant. The goods were distributed at Cruz Cassa, a hill located in Surumi, within Macha territory, which, according to ethnographic fieldwork, is considered to be home to a *cerro protector* (mountain spirit) (Pacheco Balanza and Guerrero Peñaranda 1994: 127, 137).

12 ANB, SGI, 1781, 11, f. 11; "Confession of Nicolás Catari," 729–30.

13 The militia was intercepted before reaching Pocoata, and two soldiers were killed (Francisco Serrano to audiencia, August 28, 1780, AGN, IX, Interior, Leg. 10, Exp. 1, ff. 127–29, 186–92).

14 AGN, IX, Criminales, Leg. 18, Exp. 3, ff. 61–69. On the current symbolic importance of Ocurí as the border area between the Machas and the Yamparas (a denomination that includes most of the residents of the southeastern valleys of the colonial province of Chayanta and Quilaquila), see Pacheco Balanza and Guerrero Peñaranda 1994: 40, 101, 134.

15 "Confession of Nicolás Catari," 724.

16 ANB, SGI, 1781, 47, f. 1. Nicolás Katari's scribe was named Bartolomé and had had some relationship with Sánchez Morato ("Confession of Nicolás Catari," 727).

17 As summed up in 1761, Andean peasants "could not have two levies at the same time" (ANB, TI, 1761, 30, f. 10) (cf. chapter 1). Regarding the tribute, Dámaso Katari even mentioned that a clash had occurred with a Condocondo Indian because he had published a tribute reduction without Dámaso's or Nicolás's authorization ("Confession of Dámaso Catari," 688).

18 Opposition to these taxes proved to be effective. In May 1781, the junta de diezmos of La Plata reported that as a result of rebels' edicts and threats, there were no tax farmers willing to serve in the Chayanta province (ANB, SGI, 1781, 153).

19 Dámaso used this title in a letter to the Indians of Tacobamba in March 1781 (ANB, SGI, 1781, 59). Nicolás Katari deployed the title in a letter appointing an alcalde mayor (in Lewin 1957: 558–59).

20 Nicolás reportedly did this in Pitantora (AGN, IX, Criminales, Leg. 18, Exp. 3, ff. 85–86). While in Quilaquila (province of Yamparáez) Dámaso issued, through his scribe Juan Peláez, several letters, appointing new authorities of communities outside Chayanta ("Confession of Dámaso Catari," 688).

21 ANB, SGI, 1781, 193, ff. 1–2 (italics mine).

22 ANB, SGI, 1781, 42. On these events, see also Abercrombie 1998: 296–99; Penry 1996: 396–402.

23 AGN, IX, Criminales, Leg. 18, Exp. 3, ff. 71–75.

24 Ibid., ff. 132–33.

25 Two of the victims, Vicente and Bernardo Bernal, might have been relatives of Pitantora cacique Anselmo Bernal (AGN, IX, Criminales, Leg. 18, Exp. 3, ff. 86–91).

26 Ibid., ff. 84–85.

27 Ibid., ff. 85–86. Regarding the murder of a mestizo named Ignacio Choque, the Indians explained that it was said he "wanted to kill our women" (f. 89).

28 Ibid., ff. 99–101. Cruz was a Tinquipaya Indian.

29 ANB, SGI, 1782, 3, ff. 7–8.

30 An all-out assault occurred in La Paz on March 26. Túpac Katari's troops, however, did not thereafter conduct a new frontal, massive attack.

31 On the siege of La Paz, see Valle de Siles 1990; Thomson 1996. On Cuzco, see Campbell 1978: 126–29; Walker 1999: 45–46.

32 Certainly, alcaldes, informal ringleaders, captains, and more-or-less spontaneous forms of community mobilization must have played an important role. Naturally enough, in times of great political turmoil, political solidarity did not necessarily match ethnic identities.

33 Although the reported number of casualties is unreliable, the disparity is still striking. For instance, in the Pocoata battle on August 26, 1780, a witness reported that twenty-four Spaniards or mestizos died ("Diario de Juan Gelli," cited in Lamas 1849: 367), while, according to Tomás Katari, around three hundred Indians died (cited in Lewin 1957: 820). During the first failed Spanish assault on La Punilla, reportedly two soldiers and eighty or ninety Indians were killed ("Relación" 1900: 167).

34 "Confession of Dámaso Catari," 690–91.

35 This information was provided by Merlos. He had been informed in La Plata that Dámaso was in Quilaquila "trying to find out whether his brother Tomás's death was true because there were rumors among the natives that he had resuscitated" (Merlos to Vértiz, February 15, 1781, AGN, IX, Tribunales, Leg. 124, Exp. 3).

36 The importance of this has been pointed out by Arze (1991: 104–5).

37 On Carnival, see Harris 2000: 27–50; Rasnake 1988: 242–59.

38 "Confession of Dámaso Catari," 693.

39 "Confession of Nicolás Catari," 727–28. Nicolás was not present when Dámaso decided to attack La Plata in Quilaquila either. Although from both Quilaquila and La Punilla, Dámaso, through his amanuense Juan Peláez, wrote several letters that he signed with his own name and that of Nicolás, the latter was not there.

40 "Confession of Nicolás Catari," 725.

41 Ibid., 725, 734.

42 AGN, IX, Criminales, Leg. 19, Exp. 23, ff. 5–6. The missive was addressed to the acting president of the audiencia, Gerónimo Manuel de Ruedas, and the "king fiscal," Juan del Pino Manrique.

43 ANB, IX, Tribunales, Leg. 124, Exp. 3. The city of La Plata had approximately ten thousand inhabitants (Lewin 1957: 550).

44 Dámaso demanded also that "the thief corregidor Alós and the Jew lieutenant Núñez" be handed over (AGN, IX, Criminales, Leg. 19, Exp. 23, ff. 21–22). As a result, Alós fled La Plata for Tucumán (AGN, IX, Interior, Leg. 12, Exp. 5). He then traveled to Buenos Aires, where he was placed in house detention for his behavior as corregidor (AGN, IX, Interior, Leg. 11, Exp. 11).

45 The attack was led by two prominent Spanish officials, oidor Alonso González Pérez, and the administrator of the royal tobacco monopoly, Francisco de Paul Sanz, despite the opposition of Charcas military commander Ignacio Flores (Lewin 1957: 552–53).

46 The two priests were Josef Bartolomé Guerra and Nicolás Malendro (AGN, IX, Interior, Leg. 10, Exp. 12).

47 From Quilaquila, the Indians mentioned "a little box with papers" seized at the time of Tomás Katari's death (AGN, IX, Criminales, Leg. 19, Exp. 23, f. 5). Dámaso said that the Quilaquila priest had sent this box to the audiencia shortly after the death of Acuña and Tomás. This information was accurate (AGN, IX, Interior, Leg. 11, Exp. 6, ff. 5–6). These papers were not limited to the decree obtained in Buenos Aires in 1779. It should be noted that Joaquín Alós had signed edicts dealing with a reduction in repartos, and that documents regarding the church tariff list, mitayos' tribute exemption, and so forth had been exhibited by the Indians during 1780. In one of his missives to the audiencia, Dámaso explicitly mentioned that some of these documents were among his brother's papers (cited in Lewin 1957: 554–55).

48 "Confession of Dámaso Catari," 695–96.

49 Katari quoted in Lewin 1957: 554–55.

50 Lewin 1957: 554–55.

51 A Spanish official reported that the Moromoro Indians were in La Punilla "until a priest and a fray went there to issue the pardon" ("Confession of Dámaso Catari," 686). Some months later, the Moromoro's cacique lieutenant confirmed that they had accepted the pardon, leaving La Punilla before the final battle (ANB, SGI, 1781, 11, ff. 5, 11).

52 "Confession of Dámaso Catari," 703.

53 AGN, IX, Criminales, Leg. 19, Exp. 23, ff. 147–48. See also, "Relación" 1900: 206. Rebellions invoking the names of Túpac Amaru and Túpac Katari would later erupt in Cochabamba (Fisher 1966: chap. 7; Larson 1997: 167–70).

54 "Relación histórica de los sucesos de la rebelión de José Gabriel Tupac Amaru," in de Angelis 1971: 221.

55 The complete edict is transcribed in AGN, IX, Criminales, Leg. 18, Exp. 3, ff. 153–54. The Indians who petitioned the edicts in Oruro were Tiburcio Ríos, Asencio Pinaya, Asencio Copali, Juan Quispi (cacique lieutenant of Caracha), Carlos Condori "and his community," Bernabe Pascual, and Antonio Suturi. Pablo Guarachi also traveled to Oruro. The edict was handed over after a meeting with Jacinto Rodríguez (ff. 120–23).

56 "Confession of Dámaso Catari," 684, 689–90.

57 Missives regarding military preparations among the Indians of Yura, Condocondo, Tacobamba, Tomave, Coroma, and Tupiza are in ANB, SGI, 1781, 61; ANB, SGI, 1781, 59. For an analysis of the events in Paria and Yura at the time, see Abercrombie 1998: 296–401; Rasnake 1988: 144–48.

58 "Confession of Dámaso Catari," 690.

59 "Confession of Dámaso Catari," 690. On the relationship between Catholicism and insurgent ideology during the Túpac Amaru rebellion, see Szeminski 1987.

60 Testimony of Norberto Osinaga. Another witness made reference to the holy host as made up of flour, but the allusion to Tomás Katari as "Nuestro Dios y Rey" appears only in Osinaga's testimony (AGN, IX, Criminales, Leg. 18, Exp. 3, ff. 42–49).

61 Testimony of Ancelmo Arsibia, AGN, IX, Criminales, Leg. 18, Exp. 3, ff. 42–49.

62 Merlos had been imprisoned on his arrival in La Plata for his complicity with the rebellion. From jail, he firmly defended Tomás Katari's behavior, warning about the ominous consequences of his arrest and murder (AGN, IX, Criminales, Leg. 21, Exp. 17, Exp. 23). On Merlos, see Adrián 1993: 29–54.

63 As Merlos volunteered to ask for a pardon, the Indians replied that he could do so "but that it was not desirable that the judge [Ignacio Flores] come with many soldiers because they would confront them" (AGN, IX, Interior, Leg. 12, Exp. 5). AGN, IX, Interior, Leg. 12, Exp. 5.

64 On his way back to La Plata, Merlos was intercepted by large groups of Machas armed with slings and clubs from whom he received two "insulting" letters from Nicolás Katari (AGN, IX, Interior, Leg. 12, Exp. 5. See also AGN, IX, Interior, Leg. 11, Exp. 6, ff. 3–4, 12–13; AGN, IX, Criminales, Leg. 19, Exp. 23, f. 27).

65 AGN, IX, Criminales, Leg. 18, Exp. 3, ff. 80–83; AGN, IX, Criminales, Leg. 21, Exp. 17, ff. 13–16.

66 Idem. This despite that, in searching to reunify again the Macha and Chayrapata parishes, Nicolás Katari and other rebel Indians proposed that Arzadum be appointed in the place of Merlos (AGN, IX, Criminales, Leg. 19, Exp. 3, ff. 19–20). In February 1781, when passing through Ocurí, the Machas told Merlos that Chayrapata's priest's assistant was not to come back to Chayrapata because they "did not want this parish separated from the one of Macha" (AGN, IX, Interior, Leg. 11, Exp. 6, ff. 3–4).

67 Priests Gerónimo de Cardona y Tagle (San Marcos de Miraflores), Juan de la Cruz Serrano (Moscari), Clemente de Montoya y Miranda (Micani), and Dionisio Larrazabal (Carasi) to the archbishop, January 21, 1780, AGN, IX, Criminales, Leg. 21, Exp. 17. The Carasi priest, Dionisio Larrazabal, had been the object of the first protests during the struggles over ecclesiastical fees in the early 1770s (cf. chapter 3).

68 ANB, SGI, 1782, 3, ff. 7–8.

69 AGN, IX, Criminales, Leg. 21, Exp. 17, ff. 13–15.

70 ANB, SGI, 1781, 19, f. 4.

71 Blas Colque, one of the ethnic chiefs later executed for his involvement in Cortés's death, had asked Joseph Roque to attend Candlemas because "the reduction of church fees and other levies would be announced" (ANB, SGI, 1781, 19, f. 7).

72 It was also reported that about fifty Indians invaded the mining center of Capacirca, located near the village of Aymaya, but no casualties were mentioned (AGN, IX, Criminales, Leg. 18, Exp. 3, ff. 146–47).

73 ANB, SGI, 1781, 19, f. 1.

74 AGN, IX, Criminales, Leg. 18, Exp. 3, ff. 140–41. The ethnic authorities reportedly involved in this event were Josef Roque, Pedro Calle, Blas Santos, and Pedro Nolasco Gallego (the latter cacique of the group Aymaya). Alguaciles, alcaldes, and cacique lieutenants also participated in

killing Cortés and distributing his goods. The alcalde Gregorio Mamani said that he brought his bastón (staff of authority) to the attack (ff. 145–46).

75 AGN, IX, Criminales, Leg. 18, Exp. 3, ff. 56–58.

76 Ibid., ff. 140–41.

77 Captain Gavino de Hoyos, AGN, IX, Interior, Leg. 12, Exp. 8. The author of "Relación" (1900: 171) estimated twelve hundred dead. The acting president of the audiencia, Gerónimo Manuel de Ruedas, estimated that more than four hundred persons, of all ages and genders, had been killed (AGN, IX, Interior, Leg. 13, Exp. 11).

78 One of the assailants explained that only "a few women" were spared (AGN, IX, Criminales, Leg. 18, Exp. 3, ff. 111–14). The Auquimarca cacique noted that *nenes de pecho* (breast-fed babies) were also killed; indeed, just seven persons survived (ff. 114–20). A Moscari Indian recalled that he was assigned to guard one of the church windows to insure that nobody escaped (ff. 124–25).

79 AGN, IX, Criminales, Leg. 18, Exp. 3, ff. 114–20; see also ff. 131–32.

80 The quote is from ANB, SGI, Rück No. 96, f. 11. For the rest of the references see Gavino de Hoyos, AGN, IX, Interior, Leg. 12, Exp. 8; "Relación" 1990: 171; and *Comisión* 1971: 693. Regarding the latter — a report signed in Arequipa in May 1781 — it is worth noting that it refers to Simón Castillo as Herrera's killer, when he was not present at the attack.

81 AGN, IX, Criminales, Leg. 18, Exp. 3, ff. 111–14. Another Indian said he "saw that [San Pedro's central square] was covered by the dead bodies of Spaniards and Indians, and the church's roof and its roof tiles [were] reduced to pieces because of the countless rocks that Indians launched" (ff. 101–11).

82 AGN, IX, Criminales, Leg. 18, Exp. 3, ff. 114–20.

83 Ibid., ff. 120–23, 134–39.

84 Pascual Tola mentioned that he was accompanied during the attack by the Auquimarca's hilacata Pablo Pique and alcalde Pablo Huma (AGN, IX, Criminales, Leg. 18, Exp. 3, ff. 114–20). Moscari Indians were also led by their cacique, Marcos Colque, hilacatas Carlos Conti and Pascual Guacama, and alcaldes Antonio Nuguali and Basilio Betusco (ff. 111–14). A Sicoya Indian mentioned hilacatas Julián Cuñaca, Manuel Gualpa, and Nolasco Cañuma as the leaders (ff. 128–29).

85 See, for instance, ANB, SGI, 1781, 1a. Marcos Colque had participated in previous disputes with Florencio Lupa in alliance with the Moscari priest (Penry 1996: 403). This did not deter him from collaborating in this massacre.

86 AGN, IX, Criminales, Leg. 18, Exp. 3, ff. 101–11.

87 Ibid., ff. 111–14.

88 Information on the death of Manuel Puma is an ANB, SGI, 1784, 63. Information on Apolonia Hinojosa's death is in "Relación" 1900: 17.

89 AGN, IX, Criminales, Leg. 18, Exp. 3, ff. 52–53.

90 Ibid., ff. 139. Note that figure named Caracara, the only one who did not take shelter inside the church, was most certainly the Chullpa cacique Miguel Caracara, who had led collective protests in the late 1740s and early 1770s (cf. chapter 1).

91 AGN, IX, Criminales, Leg. 21, Exp. 17, ff. 14–16.

92 ANB, SGI, 1781, No 1a.

93 ANB, SGI, 1781, 30, f. 6.

94 AGN, IX, Criminales, Leg. 18, Exp. 3, ff. 114–20.

95 Ibid., ff. 124–25, 131–32.

96 Ibid., ff. 54–56, 143–45.

97 Ibid., ff. 175–77.

98 AGN, IX, Criminales, Leg. 18, Exp. 3, ff. 101–11.

99 Dámaso and Nicolás Katari identified themselves as "brothers and governors of the towns of Macha and Chayrapata." The document is presented in the name of "all our community" and the towns of Chayanta, Pitantora, Moromoro, Panacachi, Sacaca, Acacio, San Pedro de Buena Vista, Auquimarca, Moscari, and Micani (ANB, SGI, 1781, 249b).

100 ANB, SGI, 1781, 50. As far as I know, letters of Nicolás Katari ordering not to pay tributes were never exhibited.

101 The letter, sent from Macha, is signed by "las comunidades e Indios originarios tributarios de su Magestad y vecinos de esta Provincia de Charcas" (the communities and originario and tributary Indians resident in this province of Charcas).

102 "Relación" 1900: 181. Dámaso Katari had tried to gain the Pocoatas's collaboration by sending them an emissary with Túpac Amaru's edict ("Confession of Dámaso Catari," 689).

103 ANB, SGI, 1781, 1a, f. 3.

104 On the ayllu Majapicha, see cacique Antonio Vázquez and the Indians of Majapicha to Ignacio Flores in La Plata, April 4, 1781, ANB, SGI, 1781, 249c. On Salvador Torres, see ANB, SGI, 1782, 10, ff. 9–10. On Sebastián Colque, see AGN, IX, Criminales, Leg. 18, Exp. 3, ff. 168–69. At least two Majapicha Indians, Ventura and Silvestre Colque, were imprisoned on arriving in La Plata because of their previous involvement in the rebellion. On the active involvement of Antonio Vázquez, the Majapicha Indians, and Sebastián Colque in protest movements during 1778–1780, see, for instance, AGN, IX, Tribunales, Leg. 54, Exp. 54, ff. 1–3; June 25, 1779, AGN, IX, Tribunales, Leg. 128, Exp. 29, ff. 15–17; AGN, IX, Interior, Leg. 11, Exp. 8, ff. 34–37. On the capture of Castillo and Ríos, see AGN, IX, Criminales, Leg. 18, Exp. 3, ff. 152–53; on Aymaya, see ANB, SGI, 1781, 19, f. 8.

105 For instance, the Macha Indians of Majapicha said that Nicolás had managed to excape from Aullagas after they had handed him to the authorities (ANB, SGI, 1781, 249c). Likewise, Sebastián Colque said that his group had had two violent confrontations with Nicolás's entourage (AGN, IX, Criminales, Leg. 18, Exp. 3, ff. 168–69). Nicolás Katari, in turn, accused Sebastián Colque "of wanting to obtain [Macha's] government, offering brandy, as he did during the past *carnestolendas* (carnival), and letting others give him offerings and address him as cacique" (ff. 35–42).

106 AGN, IX, Interior, Leg. 13, Exp. 11. On the granting of medals, see also "Relación" 1990: 185.

107 AGN, IX, Criminales, Leg. 18, Exp. 3, ff. 63–66.

108 "Relación," 183.

109 Quoted in Lewin 1957: 557.

110 Confession of Nicolás Catari," 718. Nicolás said that Tomás only spoke of tribute reductions when reading his appointment as cacique in early September 1780. It was not asked whether this was related to that false viceregal order, or to the tributary exemption of mita workers and ritual sponsors that Indians then demanded of Juan Antonio Acuña.

111 AGN, IX, Criminales, Leg. 18, Exp. 3, ff. 134–39.

112 AGN, IX, Interior, Leg. 14, Exp. 7, f. 8.

113 "Confession of Dámaso Catari," 704.

114 AGN, IX, Interior, Leg. 12, Exp. 3.

Conclusion

1 See also Guibovich 1990–92; Mazzotti 1998.

2 Rowe 1954; Flores Galindo 1987. On the *colegio de caciques*, see Brading 1991: 342; O'Phelan Godoy 1995: 31–32. On the Indian leaders' appeal to precolonial noble lineage, see Sala i Vila 1995: 54–57.

3 It must be noted that this regional analysis points to general trends. Given the wide ecological and social variances characteristic of the Andes, even the province level is not a totally adequate unit of analysis, as Mörner and Trelles (1987), among others, have pointed out. Particularly in the area between Cuzco and Lake Titicaca, as one of Duke Press's readers has rightly noted, the social and political dynamics reflect many of the patterns that we find in La Paz or northern Potosí.

4 See Hidalgo Lehuede 1983: 117–38; Szeminski 1984; Campbell 1987: 110–39; Flores Galindo 1987: 127–57.

5 On the Bourbon violation of Spanish traditional contract notions, see Guerra 1992: 56; on the Habsburg model of rule and the Indian rebels, see Sala i Vila 1995: 300; O'Phelan Godoy 1995: 44.

6 On Túpac Amaru's overall aim as "a cross-racial Peruvian nationalist project," see Thomson 1996: 245; Walker 1999: 40.

7 In his study of Andagua, Arequipa, in the mid-eighteenth century, Frank Salomon (1987: 163) provides an excellent example of the dichotomic worldview prevailing among other Andean peoples.

8 On the composition of the rebel leadership, see Campbell 1981; O'Phelan Godoy 1988: 268. On parish priests in the Cuzco rebellion, see Stavig 1999: 242; O'Phelan Godoy 1995: 122–23. For an interesting study questioning the extent of the involvement of the priests in the insurrection, see Garzón Heredia 1995: 245–71.

9 See Campbell 1987: 120–24; Szeminski 1987: 171–74; Stavig 1999: 208.

10 See Méndez 1993; Thurner 1997: 110–12; Walker 1999: 145–50, 193–201; Poole 1997: 146–51. On creole uses of pre-Columbian history, see Pagden 1990: 91–132; Brading 1991: 447–64.

11 On the ambivalent meaning of colonial artistic evocations of the Inca past and Catholic festivals, see Espinoza 1995 and Cahill 1996.

12 Stavig (1999: 235) has argued that rebellion was originated in peasants' wonders about "their ability to culturally survive."

13 For a critique of the "purposive image" of the process by which revolutions develop, see Skocpol 1979: 15–17; Scott 1985: 341–44.

14 See Thomson 1996: 246–54; see also Cornblit 1995: 137–72.

15 On the importance of these demands, see O'Phelan Godoy 1992: 91; Fisher 1976: 118.

16 See Brading 1991: 491; Rowe 1954: 35–36; Campbell 1987: 118.

17 Quoted in Valle de Siles 1990: 598. The attorney of the viceregal court of Buenos Aires supported Flores's proposal (Valle de Siles 1990: 612). Even at the height of rural insurgency in 1780, the acting president of the audiencia, Gerónimo Manuel de Ruedas, pondered this idea

in his correspondence with the Buenos Aires viceroy (letters of Ruedas to Viceroy Vértiz, October–November, 1780, AGN, IX, Tribunales, Leg. 124, Exp. 2 and Exp. 3, respectively), and he also consulted Macha priest Merlos. In May 1781, when the rebellion had mostly been suppressed, Ruedas reiterated the proposal to Viceroy Vértiz, arguing that "the increase of the tribute, along with the extinction of repartos and the accuracy in the revisitas (population recounts) will give the treasury more revenues" (AGN, IX, Intendencia, Leg. 8). The corregidor's lieutenant of the Yamparáez province, Manuel Martínez, had also stated in November 1780 that the rebellion "was caused by the large repartos of the corregidores, and the Indians want to pay one peso more in the tributes if they are freed from that tyranny." Martínez, who had been assaulted by the Indians, had also discussed the issue of repartos with Ruedas.

18 Flores quoted in Valle de Siles 1990: 596.

19 Ibid., 605.

20 See, for instance, the testimony of the bishop of Cuzco, Juan Manuel de Moscoso, in Garzón Heredia 1995: 247; and the testimony of the creole Melchor de Paz in Brading 1991: 487.

21 Cf. chapter 4. See also Thomson 1996: 279–309.

22 This is not to imply that these issues had not been discussed before. A good example is the wide circulation in the Spanish court of the report on the mistreatment of the Indians prepared by the scientific voyagers Jorge Juan y Santilla and Antonio de Ulloa in the late 1740s titled *Noticias Secretas de América*. See also Andrien 1998. Yet, it was only after the rebellion that the crown took measures to address some of these problems.

23 Flores quoted in Lewin 1957: 843.

24 Gálvez quoted in Fischer 1976: 119–20.

References

Abercrombie, Thomas. 1991. "Articulación doble y etnogénesis." In *Reproducción y transformación de las sociedades andinas*, ed. Segundo Moreno Yañez and Frank Salomon. Quito: ABYA-YALA.

———. 1998. *Pathways of Memory and Power. Ethnography and History among an Andean People*. Madison: University of Wisconsin Press.

Adrián, Mónica. 1993. "Sociedad civil, clero y axiología oficial durante la rebelión de Chayanta: Una aproximación a partir de la actuación del cura doctrinero de San Pedro de Macha." *Boletín del Instituto de Historia Americana "Dr. E. Ravignani"* (segundo semestre): 29–54.

———. 1995. "Reformas borbónicas y políticas locales: Las doctrinas de Chayanta durante la segunda mitad del siglo XVIII." *Revista del Instituto de Derecho* 23: 11–35.

———. 1996. "Los curatos en la provincia de Chayanta durante la segunda mitad del siglo XVIII." *Data* 6: 97–117.

———. 1997. "Identidad andina y doctrinas de aborígenes en la comunidad de Chayanta a fines del XVIII." Cuaderno de Trabajo No. 2, Universidad Nacional de Luján.

Andrade, Claudio Padilla. 1994. *La rebelión de Tomás Katari*. Sucre: CIPRES.

Andrien, Kenneth. 1998. "The *Noticias Secretas de América* and the Construction of a Governing Ideology for the Spanish American Empire." *Colonial Latin American Review* 7: 175–92.

Arze, Silvia. 1991. "La rebelión de los ayllus de la provincia colonial de Chayanta (1777–1781)." *Estado y Sociedad* 8: 89–110.

Arze, Silvia, and Ximena Mendinaceli. 1991. *Imágenes y presagios: El escudo de los Ayaviri, Mallkus de Charcas*. La Paz: HISBOL.

Assadourian, Carlos Sempat. 1979. "La producción de la mercancía dinero en la formación del mercado interno colonial: El caso del espacio peruano, siglo XVI." In *Ensayos sobre el desarrollo ecónomico de México y América Latina*, ed. Enrique Florescano. Mexico City: FCE.

———. 1982. *Sistema de la economía colonial: mercado interno, regiones y espacio económico*. Lima: IEP.

Baker, Keith. 1987. "Politics and Public Opinion under the Old Regime: Some Reflections." In *Press and Politics in Pre-Revolutionary France*, ed. Jack Censer and Jeremy Popkin. Berkeley: University of California Press.

Bakewell, Peter. 1984. *Miners of the Red Mountain. Indian Labor in Potosí, 1545–1650*. Albuquerque: University of New Mexico Press.

Barragán Romano, Rossana. 1985. "En torno al modelo comunal mercantil: 1985 el caso de Mizque (Cochabamba) en el siglo XVII." *Revista Chungara* 15.

Barragán Romano, Rossana, and Sinclair Thomson. 1993. "Los lobos hambrientos y el tributo a Dios: Conflictos sociales en torno a los diezmos en Charcas colonial." *Revista Andina* 2: 305–48.

Bhabha, Homi. 1984. "Of Mimicry and Man: The Ambivalence of Colonial Discourse." *October* 28: 125–33.

——. 1985. "Signs Taken for Wonders: Questions of Ambivalence and Authority under a Tree outside Delhi, May 1817." *Critical Inquiry* 12: 144–65.

Borah, Woodrow. 1983. *Justice by Insurance: The General Indian Court of Colonial Mexico and the Legal Aides of the Half-Real*. Berkeley: University of California Press.

Bourdieu, Pierre. 1977. *Outline of a Theory of Practice*. Cambridge: Cambridge University Press.

——. 1987. "The Force of Law: Toward a Sociology of the Juridical Field." *The Hastings Law Journal* 38: 814–53.

Bouysse Cassagne, Therese. 1987. *La identidad Aymara: Una aproximación histórica*. La Paz: Hisbol-IFEA.

Brading, David. 1975. *Mineros y comerciantes en el México borbónico (1763–1810)*. Mexico City: FCE.

——. 1991. *The First America: The Spanish Monarchy, Creole Patriotism, and the Liberal State, 1492–1867*. Cambridge: Cambridge University Press.

Brewer, John, and John Styles, eds. 1983. *An Ungovernable People: The English and Their Law in the Seventeenth and Eighteenth Centuries*. New Brunswick: Rutgers University Press.

Buechler, Rose Marie. 1981. *The Mining Society of Potosí, 1776–1810*. Syracuse: Syracuse University Press.

Burga, Manuel. 1988. *Nacimiento de una utopía: Muerte y resurrección de los Incas*. Lima: Instituto de Apoyo Agrario.

Burkholder, Mark, and D. S. Chandler. 1977. *From Impotence to Authority: The Spanish Crown and the American Audiencias, 1697–1801*. Columbia: University of Missouri Press.

——. 1982. *Biographical Dictionary of Audiencia Ministers in the Americas, 1687–1821*. Westport, Conn.: Greenwood Press.

Cahill, David. 1984. "*Curas* and Social Conflict in the *Doctrinas* of Cuzco, 1780–1814." *Journal of Latin American Studies* 16: 241–76.

——. 1990. "Taxonomy of a Colonial 'Riot': The Arequipa Disturbances of 1780." In *Reform and Insurrection in Bourbon New Granada and Peru*, ed. John Fisher, Allan Kuethe, and Anthony McFarlane. Baton Rouge: Louisiana University Press.

——. 1996. "Popular Religion and Appropriation: The Example of Corpus Christi in Eighteenth-Century Cuzco." *Latin American Research Review* 31: 67–110.

Campbell, Leon. 1978. *The Military and Society in Colonial Peru, 1750–1810*. Philadelphia: American Philosophical Society.

——. 1979. "Recent Research on Andean Peasant Revolts, 1750–1820." *Latin American Research Review* 14: 3–49.

——. 1981. "Social Structure of the Túpac Amaru Army in Cuzco, 1780–81." *HAHR* 61: 3–49.

——. 1987. "Ideology and Factionalism during the Great Rebellion, 1780–1782." In *Resistance, Rebellion, and Consciousness*, ed. Steve Stern. Madison: University of Wisconsin Press.

Cangiano, María Cecilia. 1987. "Curas, caciques y comunidades en el Alto Perú: Chayanta a fines del siglo XVIII."

Celestino, Olinda, and Albert Meyers 1981. *Las cofradías en el Perú: Región central*. Frankfurt: Klaus Dieter Vervuert.

Chartier, Roger. 1991. *The Cultural Origins of the French Revolution*. Durham: Duke University Press.

Chatterjee, Partha. 1993. *The Nation and Its Fragments: Colonial and Postcolonial Histories*. Princeton: Princeton University Press.

Choque, Roberto. 1978. "Pedro Chipana: Cacique comerciante de Calamarca." *Avances* 1: 28–32.

Coatsworth, John. 1982. "The Limits of Colonial Absolutism: The State in Eighteenth-Century Mexico." In *Essays in the Political, Economic, and Social History of Colonial Latin America*, ed. Karen Spalding. Newark: University of Delaware Press.

——. 1988. "Patterns of Rural Rebellion in Latin America: Mexico in Comparative Perspective." In *Riot, Rebellion, and Revolution: Rural Social Conflict in Mexico*, ed. Friedrich Katz. Princeton: Princeton University Press.

Cole, Jeffrey. 1985. *The Potosí Mita, 1573–1700: Compulsory Indian Labor in the Andes*. Stanford: Stanford University Press.

Colección documental de la independencia del Perú. 1971. Tomo 2, vol. 2. Lima: Comisión Nacional del Sespuicentario de la Independencia del Perú.

Comaroff, Jean, and John Comaroff. 1991. *Of Revelation and Revolution: Christianity, Colonialism, and Consciousness in South Africa*. Vol. 1. Chicago: University of Chicago Press.

Cornblit, Oscar. 1995. *Power and Violence in the Colonial City: Oruro from the Mining Renaissance to the Rebellion of Túpac Amaru (1740–1782)*. New York: Cambridge University Press.

Corrigan, Philip, and Derek Sayer. 1985. *The Great Arch: English State Formation as Cultural Revolution*. Oxford: Basil Blackwell.

Davis, Natalie Zemon. 1975. "The Rites of Violence." In *Society and Culture in Early Modern France*. Stanford: Stanford University Press.

de Angelis, Pedro. 1971 [1836]. *Colección de obras y documentos relativos a la historia antigua y moderna de las provincias del Río de la Plata*. Buenos Aires: Plus Ultra.

de Certeau, Michel. 1984. *The Practice of Everyday Life*. California: University of California Press.

Del Río, Mercedes. 1995. "Estructuración étnica Qharaqhara y su desarticulación colonial." In *Espacios, etnias, frontera: Atenuaciones políticas en el sur del Tawantinsuyu, siglos XV–XIII*, ed. Ana María Presta. Sucre: Ediciones Asur.

Dillon, Mary, and Thomas Abercrombie. 1988. "The Destroying Christ: An Aymara Myth of Conquest." In *Rethinking History and Myth: Indigenous South American Perspectives on the Past*, ed. Jonathan Hill. Urbana: University of Illinois Press.

Espinoza, Carlos. 1995. "Colonial Visions: Drama, Art, and Legitimation in Peru and Ecuador." In *Native Artists and Patrons in Colonial Latin America*, ed. Emily Umberger and Tom Cummins. Tempe: Arizona State University.

Estenssoro Fuchs, Juan Carlos. 1995. "La plebe ilustrada: El pueblo en las fronteras de la razón." In *Entre la retórica y la insurgencia: Las ideas y los movimientos sociales en los Andes, siglo XVIII*, ed. Charles Walker. Cusco: Centro de Estudios Regionales Andinos Bartolomé de las Casas.

Farriss, Nancy. 1968. *Crown and Clergy in Colonial Mexico 1759–1821: The Crisis of Ecclesiastical Privilege*. London: Athlone Press.

Fisher, John, 1976. "La rebelión de Túpac Amaru y el programa imperial de Carlos III." In *Túpac Amaru II-1780*, ed. Alberto Flores Galindo. Lima: Retablo de Papel Ediciones.

——. 1977. *Minas y mineros en el Perú colonial, 1776–1824*. Lima: IEP.

Fisher, John, Allan Kuethe, and Anthony McFarlane, eds. 1990. *Reform and Insurrection in Bourbon New Granada and Peru*. Baton Rouge: Louisiana State University Press.

Fisher, Lillian E. 1966. *The Last Inca Revolt, 1780–1783*. Norman: University of Oklahoma Press.

Flores Galindo, Alberto. 1981. "La revolución tupamarista y los pueblos andinos (una crítica y un proyecto)." *Allpanchis* 17/18: 153–65.

——. 1987. *Buscando a un Inca: Identidad y utopía en los Andes*. Lima: Instituto de Apoyo Agrario.

Foucault, Michel. 1982. "The Subject and Power." In *Michel Foucault: Beyond Structuralism and Hermeneutics*, ed. Hubert Dreyfus and Paul Rabinow. Chicago: University of Chicago Press.

Garzón Heredia, Emilio. 1995. "1780: Clero, elite local y rebelión." In *Entre la retórica y la insurgencia*, ed. Charles Walker. Cusco: Centro de Estudios Bartolomé de las Casas.

Glave, Luis Miguel. 1989. *Trajinantes: Caminos indígenas en la sociedad colonial, siglos XVI/XVII*. Lima: Instituto de Apoyo Agrario.

Glave, Luis Miguel, and María Isabel Remy. 1983. *Estructura agraria y vida rural en una región andina: Ollantaytambo entre los siglos XVI y XIX*. Cusco: Centro Bartolomé de las Casas.

Godoy, Ricardo. 1990. *Mining and Agriculture in Highland Bolivia: Ecology, History, and Commerce among the Jukumanis*. Tucson: University of Arizona Press.

Golte, Jürgen. 1980. *Repartos y rebeliones: Túpac Amaru y las contradicciones de la economía colonial*. Lima: IEP.

Greenblatt, Stephen. 1981. "Invisible Bullets: Renaissance Authority and Its Subversion." In *Glyph 8*, ed. Walter Michaels. Baltimore: Johns Hopkins University Press.

Grieshaber, Erwin. 1977. "Survival of Indian Communities in Nineteenth-Century Bolivia." Ph.D. dissertation, University of North Carolina.

Gruzinski, Serge. 1989. *Man-Gods in the Mexican Highlands: Indian Power and Colonial Society 1520–1800*. Stanford: Stanford University Press.

——. 1993. *The Conquest of Mexico: The Incorporation of Indian Societies into the Western World, Sixteenth–Eighteenth Centuries*. Cambridge: Polity Press.

Guerra, Francois-Xavier. 1992. *Modernidad e independencias: Ensayos sobre las revoluciones hispánicas*. Mexico: MAPFRE.

Guha, Ranajit. 1983. *Elementary Aspects of Peasant Insurgency in Colonial India*. Delhi: Oxford University Press.

——. 1988. "The Prose of Counter-Insurgency." In *Selected Subaltern Studies*, ed. Ranajit Guha and Gayatri Spivak. Delhi: Oxford University Press.

Guibovich Pérez, Pedro. 1990–92. "Lectura y difusión de la obra del Inca Garcilaso en el virreinato peruano (siglos XVII–XVIII): El caso de los *Comentarios Reales*." *Revista Histórica* 37: 103–20.

Haitin, Manuel. 1983. "Late-Colonial Lima: Economy and Society in an Era of Reform and Revolution." Ph.D. dissertation, University of California, Berkeley.

Harris, Olivia. 1986. "From Asymmetry to Triangle: Symbolic Transformation in Northern Potosí." In *Anthropological History of Andean Polities*, ed. John V. Murra, Nathan Wachtel, and Jacque Revel. Cambridge: Cambridge University Press.

——. 2000. *To Make the Earth Bear Fruit: Ethnographic Essays on Fertility, Work, and Gender in Highland Bolivia*. London: Institute of Latin American Studies.

Hidalgo Lehuede, Jorge. 1983. "Amarus y cataris: Aspectos mesiánicos de la rebelión indígena de 1781 en Cusco, Chayanta, La Paz y Arica." *Revista Chungara* 10: 117–38.

Hill, Christopher. 1972. *The World Turned Upside Down*. New York: Viking.

Hobsbawm, Eric. 1973. "Peasant Politics." *Journal of Peasant Studies* 1: 3–22.

Hunefeldt, Christine. 1982. *Lucha por la tierra y protesta indígena: Las comunidades indígenas del Perú entre colonia y república*. Bonn: Bonner Americanische Studien.

Hunt, Lynn. 1984. *Politics, Culture, and Class in the French Revolution*. Berkeley: University of California Press.

Irurozqui, Marta. 2000. "The Sound of the Pututos: Politicisation and Indigenous Rebellions in Bolivia, 1826–1921." *Journal of Latin American Studies* 32: 85–114.

Juan y Santilla, Jorge, and Antonio de Ulloa. 1953. *Noticias Secretas de America*. Buenos Aires: Mar Océano.

Joseph, Gilbert, and Daniel Nugent, eds. 1994. *Everyday Forms of State Formation: Revolution and the Negotiation of Rule in Modern Mexico*. Durham: Duke University Press.

Katz, Friedrich. 1988. "Rural Uprisings in Preconquest and Colonial Mexico." In *Riot, Rebellion, and Revolution: Rural Social Conflict in Mexico*. Princeton: Princeton University Press.

Klein, Herbert. 1992. *Bolivia: The Evolution of a Multi-Ethnic Society*. New York: Oxford University Press.

——. 1993. *Haciendas and Ayllus*. Stanford: Stanford University Press.

LaCapra, Dominick. 1985. "The 'Cheese and the Worms': The Cosmos of a Twentieth-Century Historian." In *History and Criticism*. Ithaca. Cornell University Press.

Lamas, Andrés. 1849. *Colección de Memorias y Documentos para la Historia y Geografía de los Pueblos del Río de la Plata*. Vol. I. Montevideo.

Langer, Erik. 1990. "Andean Rituals of Revolt: The Chayanta Rebellion of 1927." *Ethnohistory* 37: 227–53.

Larson, Brooke. 1979. "Caciques, Class Structure, and the Colonial State." *Nova Americana* 2: 197–235.

——. 1989. "Exploitation and Moral Economy in the Southern Andes: A Critical Reconsideration." Columbia-New York University, occasional papers, no. 8.

——. 1997. *Colonialism and Agrarian Transformation in Bolivia: Cochabamba, 1550–1900*. Durham: Duke University Press.

Larson, Brooke, and Olivia Harris with Enrique Tandeter. 1995. *Ethnicity, Markets, and Migration in the Andes: At the Crossroads of History and Anthropology*. Durham: Duke University Press.

Lehn, Zuelma. 1987. "La lucha comunaria en torno a la contribución territorial y a la prestación de servicios gratuitos durante el período republicano (1920–1925)." Taller de Historia Oral Andina.

Levi, Giovanni. 1988. *Inheriting Power: The Story of an Exorcist*. Chicago: University of Chicago Press.

Lewin, Boleslao. 1957. *La rebelión de Túpac Amaru y los orígenes de la emancipación americana*. Buenos Aires: Hachette.

Lynch, John. 1992. "The Institutional Framework of Colonial Spanish America." *Journal of Latin American Studies* 24 (quincentenary supplement): 69–81.

Macera, Pablo. 1971. "Feudalismo colonial americano: El caso de las haciendas peruanas." *Acta Histórica* 35 (Szeged): 3–43.

MacLachlan, Colin. 1988. *Spain's Empire in the New World: The Role of Ideas in Institutional and Social Change*. Berkeley: University of California Press.

Mallon, Florencia. 1995. *Peasant and Nation: The Making of Postcolonial Mexico and Peru*. Berkeley: University of California Press.

Markoff, John. 1996. *The Abolition of Feudalism. Peasants, Lords, and Legislators in the French Revolution*. University Park: Pennsylvania State University Press.

Mazzotti, José Antonio. 1998. "Garcilaso y los orígenes del garcilasismo: El papel de los *Comentarios Reales* en el desarrollo del imaginario peruano." *Fronteras* 3: 13–35.

Méndez, Cecilia. 1993. *Incas sí, indios no: Apuntes para el estudio del nacionalismo criollo en Perú*. Lima: IEP.

Moreno Cebrián, Alfredo. 1977. *El Corregidor de Indios y la economía peruana del siglo XVIII (Los repartos forzosos de mercancías)*. Madrid: Instituto González Fernández de Oviedo.

Mörner, Magnus, and Efraín Trelles. 1987. "A Test of Causal Interpretations of the Túpac Amaru Rebellion." In *Resistance, Rebellion, and Consciousness*, ed. Steve Stern. Madison: University of Wisconsin Press.

Murra, John. 1975. *Formaciones económicas y políticas del mundo andino*. Lima: IEP.

O'Phelan Godoy, Scarlett. 1983. "Tierras comunales y revuelta social: Peru y Bolivia en el siglo XVIII." *Allpanchis* 22: 75–91.

——. 1986. "Aduanas, Mercado Interno y Elite Comercial en el Cuzco antes y después de la Gran Rebelión de 1780." *Apuntes* 19: 53–72.

——. 1988. *Un siglo de rebeliones anticoloniales: Perú y Bolivia 1700–1778*. Cusco: Centro Bartolomé de las Casas.

——. 1992. "Tradicion y modernidad en el proyecto de Túpac Amaru." In *Tres levantamientos populares: Pugachóv, Túpac Amaru, Hidalgo*, ed. Jean Meyer. Mexico City: CEMCA.

——. 1995. "Algunas reflexiones sobre las Reformas Borbónicas y las rebeliones del siglo XVIII." In *Entre la retórica y la insurgencia*, ed. Charles Walker. Cusco: Centro Bartolomé de las Casas.

——. 1995. *La gran rebelión en los Andes: De Túpac Amaru a Túpac Catari*. Cusco: Centro Bartolomé de las Casas.

——. 1998. *Kurakas sin sucesiones: Del cacique al alcalde de indios (Perú y Bolivia 1750–1835)*. Cuzco: Centro Bartolomé de las Casas.

Ossio, Juan, ed. 1973. *Ideología mesiánica del mundo andino*. Lima: Prado Pastor.

Pacheco Balanza, Diego, and Edgar Guerrero Peñaranda. 1994. *Machas, Tinkipayas y Yamparas, Provincia Chayanta (Norte Potosí)*. Sucre: CIPRES.

Pagden, Anthony. 1990. *Spanish Imperialism and the Political Imagination*. New Haven: Yale University Press.

Pease, Franklin. 1992. *Curacas, reciprocidad y riqueza*. Lima: Pontificia Universidad Católica del Perú.

Penry, Elizabeth. 1996. "Transformations in Indigenous Authority and Identity in Resettlement Towns of Colonial Charcas (Alto Peru)." Ph.D. dissertation, University of Miami.

Phelan, John Leddy. 1967. *The Kingdom of Quito in the Seventeenth Century*. Wisconsin: University of Wisconsin Press.

——. 1978. *The People and the King: The Comunero Revolution in Colombia, 1781*. Madison: University of Wisconsin Press.

Pietschmann, Horst. 1987. "Estado colonial y mentalidad social: El ejercicio del poder frente a los distintos sistemas de valores, siglo XVIII." In *America latina: Dallo stato coloniale allo stato nazione*, ed. Antonio Annino. Milan: Franco Angeli.

Platt, Tristan. 1978. "Mapas coloniales de la provincia de Chayanta: dos visiones conflictivas de un solo paisaje." In *Estudios bolivianos en homenaje a Gunna Mendoza L.*, ed. Marta V. de Apuirre et al. La Paz: n.p.

——. 1982a. "El rol de ayllu andino en la reproducción del régimen mercantil simple en el norte de Potosí (Bolivia)." In *Identidades andinas y lógicas del campesinado*, Lucy Therina Briggs, et al. Lima: Mosca Azul Editores.

——. 1982b. *Estado boliviano y ayllu andino: Tierra y tributo en el norte de Potosí.* Lima: IEP.

——. 1983. "Conciencia andina y conciencia proletaria: Qhuyaruna y ayllu en el norte de Potosí." *HISLA* 2: 47–73.

——. 1984. "Liberalism and Ethnocide in the Southern Andes." *History Workshop Journal* 17: 3–18.

——. 1986. "Mirrors and Maize: The Concept of 'Yanatin' among the Macha of Bolivia." In *Anthropological History of Andean Polities*, ed. John V. Murra, Nathan Wachtel, and Jacques Revel. Cambridge: Cambridge University Press.

——. 1987a. "The Andean Experience of Bolivian Liberalism, 1825–1900: Roots of Rebellion in Nineteenth-Century Chayanta (Potosí)." In *Resistance, Rebellion, and Consciousness*, ed. Steve Stern. Madison: University of Wisconsin Press.

——. 1987b. "The Andean Soldiers of Christ: Confraternity Organization, the Mass of the Sun, and Regenerative Warfare in Rural Potosí (18th–20th Centuries)." *Journal de la Société des Americanistes* 73: 139–91.

——. 1987c. "Entre 'ch'axwa'y 'muxsa': Para una historia del pensamiento político aymara." In *Tres reflexiones sobre el pensamiento andino*, ed. Thérès Bouysse-Cassagne et al. La Paz: HISBOL.

Polo Laborda, Jorge. 1981. "Pachachaca, una hacienda feudal, autoabastecimiento y comercialización." In *Hacienda, comercio, fiscalidad y luchas sociales (Perú Colonial)*, ed. Javier Tord Nicolini and Carlos Lazo. Lima: BPHES.

Poole, Deborah. 1992. "Antopología e historia andinas en los EE.UU: Buscando un reencuentro." *Revista Andina* 10: 209–45.

——. 1997. *Vision, Race, and Modernity: A Visual Economy of the Andean Image World.* Princeton: Princeton University Press.

Powers, Karen. 1995. *Andean Journeys: Migration, Ethnogenesis, and the State in Colonial Quito.* Albuquerque: University of New Mexico Press.

Rama, Angel. 1996. *The Lettered City.* Durham: Duke University Press.

Ramos, Gabriela, ed. 1994. *La venida del reino.* Cuzco: Centro Bartolomé de las Casas.

Rancière, Jacques. 1992. "Politics, Identification, and Subjectivation." *October* 61: 48–64.

Rasnake, Roger. 1988. *Domination and Resistance: Authority and Power among an Andean People.* Durham: Duke University Press.

"Relacion de los hechos más notables de la sublevación de José Gabriel Túpac Amarn, 1780 a 1782" 1900. *Revista de Archivos y Bilbliotecas Nacionales* (Año III) 5.

Rivera Cusicanqui, Silvia. 1978. "El mallku y la sociedad colonial en el siglo XVII: El caso de J. De Machaca." *Avances* 1: 7–27.

——. 1984. *"Oprimidos pero no vencidos," luchas del campesinado aymara y qhechwa de Bolivia, 1900–1980.* La Paz: HISBOL-CSUTCB.

——. 1992. *Ayllus y proyectos de desarrollo en el norte de Potosí.* La Paz: Ediciones Aruwiyri.

Root, Hilton. 1987. *Peasants and King in Burgundy: Agrarian Foundations of French Absolutism.* Berkeley: University of California Press.

Rostworowski de Diez Canseco, María. 1961. *Curacas y sucesiones: Costa Norte.* Lima: Minerva.

Rowe, John. 1954. "El movimiento nacional inca del siglo XVIII." *Revista Universitaria* (Cusco) 107: 17–47.

Saignes, Thierry. 1983. "Las etnías de Charcas frente al sistema colonial (siglo XVII): Ausentismo y fugas en el debate sobre la mano de obra indígena (1595–1665)." *Jahbuch fur Geschichte von Staat, Wirtshaft and Gesellschaft Lateinamerika* 21: 27–75.

———. 1987. "De la borrachera al retrato: Los caciques de Charcas entre dos legitimidades." *Revista Andina* 5: 139–70.

———. 1991. "Lobos y ovejas: Formación y desarrollo de los pueblos y comunidades en el sur andino (siglos XVI–XX)." In *Reproducción y transformación de las sociedades andinas*, ed. Segundo Moreno Yáñez and Frank Salomon. Quito: Ediciones ABYA-YALA.

———. 1995. "Indian Migration and Social Change in Seventeenth-Century Charcas." In *Ethnicity, Markets, and Migration in the Andes*, ed. Brooke Larson and Olivia Harris, with Enrique Tandeter. Durham: Duke University Press.

Sala i Vila, Núria. 1995. "La rebelión de Huarochirí en 1783." In *Entre la retórica y la insurgencia*, ed. Charles Walker. Cusco: Centro Bartolomé de las Casas.

———. 1996. *Y se armó el tole tole: Tributos indígenas y movimientos sociales en el virreinato del Perú, 1784–1814*. Cusco: IER.

Salomon, Frank. 1987. "Ancestor Cults and Resistance to the State in Arequipa, ca. 1748–1754." In *Resistance, Rebellion, and Consciousness*, ed. Steve Stern. Madison: University of Wisconsin Press.

———. 1994. "A 'Personal Visit': Colonial Political Ritual and the Making of Indians in the Andes." *Colonial Latin American Review* 3: 1–34.

Sánchez-Albornoz, Nicolas. 1978. *Indios y tributos en el Alto Perú*. Lima: IEP.

Santamaría, Daniel. 1977. "La propiedad de la tierra y la condición social del indio en el Alto Perú, 1780–1810." *Desarrollo Económico* 66: 253–71.

———. 1983. "Iglesia y economía campesina en el Alto Perú, siglo XVIII." Florida International University, occasional paper series.

Scott, James. 1985. *Weapons of the Weak: Everyday Forms of Peasant Resistance*. New Haven: Yale University Press.

———. 1990. *Domination and the Arts of Resistance: Hidden Transcripts*. New Haven: Yale University Press.

Serulnikov, Sergio. 1988. "Tomás Catari y la producción de justicia: Análisis de un interrogatorio al líder de la rebelión indígena de Chayanta." *Documentos CEDES* 10.

———. 1989. "Reivindicaciones indígenas y legalidad colonial: La rebelión de Chayanta (1777–1781)." *Documentos* CEDES 20.

———. 1998. "Peasant Politics and Colonial Domination: Social Conflicts and Insurgency in Northern Potosí, 1730–1781." Ph.D. dissertation, State University of New York at Stony Brook.

———. 1999. "Customs and Rules: Social Conflicts in the Age of Bourbon Reformism (Northern Potosí in the 1770s)." *Colonial Latin American Review* 8: 245–74.

———. 2000. "Conflictos agrarios y políticos intra-étnicos en el norte de Potosí (el caso de Pocoata, siglo XVIII)." *Revista Andina* 17: 65–99.

———. 2003. "De forasteros a *hilacatas*: una familia andina del grupo Chullpa, provincia de Chayanta, siglo XVIII." *Jahrbuch fur Geschichte Lateinamerikas* 40.

Skocpol, Theda. 1979. *States and Social Revolutions: A Comparative Analysis of France, Russia, and China*. Cambridge: Cambridge University Press.

Socolow, Susan. 1987. *The Bureaucrats of Buenos Aires, 1769–1810: Amor al Real Servicio*. Durham: Duke University Press.

Spalding, Karen. 1974. *De indio a campesino: Cambios en la estructura social del Peru colonial*. Lima: IEP.

———. 1984. *Huarochirí: An Andean Society under Inca and Spanish Rule*. Stanford: Stanford University Press.

Stavig, Ward. 1988. "Ethnic Conflict, Moral Economy, and Population in Rural Cuzco on the Eve of the Thupa Amaro II Rebellion." *HAHR* 68: 737–70.

———. 1999. *The World of Túpac Amaru: Conflict, Community, and Identity in Colonial Peru*. Lincoln: University of Nebraska Press.

———. 2000. "Ambiguous Visions: Nature, Law, and Culture in Indigenous-Spanish Land Relations in Colonial Peru." *HAHR* 80: 77–111.

Stein, Stanley. 1981. "Bureaucracy and Business in the Spanish Empire, 1759–1804: Failure of a Bourbon Reform in Mexico and Peru." *HAHR* 61: 2–28.

Stern, Steve. 1982. *Peru's Indian Peoples and the Challenge of Spanish Conquest: Huamanga to 1640*. Madison: University of Wisconsin Press.

———. 1987a. "New Approaches to the Study of Peasant Rebellion." In *Resistance, Rebellion, and Consciousness*, ed. Steve Stern. Madison: University of Wisconsin Press.

———. 1987b. "The Age of the Andean Insurrection, 1742–1782: A Reappraisal." In *Resistance, Rebellion, and Consciousness*, ed. Steve Stern. Madison: University of Wisconsin Press.

———. 1995. "The Variety and Ambiguity of Native Andean Intervention in European Colonial Markets." In *Ethnicity, Markets, and Migration in the Andes*, ed. Brooke Larson and Olivia Harris, with Enrique Tandeter. Durham: Duke University Press.

Szeminski, Jan. 1984. *La utopía tupamarista*. Lima: Pontífica Universidad Católica.

———. 1987. "Why Kill the Spaniards? New Perspectives on Andean Insurrectionary Ideology in the Eighteenth Century." In *Resistance, Rebellion, and Consciousness*, ed. Steve Stern. Madison: University of Wisconsin Press.

Tandeter, Enrique. 1992. *Coacción y mercado: La minería de la plata en el Potosí colonial, 1692–1826*. Cusco: Centro Bartolomé de las Casas.

———. 1995. "Población y economía en los Andes (siglo XVIII)." *Revista Andina* 13: 7–22.

———. 1997. "Teóricamente ausentes, teóricamente solas: Mujeres y hogares en los Andes coloniales (Sacaca y Acasio en 1614)." *Andes: Antropología e Historia* 8: 11–25.

Tandeter, Enrique, and Nathan Wachtel. 1989. "Price and Agricultural Production: Potosí and Charcas in the Eighteenth Century." In *Essays on the Price History of Eighteenth-Century Latin America*, ed. Lyman L. Johnson and Enrique Tandeter. Albuquerque: University of New Mexico Press.

Taylor, William. 1979. *Drinking, Homicide, and Rebellion in Colonial Mexican Villages*. Stanford: Stanford University Press.

———. 1985. "Between Global Process and Local Knowledge: An Inquiry into Early Latin American Social History, 1500–1900." In *Reliving the Past: The Worlds of Social History*, ed. Olivier Zunz. Chapel Hill: University of North Carolina Press.

———. 1996. *Magistrates of the Sacred: Priests and Parishioners in Eighteenth-Century Mexico*. Stanford: Stanford University Press.

Thomson, Sinclair. 1996. "Colonial Crisis, Community, and Self-Rule: Aymara Politics in the Age of Insurgency." Ph.D. dissertation, University of Wisconsin.

——. 1999. "'We Alone Will Rule . . . ': Recovering the Range of Anticolonial Projects among Andean Peasants (La Paz, 1740s to 1781)." *Colonial Latin American Review* 8: 275–99.

Thurner, Mark. 1991. "Guerra andina y política campesina en el sitio de La Paz." In *Poder y Violencia en Los Andes*, ed. Henrique Urbano. Lima: Centro Bartolomé de las Casas.

——. 1997. *From Two Republics to One Divided: Contradictions of Postcolonial Nation-Making in Andean Peru*. Durham: Duke University Press.

Tilly, Charles. 1978. *From Mobilization to Revolution*. Reading, Mass.: Addison-Wesley.

——. 1981. "How (and, to Some Extent, Why) to Study British Contention." In *As Sociology Meets History*. New York: Academic Press.

——. 1989. "Routine Conflicts and Peasant Rebellions in Seventeenth-Century France." In *Power and Protest in the Countryside: Studies of Rural Unrest in Asia, Europe, and Latin America*, ed. Robert P. Weller and Scott Guggenheim. Durham: Duke University Press.

Tord Nicolini, Javier. 1974. "El corregidor de indios del Perú: Comercio y tributos." *Historia y Cultura* 8: 173–214.

Valle de Siles, María Eugenia. 1990. *A rebelión de Túpac Catari, 1781–1782*. La Paz: Editorial Don Bosco.

Van Young, Eric. 1989. "The Raw and the Cooked: Elite and Popular Ideology in Mexico, 1800–1821." In *The Middle Period in Latin America: Values and Attitudes in the Seventeenth to Nineteenth Centuries*, ed. Mark Szuchman. Boulder: Lynne Rienner Publishers.

——. 2001. *The Other Rebellion: Popular Violence, Ideology, and the Mexican Struggle for Independence, 1810–1821*. Stanford: Stanford University Press.

Voekel, Pamela. 1992. "Peeing on the Palace: Bodily Resistance to Bourbon Reforms in Mexico City." *Journal of Historical Society* 5: 183–208.

Walker, Charles F. 1999. *Smoldering Ashes: Cuzco and the Creation of Republican Peru, 1780–1840*. Durham: Duke University Press.

Wightman, Ann. 1990. *Indigenous Migration and Social Change. The Forasteros of Cuzco, 1520–1720*. Durham: Duke University Press.

Young, Robert. 1990. *White Mythologies. Writing History and the West*. London: Routledge.

Zulawski, Anne. 1987. "Forasteros y yanaconas: La mano de obra de un centro minero en el siglo XVII." In *La Participación indígena en los mercados surandinos: Estrategias y reproducción social, siglos XVI a XX*, ed. Olivia Harris, Brooke Larson, and Enrique Tandeter. La Paz: CERES.

Coatsworth, John, 124, 229 n.4, 251 n.82

Coca (family), 169, 255 n.73

Cochabamba, 11, 27, 164–65, 199, 208, 209, 222, 231 n.22, 261 n.53

Cofradías, 232 nn.12, 13. *See also* Alférez/ alfareces; Priests; Ritual celebrations

Colcha, 164, 168–69, 199

Cole, Jeffrey, 234 n.32

College of San Francísco de Borja, 216

Colonial government: Caja de Censos, 29–30, 32; Catholic Church and, 96–103, 245 n.59; ecclesiastical fee schedule (arancel) and, 96–103, 245 n.59; Indian legal strategies and, 31, 124, 133, 147, 248 n.28; internal rivalries within peasant society, 175–76; messianism, 125, 153, 187, 195–96, 217, 221–22; monarchy and, 187, 188, 195, 217; pact of reciprocity with native communities, 31–32, 139–40, 174; pardon requests and, 178–80, 182–83, 193, 210, 258 n.133; provincial authorities' relations with, 35–52, 41–43, 237 n.106; public ceremony and, 178–79, 180, 257 nn.117, 121; social hierarchies and, 180, 257 n.121; viceregal court and, 128–30, 132–33, 135–37, 145, 248 n.14. *See also* Chayanta rebellion; Insurrection, Andean; Reparto de mercancías; Taxation; Tribute system

Colque, Blas, 105, 108, 262 n.71

Colque, Marcos, 206, 238 n.19, 263 nn.84, 85

Colque, Sebastián, 189, 211, 264 nn.104, 105

Colquerunas, 29, 89–90, 92, 94, 234 n.32

Comaroff, Jean, 249 n.45

Comaroff, John, 249 n.45

Condocondo, 29, 160–61, 183, 189, 230 n.10, 245 n.82, 252 n.8, 258 n.133, 261 n.57

Cook, Noble David, 12

Cori, Blas, 20, 40, 44

Cornblit, Oscar, 45, 265 n.14

Coroma (Porco community), 183

Corregidores: aranceles and, 53, 244 n.47; audiencia, relations with, 12, 51–52, 127–28, 132, 147, 152, 248 n.8; Chayanta rebellion and, 42, 132, 142–44; indigenous peoples'

dissent and, 21–22; jurisdiction over Indian villages, 129; Tomás Katari and, 129, 133; land distribution by, 14–15, 232 n.25; legitimacy of, 146; mita labor and, 89–90, 149–50; reparto system and, 12, 49–50, 127–29, 144, 150, 163, 197, 250 n.71, 251 n.86, 261 n.47; tribute collection and, 47–48

Corrigan, Philip, 44, 226

Cortés, Dionisio, 101, 104–6, 108, 162–63, 173, 203–4, 205, 208, 211, 244 n.47, 262 nn.71, 74

Creoles, 200, 218, 223, 265 n.8

Cult of ancestors, 98, 244 n.44

Curas doctrineros. See Priests

Cuzco: anticolonial warfare, 186–89; aristocracy in, 216–17, 220–21; Inca culture in, 215–16, 221, 223–24; Indian subalternity in, 223–24; insurrection of, 217–18; interracial relations in, 215–18, 220–21; priests and, 162, 252 n.17; taxation in, 231 n.22. *See also* Inca headings; La Paz; Túpac Amaru

Davis, Natalie Zemon, 123

de Angelis, Pedro, 240 n.82, 251 n.85, 256 n.93, 257 n.114

de Certeau, Michel, 249 n.45

Del Río, Mercedes, 229 n.7

Dillon, Mary, 155

Dorado, Antonio, 165, 173

Ecclesiastical fee schedule (arancel), 53, 78, 95–106, 163, 166–73, 203, 244 n.47, 245 n.59

Escobar, Martínez de, 80, 241 n.91

Escobedo, Jorge, 130, 193

Espinoza, Carlos, 265 n.11

Espinoza, Melchor (Macha Indian), 116, 117, 243 n.28, 247 n.118

Estenssoro Fuchs, Juan Carlos, 97

Ethnic groups: in demographic surveys, 68–70; forasteros and, 13, 14, 68, 231 nn.22, 23, 242 n.12; land claims, 230 nn.11, 12; mestizos, 20, 61, 67–69, 107–8, 254 n.54; migration and, 13, 14, 231 nn.14, 22, 23, 242 n.12; multi-ethnic chieftainships, 52, 80–84; reparti-

Insurrection, Andean (*cont.*)
    livelihood and, 209; priests and, 170–71, 201–2, 203, 254 n.69; property rights, 168–69; punishment of rebel leaders, 208–9, 211–12; Spanish accounts of, 176–78, 225–27, 257 nn.113, 115; Spanish monarchy and, 225, 226, 227. *See also* Katari headings; Túpac Amaru
Iruzoqui, Marta, 229 n.1

Jorge, Matheo, 77, 79, 80, 241 n.91
Joseph, Gilbert, 229 n.5, 242 n.4
Jukumani (ethnic group): cacique relations, 36, 40–41; ethnic identity and ecological complementarity and, 230 n.12; land ownership disputes, 36; in Micani (valley district), 7, 9, 20, 27, 101, 104; priests and, 100–101; rebellion and, 203–4; tribute collection in, 91

Katari, Dámaso: execution of, 211–12, 214; La Plata siege and, 196–97, 208; pardon request, 210; peasant mobilization and, 195, 260 n.32; political influence of, 192, 208; tribute payments, 194, 200, 259 n.17
Katari, Nicolás: capture of, 211, 264 n.105; confessions of, 213, 264 n.110; La Plata siege and, 196–97, 208; pardon request, 210; peasant mobilization and, 193, 195, 260 n.32; political influence of, 192, 208; tribute payments, 194; Túpac Amaru allegiance of, 197
Katari, Tomás: Juan Antonio de Acuña and, 179–80, 184, 197–98, 257 nn.114, 121; background of, 116–17, 247 nn.116, 119; in Buenos Aires, 129, 135, 151, 210, 261 n.47; Condocondo Indians and, 160, 183, 258 n.133; corregidores and, 119, 129, 133, 152, 179–80, 184; death of, 184–85, 189–91; imprisonment of, 122, 129–31, 142, 145–46, 184, 250 n.74; leadership of, 131, 150, 153, 172, 174–76, 183–84, 187–88, 256 nn.99, 101; papers of, 197, 261 n.47; priests and, 172–73, 202, 262 n.62; tribute collection and, 129–30, 133–36, 183–84, 210, 213, 256 n.99, 257 nn.114, 123, 264 n.110

Katz, Friedrich, 124
Klein, Herbert, 58–60, 231 n.23, 232 n.28, 239 n.53
Kuethe, Allan, 217

LaCapra, Dominick, 249 n.39
Lamas, Andrés, 251 n.84, 260 n.33
Land: ayllus, 6, 24–26, 31–34, 60, 74, 231 n.23, 247 n.6; caciques and, 28–32, 74–76, 234 nn.24, 31; collective cultivation (comunes), 11, 24, 62, 89–90, 94; for ecclesiastical obligations, 96, 99, 243 n.36; forasteros and, 13, 14, 28, 68, 231 nn.22, 23, 242 n.12; land tenure model, 7–8; mita laborer support, 29, 94, 234 nn.36, 38; originarios and, 13, 14, 57, 230 n.11, 231 n.22, 257 n.123; population distributions and, 7, 9, 13–15, 57–60, 68–73; in tribute system, 71, 239 n.53; valley parishes and, 10, 68, 230 n.11, 231 n.14
Landaeta, Tomás, 47, 48, 49
Langer, Erik, 229 n.1, 249 nn.39, 43
La Paz siege, 188–89, 194–96, 209, 219–20
La Plata siege, 189, 194–97, 214
La Punilla, 195, 197, 198–99, 260 n.39, 261 nn.45, 51
Larrazabal, Dionisio, 97–100, 262 n.67
Larreategui, Gabriel de, 51–53
Larson, Brooke, 11, 164, 231 nn.16, 22, 232 nn.12, 25, 233 nn.20, 23, 237 n.9, 248 n.7, 249 n.42, 261 n.53
Laymi (ethnic group): caciques of, 81, 108; in Carasi, 97, 179; in Chayanta (town), 23–24, 38, 43–44, 170; Chico, Manuel, 36; Indian dissent in, 20; Laymi-Puraca (ethnic group), 22, 162, 169, 177, 230 n.12; in Micani (valley district), 9, 23, 165; mita labor and, 68; tribute collection in, 91. *See also* Puraca
Lehn, Zuelma, 249 n.43
Levi, Giovanni, 242 n.23
Lewin, Boleslao, 65, 197, 229 n.2, 248 nn.14, 15, 251 nn.84, 86, 257 n.114, 260 n.33, 261 nn.45, 47
Lima. *See* Viceroyalty of Peru

Moscari (*cont.*)
75; migration, 66–74; rebellion in, 159–60, 206; tax collection in, 60; tribute collection and, 58, 71–72. *See also* Lupa, Florencio

Moscoso, Juan Manuel de, 224

Murra, John, 7

Navarro, Juan Francisco, 68, 72, 75, 239 n.59

Ninavia, Manuel, 29, 78, 89, 244 n.47

Ninavia, Martín, 27, 30, 32, 49, 79

Nugent, Daniel, 229 n.5, 242 n.4

Núñez, Luis, 141, 145, 148, 259 n.11, 261 n.44

Ocurí, 48, 49, 161, 193, 195

O'Phelan Godoy, Scarlett, 26, 138, 216, 217, 232 n.12, 243 n.34, 244 nn.41, 47, 247 n.47, 248 n.11, 265 n.8

Originarios, 13, 14, 57, 230 n.11, 231 n.22, 257 n.123

Orsinaga, Norberto, 140, 149, 262 n.60

Ortuño, Manuel, 172, 255 nn.73, 76

Oruro, 45, 62, 196, 199, 200, 212, 223, 261 n.55

Osa Palacios, Josef de, 77, 79, 240 nn.78, 80

Osinaga, Norberto, 248 n.9, 262 n.10

Ossio, Juan, 229 n.6

Pacajes (province), 30, 60

Pacheco, Jorge, 135–36

Pacheco Balanza, Diego, 230 n.12, 244 n.44, 258 n.135, 259 nn.10, 11

Pagden, Anthony, 265 n.10

Panacachi (ethnic group), 9, 22, 60, 68, 81, 91, 112

Paria (province), 28, 67, 183, 186, 199, 232 n.13. *See also* Condocondo; Challapata

Parishes (valley districts), 9

Paucartambo, 186

Paula Sanz, Francisco de, 261 n.45

Peláez, Juan, 260 nn.20, 39

Penry, Elizabeth, 35, 65, 229 n.2, 230 n.11, 232 n.13, 233 n.15, 243 nn.34, 35, 245 n.82, 252 n.8, 253 n.35, 256 n.92

Pereira de Castro, Pedro, 91, 113

Pérez de Vargas, Agustín, 19–20, 35, 38, 43–44, 46, 53

Phelan, John Leddy, 42, 251 n.96

Pietschmann, Horst, 242 n.3, 248 n.28

Pirapi, Juan, 175, 256 nn.100, 101

Pirapi, Lucas, 247 n.118

Pisaca ayllu (Pocoata), 110, 241 n.96

Pitantora, 161–64, 190–91, 193–94, 195, 213, 259 n.13

Pitunisa, 166–69, 204, 253 n.35

Platt, Tristan, 11, 14, 30–31, 61, 68, 209, 229 n.1, 230 nn.9, 11, 12, 232 nn.11, 12, 13, 233 n.14, 236 n.91, 237 n.113, 243 nn.35, 39, 244 n.44, 247 n.6, 249 nn.39, 43

Pocoata (ethnic group): agrarian revenues, 90; ayllus of, 7, 9, 14, 107, 114, 241 n.96; capture of Dámaso Katari, 211; Carasi and, 97, 179; Chayala, 81; colquerunas in, 94; Florencio Lupa and, 81–83, 107–14, 241 nn.95, 97, 98, 245 n.82; grain cultivation, 11; Indian assault in, 148–50, 163, 251 n.85; Machas and, 116, 173, 255 n.83; in Pitunisa, 167; population distribution of, 81–83; Poroma invasion and, 161; self-rule in, 81–83, 106–15, 241 nn.95, 97, 98; tax collection in, 60; tribute payments of, 93, 94, 109–13, 174, 246 n.89, 255 n.91; village, 131, 148, 160–61, 173

Policario (family), 27–28, 30, 40, 36, 49–50

Polo Laborda, Jorge, 237 n.9

Poole, Deborah, 126, 265 n.10

Porco (province), 161, 183, 186, 199, 232 n.13, 261 n.57

Poroma (Yamparáez province), 161, 185, 193

Potosí: anti-cacique testimony in, 30; mining, 15; mita labor in, 29–30; peasant mobilization in, 193; tribute payments to royal treasury in, 130

Powers, Karen, 25, 231 n.22

Priests: alférez/alféreces and, 10, 92, 96–97, 98, 243 n.38, 245 n.59; arancels and, 96–103, 170, 173, 244 n.47, 245 n.59; caciques and, 38, 77–78, 167, 240 nn.78, 79, 80, 82; cofradías, 232 nn.12, 13; Cortés, Dionisio,

Sergio Serulnikov is Assistant Professor in the
Department of History at Boston College.

Library of Congress Cataloging-in-Publication Data
Serulnikov, Sergio.
Subverting colonial authority : challenges to Spanish rule in
eighteenth-century southern Andes / Sergio Serulnikov.
Includes bibliographical references and index.
ISBN 0-8223-3110-1 (cloth : alk. paper)
ISBN 0-8223-3146-2 (pbk. : alk. paper)
1. Aymara Indians — History — 18th century. 2. Aymara Indians —
Wars. 3. Aymara Indians — Government relations. 4. Katari
Marâia, Tomâas, ca. 1740–1781. 5. Chayanta (Bolivia : Province) —
History — 18th century. 6. Indians of South America — Wars —
Andes Region. I. Title.
F2230.2.A9S46 2003   984'.1403 — dc2   2002156641